D0930006

THE EUROPEAN VOTER

COMPARATIVE POLITICS

Comparative Politics is a series for students and teachers of political science that deals with contemporary issues in comparative government and politics. As Comparative European Politics it has produced a series of high quality books since its foundation in 1990, but now takes on a new form and new title for the new millennium—Comparative Politics. As the process of globalization proceeds, and as Europe becomes ever more enmeshed in world trends and events, so it is necessary to broaden the scope of the series.

The General Editors are Max Kaase, Vice-President and Dean of Humanities and Social Sciences, International University, Bremen; and Kenneth Newton, Professor of Comparative Politics, University of Southampton. The series is published in association with the European Consortium for Political Research.

OTHER TITLES IN THIS SERIES

Democratic Challenges, Democratic Choices
Russell J. Dalton

Environmental Protest in Western Europe
Edited by Christopher Rootes

Democracy Transformed?
Edited by Bruce E. Cain, Russell J. Dalton, and Susan E. Scarrow

Losers' Consent
*Christopher J. Anderson, André Blais, Shaun Bowler,
Todd Donovan, and Ola Listhaug*

The Presidentialization of Politics
Edited by Thomas Poguntke and Paul Webb

The European Voter

A Comparative Study of Modern Democracies

edited by

JACQUES THOMASSEN

OXFORD
UNIVERSITY PRESS

OXFORD

UNIVERSITY PRESS

Great Clarendon Street, Oxford OX2 6DP

Oxford University Press is a department of the University of Oxford.
It furthers the University's objective of excellence in research, scholarship,
and education by publishing worldwide in

Oxford New York

Auckland Cape Town Dar es Salaam Hong Kong Karachi
Kuala Lumpur Madrid Melbourne Mexico City Nairobi
New Delhi Shanghai Taipei Toronto

With offices in

Argentina Austria Brazil Chile Czech Republic France Greece
Guatemala Hungary Italy Japan Poland Portugal Singapore
South Korea Switzerland Thailand Turkey Ukraine Vietnam

Oxford is a registered trade mark of Oxford University Press
in the UK and in certain other countries

Published in the United States
by Oxford University Press Inc., New York

British Library Cataloguing in Publication Data

Data available

Library of Congress Cataloging in Publication Data

Data available

Typeset by SPI Publisher Services, Pondicherry, India
Printed in Great Britain
on acid-free paper by
Biddles Ltd., King's Lynn, Norfolk

ISBN 0-19-927321-9
978-0-19-927321-8

1 3 5 7 9 10 8 6 4 2

Preface

The prehistory of this book project goes as far back as the ECPR research sessions in Rimini (Italy) in 1988. It was there and then that the International Committee for Research into Elections and Representative Democracy (ICORE) was founded. Its founding fathers were the study directors of the older national election studies programmes in Western Europe, particularly in Britain, Denmark, Germany, Norway, the Netherlands, and Sweden. All but one of them are among the authors of this volume.

ICORE was founded with the purpose to promote cross-national research into electoral behaviour and representative democracy. We were particularly interested in the study of electoral change. As representatives of the oldest election studies in Europe we were very much aware that together we were sitting on a unique data treasure that was extremely suitable for that purpose. But we were also aware that there was no easy access to this goldmine, at least not when we wanted to use it for comparative purposes. The number of logistical problems was almost prohibitive for the use of the various national election studies in cross-national research. To mention only the most obvious one: for a number of studies written documentation, even the questionnaires, were only available in the original language and not in English, the modern lingua franca. In order to remove these logistical barriers ICORE started its activities by creating a European National Elections Database consisting of all the national election studies documented in English. As a start all available election studies data sets were collated at the ZA-EUROLAB, a Data Laboratory for Comparative Social Research of the Central Archive for Empirical Social Research at the University of Cologne.

At first we never had the intention to write a book on the basis of this wealth of data. Our only intention was to make these data easily accessible for secondary analysis to the international scholarly community. However, I clearly remember how two people simply could not understand this. One of them was Henry Valen. He told us in his characteristic profane language that it would be a shame not to write a comparative volume as part of the effort to create a European National Elections Database. The second one was Ekkehard Mochmann, the administrative director of the Central Archive. His encouragement and his hospitality enabling us to meet several times with all authors at the archive was invaluable for this project. The development of the dataset for this book was supported by the Improving Human Potential (IHP) programme—Access to Research Infrastructures (ARI) Activity of the European Commission.

The decision to write this volume coincided with the start of the Training and Mobility of Researchers (TMR) network 'Political Representation and Party Choice in the European Union', directed from the University of Mannheim by Hermann Schmitt. In addition to the European Elections Study (EES), ICORE was one of the two constituent research projects of this network. Writing this book was promised as one of the 'deliverables' of the TMR project. As a consequence the consecutive meetings of this project were an important venue to work on the book. The basic philosophy of the TMR network was to train a new generation of scholars in empirical political science by immersing them in research projects jointly with senior and more experienced colleagues. This formula turned out to be highly successful and is reflected in the authorship of this volume. Several chapters are co-authored by senior and junior scholars.

The decision to write this volume had an important feedback on the development of a common database. In order to achieve the objectives of this book we needed (a) to define a set of common concepts for which measures were required for each country, (b) to construct from the original data sources for each country files in which variables that operationalize these common concepts are measured over time in as identical a fashion as possible. In addition to the study directors who made the original data available several people were very helpful in creating this common database. Among them are Sarinder Hunjan (Britain), Jørgen Goul Andersen and Johannes Andersen (Denmark), Tanja Binder (Germany), Pieter van Wijnen (the Netherlands), Frode Berglund (Norway), and Per Hedberg (Sweden). Ingvill C. Mochmann and Wolfgang Zenk-Möltgen helped us to realize the original purpose of this project, that is to make these data available and accessible to the scientific community. They integrated and stored all data and documentation relevant for this project in a database under the ZA Codebook Explorer. This database is now in the public domain (see appendix 2 for details).

I wrote and edited several parts of this book when I was a fellow at NIAS—the Netherlands Institute for Advanced Study in the Humanities and Social Sciences. I am grateful to the rector and staff of this wonderful institute for their hospitality and help.

Claire Croft at Oxford University Press proved to be an understanding and patient editor. Last but not least, I would like to acknowledge the help of Janine van der Woude, my secretary, who prepared the typescript and kept me organized.

Jacques Thomassen

Enschede
October 2004

Contents

List of Figures

List of Tables

Contributors

Bernt Aardal is Research Director at the Institute for Social Research in Oslo, Norway, and Adjoint Professor in Political Science at the University of Oslo. He has published a number of books and articles on voting behaviour, public opinion and electoral systems. His publications include *I valgkampens hete* (2004, ed. with A. Krogstad and H.M. Narud), *Velgere i villrede...* (2003, ed.), 'Electoral Systems in Norway', in B. Grofman and A. Lijphart (eds) *The Evolution of Electoral and Party Systems in the Nordic Countries*, 2002.

Kees Aarts is Associate Professor of Research Methods and Statistics in the School of Business, Public Administration and Technology, University of Twente. His research focuses on elections and electoral behaviour, in the Netherlands as well as in comparative perspective.

Frode Berglund is researcher at the Norwegian Institute for Urban and Regional Research. His thesis dealt with party identification and political change, and his main fields of interest are political behaviour and public opinion.

Tanja Binder is a researcher and Ph.D. candidate at the Wissenschaftszentrum Berlin für Empirische Sozialforschung, Germany. She has published on the meaning of party leaders for vote choices, and on the discrepancy between political parties issue emphasis in EP election manifestos and their voters issue concerns.

John Curtice is Professor of Politics and Director of the Social Statistics Laboratory at the University of Strathclyde, and Deputy Director of the Centre for Research into Elections and Social Trends. Co-director of the British Election Study between 1983 and 1997 and a co-editor of the British Social Attitudes studies since 1994, his publications include *The Rise of New Labour* (with Anthony Heath and Roger Howell), *On Message* (with Pippa Norris and others) and *Devolution—Scottish Answers to Scottish Questions* (co-edited with Catherine Bromley and others).

Sören Holmberg is Professor of Political Science and Election Research at Göteborg University. Since 1979 he has been the leader of the Swedish Election Studies. He is also a co-leader of the SOM Institute. Among his publications in English are *The Political System Matters* (1988, co-authored with Donald Granberg) and *Representation from Above* (1996, co-authored with Peter Esaiasson).

Hans-Dieter Klingemann is directeur de recherche associé at Sciences Po in Paris, France. He has published widely on electoral behaviour, political attitudes and democratic politics. His publications include *Parties, Policies and Democracy*

(1994, with Richard I. Hofferbert and Ian Budge), *Citizens and the State* (1995, with Dieter Fuchs), *A New Handbook of Political Science* (1996, with Robert E. Goodin), *Mapping Policy Preferences* (2001, with Ian Budge, Andrea Volkens et al.) and *The State of Political Science in Central and Eastern Europe* (2002, with Annette Legutke and Ewa Kulesza).

Oddbjørn Knutsen is Professor of Political Science at the University of Oslo. His research interests are in the fields of comparative politics with special interest in Western Europe, political sociology and electoral behaviour, value orientations and ideology, and methodology and statistics. He has published several comparative articles in international journals on value change, value orientations and party choice, political cleavages and political ideology.

Staffan Kumlin is a researcher at the Department of Political Science at Göteborg University. He is the author of *The Personal and the Political: How Personal Welfare State Experiences Affect Political Trust and Ideology* (2004). His work has previously appeared in journals such as *Comparative Political Studies* and *European Journal of Political Research*.

Ola Listhaug is Professor of Political Science at the Norwegian University of Science and Technology, Trondheim and working group leader, Centre for the Study of Civil War, PRIO. His main fields of interest are trust in government, voting behaviour, value change, and values and violence. He is the author (with Chris Anderson, Shaun Bowler, André Blais, and Todd Donovan) of *Losers Consent: Elections and Democratic Legitimacy* (2005).

Ingvill C. Mochmann is coordinator of the ZA-EUROLAB at the Central Archive for Empirical Social Research at the University of Cologne, Germany. Her research interests include comparative electoral research and human rights and war children. Her publications include *Inventory of National Election Studies* (1998, with E. Mochmann and R. Mauer), *Continuity Guide der deutschen nationalen Wahlstudien 1949–1998* (2000, with E.Mochmann, R.Mauer and W. Zenk-Möltgen) and *Lifestyles, social milieus and voting behaviour in Germany*, 2003.

Maria Oskarson is associate professor in political science at Göteborg university, Sweden. Her publications are mainly in the field of political sociology and covers areas such as class voting, gender and politics and attitudes towards the European Union.

Hermann Schmitt is a research fellow of the Mannheim Centre for European Social Research and a Privatdozent for Political Science at the Free University of Berlin. He has published widely on multilevel electoral systems, political parties and political representation. His publications include (with Jacques Thomassen) *Political Representation and Legitimacy in the European Union* (1999), *Politische Repräsentation in Europa* (2001), and (with Kees Aarts and André Blais) *Political Leaders and Democratic Elections* (2005).

Jacques Thomassen is professor of political science at the University of Twente, Netherlands. His main fields of interests are electoral behaviour, political representation, democratic theory and European Union politics. His publications include *Political Representation and Legitimacy in the European Union* (1999, with Hermann Schmitt) and *Policy Representation in Western Democracies* (1999, with Warren E. Miller et al.).

Cees van der Eijk is Professor of Social Science Research Methods at the University of Nottingham (UK). His main interests are in the fields of comparative political behaviour and methodology. Among his publications are *Choosing Europe?* (with Mark Franklin), *European Elections and Domestic Politics* (with Wouter van der Brug) and *Electoral Change in the Netherlands* (with Kees Niemöller).

Pieter van Wijnen has been a Ph.D. student and postdoctoral researcher at the University of Twente. He has published mainly on the impact of issues and ideology on voting behaviour. Currently he is a researcher at MKB-Nederland employers organization.

Bernhard Wessels is senior research fellow at the Social Science Research Center Berlin (WZB) and teaching political science at the Free University of Berlin. He has published widely on electoral behaviour, political representation and interest intermediation. His publications include *The European Parliament, the National Parliaments, and European Integration* (1999, ed. with Richard S. Katz), *Policy Representation in Western Democracies* (1999, with Warren E. Miller et al.), and *Wahlen und Wähler—Analysen aus Anlass der Bundestagswahl* (2002, ed. with Jürgen W. Falter and Oscar W. Gabriel).

Wolfgang Zenk-Möltgen is head of the IT department at the Central Archive for Empirical Social Research at the University of Cologne, Germany. He has worked on several database developments for survey documentation, especially the ZA CodebookExplorer. His publications include the *Continuity Guide to German Election Studies* (2000, with E. Mochmann), the *European Values Study 1999/2000* (2003, with R. Luijkx and E. Brislinger) and *The Central and Eastern Eurobarometer 1990–1997* (2004, with B. Hausstein and M. Moschner).

1

Introduction

Jacques Thomassen

1.1 INTRODUCTION

The purpose of this book is to systematically describe and explain the electoral changes that have occurred in a number of West European countries in the second half of the twentieth century. As such it intends to fill an obvious gap in European comparative electoral research. At first sight, electoral research is one of the best-developed and best-integrated sub-disciplines in political science. A growing number of countries have an established programme of academically directed election studies, based on national probability samples of the electorate. Between the end of the 1950s and the early 1970s a national programme of election studies was established in the Scandinavian countries, Britain, Germany, and the Netherlands. Other European countries followed later.

All these national election studies had two characteristics in common:

- First, from the very beginning they were set up as a time series, that is a core of survey questions is replicated at each election.
- Second, all these election studies were based on more or less the same theoretical framework and methodology, partly based on a socio-logical approach of political behaviour as developed by Rokkan et al. and partly derived from the so-called Michigan School of Electoral Research.

Because of these common intellectual roots, the similarity of most of these studies, both in their theoretical and methodological features, is striking. This similarity suggests a well-developed programme of comparative research. However, such a programme does hardly exist. Despite the common intellectual roots of most European election studies, comparative research is remarkably rare (Thomassen 2000).

Basically, there are two main reasons for doing comparative electoral research (Thomassen 2000). The first one is generalization: comparative analysis opens the door to discovering whether theories developed in one context are equally valid in another context. It forces scholars to formulate more general propositions, which are valid beyond the particular circumstances of a single political system. However, a second reason for doing comparative electoral research is at least as important. To quote one of the pioneers of electoral research, Warren E. Miller (1994):

[T]he essential uniqueness of political science is to be found in the need to understand the contributions, the roles and the impact of the institutions of politics and government. In the study of mass behaviour it is, of course, the impact of institutions on the attitudes and behaviour of citizens that is of central interest.

How the institutional arrangements that govern elections affect voters in a particular polity can only be appreciated through comparative research. Without variation in institutional arrangements, it is impossible to learn how any particular configuration of institutions structures votes, public opinion, and political participation. Comparative research offers the opportunity to see to what extent relations at the micro-level are influenced by factors at the system level, to what extent there is an interaction between the macro- and the micro-level. Discovering the interactions between variables at the macro- and micro-level is the real challenge of comparative research (Przeworski and Teune 1970).

This second, and perhaps most important objective of comparative research was neglected in most previous comparative studies of electoral behaviour, which makes them vulnerable to the criticism of suffering from a sociological determinism. In his crusade against what he calls 'modernism' in political behaviour research, Dunleavy (1996) criticizes longitudinal election study programmes for not taking the political context into account:

Once a series of consistent studies had been created, and overtime panel surveys had been set up, these researchers held data-sets which could be and were analysed as if they stood outside time. Many of these studies were explicitly premised on the view that the political context of the whole 'modern' period has been so uniform as to render unnecessary any detailed cross-referencing between voters' responses to survey questions and their immediate political environment.

In this book we will try to reach both objectives of comparative research. First, we will develop and test a dynamic explanatory model of party choice, enabling a comprehensive test of modernization theory. Later in this chapter we will spell out this theory and its implications for electoral behaviour in more detail. In a nutshell it implies that over time the explanatory power for electoral behaviour of more or less stable structural variables as social class and religion will yield to more short-term factors. The explanatory model developed in this book makes it possible to describe and explain both the decline of the importance of traditional factors determining party choice and the possible increase of the relevance of factors replacing these traditional factors.

Second, throughout this book we will see to what extent differences in the political–institutional context, both between countries and within countries between different elections, affect people's political behaviour. As we will see, it has been argued that modernization theory is wrong in assuming that changes in electoral behaviour are due to an autonomous societal process, independently from the political–institutional context. The alternative explanation is that differences in the development of electoral change between countries and fluctuations within countries are entirely, or a least partly, due to differences or changes in the political–institutional context. In this book we will confront both explanations.

The progress thus being made compared to previous studies is not only a matter of intellectual progress, but also of the availability of data. For a long time a number of logistical problems bedevilled using existing data in international comparative electoral research. To mention only the most obvious one: For a number of studies, written documentation or even the questionnaires were not available in English.

Awareness of these problems led to the initiative to establish the International Committee for Research into Elections and Representative Democracy (ICORE). It was founded at the end of the 1980s, its founding fathers being the study directors of some of the older national election studies programmes in Western Europe, in particular Norway, Sweden, Britain, the Netherlands, Denmark, and Germany.[1] Most of them are among the authors of this book. The aim of ICORE is to promote cross-national research into electoral behaviour and representative democracy. One of ICORE's first priorities was to overcome the logistical problems making the use of existing data difficult. In order to solve them a European Elections Database was created, consisting of all the national election studies documented in English. As a result of these efforts the data of most of the major European election studies, documented in English, are now available at the Central Archive in Cologne (Mochmann et al. 1998). In order to facilitate the systematic study of trends in electoral behaviour and its correlates across countries, comparable measures across time within countries for each of our key concepts were developed. This huge investment in time and other resources made it possible to reach beyond the possibilities of previous comparative longitudinal studies of electoral behaviour.

In the next section we will first give an impression of the major changes in electoral behaviour occurring in West European countries. Then we will introduce the theory of modernization and the effects we expect the process of modernization to have on people's electoral behaviour. Next we will explain to what extent the political–institutional context will be used throughout this book as an additional or alternative explanatory theory of change. At the end of the chapter we will explain the structure of the book. Appendix 2 contains a detailed description of the database used.

1.2 POLITICAL CHANGE IN EUROPE

At the turn of the century, flux rather than stability seems to characterize politics in the well-established democracies of Western Europe. Until shortly in most of these countries the outcomes of elections were quite predictable, based as they were on historical and stable cleavages. In recent decades the electoral behaviour of the citizens of Europe has become less predictable. A case in point is the 2002 parliamentary election in the Netherlands. The Netherlands once were the proto-type of a country where elections were hardly contentious and where elections were not much more than a census measuring the strength of the several segments (or *zuilen*) in society, the members of which usually massively voted for the political parties associated with them. As the social composition of the country hardly changed between two elections the extreme proportional electoral system guaranteed that the shifts from one election to the next were very limited indeed. However, this situation has totally changed. The 2002 parliamentary elections were dominated by the rise of a new political movement, the 'list Pim Fortuyn', named after its flamboyant leader who had decided to enter politics less than half a year before the elections. Had he not been murdered ten days before the elections, he might have entered parliament as leader of the biggest party after the elections, which would have given him the initiative in forming a new government coalition. But even without their leader the new movement managed to pull off the largest landslide in Dutch history, winning 26 of the 150 seats in the Lower House of Dutch parliament. Similar, although not always equally spec-tacular, changes could be observed in other West European countries.

However, it is not our intention to describe the idiosyncratic patterns of change at particular elections in individual countries in any detail. (For a detailed description of the development of the electoral strength of individual parties, see Appendix 1.) It is the purpose of this book to describe and explain the *commonalities* in electoral changes that have occurred in the established European democracies of Northern Europe in the second half of the twentieth century.

This time period was chosen for two reasons. First, there seems to be a general understanding that as far as secular changes in the electoral fortunes of major political party families and the underlying behaviour of the electorate have occurred, these changes did not occur until after the middle of the century. The somewhat obligatory opening sentences of many publications on electoral change in Western democracies refer to Lipset and Rokkan's famous dictum that 'the party systems of the 1960s reflect, with few but significant exceptions, the cleav-age structures of the 1920s' (Lipset and Rokkan 1967). The persistence of the party systems was based on the stability of party preferences of most voters, and their firm position in the cleavage structure in a particular country. However, Lipset and Rokkan's characterization of the party systems of Western Europe already was losing its validity at the moment it was written. It is somewhat ironic that as 'this theme of stable, cleavage-based voting became the conventional wisdom, dramatic changes began to affect these same party systems. Within a decade the dominant question changed from explaining the persistence of electoral politics to explaining electoral change' (Dalton 1996: 344).

Therefore, if there is a kind of watershed in the 1960s, dividing a period of stability in party systems and electoral behaviour from a period of flux, a systematic study of political change should start no later than the 1960s. A second reason to limit ourselves to the second half of the twentieth century is of a more pragmatic nature. In order to understand the individual choices underlying the changes in the electoral fortune of political parties across time and across countries, we need to analyse them at the micro-level, that is at the level of the individual voter. The standard instrument to study the electoral choices of individual citizens is survey research. In order to study political changes since the time party systems and voters' preferences were more or less frozen, we need regular surveys around successive elections enabling us to measure changes over such a long period of time, that is from the early 1960s on. Also, in order to understand changes across time and across countries we need comparable measurements across time and across countries. There are only a few countries where election studies have been conducted for such a long time. Therefore we decided to limit this study to those countries where election studies have been conducted on a regular and comparable basis since the 1960s or at least the 1970s. These countries are Denmark, (West) Germany, Britain, the Netherlands, Norway, and Sweden. Therefore, the more specific purpose of this book is to describe and explain the commonalities in the electoral changes in the second half of the twentieth century in these six countries.

1.3 MODERNIZATION AND POLITICAL CHANGE

Stability and change in the mutual strength of political parties depend on two consecutive decisions individual citizens make. First, the decision whether to vote, and second, the choice of a particular party. We will study both. In this chapter we first develop the conceptual framework that not only defines the structure of this book, but also enables us to predict the kind of changes we can expect over time and across countries.

The basic hypothesis to be tested in this book is that changes in electoral behaviour in advanced West European democracies are caused, first by a secular trend in the development of society in these countries, and second by the political–institutional context. Moreover, we expect that the main societal developments leading to changes in people's voting behaviour will make their behaviour more amenable to (changes in) the political–institutional context.

In this section we will first give a short description of the developments in society we expect to be the main determinants of changes in electoral behaviour.

Next, we will argue in more detail what consequences we expect these social changes to have on changes in voting behaviour, first on turnout and more in general on political involvement and second on party choice.

The changes that have occurred in advanced industrial democracies are usually summarized as the *process of societal modernization*. The theoretical notions connecting these changes in society to changes in politics are often referred to as the modernization theory or hypothesis. Both the process of modernization and the impact these processes are supposed to have on politics, and more in particular on the attitudes and behaviour of individual citizens, are extensively documented elsewhere (Inglehart 1977; Fuchs and Klingemann 1995; Dalton 2002). Economic development, the growing size and diversity of the mass media, the enormous rise of the average level of education, the development of the welfare state, the growing importance of the service sector, and increasing geographical and social mobility have led to changes at the level of individual citizens which in turn might be indicated as *individual modernization*. Following Inkeles, Fuchs and Klingemann describe a personality with a high degree of modernity as an informed participant citizen with a marked sense of personal efficacy, being highly independent and autonomous in his relations to traditional sources of influence. This development will have consequences for both turnout and the determinants of party choice (Fuchs and Klingemann 1995).

1.4   DECLINING TURNOUT?

Several authors have observed 'a puzzle of political participation' (Brody 1978; Dalton 2002). The secular decline in turnout in most advanced industrial democracies that several empirical studies seem to indicate is at odds with the traditional insight that political participation, including turnout, is a function of people's personal resources. Among these resources are education and information. Due to increase in education and the explosion of information via the media the resources of the average citizen have increased enormously. Therefore, it is a matter of logic to expect an increase in turnout. Why then would it decline? Modernization theory pretends to have the answer. According to this theory there are two reasons to expect a decline in turnout.

First, rising levels of education, better information, and an increase of people's self-confidence—in general the increase in personal skills—might lead to a relativization of what we might call *electoral democracy*. Elections as the institutionalized way for citizens to exert political influence will become less important. In electoral democracy, political parties have a pivotal role as an intermediary between citizens and the state. Citizens depend on them because only political parties are capable of transforming diverse wants and interests into the will of the people. However, highly competent 'new citizens' are more and more inclined to manage their own affairs and to get themselves—alone or in cooperation with others—directly involved in the process of political decision-making. As a consequence, citizens will be inclined to become more rather than less politically active. However, conventional forms of political participation will be replaced by less conventional ones. Political activities directly or indirectly related to elections will become less important within the repertory of political actions (Barnes and Kaase 1979; Inglehart 1977; Fuchs and Klingemann 1995). As turnout at elections is the most essential element of conventional participation this development will lead to a secular decrease in turnout.

Second, individual modernization will lead to an increasingly *instrumental* orientation towards politics. Citizens will choose that mode of political participation which suits their purposes best. Voting is something they will do only when there is a real choice, that is, when it makes a difference to them which party or parties come to power, or when it is clear to them that elections matter for the allocation of power (Van der Eijk and Franklin 1996). This instrumental orientation implies that voters will decide from election to election whether they will vote. Traditionally, turnout was only to a limited extent based upon an individual calculus of the utility of voting, but more on sociological characteristics like a sense of citizen duty and party affiliation (Kaase and Bauer-Kaase 1998). However, the number of people identifying with a particular political party is declining and due to the process of individualization the norm that voting is a citizen duty, is less enforced by social control (Kühnel and Fuchs 1998). A more instrumental orientation of citizens will make people's decision to vote more dependent on their assessment of the importance of the outcome of a specific election. As argued later, that importance will be defined at least as much by political–institutional factors as by the characteristics of individual voters. A more instrumental orientation towards politics does not necessarily mean that turnout will decline. However, it might make the *paradox of voting* more relevant for the real world of politics. If voters' decision to vote or not to vote purely depends on instrumental orientations, on the calculus of individual costs and benefits, the costs of voting almost always will be higher than the possible benefits, making the act of voting into an irrational political activity.[2]

1.5 THE EXPLANATION OF PARTY CHOICE

The same aspects of the process of modernization that might lead to a change in the political involvement of citizens and a decline of turnout are expected to cause a change in the factors determining voters' party choice. Due to changes both in the composition of the electorate and the relationship between social position and electoral behaviour, the once strong relationship between social structure and politics, between social position and party choice will diminish. For the same reason it will no longer be evident that people for their life time will be loyal to a particular party. Ideologies reflecting traditional cleavages will become less important as a factor determining people's political attitudes and party choice. Voters will decide from election to election what party they will vote for, taking into account the issues of the day, the performance of the incumbent government and their confidence in individual political leaders. This can lead to large fluctuations in election outcomes. However, this is not necessarily a sign of a lack of political interest, but reminds us of the almost forgotten informed and rational voter from classic democratic theory (Dalton 1996).

As the supposed consequences of the modernization process form the conceptual framework and the main organizing principle of this book we will expand on it in some more detail. The conceptual framework and the organizing principle of the book are represented schematically in Fig. 1.1. It might be clear that this scheme is not very different from the *funnel of causality* as developed in the Michigan tradition of electoral research. However, this is mainly so because of the general and all-embracing nature of the Michigan framework. It would be hard to think of any theoretical approach or set of variables that would not fit into this general scheme. The scheme might not only be seen as a comprehensive and theoretically organized summary of the main sets of variables, but also of the main theoretical approaches figuring in electoral research. The supposition that people's electoral behaviour is mainly determined by their position in the social structure is the main element of the political–sociological approach in electoral research, usually associated with the Columbia School of Berelson, Lazarsfeld and their associates. In the European literature the seminal introduction to Lipset and Rokkan's *Party Systems and Voter Alignments* is usually considered as the theoretical basis of the political–sociological approach. In this approach the cleavage structure is reflected in differences in value orientations. The central position of party identification as the main determinant of people's political

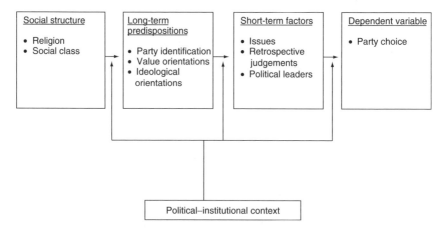

Fig. 1.1. *Conceptual framework*

attitudes, perceptions, and political behaviour is the core element of the political–psychological school, or Michigan School, whereas the idea of an ideological continuum, the left–right dimension as an information costs saving device for voters and political parties alike is the core element of Downs' economic theory of democracy. The assessment of parties and candidates in relation to political issues and government performance are a key element in any explanatory model assuming—if one wants to avoid the rational choice vocabulary—that citizens act instrumentally on the basis of their own purposes (Carmines and Huckfeldt 1996).

Modernization theory can be translated into the hypothesis that over time the explanatory power of the variables in this causal scheme gradually shifts from left to right in Fig. 1.1. This is tantamount to saying that over time a sociological model will become less powerful in explaining the variation in party choice, a fate it has in common with any other model having long-term predispositions as its backbone. At the same time models emphasizing instrumental orientations towards politics should become more successful over time. However, presenting these different approaches as competing models would be missing the point. The basic proposition is that the sets of variables further to the right in Fig. 1.1, *controlling for the preceding sets of variables* will gradually become more powerful as explanatory factors of voting behaviour. In statistical terms: if we think of Fig. 1.1 as a model of stepwise regression, the variables further to the right will gradually contribute more to the explained variance. In the remaining parts of this section we will try to underscore this general argument.

1.5.1   Social Structure and Party Choice

As noted, the political–sociological approach in Europe, the idea that electoral choices are based on a limited number of social cleavages, is strongly based on Lipset and Rokkan's famous dictum that 'the party systems of the 1960s reflect, with few but significant exceptions, the cleavage structures of the 1920s' (Lipset and Rokkan 1967). They argue that the party systems that came into existence at the time of the introduction of universal suffrage in the countries of Western Europe reflected four historical cleavages, between Centre and Periphery, between State and Church, between Land and Industry, and between Owner and Worker, and that almost without exception these party systems withstood the turbulent political events of the first half of the century. Of these four historical conflict dimensions social class (owner and worker) and religion (state and church) have been the most important and persistent in most West European countries.

There is a general understanding that Lipset and Rokkan's characterization of the party systems of Western Europe already was losing it's validity at the moment it was written. As early as the 1950s, that is, even before Lipset and Rokkan published their seminal study, a debate had started on the relative importance of the class cleavage for politics. In 1958 Dahrendorf maintained that class conflicts were declining at the same time as they proved to be easier to solve in welfare societies. At the same time US scholars in particular (including Lipset) argued that ideologies based on class cleavages were or would be fading away, the slogan being the end of ideology (Lane and Ersson 1999). Still in the 1960s Kirchheimer (1966) developed his well known argument that

Under present conditions of spreading secular and mass consumer-goods orientations, with shifting and less obtrusive class lines, the former class–mass parties and denominational mass parties are both under pressure to become catch-all people's parties.

As argued before, one of the hypotheses to be tested in this book is that in the second half of the twentieth century traditional cleavages, in particular social class and religion, have become less important for people's party choice. According to the empirical literature, the outcome of that assessment leaves little room for doubt. Major comparative studies on this question (Dalton et al. 1984; Franklin et al. 1992), all find evidence for such a secular trend. There is strong evidence that the impact of social cleavages substantially declined in a twofold fashion. First, because of a composition effect: the number of those integrated into a cleavage at all shrinks because of social change (the most telling example is the decrease in the number of Catholics who regularly attend church). Second, because the relationship between belonging to a particular segment of society and party choice has been declining (for instance because the Catholics who still go to church no longer vote for a Catholic or Christian-democratic party (Kaase and Klingemann 1994).

However, this conclusion of a decline of the importance of the social cleavage structure for electoral politics is anything but uncontested. As late as in 1990 Bartolini and Mair argued that the frozen party hypothesis still applied (Bartolini and Mair 1990). Even more recently the decline of class hypothesis has been challenged in the context of the British election study. Moreover, proponents of the decline of the importance of social cleavages have been accused of taking a sociological–determinist approach to the evolution of political cleavages, neglecting the importance of the political–institutional context for the politicization of social cleavages (De Graaf et al. 2001). Long-term change in electoral behaviour is regarded as the product of long-term gradual secular social change without reference to potentially fluctuating political circumstances (Curtice 2002: 164). In the context of the British parliamentary elections some evidence was presented to suggest that, from 1970 onwards, the strength of the relationship between class and vote in Britain has fluctuated in line with the varying policy distance between the Conservative and Labour parties (Curtice 2002: 164; Evans 1999). Therefore, according to Curtice, rather than simply looking for linear trends over time we should regard elections as independent events whose political context needs to be measured and impact evaluated. This is in line with our own emphasis on the political–institutional context to which we will come back later in this chapter.

However, certainly in the 1970s there was still more consensus on the declining importance of social structure for voting behaviour than on what was replacing it. It has been argued that students of voting behaviour where so preoccupied with stable alignments, with the stability of voting behaviour, that they almost instinctively assumed that dealignment should be followed by realignment according to new conflict dimensions (Andeweg 1982). Only gradually the insight developed that dealignment is not necessarily followed by realignment, but might be a permanent state of affairs (Dalton et al. 1984). In the literature a great number of possible new cleavages passed in revue, like the cleavages between workers in the public and private sector, between house owners and tenants, and between men and women. But none of these possible cleavage lines seem to be of permanent importance (Franklin et al. 1992; Rose and McAllister 1986).

1.5.2 Party Identification

However, a stable party system and more or less stable relations between political parties and voters are not necessarily based upon the social position of voters. *Party identification*, the central concept in the Michigan tradition of electoral research is supposed to have the same function. Party identification is a long-term, affective, psychological identification with one's preferred political party. These party attachments are distinct from voting preferences, which explains why some Americans vote for the presidential candidate of one party while expressing loyalty to another party. Indeed, it is the conceptual independence of voting and party identification that initially gives the latter its theoretical significance (Dalton 2000a). Certainly, this is precisely why in the 1970s the concept of party identification met some scepticism among European electoral researchers. The answers to the question on party identification appeared to reflect current voting intentions rather than a long-standing commitment to a party. As in most countries party identification tended to change in tandem with party choice, some of the most important analytical virtues of the concept apparently did not apply. In particular the concept of a normal vote as a baseline for people's party preference, making the explanation of deviations from this baseline into one of the most important empirical questions at each election, seemed to be a trivial concept in the context of European elections (Thomassen 1976). However, other aspects of the concept proved more useful. The objections mainly applied to the *directional* and far less to the *strength* dimension of party identification. Early on it was recognized that the strength of partisanship was an important predictor of people's political attitudes and behaviour, including the stability of party choice and turnout. Partisan ties help orient the individual to the complexities of politics, and provide a framework for assimilating political information, understanding political issues, and making political judgements. Furthermore, partisan ties mobilize individuals to participate in parties, elections, and the processes of representative government (Dalton 2000*a*).

Why party identification seemed to be less important for European than US voters is an interesting puzzle. A possible solution to that puzzle might be *the functional model of party identification*, as initially developed by Shively. He explains the development of party identification because of the party's function of providing political cues to voters who feel themselves in need of guidance because they must make political decisions under confusing circumstances. Just like ideology in Downs' theory of democracy, party identification in his view is a cost saving device, providing people with a short cut to all kinds of decisions, including the decision for which party or candidate to vote. However, this short cut is not necessarily provided by party identification. Other short cuts might have the same function. According to Shively, the weak direct ties to political parties in post-war Europe have resulted from the prevalence of strong ties to a class or religion, which have obviated the need for direct ties to any party, per se. If a voter is a conscious member of a social class or religion, and if that class or religion is represented by a particular political party, then there may be no need for the voter to develop any identification with a party per se; such voters can simply base their electoral choice on their class or religion. Expressed partisanship, then, will be synonymous with the vote and parties as such will not serve as guides to organize behaviour (Shively 1979; Thomassen 1976).

A logical extension of that argument might be that once the importance of the traditional cleavage structure declines and voters are deprived of their traditional short-cutting device, they will develop party identification in the same way as their American counterparts. However, it is the very same functional theory that contradicts this prediction. The need of an information costs saving device is supposed to be a function of the political skills of the voters. Modernization and in particular the cognitive mobilization of citizens have dramatically increased these skills. According to Dalton, the dramatic spread of education in advanced industrial democracies has produced a qualitative change in the political sophistication of citizens. At the same time, these societies have experienced an information explosion through the mass media. Both developments have led to a substantial decrease of information costs. Because of this cognitive mobilization, more voters now are able to deal with the complexities of politics and make their own political decisions. Thus, the functional need for partisan cues to guide voting behaviour is declining for a growing number of citizens (Dalton 1984). As a consequence, we should expect a decline in the level of party identification. This is the hypothesis we will put to a test in this book. However, as the argument derived from the functional model of party identification is anything but uncontested (Barton and Döring 1986) we will test the underlying assumptions at the micro-level as well.

1.5.3 *Ideological and Value Orientations*[3]

Party identification is not the only possible alternative to social cleavages as a base for more or less stable relations between political parties and voters. A somewhat similar argument applies to the role of values. In order to clarify the role of value orientations as a possible source for stable relations between parties and voters we should discuss the relations between social structure, values, and party choice in somewhat more detail.

Our reproduction of Lipset and Rokkan's cleavage theory might suggest the implication that people's electoral choices are defined by group membership irrespective of their value orientations. However, such an interpretation of the cleavage model is missing the point. In Lipset and Rokkan's view the traditional, historically defined cleavages between different interests were the basis for the development of different ideologies or *Weltanschauungen* (Lipset and Rokkan 1967). For them, the group conflicts and accompanying ideological confrontations typical of mass politics in Western Europe are less about the 'specific gains and losses' of particular groups than about 'conceptions of moral right and interpretations of history and human destiny' (Knutsen and Scarbrough 1995: 494). According to Knutsen and Scarbrough the concept of a cleavage encompasses three distinct phenomena. First, a cleavage is rooted in a relatively persistent social division which gives rise to 'objectively' identifiable groups within a society—according to class, religion, economic, or cultural interests, or whatever. Second, a cleavage engages some set of values common to members of the group; group members know a 'common life' in so far as they share the same value orientation. Third, a cleavage is institutionalized in some form of organization—most commonly a political party, but also in churches, unions, and other associational groups. Thus voting for a party out of 'objective' group interests without sharing the values of the party does not constitute cleavage politics; nor does voting for a party out of shared values without being a member of the associated social group. Structural variables or value orientations may yield intelligible accounts of voting, but they do not amount to accounts of 'cleavage politics' (Knutsen and Scarbrough 1995: 494–5).

The ideological orientation connected to the class cleavage is traditionally conceived in terms of the concepts of *Left and Right*. Differences between left and right are reflected in the twin concepts: *economic equality* and *inequality* and the *role of government and the market* (Downs 1957; Knutsen 1995a). The second major cleavage that we will consider in this volume, religion, is primarily reflected in the role of religion and the church in society and secondly in views on moral issues. The value orientations connected with these views are reflected in the distinction between a *libertarian* and a *traditional* value orientation.

Although these value orientations historically were part of the social cleavage structure, this is not to say they should lose their political significance once the social cleavages behind them do. More or less stable political cleavages can be based directly on these value orientations (Bartolini and Mair 1990; Rose and McAllister 1986). In general, people's value orientations are formed during their adolescence and are quite persistent during the rest of their lifetime (Inglehart 1977). As a consequence, changes in value orientations among the population at large will only gradually change and will continue to be of importance for people's party choice even when these value orientations are no longer, or at least less, anchored in the social structure. Therefore, we expect that the impact of traditional value orientations—controlled for social background variables—will gradually increase.

Because of the persistence of value orientations during people's lifetime, a change in values will mainly occur by generation replacement. This is a main element in Inglehart's theory of value change. His point of departure is that value orientations related to the traditional cleavage structure have lost much of their significance in the second half of the twentieth century. Older generations of voters who have experienced the economic crisis of the 1930s and the Second World War, grew up with the experience that material well being and security are scarce goods. As a consequence these goods have a high utility to them. The post-war generation grew up with a totally different experience. Material well being and physical security are almost self-evident to them. This is not to say that they do not appreciate these goods, but their marginal utility is low. Therefore, they are more open to other, post-materialist values. Of course, older generations have equally benefited from the growing prosperity and security after the war, but this does not essentially change their value orientations anymore. People tend to stick to the values they have been socialized in during their adolescence. Equally, the value orientations of the younger generations will not easily change when they endure an economic setback. Inglehart foresees a *silent revolution* by which materialist generations gradually will be replaced by generations with dominantly a post-materialist orientation. This revolution will lead to a realignment: post-materialists will base their party choice on issues related to their value orientation, like environmental issues (Inglehart 1977).

The argument in this section leads to two hypotheses:

Hypothesis 1. The independent impact of value orientations, that is controlling for social background, will gradually increase;

Hypothesis 2. The impact of traditional value orientations based on the class and religious cleavage will gradually yield to the material–post-material conflict dimension.

A somewhat different approach of value orientations puts an emphasis on a single ideological continuum, the left–right dimension, as the main source of stability in people's political preferences, although not necessarily in the preference for a particular party. The distinction between left and right as an important organizing principle of politics has its origin in French politics and is still deeply embedded in French political culture. At the time of the French revolution, the radicals sat to the left of the president's box in the French legislative assemblies, and the conservatives to the right, giving rise to the political connotations of the terms. Since the early traditions of French electoral research it has been an important question to what degree left–right orientations provide French voters with elements of meaning and long-term stabilization which are effective substitutes for party loyalties (Converse and Pierce 1986). As an alternative to the central concept of party identification at least the hypothesis was presented that French voters would be more inclined to identify with a particular *tendance*, a particular stretch on the left–right dimension, rather than with a particular political party as assumed in the Michigan tradition.

Over the years several authors have 'asserted that the left–right dimension obtains a superior all-inclusive status within the hierarchy of cleavages' (Sani and Sartori 1983). According to this view the traditional structural cleavages have to a large extent been replaced by a new one, which reflects voters' substantive political ideals, largely captured by their position in terms of left and right (Van der Eijk and Niemöller 1994). Van der Eijk and Niemöller (1992) interpret the decline of the influence of social determinants of the vote as a process of political emancipation of voters as individuals who can now choose on the basis of their own preferences and orientations, rather than merely express with their vote that they are part of a particular segment of society. They argue that the major political determinant of the vote, voters' left–right ideological orientation, cannot be regarded as a mere reflection, or common political translation, of their social position. At least for the Netherlands they find the relationship between social structure and ideology, such as the effect of income on left–right ideology, to be very weak or even not significant at all. Substantively this means that not only party choice but also voters' ideological orientations are to a large extent independent of their location in the social structure.

In contrast to the previous approach this tradition in electoral research usually assumes that both the competition between political parties and people's long-term political identifications can be represented by a one-dimensional space, the left–right continuum. The popularity of this approach is most certainly enhanced by the fact that it offers a manageable instrument to test rational choice theory in the Downsian tradition, according to which voters are supposed to vote for the party being located at the smallest distance from the voter's own location on the left–right continuum. 'Rational' voting in the Downsian tradition might be interpreted as a direct consequence of cognitive mobilization, as an indication of the emancipation of voters. Therefore, just as we concluded in the case of value orientations, we should expect an increase of the independent impact of left–right orientations on the vote, at least initially.

1.5.4   The Individualization of Politics

Only initially, because even the significance of value or ideological orientations in whatever form is challenged by an alternative view on the developments among the electorate, or rather by later developments among the electorate. According to this view dealignment of structural cleavages is not, or at least no longer, followed by any realignment according to whatever value dimension, but only by de-ideologization and dealignment. The traditional social cleavages as determinants of political judgements and party preferences will not be followed by any new structural dividing lines, but by an *individualization of politics*. This can be defined as:

a shift away from a style of electoral decision-making based on social group and/or party cues toward a more individualized and inwardly oriented style of political choice. Instead of depending upon party élites and reference groups, more citizens now try to deal with the complexities of politics and make their own political decisions. What is developing is an eclectic and egocentric pattern of citizen decision-making. Rather than socially structured and relatively homogeneous personal networks, contemporary publics are more likely to base their decisions on policy preferences, performance judgements, or candidate images. (Dalton 1996: 346)

This development will be reflected in a rising heterogeneity of the political issues voters deem important. Citizens are becoming fragmented into a variety of distinct issue publics. 'Rather than politics being structured by a group benefits framework, which often reflected socially derived cues, citizens now tend to focus on specific issues of immediate or personal importance' (Dalton 1996: 347).

   We expect that the increasing importance of these more idiosyncratic orientations will be accompanied by a gradual decline of the explanatory power of value orientations, whether in the form of value orientations related to the old social cleavages, left–right or even materialist–post-material value orientations. In the case of left–right orientations this argument was already implied in our reflection on the development of party identification. Downs explicitly introduced the left–right continuum as an information costs saving device. Just as in the case of party identification we should expect the need of such a device to decrease with the increase of political skills. The expectation that the importance of a post-materialist value orientation will gradually decrease just like any other value orientation, is clearly at odds with the expectations still maintained by Inglehart. The core of his argument is that materialism–post-materialism is a new cleavage, gradually replacing the traditional cleavages on which traditional value orientations were based (Inglehart 1977).

   If our argument is correct, the autonomous explanatory power of the variables in the third box of Fig. 1.1, that is voters' opinions on political issues, the evaluation of the performance of political parties and political leaders and the evaluation of government policy, will increase. However, we first should clarify what kinds of issues belong in this box and which ones do not. A classic distinction is between position and valence issues (Stokes 1963; Van Wijnen 2001). Position issues refer to public conflicts on policy goals or policy means. As such they often are a reflection of the same domains of conflict as the value dimensions just discussed. Typical examples are opinions on the equality of incomes as a reflection of the left–right dimension, or moral issues like abortion. Instead of being considered as short-term factors, in the sense of the issues of the day, they should be considered as a reflection or proxy of the underlying value orientations. To the extent that these underlying value orientations become less decisive this will apply to related issues as well. The logic of this argument is that the importance of such position issues will gradually be taken over by issues that are not necessarily constrained by any ideological orientation and in particular by valence issues. Valence issues refer to policy goals that are shared almost unanimously. Public controversy on valence issues pertains to the priority that should be given to solving each of several problems and to the perceived competence of parties to solve the problem (Van Wijnen 2001). For the same reason we expect that in explaining voters' party choice *accountability* will gradually become more important. As Manin (1997: 221) puts it, 'the age of voting on the candidates' platforms is probably over, but the age of voting on the incumbents' records may be beginning.' This prediction is based on the observation that both the scope and the complexity of governmental activities have increased substantially over the last hundred years. Still according to Manin, the problems, which politicians have to confront once in office, become less and less predictable. Therefore, when standing for office, politicians know they will have to face the unforeseen; so they are not inclined to tie their hands by committing themselves to a detailed platform (Manin 1997). Voters, less than in the past being driven by party loyalties and value orientations, will be inclined to judge politicians and political parties on their performances in office, rather than on their promises. This means that people's assessment of government policy and their perception of the responsibility of the incumbent government for the state of society, in particular the economy, will become more important. As responsibility is attributed, not only to political parties, but to political leaders as well, and probably increasingly so, we also expect an increasing effect on vote choice of people's confidence in respective *political leaders*.

1.6 DOES POLITICS MATTER?

In the previous sections the implications of the theory of modernization for electoral behaviour were spelt out. Testing this theory and its behavioural implications is the first major objective of this project. The modernization thesis is of a general nature and in principle applies to all advanced industrial democracies. Therefore, the significant test is to what extent we can observe a common trend in advanced western democracies as predicted by the theory of modernization.

However, as we observed in Section 1.1, by predicting common secular trends across countries, modernization theory seems to neglect differences in the political–institutional context, making itself vulnerable to the criticism of suffering from a sociological determinism.

It is hard to deny that the political–institutional context has not always been at the forefront of electoral research. Traditionally, most models trying to explain the two most important choices voters make, whether to vote, and if so, for which party, tend to rely on the personal characteristics of voters. And it is true indeed that as far as secular changes have been observed in the motives underlying voting choices these usually are related to societal changes, like the process of modernization.

Of all possible explanations for the traditional neglect of the political–institutional context, two might be mentioned here. First, for a long time it was possible to explain a great deal of the variation in voting behaviour using a sociological model. Knowledge of a limited number of social characteristics was sufficient to explain most people's voting behaviour.[4] Second, many election studies refer to a single election in a single country. Political–institutional characteristics usually are characteristics of the political system as such. Therefore, as long as research refers to the behaviour of individual voters in a single election, these characteristics are not a variable but a constant and therefore cannot contribute to the explanation of the variation in the dependent variable, party choice or turnout. Without variation in institutional arrangements, it is impossible to learn how any particular configuration of institutions structures votes, public opinion, and political participation.

However, as far as these explanations ever were a valid excuse, they no longer are. First, as soon as the explanation of voting behaviour needs to be found further to the right in Fig. 1.1, neglecting a possible impact of the political–institutional context can no longer be justified. The possibility for voters to make their party choice dependent on their distance to the several parties in terms of ideological or value orientations or political issues, is at least partly defined by the extent to which political parties distinguish themselves on the same value or issue dimensions. If political parties do not make it clear where they politically stand or if there are hardly policy differences between political parties, it will be close to impossible for voters to decide their party choice on the basis of policy orientations. Also, the extent to which individual voters can base their vote choice on their assessment of the qualities and performances of political candidates or leaders and their evaluation of the incumbent government will be related to the electoral system and the clarity of who or which party or parties are responsible for government policy. Therefore, to the extent that the short-term factors in the third box of Fig. 1.1 become more important, we should also expect an increasing interaction effect of the political–institutional context on these relationships.

Moreover, even the hypothesis that the decline of the impact of long-term factors on the left side of Fig. 1.1 is mainly due to more or less autonomous developments in society and is hardly related to the political–institutional context is anything but uncontested. As noted, from 1970 onwards, the strength of the relationship between social class and vote in Britain was shown to fluctuate in line with the varying policy distance between the Conservative and Labour parties (Curtice 2002: 164; Evans 1999). Schmitt and Holmberg (1995) developed a similar argument with respect to party identification. They claim that developments and variations in the level of party identification are related to changes and variations in the ideological polarization between parties rather than to developments in society.

Also, for the same reason we can expect the political–institutional context to become more important for the decision whether to vote at all. Traditionally, turnout was less dependent on an individual utility calculus and more on what one might call sociological factors like a sense of citizen duty and the bond to a particular party (Kaase and Bauer-Kaase 1998; Kühnel and Fuchs 1998). However, ever less citizens are bound to a specific party and the norm that voting is a citizen duty is ever less enforced by social control because of increasing individualization (Kühnel and Fuchs 1998). A more instrumental orientation towards politics will make the decision whether to vote more dependent upon what is at stake in a particular election, that is, on how important people think the outcome of the election is. That importance will be defined at least as much by political–institutional factors than by individual characteristics of voters. First, turnout will be influenced by the importance people attach to the level of government concerned. In most countries the difference in turnout between elections for the national parliament and all other levels of government are of such magnitude that the latter have become known as *second order national elections* (Reif and Schmitt 1980; Van der Eijk and Franklin 1996). As this book is exclusively on national parliamentary elections, this factor is not very relevant for our analyses. A second important factor is to what extent the outcome of elections defines who or which party or parties will come to power after the elections (Franklin 1996). A third possibly important contextual factor is the degree of polarization between political parties. The more pronounced the ideological and policy differences between political parties, the more important the outcome of the elections will be for citizens and the more they will be inclined to vote (Downs 1957; Grofman 1996; Powell 1986).

Therefore, it should be obvious that the necessity to take the political–institutional context into account is a direct consequence of the development of an electorate making both voting decisions ever more dependent on instrumental orientations.

The theory of modernization is not necessarily at odds with a more political–institutional approach. First, it predicts a gradual shift towards more instrumental orientations in politics. As a consequence one might expect an increasing relevance of the political–institutional context as this will be of great significance for the calculus of individual citizens in deciding whether they would vote and if so for which party or candidate. Therefore, although in the theory of modernization a political–institutional perspective does not play a significant role in explaining the predicted secular trends in advanced industrial democracies, this perspective becomes evermore important in explaining political behaviour once the process of modernization is well on its way. Second, modernization theory by its very nature can only predict similar linear trends in all countries to which the modernization theory applies. However, even if such trends are observed, it is highly unlikely that there would be no fluctuations around the trend line representing the development predicted by modernization theory. Again a political–institutional perspective might be an effective approach in explaining these fluctuations. Combining the two perspectives of modernization theory and a political–institutional perspective asks for a particular research strategy. Testing the predictions of modernization theory asks for comparable time series of election studies going back to the 1960s or at least the 1970s. Testing the impact of the political–institutional context asks for sufficient units of analysis (i.e. elections) to enable the assessment of variations in the political–institutional context. These two requirements are somewhat at odds. The requirement of a long time series limits the number of countries to those with a continuous programme of election studies since the 1960s. Only six countries qualify according to this requirement: Britain, Denmark, (West) Germany, the Netherlands, Norway, and Sweden. As the main focus of this book is on political change we decided to limit our analysis to these six countries. This, of course, means that variations in the political–institutional structure are very limited, at least as far as this context refers to formal institutions like the electoral system. However, variations in the political context, like the polarization between political parties cannot only vary between countries, but between different elections within countries as well. Therefore, in those cases each election rather than each country can be taken as the unit of analysis, which considerably increases the number of cases. Chapter 2 describes in more detail the possibly relevant developments in the party systems of each of the six countries involved.

Because of the limited number of countries in our study and the always disputable functional equivalence of survey instruments in different languages and countries, we have abstained from attempts to explain differences in level on any variable. Instead we focus on trends within countries, trying to explain both fluctuations within countries and differences in trends between countries.

1.7 STRUCTURE OF THE BOOK

The successive chapters follow the argument developed in this chapter. In order to do justice to our ambition to take into account the political–institutional context in the explanation of electoral behaviour, Chapter 2 will present an overview of the development of the party system in each of the six countries. By presenting developments on a number of indicators, the number of (relevant) parties, fragmentation, polarization and volatility, the chapter enables the authors of later chapters to take these developments into account in their attempt to explain electoral behaviour.

Chapter 3 is on turnout. It first describes the trends in turnout. Is there a secular decline in turnout as modernization theory predicts? If not, what is the validity of the underlying theory at the micro-level? To what extent can fluctuations and trends in turnout be explained by the political–institutional context rather than societal developments?

Chapters 4–10 follow the logic of Fig. 1.1. Each of them tries to describe the explanatory power of one of the variables in this figure, and in particular the development of this power over time. These chapters together test the main hypothesis that over time the explanatory power of the variables in Fig. 1.1 will move from left to right in the figure. Also, each of these chapters will explicitly test the alternative hypothesis that the political–institutional context rather than changes in society are responsible for changes and fluctuations in the explanatory power of each of these variables.

In Chapter 11 the findings of the previous chapters will be confronted with the expectations developed in Chapter 1.

Notes

1. The present membership includes most West European countries, but also the national election studies of Canada, the United States, Australia, and New Zealand. So in the meantime it has become a worldwide endeavour.
2. For a more nuanced amendment to Downs' original proposition see a.o. Grofman 1996.
3. Value and ideological orientations are used here as synonyms. Van Deth and Scarbrough (1995: 28) define values as 'conceptions of the desirable'. This is almost identical to 'a verbal image of the good society', as Downs (1957: 96) defines an ideology.
4. It is interesting to note here that the goal of one of the earliest election studies in the United States, the Erie County study by Lazarsfeld et al. was to study 'votes in the making': How do voters make up their minds, and what is the role of the mass media in that process, i.e. during the campaign? However, as it turned out nine out of ten voters had made their decision well before the start of the campaign. It was only then, more or less out of frustration with the failure of their original design that Lazarsfeld et al. developed the famous Index of Predisposition, explaining voting choices from only three social characteristics (Lazarsfeld et al. 1948: 137ff; Visser 1998: 26–7).

Political Parties and Party Systems

Hans-Dieter Klingemann[1]

2.1 INTRODUCTION

Most of the analyses presented in this volume are concerned with causes and correlates of individual-level voting behaviour. As stated in Chapter 1 propositions tend to be general, clearly transcending national particularities. This chapter is different in two respects: (1) it is primarily concerned with macro-level characteristics of national party systems and because the number of cases is small (2) it will not be possible to explain general trends in party system development. Thus, by necessity the analysis is mostly descriptive. It proceeds in two steps. First, it provides an overview of the political parties in the various countries and classifies them by party family. A detailed country-by-country account is presented in the appendix. Second, it deals with three aspects of interparty competition which have been singled out as important by previous research efforts: (1) the number of political parties (fragmentation), (2) the ideological distance between parties (polarization), and (3) the degree of electoral change (volatility). Measures of these characteristics allow a basic description of structure and dynamics of these party systems. The empirical analysis is restricted to the level of the parliament. No attempt is made to portray the party system at the voter level. This task will be tackled in the remaining chapters of the volume.

The literature about West European party systems is quite extensive. There is no possibility for a detailed summary of theoretical approaches and empirical findings. Thus, the general picture has to be painted with the broad brush. Selection of fragmentation and polarization as basic indicators of party systems is guided by Sartori's seminal work (1976) on Parties and Party Systems. Concept and measurement of volatility capitalizes from Pedersen's (1979) efforts to develop an indicator to capture party system dynamics. Innovative and major stocktaking volumes such as those edited by Lipset and Rokkan (1967), Crewe and Denver (1985), Wolinetz (1988), Mair and Smith (1990), Bartolini and Mair

[1]The author wants to thank Jørgen Goul Andersen, John Curtice, Sören Holmberg, Oddbjorn Knutsen, and Jacques Thomassen for helpful comments.

(1990), Lane and Ersson (1994), and Pennings and Lane (1998)—to name just a few—have greatly helped to provide theory and empirical background. With the possible exception of the United Kingdom where the party system—to a large extent—is stable by institutional design (Budge 1998) most country studies report particular events as correlates of major changes or 'earthquake' elections (Ersson and Lane 1998: 36). Often cited historical events of this type are, for example, the reaction to growing secularization and dealignment of the Dutch denominational parties in the mid-1970s (e.g. Tromp 1990), the impact of EU-membership and opposition to the welfare state on the Danish and Norwegian party systems in the early 1970s (e.g. Bille 1990; Heidar 1990) or, in the German case, reunification in 1990 (e.g. Niedermayer 1998; Wessels 2004). Thus, there are good reasons to expect genuine country differences in the dynamics of the party systems under study.

However, theory has also developed arguments which lead to the expectation of general tendencies of party system development. Basically one can distinguish three types of hypotheses. The first one is the well-known 'stability hypothesis'. In their classical study of West European party systems Lipset and Rokkan (1967: 50) state that '...the party systems of the 1960s reflect, with few but significant exceptions, the cleavage structures of the 1920s.' They argue that the high degree of continuity is caused by stable relationships between parties and their constituencies which tend to remain intact from one election to another. Supportive evidence has been provided by Rose and Urwin (1970) and Bartolini and Mair (1990). The second hypothesis predicts long-term secular change. Considering evidence from the early 1970s to the early 1980s authors such as Dalton et al. (1984: 451) expect that 'Electoral alignments are weakening, and party systems are experiencing increased fragmentation and electoral volatility.' They assume that value-orientations of voters have changed from a materialist to a post-materialist orientation causing shifts in the long-term value bases of party support. The rise of the Greens and of new Left-Socialist parties are often cited as typical examples to demonstrate the plausibility of the 'long-term secular change hypothesis'. Short-term non-linear developments—sometimes also called 'erratic'—are expected by the third hypothesis. This theory stresses the importance of strategies of party elites to gain voter support. Ersson and Lane (1998: 24), for example, ascribe voters a high probability of disappointment with any kind of problem solution offered by party government—be it market-oriented or state-based. This logic would explain why periods of political stability are followed by periods of instability.

There are good reasons to believe that the stability hypothesis does not square with current analyses of party system development. A most recent comprehensive comparative study which considers empirical data up to the turn of the century comes to the following conclusion: 'The Lipset–Rokkan model should be abandoned in relation to today's realities, where the crucial question is whether countries remain at a high level of party system instability after the occurrence of an earthquake election or move back to a temporary stable state, as the circular model predicts' (Ersson and Lane 1998: 36). This seems to be a fair summary of results of cutting edge party system research. However, one important caveat should be made. Mair (1990: 175) distinguishes between two types of vote change. The first type would count all changes between individual political parties. The second type would qualify vote change taking place within or across specific blocs or families of parties. This is, indeed, a crucial distinction between two possible processes of change with quite different systemic implications:

In the one case, the individual party volatilities result exclusively from an exchange of votes between the parties of a given political family while, at the same time, leaving the overall alignment wholly unscathed. In the other case, the individual party volatilities are the exclusive result of an exchange of votes across the broader blocs and thus involve a major shift in the balance of the overall alignment. (Mair 1990: 175–6)

This study will not follow up this important insight in its empirical analysis. However, the three general hypotheses described above lead to a set of expectations with which empirical results can be confronted.

In the first part of the chapter, party systems are briefly characterized and the individual parties classified by party family. By distinguishing different phases or periods of the party systems a first description of party system dynamics is attempted. In the second part of the chapter, the party systems will be characterized by degree of fragmentation, polarization, and volatility of parties in parliament.

2.2 POLITICAL PARTIES AND PARTY FAMILIES

Each of the countries under study is home to a large number of political parties. Political parties are the basic elements of any party system. There is no way to include all of them in this study. Parties which are important enough to be included in the analysis are identified by the criterion of electoral strength. Electoral strength is measured by the proportion of seats in parliament gained in an election. This is a pragmatic decision which follows Mackie and Rose (1991). To be sure, there are different thresholds set by the various electoral laws which have to be overcome by parties to enter parliament. However, it is fair to say that parties in parliament have a better chance to influence political decision-making than parties outside parliament. Thus, the criterion stresses the ability of parties to influence binding-decisions. All parties which have entered parliament in any one of the elections in the time period under study will be included in the analysis of party system fragmentation and volatility. Tables have been constructed for vote and seat distributions mostly relying on the third edition of the *International Almanac of Electoral History* compiled by Mackie and Rose (1991). Measures of number of parties in parliament, fragmen-

TABLE 2.1. *Time period covered by the analysis*

Country	Time period	Number of elections
Sweden	Sept. 1944–Sept. 1998	18
Norway	Oct. 1945–Sept. 1997	14
Denmark	Oct. 1945–Nov. 2001	23
Netherlands	May 1946–May 1998	16
Germany	Aug. 1949–Sept. 1998	14
United Kingdom	July 1945–June 2001	16
Total N elections		101

tation, and volatility are based on these tables which are documented in Appendix 1 of this book.

Table 2.1 shows time span and number of elections covered in the analysis. In general the investigation roughly spans the time from the end of the Second World War to the year 2000.

All in all 101 national parliamentary elections have taken place during this period ranging from 14 in Germany and Norway, to 23 in Denmark; 93 different political parties returned deputies to these parliaments. Numbers of political parties meeting the electoral strength citeria range from 8 in Sweden to 25 in the Netherlands. A brief characterization of individual parties is compiled in Appendix 1 of this book. This characterization relies on many sources. Three general sources have been particularly helpful. The first one consists of the volumes of the *Political Handbook of the World* (edited by Banks; Mallory; Stebbins). The second one *Political Parties of the World* has been compiled by Alan J. Day, and the third one *Lexikon zur Geschichte der Parteien in Europa* by Frank Wende. These works deserve special mention because this analysis capitalizes on their documentation.

To ease comparability across countries parties are not only described by their basic programmatic characteristics, coalition behaviour and seat-share in parliament but also by party family. Following are the party families:

- Communists (5 parties)
- Left Socialists (12 parties)
- Socialists (9 parties)
- Ecologists (2 parties)
- Liberals (18 parties)
- Conservatives (5 parties)
- Religious (15 parties)
- Discontent (10 parties)
- Regional (14 parties)
- Single Issue (3 parties)

Most of these party families are well known and there is not much disagreement between experts about party family classification (Mair and Mudde 1998). Two 'families' used here, suggested by Lane and Ersson (1987), have fuzzy boundaries: the 'Left Socialists' and the 'Discontent parties'. Left-Socialist parties typically originate from either socialist or communist parties from which they have split. Most of the new Left-Socialist parties also display elements of an environmentalist ideology. 'Besides the ideological criterion is not clear-cut as the emergence of an environmentalist ideology has attracted the attention of left-wing groupings . . .' (Lane and Ersson 1987: 101). The notion of a 'Discontent party' is not generally accepted either:

> Yet, the phenomena that we intend to cover with the concept are well known. Often these parties have been formed around some concrete issue as the starting point channelling people's discontent. The element of populism in the programmes of these parties is also obvious. Another characteristic is that the discontent parties are headed by charismatic leaders. (Lane and Ersson 1987: 103)

There is an additional problem with party family classification in general. Over time, party family membership may change. For example, a Discontent party may enter the ranks of the Liberal or Conservative party families at a later point in time. No effort is made to address the issue of individual-level party change of party family classification in this analysis.

Classification of parties by party families allows cross-national comparison of their representation in the various parliaments. It is expected that the basic cleavage structure of a country is revealed by averaging proportions of seats for each party family for the time period under investigation. This expectation assumes stability of the general structure of conflict not, however, stability of individual parties which politicize and represent the conflicting interests. Table 2.2 presents an overview of the party families in each country. The number of parties in the various party families is shown in parentheses.

The development of individual parties is not discussed in this chapter, it is extensively described in Appendix 1 of this book. However, the structure and main changes in the party systems of each country are sketched out at the level of party families in the following sections.

2.2.1   *Sweden*

Table 2.A.1 of the appendix to this chapter shows the relative strength of the party families in Sweden. For a comparison the total time period under study has been divided by the election of 1988. The Social Democrats dominate the party system gaining 46.2 per cent of seats on average. The Liberals (28.7 per cent) and the Conservatives (17.8 per cent) follow far behind. These 'old' parties command 96 per cent of the seats during the 1944 to 1985 period and 93 per cent of seats in the period thereafter. Thus they have incurred a slight loss caused by the emer-

TABLE 2.2. *Average proportion of seats and number of parties by party family and country in the time period under consideration: a cross-country comparison*

Party family	Sweden	Norway	Denmark	Netherlands	Germany	United Kingdom	United Kingdom*	Average
Communists	—	0.7 (1)	2.0 (1)	3.1 (1)	0.3 (1)	0.0 (1)	0.0 (1)	1.0
Left Socialists	4.7 (1)	3.2 (2)	7.5 (4)	2.9 (4)	0.9 (1)	—	—	3.2
Socialists	**46.2** (1)	**46.4** (1)	**36.4** (1)	**30.5** (2)	**39.2** (1)	**48.4** (3)	**42.5** (3)	**41.2**
Ecologists	0.9 (1)	—	—	—	2.1 (1)	—	—	0.5
Liberals	**28.7** (2)	**16.1** (3)	**31.7** (7)	**19.2** (2)	**9.2** (1)	2.6 (3)	**11.9** (3)	**17.5**
Conservatives	**17.8** (1)	**20.9** (1)	**15.8** (1)	—	0.8 (1)	**46.8** (1)	**41.6** (1)	**16.9**
Religious	1.3 (1)	**9.7** (1)	1.4 (1)	**43.1** (10)	46.5 (2)	—	—	**17.0**
Discontent	0.4 (1)	2.9 (2)	5.1 (1)	0.9 (4)	0.3 (2)	—	—	1.6
Regional	—	0.1 (2)	0.1 (1)	—	0.3 (2)	1.9 (9)	2.5 (9)	0.4
Single Issue	—	—	—	0.3 (2)	0.4 (1)	—	—	0.1
Other	—	—	—	—	—	0.3 (?)	1.5 (?)	

*Average proportion of votes.
Figures in parentheses, number of parties.

gence of the new parties. Of the two big political blocks the left one (−2.1 per cent points) has suffered much less than the right one (−9.5 per cent points). The big losses of the two liberal parties (−15.0 per cent points) could not be balanced by the gains of the Conservatives (+5.2 per cent points). On the left, however, the losses of the Social Democratic Labour Party (−5.4 per cent points) were largely offset by the gains of the Left Party (−3.3 per cent points). Although still quite small, the Christian Democrats (7.9 per cent of seats on average) and the Ecologists (5.2 per cent of seats on average) seem to have a good chance to become a permanent feature of the Swedish party system. There may also be a possibility for a Discontent party to intrude into the system. At least the Progress Party—the Swedish Discontent Party—was able to gain on average 7.2 per cent of parliamentary seats during 1988–98. The number of parties in parliament has gone up from five in the first period to eight in the second period—a development which will be discussed in Section 2.3 in greater detail.

2.2.2   Norway

An overview of the relative strength of Norwegian party families in parliament is presented in Table 2.A.2 of the appendix. The time periods before and after the 1973 election are contrasted. As in Sweden, the Labour Party is by far the strongest both in terms of votes and in terms of seats. The Conservatives (20.9 per cent), the Liberals (16.1 per cent) and the Christians (9.7 per cent) are trailing behind. A comparison of the two time periods shows that the parties on the left lose 4.1 per cent points. As in Sweden, part of the losses of the Labour Party (−8.6 per cent points) were set off by the growth of the Left Socialists (+4.7 per cent points). On the right the Liberal parties incurred the greatest losses (−9.9 per cent points). Their share of parliamentary seats almost halved. In contrast, both the Conservative Party (+5.1 per cent points) and the Christian People's Party (+3.1 per cent points) did better in the second than in the first period. The populist Progress Party which entered parliament in 1973 could secure 6.8 per cent of the seats on average in the six legislatures they attended. As in Sweden, the number of parties in parliament was on the rise. It rose from seven in the time period from 1945 to 1969 to eleven in the time period from 1973 to 1997.

2.2.3   Denmark

The development of strength of party representation in parliament by party families is shown in Table 2.A.3 of the appendix. The time period has been divided by the 'earthquake' election of 1973. On the left the Social Democrats (44.4 per cent on average) have been the strongest party in parliament by far. However, they lost more than 6 per cent points (−6.2) compared to the early years. The smaller Communist Party also lost seats (−2.1 per cent points) whereas the Left-Socialist parties taken together gained 2.6 per cent points. The overall losses in seats of the left parties combined, however, are rather small (−1.4 per cent points). The emergence in parliament of the Progress Party and the Danish People's Party (Discontent) winning on average 9.9 per cent of the seats in the 1973–2003 period has hit the parties of the Liberal party family as well as the Conservative Party. The combined Liberals commanded 31.7 per cent of seats on average; the Conservatives 15.8 per cent. The Liberals lost 7.2 per cent points of their seat share; the Conservatives 3.8 per cent points. The Christian People's Party, representing the Religious party family, won 2.9 per cent of the seats on average in the time period after 1973. There was a modest rise in the number of parties in parliament. Twelve parties were counted between 1945 and 1971, fourteen parties between 1973 and 2001.

2.2.4 Netherlands

The strength of party families in the Dutch parliament are summarized in Table 2.A.4 of the appendix. The time period has been divided by the 1977 election. The general picture shows great stability as far as the left parties are concerned. Comparing the two time periods their proportion of seats was 36.6 and 36.5 per cent points on average. Results for each one of the three left party families signal a decline for the Communists and slight gains for Left Socialists and Socialists. On the right the combined Liberals (19.2 per cent on average) increase their average proportion of seats from 12 to 28.4 per cent. To an overwhelming degree this increase can be accounted for by the electoral success of the newly formed Democrats 66. The difference of 16.4 per cent points is almost equal to the losses the combined Religious parties (43.1 per cent on average) incurred from the first to the second time period (−17.0 per cent points). Thus, the religious parties have been the bigger losers of the triangular game. The Single-Issue parties, campaigning for the interests of the elderly reached 4.7 per cent of the seats in the 1994 parliament. Number of parties in parliament increased from sixteen to nineteen from the first to the second period.

2.2.5 Germany

The development of the German party system is often divided in different periods such as the formative period (1949–57), the stable period (1961–80) and a period of differentiation, starting in 1983. This division, which could be further subdivided to isolate the impact of unification, is used to describe the development of strength of party families in parliament for the time period under study. On average the Christian Democrats occupied 46.5 per cent of the seats, the Social Democrats 39.2 per cent and the Liberals 9.2 per cent. The biggest change shown by Table 2.A.5 in the appendix relates to the 10.4 per cent point increase of the Social Democrats from the first to the second period. Closer inspection of election results reveals that the party could continuously win an increased number of seats until 1972—a development often labelled as caused by 'Genosse Trend'. Otherwise, the changes between time periods are moderate. The Social Democrats lose 4 per cent points from the second to the third time period. Stable between the first and the second period the Liberals lose 1.1 and the Christian Democrats 3.3 per cent points. The losses in seats of the old parties are made up by the Greens and the Party of Democratic Socialism in the third period. The number of parties in parliament has drastically decreased from the formative to the stable period of the party system. Of the eleven parties in the 1949 parliament there remained just three in 1961. Two new parties were added to the parliament in the period of differentiation. The Greens first gained seats in the 1983 parliament and the Party of Democratic Socialism entered parliament in the 1990 all-German election.

2.2.6   United Kingdom

Table 2.A.6 of the appendix summarizes strength of party families in the United Kingdom. Unlike for the other countries, proportion of votes is added to the information about proportion of seats to show the effects of plurality voting. The time period is divided in a first period up to 1974, followed by the period of the rule of the Conservatives beginning with Margaret Thatcher's premiership in 1979 and ending with John Major's tenure in 1992. The last period covers the Labour governments of Tony Blair.

Vote and seat shares of the smaller parties of the left, the Communists, the Independent Labour Party, and the Social Democratic Party, leave the proportions reached by Labour unchanged. On average, Labour (votes: 42.5 per cent; seats: 48.4 per cent) and Conservatives (votes: 41.6 per cent; seats: 46.8 per cent) are almost equal as far as votes and seats are concerned. The Liberals reach an average of 11.9 per cent of the vote and just 2.6 per cent of the seats. In contrast to the Liberals, vote and seat shares correspond for the national-regional parties (votes: 2.5 per cent; seats 2.2 per cent). As expected, changes of votes are much less expressed than changes in seats. Labour has lost 6.7 per cent points of the vote from the first to the second period and gained 4.2 per cent points from the second to the third. However, the vote change from the first to the second period translated into a reduction of seats in the order of 11.3 per cent points and the increased vote share from the second to the third period resulted in a 26.8 per cent point change of seats (that is, by a factor of 2.4). The almost similar average vote share of the Conservatives (−0.7 per cent points) in the first and second period nevertheless led to an 8.6 per cent point increase of Conservative seats and the party's vote loss from the second to the third period reduced the number of their seats by a factor of 2.7 (−30.9 per cent points). The trend towards an increase in the number of (small national-regional) parties does not show because of the particular cutting of the time periods.

Similarities and differences between the party systems are reflected in Table 2.2 shown earlier. Characteristic for the parliaments of Sweden and Denmark is the strong representation of Socialists, Liberals (Agrarians), and Conservatives. In Germany and the Netherlands the Religious parties, the Socialists, and the Liberals dominate the general pattern—although the Dutch Liberals are much stronger than their German counterpart. As expected, average seat shares in the House of Commons show the dominance of Labour and Conservatives—a pattern not shared by any of the other countries under investigation. Comparing the average vote share, however, reveals a more differentiated conflict structure in the United Kingdom signalling the relative strength of the Liberal Democrats and regional interests in Scotland, Wales, and Northern Ireland. This underlines, again, the importance of the way votes are translated into seats. Unlike the other countries, Norway represents four party families in its parliament. In addition to the Socialists, there are the Conservatives, Liberals (including the Agrarians), and a Religious party. The religious party is the smallest, however, it reaches the size of the German Liberals. In general, the overall pattern of party families assembled in parliament reflect the major cleavages underlying the party systems in the various countries quite well.

Although structurally still dominant it can be demonstrated that these old patterns change in at least five different ways. First, parties of the old Communist party family have disappeared from the parliaments. Second, Left-Socialist parties have gained strength instead. This is true for all countries except the United Kingdom. Third, Green ecology parties entered the parliaments of Germany and Sweden. Fourth, a centre–periphery conflict finds expression in the German and British parliaments. Fifth, Discontent parties have cropped up in the Scandinavian parliaments. Finally, it is noted that Single-Issue pensioners' parties gained access to the Dutch parliament. These are signs of change which have altered the structure of party competition.

2.3 PATTERNS OF PARTY SYSTEM CHANGE

Patterns of party system change as observed at the level of parliament will be discussed in this section. As described in Chapter 1, results of party system development will be compared with different expectations identified in the literature. The stability hypothesis would predict no change, the long-term secular change or dealignment hypothesis would expect increased fragmentation and volatility, whereas short-term non-linear fluctuations would be interpreted as evidence in favour of the action-oriented hypothesis of the importance of party elite strategies.

The analysis proceeds in three steps. In the first step, number and relevance of parties are addressed. This relates to a basic dimension of party systems because the number of parties in the system determines the complexity of their interaction patterns. A growing number of parties over time would be interpreted as a correlate of modernization processes and supportive of the long-term secular change or dealignment hypothesis. In terms of Fig. 1.1 of the general introductory chapter this perspective relates to the boxes 'social structure' and 'long-term predispositions'. In that logic, parties are conceptualized as expressions of the underlying basic structural cleavages and the emergence of new parties is taken both as an indication of change of cleavage structures as well as the related change in long-term attitudinal predispositions of voters such as party identification or ideological orientations. In the second step, party systems are described by their levels of polarization. Polarization is considered as an indicator for the degree of conflict or consensus in the party system. High polarization indicates conflict; low polarization indicates consensus. This part of the analysis relies on

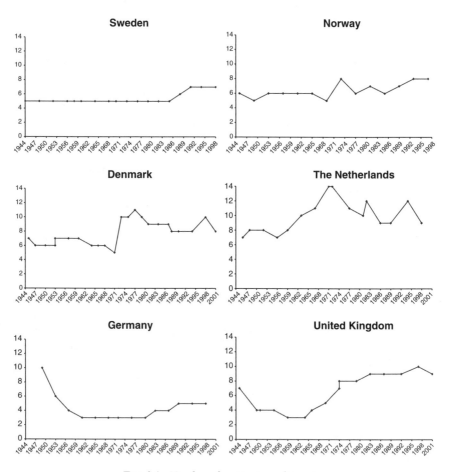

FIG. 2.1. *Number of parties in parliament*

'relevant' parties only and it focuses solely on the left–right party policy dimension. In the tradition of Sartori (1976) the relevance criterion is linked to a party's coalition potential. The justification for the focus on relevant parties is not just pragmatic, because, for example, data may not be available for smaller parties entering parliament. Rather, this limitation adds substantive information. It portrays the party system as an ensemble of parties which either have participated in or supported governments and in that role contributed to make binding decisions. There are many ideological or policy dimensions which may contribute to levels of party system polarization. This analysis locates parties on the left–right party policy dimension which has been identified as the most important dimension by many observers (Fuchs and Klingemann 1990; Knutsen 1988, 1998; Volkens and Klingemann 2003). There are conflicting expectations regarding the development of polarization in party systems over time. The end of ideology hypothesis (Bell 1988) would predict declining levels of polarization for reasons of structural development. Social cleavages lose their grip on both voters and parties in the process of societal modernization. Authors such as Downs (1957) or Kirchheimer (1966) also hypothesize declining levels of polarization. However, their arguments are based on changes in the parties' strategies for electoral competition. Because all parties chase the median voter (who is thought to be of centrist orientation) their programmatic similarities should grow. It is a plausible assumption to link policy polarization to strategies of party competition. Disregarding specific theories of party behaviour, such as the one proposed by Downs, the expectation would be that levels of polarization change as a consequence of changing party policies announced in different elections. This moves the analysis from the box of long-term predispositions to the one of short-term factors. In the third—and last—step, the analysis deals with the development of volatility, defined as changes in seat shares between two adjacent elections. Levels of volatility are expected to be related to both changes in social cleavages and long-term predispositions as well as the short-term forces of politics.

2.3.1 Fragmentation

As has been indicated earlier, number of parties is defined here as number of parties represented in parliament. The calculation of degree of fragmentation is based on proportion of seats and the formula used is the one proposed by Rae (1971):

$$F = \frac{1}{\sum_{i=1}^{n} S_i^2}$$

where S_i denotes the proportion of seats in parliament for party i.

In addition—as just mentioned—an effort has been made to identify the 'relevant' among the parliamentary parties. This honours Sartori's claim (1976:

122–3) who has convincingly argued that electoral strength alone is not enough to determine a party's relevance in the party system. This argument applies, for example, to small parties some of which have coalition potential and are in a position to make or break governments while others never come close to governmental power. However, it may also apply to large extremist parties some of which may possess 'blackmail' potential as, for example, the former Italian Communist Party, while others are kept away from governing continuously. This analysis uses coalition potential as the criterion of 'relevance'. As a rule it is indicated by a party's formal participation in coalition government. However, in the case of minority governments which have been formed quite frequently in the Scandinavian countries, external support is of crucial importance. Thus, external support of minority government has also been taken into account. Data provided by Woldendorp et al. (2000) have been used for classification. A total of 150 party governments of different types have been formed in the time period under consideration. Types of governments are very different between countries. In the countries under investigation all but one of the sixty-one minority governments originated in Sweden, Norway, or Denmark. Ten of the fifteen surplus coalition governments are found in the Netherlands while nineteen out of twenty-nine single-party majority governments were formed in the United Kingdom. Only about a third of the parliamentary parties formally participated in government formation. This shows the importance of the relevance criterion when it comes to select the more important among the smaller parties. Tables 2.A.7 to 2.A.12 in the appendix of this chapter summarize the respective information. Parties which are classified as relevant but have not been part of formal government coalitions are those who have lent external support to minority government.

Results of the analysis of the development of number of parties and levels of fragmentation are summarized in Tables 2.3 and 2.4 as well as in three sets of graphs (Figs. 2.1 to 2.3). Because of the small number of cases (elections) in all countries, inspection of graphs is instructive for the interpretation of linear correlations with time.

On average the number of parties represented in parliament is lowest in Germany (4.4) and highest in the Netherlands (9.9). In the Netherlands, however, as well as in the United Kingdom, this number is greatly reduced when eliminating the non-relevant of the smaller parties. The average number of parties in parliament competing in elections which have coalition potential varies between 7.2 in Denmark and 3 in the United Kingdom. The differences between countries are mirrored by degrees in fragmentation. On average the Dutch parliament (0.78) shows the highest degree of fragmentation, closely followed by the ones in Denmark (0.77), Sweden (0.70), Norway (0.70), and the low fragmentation countries, Germany (0.62) and the United Kingdom (0.53). Correlation coefficients support the hypothesis that party systems become more differentiated and fragmentized in all countries but the Netherlands and Germany. By eliminating

TABLE 2.3. *Number of parties in parliament, number of relevant parties and relation with time*

Number of parties	Sweden 1944–98 Parl.	Sweden 1944–98 Rel.	Norway 1945–97 Parl.	Norway 1945–97 Rel.	Denmark 1945–01 Parl.	Denmark 1945–01 Rel.	Netherlands 1946–98 Parl.	Netherlands 1946–98 Rel.	Germany 1949–98 Parl.	Germany 1949–98 Rel.	United Kingdom 1945–01 Parl.	United Kingdom 1945–01 Rel.
2											2	
3											4	16
4											1	
5	14	14	2	5	1	5		12	6 (6)	6 (6)		
6	1	1	7	5	6	6		2	3 (3)	4 (3)		
7	3	3	2	4	4		2		3 (3)	4 (4)	2	
8			3		4	7	3	2	1 (1)		2	
9					3	2	3				4	
10					4	3	2		1		1	
11					1		2					
12							2					
13												
14							2					
Mean	5.4	5.4	6.4	5.9	7.8	7.2	9.9	5.5	4.4 (3.9)	3.9 (3.8)	6.4	3.0
SD	0.8	0.8	1.0	0.8	1.7	1.7	2.2	1.0	1.9 (1.0)	0.9 (0.9)	2.5	0.0
R	0.712	0.712	0.688	0.788	0.589	0.660	0.441	0.010	−0.286 (0.227)	0.341 (0.409)	0.797	†
Sign.	0.001	0.001	0.007	0.001	0.003	0.001	0.087	0.971	0.322 (0.455)	0.233 (0.165)	0.000	†
N	18	18	14	14	23	23	16	16	14 (13)	14 (13)	16	16

Parl: Number of parties in parliament; Rel: Number of relevant parties
Without the 1949 election.
†No variance.

TABLE 2.4. *Degree of party system fragmentation at the level of seat share and relation with time*

	Sweden	Norway	Denmark	Netherlands	Germany	United Kingdom
Mean	0.70	0.70	0.77	0.78	0.62 (0.61)*	0.53 (0.63)†
SD	0.03	0.04	0.04	0.04	0.05 (0.04)	0.02 (0.06)
R	0.723	0.658	0.592	−0.137	−0.035 (0.518)	0.578 (0.814)
Sign.	0.001	0.011	0.003	0.614	0.904 (0.070)	0.019 (0.000)
N	18	14	23	16	14 (13)	16 (16)

*Without the 1949 election.
†Party system fragmentation at the level of vote share.

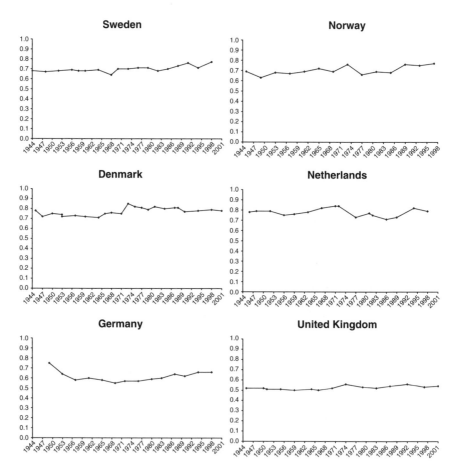

FIG. 2.2. *Degree of fragmentation of parties in parliament*

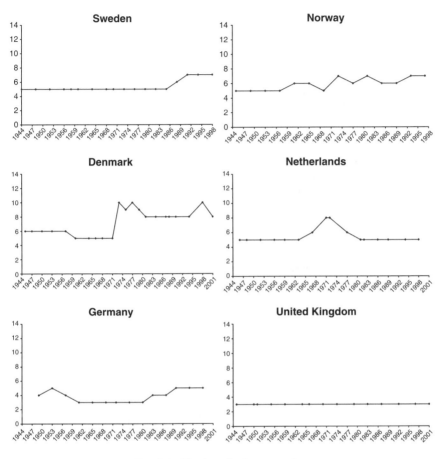

FIG. 2.3. *Number of relevant parties*

the 1949 election, which was governed by an untypical electoral law, Germany also shows an upward trend.

A closer look at the graphs highlights country differences. Concerning number of parties in parliament they show that the upward trend is not gradual. Rather, in Sweden (1988), Norway (1973), and Denmark (1973) it follows a kind of step function. The German development is characterized by a U-shaped curve indicating a period of decline (1949–61, stability (1965–80), and a period of rising numbers of parties thereafter. In the United Kingdom the picture has some similarities with the German one although the period of rising numbers of parliamentary parties already starts in 1966. Enforced by British election law the number of relevant parties remains at the level of three over the whole time period under investigation. The Dutch pattern shows a rising number of parties from 1946 to 1971–2 (both parliamentary and relevant parties), followed by a period of decline. In both periods, however, the number of relevant parties is remarkably stable. In part, this pattern is a reflection of the process of the formation of a single interconfessional party. All three measures of fragmentation are highly correlated. However, Rae's index of fragmentation is more finely tuned to the aspect of party strength and exhibits more variance than both measures of numbers of parties. Thus, as the respective graphs show, it paints the picture with a finer brush but does not change the general conclusions.

To sum up: The analysis of party system fragmentation supports the hypothesis of rising differentiation of party systems. However, results also point to the importance of institutions and actors. The impact of institutions shows clearly when untypical election laws governed the 1949 and the 1990 elections in Germany. It also shows in the United Kingdom where the plurality vote prohibits a more proportional translation of vote shares into seat shares. The impact of parties as actors in their own right is demonstrated in the Netherlands. Here the trend towards a higher degree of fragmentation in the early 1970s was stopped by the decision of party elites to merge three religious parties.

2.3.2 Left–Right Party Policy Polarization

Party system polarization captures an important characteristic of the way parties compete for citizen support. Assuming that parties seek to gain votes at elections primarily by specific policy promises, the degree of polarization reflects similarities and differences of the policies proposed. If parties offer similar policies the degree of polarization is low, if their policies are radically different the degree of polarization is high. Which policies are finally offered is up to party elites. There is a vast literature and much debate among those who investigate decision rules and strategies of party elites. No attempt is made here to discuss this literature. However, much of what has been written in the field follows either Downs (1957) or—more recently—Budge et al. (2001). While Downs attempts to deduce the choice of policies by assuming that parties compete for votes from an issue-oriented electorate, Budge tries to estimate policy positions of parties empirically by analysing party election programmes (Adams et al. 2003). Authors such as Duverger, Sartori, and others relate differing degrees of polarization to party system structure. They deduce the dynamics of party competition from structural characteristics of party systems. Duverger (1954) attributes two-party systems a low and multiparty systems a high degree of polarization. Sartori (1976) refines this consideration by distinguishing between moderate and polarized multiparty systems. This is an important theoretical step because—in addition to the number of parties in the system—the distance between poles of parties, and the interaction between such poles, whether centrifugal or centripetal, is taken into account also (Evans 2002: 156). The distinction has implications for assumptions about the dynamics of party competition. It is hypothesized that two-party and moderate multiparty systems display centripetal, polarized pluralist multiparty systems—in contrast—centrifugal patterns of competition. It is argued that parties in two-party or moderate multiparty systems compete for centrist voters whereas in polarized pluralist systems specific subsets of parties also compete for the more extremist voters on the left and the right (Evans 2002: 157). All these assumptions have come under attack and refined or different hypotheses on the nature of party competition have been proposed. To cite just a few examples: Macdonald and Rabinowitz (1998) have developed a promising approach to solve the paradox that in two-party systems parties do not usually converge at the centre as predicted by theory. Hazan (1995) has introduced the notion of 'moderate-induced polarization' to show that strong centre parties may contribute to an increase in polarization, and Pennings (1998) has argued that only by taking into account vote-, office-, and policy-related functions as well as their interdependence can one hope to tackle the problems of party system polarization successfully. Although these are interesting research perspectives this section will just focus on two rather specific questions: First, what is the pattern of the development of degree of polarization over time? Second, how can one interpret the patterns found?

As has been hinted at, there are conflicting expectations regarding development of party system polarization over time. A secular decline of levels of polarization is predicted by the end-of-ideology hypothesis. Budge (1994), in contrast, assumes a substantial degree of ideological stability of party elites as a consequence of uncertain political environments. He also expects responses to shifts in public opinion and past election results. In an empirical analysis Adams et al. (2003) confirm the response-to-public-opinion shifts hypothesis in situations where public opinion is clearly shifting away from a party's policy position. As predicted by Budge they also find a strong element of inertia but they did not find responses to past election results. Linking shifts in party strategy to shifts in polarization makes linear trends unlikely. Rather, non-linear short-term patterns of change—caused by issues, political leaders or retrospective judgements as suggested by the 'short-term factors' box of Fig. 1.1 in Chapter 1–seem to be more plausible.

A test of the assumption that party system structure has an impact on decision-making is possible both across countries as well as within some of the countries under study. United Kingdom and Germany represent party systems of moderate pluralism over the whole period of time. In the other four countries the situation is different for different elections. Applying Sartori's numerical criterion (up to five parties: moderate pluralism, six and more parties, polarized pluralism) one would expect to find centripetal tendencies, that is, lower levels of polarization, in the Swedish 1944–85 elections, in the Norwegian 1945–57, 1969 elections, in the Danish 1960–71 elections, and in the Dutch 1946–59 and 1981–98 elections. In contrast, all other elections should show centrifugal tendencies, that is, higher levels of polarization.

Most empirical studies of party system polarization and the dynamics of party competition rely on the assumption that there is one major dimension along which parties compete for votes: the left–right dimension. The substantive meaning of the left–right dimension has been conceptualized in different ways. Downs restricts its meaning to the degree of state intervention in the economy; Budge et al. (2001) propose a broader definition. Using data collected by Huber and Inglehart (1995), Knutsen (1998) has carefully analysed experts' understanding of left and right for thirteen European countries. He shows that, on average, 65 per cent of the content of the left–right dimension was defined in economic or class issues. This leaves room for other elements determining the meaning of the left and right in politics. Klingemann (1979) and Fuchs and Klingemann (1990) have presented similar findings for citizens' understanding of the terms left and right in Austria, United Kingdom, Germany, the Netherlands, and the United States. They argue that the left–right dimension represents the highest level abstraction of political communication which offers the possibility to specify and re-specify more detailed policy positions. However, with respect to content they conclude that a purely spatial ordering of political objects alone does not provide orientation and communication:

What these meanings are depends very much on the specific types of political conflict that dominated in the course of the institutionalization of the left–right symbolism in the sphere of politics. At least in the European countries it is, above all, a matter of class and religious cleavages. (Fuchs and Klingemann 1990: 233)

Bauer-Kaase (2001) has analysed changes in the understanding of left and right in politics for Germany. She demonstrates that, indeed, new meaning elements—based on new issues—have been incorporated in citizens' understanding of the terms left and right in politics. However, there were but a few of them and the pace of change was rather slow.

This study joins the mainstream in that it relies on the left–right dimension as the major generalized measure of the parties' policy positions. It is easily admitted that there are other than just the left–right party policy dimension. For example, it seems as if policy positions on the environment or on European integration vary independently of the generalized left–right party policy position. However, there are also good reasons to assume that the left–right dimension is dominant. In part that can be explained from the perspective of political communication between parties and voters. Policy supply by parties and policy demand by citizens must be communicated. Successful communication presumes a generalized exchange media which helps to simplify such complex modes of interaction (Parsons 1969; Luhmann 1981, 1984). These exchange media must be able to support long and rapid communication links and in so doing stabilize the structure of interactions. Otherwise slow and risky adjustment processes would be required. Fuchs and Klingemann (1990: 205) have argued that in most Western societies the left–right schema serves this communication function for the political system and, in addition, an orientation function for both collective actors and individual citizens.

The left–right scale designed to map party policy positions is constructed very much along the lines as the one described and used in *Mapping Policy Preferences* (Budge et al. 2001). The empirical analysis is based on quantitative content analysis of party election programmes. A detailed description of methods and technical procedures is provided by Budge et al. (2001). Thus, it is sufficient to say that the text of each election programme is divided into (quasi-) sentences (coding units) most of which contain an argument. Each of these arguments are subsequently coded using one of the fifty-six categories of the common classification scheme. Coding results are standardized by expressing the frequency of occurrence of a particular argument as a percentage of the total number of the document's coding units. The left–right scale used here has been slightly modified. It is, however, highly correlated with the original scale ($r = 0.95$). For this author the modified scale has a higher deductive quality. It also has a slightly higher discriminatory power between the parties of the various countries (η^2 'new': 0.74; η^2 'old': 0.70). The fifty-six categories of the initial 'old' classification scheme have been regrouped into four general policy fields and twenty-two categories (Table 2.5).

The left–right party policy positions displayed in each election were calculated by summing up the percentages for five 'left' and five 'right' positions and the former sum was subtracted from the latter. Theoretically, values can vary between $+100$ and -100.

If a party advocated one of the following policies, this added to its 'right' policy position:

- Freedom and human rights
- Market economy
- Traditional morality; law and order
- Welfare state, limitation
- Military strength

If, in contrast, a party advertised policies as listed below they counted for this party's 'left' policy position:

- Democracy
- Planned or mixed economy
- Cultural libertarianism
- Welfare state, expansion
- Peace and détente

On average these ten categories cover about half of the content of party election programmes (Sweden: 56.4 per cent; Norway: 51.7 per cent; Denmark: 42.9 per cent; Netherlands: 52.9 per cent; Germany: 49.9 per cent; United Kingdom: 44.9 per cent). Considered separately the categories also carry a quite different weight.

TABLE 2.5. *The classification scheme*

State Policy	CMP codes aggregated*
Freedom and Human rights	201
Democracy	202
Constitution	203, 204
Centralization	302
Decentralization	103, 301
Modes of government	303, 304, 305
Economic Policy	
Market economy	401, 402, 403, 407, 414
Planned or mixed economy	404, 405, 406, 409, 412, 413, 415
Economic infrastructure	410, 411
Environmental protection	416, 501
Agriculture	703
General economic orientation	408
Social Policy	
Traditional morality, law & order	603, 605, 608
Cultural libertarianism	604, 607
Welfare state, limitation	505, 507, 702
Welfare state, expansion	502, 503, 504, 506, 701
Social group politics	704, 705, 706
Foreign Policy	
Military strength	104
Peace and détente	105, 106
Nationalism	109, 110, 601, 606,
International cooperation	107, 108, 602
Special relationships	101, 102

*Codes as described by the Comparative Manifesto Project (Budge et al. 2001: 222–8).

On average 'Expansion of the welfare state' (20.1 per cent) and 'Market economy' (10.9 per cent) are by far the most important, followed by 'Traditional morality' (4.4 per cent), 'Planned or mixed economy' (3.3 per cent), 'Freedom' (3.1 per cent), 'Democracy' (3.0 per cent), 'Peace and détente' (2.7 per cent), 'Military strength' (1.3 per cent) while 'Limitation of the welfare state' (0.8 per cent) and 'Cultural libertarianism' trail far behind. These meaning components of the generalized left–right policy dimension prove to be pretty stable over time. Only seven out of a total of sixty possible correlations with time reach a 0.001 level of significance.

The same is not true, however, for 'new' policy positions such as advocating 'Environmental protection' or 'International cooperation' (which, in the West European context, almost exclusively refers to a pro-European Union position). 'Environmental protection' shows a highly positive correlation with time in all countries under study and so does 'International cooperation'—with one exception—the United Kingdom. This finding generally supports the claim of the emergence of a multidimensional policy space. However, whatever the 'new' policy dimensions in their importance they are still outdistanced by the 'old' left–right party policy dimension.

No matter the details, the overall placement of parties on the left–right party policy dimension should meet the test of face validity. Because of the widespread familiarity of the left–right schema not only experts 'know' where parties ought to be located. On the other hand, expert opinion, too, should be an appropriate source of validation. The expert ratings reported by Huber and Inglehart (1995) are used to evaluate the measure used in this analysis. Tables 2.6 to 2.9 provide the respective evidence.

The important face validity test is left to the reader. Comparison of placement by content analysis and experts shows a high degree of congruence in all countries (overall Pearson correlation 0.91, $N = 37$). Most of the differences in placement relate to parties of the centre. However, any differences between the two measures are small, indeed.

Two indices have been proposed in the literature to measure degree of polarization of party systems. The first one has been suggested by Taylor and Hermann (1971), the second one by Huber (1989). Both rely on deviations of left–right party policy positions from the grand mean. Details of different measurement have consequences as is shown by Knutsen (1999b) who argues that while the differences might appear trivial they, in fact, are substantial. Both indices weight (squared or non-squared) distance by vote shares. Evans (2002: 168–70) rightly argues—as part of a more comprehensive methodological critique—that with any index combining two or more variables it is impossible to discern whether shifts in polarization are due to changes in voting weights or in ideological distance.

The polarization measure used in this analysis is designed to capture the movement of parties on the left–right party policy dimension relative to each other, not relative to the grand mean. This is achieved, first, for each election, by adding the absolute distances between each pair of parties' position on the left–right party policy dimension. These absolute distances are not squared because—in an effort to portray the supply side of politics—there is no reason to privilege larger distances between pairs of parties. The sum of the absolute distances is standardized. Maximal similarity is expressed by the value of zero (all parties are located at the same left–right party policy position), maximal dissimilarity is expressed by a value of 100. The formula used here was originally suggested by Shahla and Beloussov (Social Science Research Centre Berlin). It reads as follows:

TABLE 2.6. *Mean left–right party policy position as derived from election programmes and expert location* (Huber/Inglehart 1995)

Sweden

Party	Mean party policy left–right position	SD	Huber/Inglehart Mean	Huber/Inglehart SD (N)
Left Party (18)	−32.7	13.8	2.62	0.92 (13)
Social Democratic Labour Party (18)	−29.0	15.0	4.08	0.83 (13)
Green Ecology Party (3)	−11.5	10.6	4.25	0.97 (8)
Centre Party (18)	−6.0	10.0	5.92	0.92 (13)
Christian Democratic Party (4)	−4.9	2.7	7.00	0.85 (11)
Liberal People's Party (18)	−4.2	19.9	5.92	0.62 (13)
Moderate Coalition Party (18)	32.7	19.7	8.33	0.75 (12)
New Democracy (1)	42.8	—	9.09	0.79 (11)
Total (98)	−7.3	15.8		

η^2: 0.70

Norway

Party	Mean party policy left–right position	SD	Huber/Inglehart Mean	Huber/Inglehart SD (N)
Socialist Left Party (9)	−39.4	9.1	2.55	0.89 (11)
Norwegian Labour Party (14)	−33.7	6.5	4.13	0.93 (8)
Liberal Party (12)	−21.0	11.1	5.86	0.99 (7)
Centre Party (14)	−10.6	14.9	5.33	1.15 (9)
Christian People's Party (14)	−3.0	13.0	6.55	1.08 (11)
Conservative Party (14)	1.2	10.5	8.00	0.74 (11)
Progress Party (6)	39.2	13.1	9.18	0.57 (11)
Total (83)	−12.2	11.4		

η^2: 0.77

Denmark

Party	Mean party policy left–right position	SD	Huber/Inglehart Mean	Huber/Inglehart SD (N)
Socialist People's Party (17)	−38.1	13.2	2.89	0.57 (9)
Red–Green Unity List (3)	−30.9	12.2	2.00	1.00 (2)
Danish Communist Party (9)	−28.1	7.7	No rating	
Social Democrats (23)	−23.8	11.6	4.22	0.79 (9)
Radical Party (23)	−14.2	10.0	5.67	0.47 (9)
Justice Party (9)	12.7	8.6	No rating	
Centre Democrats (11)	14.2	15.1	6.00	1.15 (9)
Danish People's Party (2)	16.4	2.0	No rating	
Christian People's Party (11)	17.4	7.9	6.22	0.79 (9)
Liberals (23)	19.3	15.2	8.11	0.31 (9)
Conservative People's Party (23)	24.1	16.0	7.56	0.50 (9)
Progress Party (11)	28.2	13.7	9.13	0.93 (8)
Total (165)	0.2	12.7		

η^2: 0.78

TABLE 2.6. (*Contd.*)

Netherlands

Party	Mean party policy left–right position	SD	Huber/Inglehart Mean	Huber/Inglehart SD (N)
Radical Political Party (6)	−32.9	10.0	No rating	
Labour Party (16)	−29.8	10.6	4.20	1.47 (10)
Green–Left (3)	−27.7	4.0	1.78	0.63 (9)
Democrats 66 (10)	−20.3	12.2	4.80	0.75 (10)
Democratic Socialists '70 (3)	−17.7	6.0	No rating	
Catholic People's Party (9)	−10.4	13.8	No rating	
Christian Democratic Appeal (7)	−8.7	8.0	6.30	0.78 (10)
Anti-Revolutionary Party (9)	0.3	12.7	No rating	
Christian Historical Union (9)	1.8	17.8	No rating	
People's Party for Freedom and Democracy (16)	7.0	8.3	7.20	0.98 (10)
Total (88)	−12.2	11.4		

η^2: 0.63

Germany

Party	Mean party policy left–right position	SD	Huber/Inglehart Mean	Huber/Inglehart SD (N)
Party for Democratic Socialism (3)	−41.5	7.8	1.50	0.50 (4)
The Greens* (5)	−27.7	8.0	2.91	1.08 (11)
Refugee Party (1)	−26.7		No rating	
Social Democrats (14)	−20.9	8.4	3.83	0.69 (12)
Free Democrats (14)	−3.7	6.4	5.64	0.77 (11)
German Party (3)	−2.3	17.5	No rating	
Christian Democratic Union (14)	7.0	13.5	6.42	0.86 (12)
Total (54)	−10.0	17.4		

η^2: 0.70
*1983–7: The Greens; 1990: The Greens/Alliance '90; 1994– : Alliance '90/The Greens

United Kingdom

Party	Mean party policy left–right position	SD	Huber/Inglehart Mean	Huber/Inglehart SD (N)
Labour Party (16)	−26.2	9.4	4.43	0.82 (14)
Liberal Democrats* (16)	−8.7	14.3	5.21	0.94 (14)
Conservative Party (16)	3.2	15.5	7.71	0.96 (14)
Total (48)	−10.5	13.3		

η^2: 0.47
*1945–79: Liberal Party; 1983 and 1987: Alliance; 1992– : Liberal Democrats

$$P = \frac{\sum\limits_{i=1}^{n-1} \sum\limits_{j=i}^{n-1} abs \left(p_{j+1} - p_i\right)}{2 \times (round(n/2) \times round \left(n/2 - 0{,}5\right))}$$

where p_i denotes the left–right policy position of the party i and p_j denotes the left–right party policy position of party j, and n denotes the number of parties.

The development of left–right party policy polarization over time is shown in Fig. 2.4. Considering the country graphs there is not much support for a linear end of ideology hypothesis. In fact none of the (linear) correlations with time is significant at the 0.05 level.

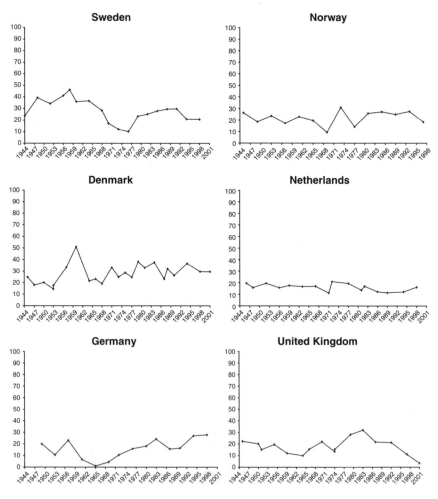

FIG. 2.4. *Degree of left–right polarization of relevant parties*

TABLE 2.7. *Average levels of polarization of relevant parties and relation with time*

Country	Average	SD	Pearson's r	Significance	N
Sweden	27.9	9.9	−0.482	0.043	18
Norway	21.9	5.9	0.148	0.614	14
Denmark	27.8	8.4	0.378	0.076	23
Netherlands	16.0	3.1	−0.506	0.046	16
Germany	15.8	8.4	0.481	0.082	14
United Kingdom	17.8	7.1	−0.126	0.642	16
Overall	21.8	7.6	0.009	0.931	101

There are, however, systematic differences between countries. Average levels of polarization are high in Denmark and Sweden, medium in Norway, and low in the United Kingdom, Germany, and the Netherlands. This finding is as expected and points to the existence of structural constraints or country specific traditions which mould competition behaviour of party elites.

However, similar differences were not found within the four countries which experienced both periods of moderate and periods of polarized pluralism. Analyses of variance did not show significant within country change. This finding would deserve further study. Obviously, polarization patterns do not change so quickly by changing numbers of parties but cling to country tradition.

It is highly plausible to assume that movements on the left–right party policy dimension reflect party elites' efforts to try to stay in touch with their voters. Left–right self-placement of voters will be discussed in Chapter 7 in more detail. However, it is indicative to note that movements of parties and movements of voters on the left–right dimension show a strong relationship overall as well as in each of the countries studied.

At least one firm conclusion can be drawn from the analysis of left–right party policy polarization: there is no long-term secular trend. Rather, it seems likely

TABLE 2.8. *Association of left–right party policy score and left–right self-placement of party voters*

Country	Pearson's r	Significance	N	Election years
Sweden	0.759	0.000	58	68, 70–98
Norway	0.688	0.000	46	73–97
Denmark	0.853	0.000	43	79, 84, 90–98
Netherlands	0.664	0.000	47	71–98
Germany	0.850	0.000	26	76, 83–98
United Kingdom	0.664	0.000	33	64–01
Overall	0.726	0.000	253	64–01

that the non-linear—sometimes cyclical—patterns are caused by policy strategies of party elites.

2.3.3   *Volatility of Parties in Parliament*

This last step of the overview on general characteristics of the party systems deals with the development of volatility. Has volatility increased or decreased over time? Volatility is in itself an indicator of change. In this case it is defined as changes of seat shares of parties in parliament. Thus, the indicator reflects stability and change of party support from one election to the next mediated by the rules which translate votes into seats. Low levels of volatility signal stability and, thus, a relatively secure environment for party elites. The reverse is the case for high levels of volatility which put party elites on shifting grounds. However, higher levels of volatility may also signal a party system's ability to adjust and adapt to changing problem agendas. It is expected that volatility of parties in parliament is both driven by changing numbers of parties—new parties entering or old parties leaving parliament—and by changing issue agendas which pull voters away from parties they have supported traditionally. The formula to calculate volatility is taken from Pedersen (1979).

$$V_t = 1/2* \left(\sum_{i=1}^{n} |p_{it} - p_{it} - 1| \right)$$

where p_{it} is the proportion of seats for party i at election t, and $p_{it} - 1$ is the proportion of seats for party i at the previous election t minus 1.

Figure 2.5 shows the development of degree of volatility of parties in parliament over time. On average the Netherlands, Denmark, and Norway show higher levels of volatility as compared to the United Kingdom, Sweden, and Germany. However, these means hide sudden peaks in the Netherlands, Denmark, and the United Kingdom which can be easily related to important political events such as the creation of the Christian Democratic Appeal as an interconfessional party and its participation in the May 1977 election: the 1973 election in Denmark which shook the foundations of the Danish party system, and the May 1997 election in the United Kingdom which drastically changed the power distribution in that country. The development of volatility over time is more gradually upwards in Sweden and Norway while it is also gradual but somehow U-shaped in Germany. The trend line for Germany would also point (slightly) upwards would one disregard the 1949 election which had a very untypical result (mainly caused by the election law). This general picture is also reflected in the correlation of degree of volatility and time. While none of the country specific coefficients is significant at the 0.001 level they all indicate a modest increase of volatility over

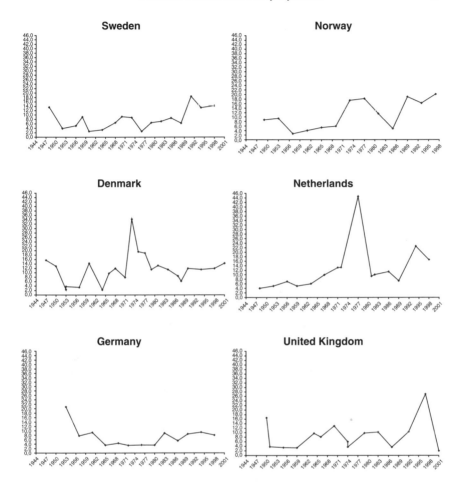

FIG. 2.5. *Degree of volatility of parties in parliament*

time, Germany being the exception. However, as suggested above, if taking away the 1949–53 seat changes, Germany falls in line, too. Thus—although not significant in statistical terms—there is a tendency of increased levels of volatility over time in all countries under study.

Checking relations with other important indicators of party system structure results mainly relate changing levels of volatility to the number of parties in parliament. In statistical terms number of parties in parliament 'explains' 21 per cent of the variance in volatility of seats in parliament. Left–right party policy polarization and left–right party policy range show no significant relations with volatility. The latter finding may, however, be due to the curvilinear trends of polarization and deserve further analytical attention.

TABLE 2.9. *Average level of volatility of parties in parliament*

Country	Average	SD	Pearson's r	Significance	N
Sweden	8.2	4.5	0.459	0.064	17
Norway	11.0	6.4	0.654	0.015	13
Denmark	11.7	7.0	0.179	0.425	22
Netherlands	12.4	10.2	0.428	0.111	15
Germany	7.4	4.6	−0.274	0.365	13
			(0.293)*	(0.355)*	(12)*
United Kingdom	8.7	6.6	0.204	0.467	15
Overall	10.0	6.8	0.268	0.009	95

*Without 1949–53.

2.4 CONCLUSIONS

The main concern of this chapter was a historical description of the development of six West European national party systems in the years after the Second World War. The focus was on political parties which gained access to parliament. Strength of types of parties constituted a major dimension of similarities and differences between countries. In Sweden and Denmark, Social Democrats, Liberals (Agrarians) and Conservatives play a major role. In contrast, the Netherlands and Germany know strong interconfessional Christian parties. The Norwegian party system shows continuous representation of all traditional party families while the British House of Commons is dominated by Labour and Conservatives. Following Sartori an effort has been made to distinguish between relevant and non-relevant parties.

Because of the small number of cases no general hypotheses of party system change could be tested in a strict sense. However, the development over time of three important characteristics of party systems could be confronted with hypotheses found in the literature. These assumptions relate to the party systems' (1) degree of fragmentation, (2) degree of polarization, and (3) degree of volatility. Regarding all three characteristics different authors have suggested three different types of hypotheses: a 'stability' hypothesis, a long-term secular change or 'dealignment' hypotheses, and a non-linear, short-term 'erratic' change hypothesis. While the first two hypotheses mainly rely on structural arguments the third one stresses the importance of strategies of party elites.

Overall, results do not support the stability hypothesis. Measures of fragmentation, polarization, and volatility show a good deal of change over time. The development of party system fragmentation—mainly the number of parties represented in parliament—comes closest to the secular change hypothesis. The number of parties increases over time signalling a process of party system differentiation. One of the consequences of this increase in number of parties is a growing level of volatility. Thus, levels of volatility are also slightly upward.

TABLE 2.10. *Correlates of volatility of parties in parliament*

		Sweden N = 17	Norway N = 13	Denmark N = 22	Netherlands N = 15	Germany N = 13	UK N = 15	Total N = 95
N parties in parliament	Pearson's r	0.719	0.711	0.534	0.377	0.810	0.217	0.459
	Significance	0.001	0.006	0.010	0.166	0.001	0.467	0.000
N relevant parties in parliament	Pearson's r	0.719	0.618	0.560	0.232	0.671		0.403
	Significance	0.001	0.024	0.007	0.405	0.012		0.000
Party system Fragmentation (parliament)	Pearson's r	0.522	0.605	0.614	−0.099	0.554	−0.035	0.308
	Significance	0.032	0.029	0.002	0.726	0.049	0.901	0.002
Party system Polarization (relevant parties)	Pearson's r	−0.073	0.231	0.109	0.128	0.125	0.119	0.087
	Significance	0.781	0.448	0.628	0.649	0.684	0.672	0.404
Left–right policy range (relevant parties)	Pearson's r	−0.057	0.321	0.176	0.201	0.174	0.119	0.137
	Significance	0.828	0.285	0.434	0.472	0.569	0.672	0.186
Election years	Pearson's r	0.458	0.654	0.179	0.429	−0.274	0.204	0.268
	Significance	0.064	0.015	0.425	0.111	0.365	0.467	0.009

However, it can also be demonstrated that in most countries major events intervene in the process of party system differentiation. This points in the direction of the importance of strategies of party elites. It seems as if development of party system polarization is particularly congruent with the assumption of elite driven change.

Finally, comparing party system structures across countries based on average scores for fragmentation, polarization, and volatility one can distinguish clearly between the United Kingdom and Germany on the one hand and Norway and Denmark on the other. The first two countries are below average on all three dimensions indicating 'moderate' party system dynamics, while the latter two are above average. Sweden scores high on fragmentation and polarization but low on volatility, a fact which may be explained by the long periods of dominance of the Social Democrats. The Netherlands combine above average fragmentation and volatility with below average polarization. The lack of a truly conservative party may explain this pattern.

APPENDIX

TABLE 2.A.1. *Proportion of parliamentary seats of party families in Sweden by time period*

Party family	1944–85 14 parl. % seats	1944–85 14 parl. N parties	1988–98 4 parl. % seats	1988–98 4 parl. N parties	1944–98 18 parl. % seats	1944–98 18 parl. N parties
Communists						
Left Socialists	4.0	1	7.3	1	4.7	1
Socialists	47.4	1	42.0	1	46.2	1
Total 'Left'	51.4	2	49.3	2	50.9	2
Ecologists	—	—	5.2 (3)*	1	5.2 (3)*	1
Liberals	32.0	2	17.0	2	28.7	2
Conservatives	16.6	1	22.1	1	17.8	1
Religious	—	—	7.9 (3)*	1	7.9 (3)*	1
Discontent	—	—	7.2 (1)*	1	7.2 (1)*	1
Regional						
Single Issue						
N parties		5		8		8

*If the number of parliaments in which the party is represented deviates from the number of parliaments in the time period it is given in brackets. In this case average proportion of seats relates to that number.

TABLE 2.A.2. *Proportion of parliamentary seats of party families in Norway by time period*

Party family	1945–69 7 parl. % seats	1945–69 7 parl. N parties	1973–97 7 parl. % seats	1973–97 7 parl N parties	1945–97 14 parl. % seats	1945–97 14 parl. N parties
Communists	3.3 (3)*	1	—	—	3.3 (3)*	1
Left Socialists	1.3 (2)*	1	6.0	2	5.0 (9)*	2
Socialists	50.7	1	42.1	1	44.4	1
Total 'Left'	52.3	3	48.2	3	50.3	4
Ecologists						
Liberals	21.0	2	11.1	3	16.1	3
Conservatives	18.4	1	23.5	1	20.9	1
Religious	8.1	1	11.2	1	9.7	1
Discontent	—	—	6.8 (6)*	1	6.8 (6)*	1
Regional	—	—	0.6 (2)*	2	0.6 (2)*	2
Single Issue						
N parties		7		11		12

*If the number of parliaments in which the party is represented deviates from the number of parliaments in the time period it is given in parentheses. In this case average proportion of seats relates to that number.

TABLE 2.A.3. *Proportion of parliamentary seats of party families in Denmark by time period*

Party family	1945–71 11 parl. % seats	1945–71 11 parl. N parties	1973–2001 12 parl. % seats	1973–2001 12 parl N parties	1945–2001 23 parl. % seats	1945–2001 23 parl. N parties
Communists	5.9 (6)*	1	3.8 (3)*	1	5.2 (9)*	1
Left Socialists	8.3 (5)*	2	10.9	4	10.1 (17)*	4
Socialists	50.7	1	42.1	1	44.4	1
Total 'Left'	46.6	4	45.2	6	45.9	6
Ecologists						
Liberals	35.4	6	28.2	4	31.7	7
Conservatives	17.8	1	14.0	1	15.8	1
Religious	—	—	2.9 (11)*	1	2.9 (11)*	1
Discontent	—	—	9.9	2	9.9 (12)*	2
Regional	0.6 (3)*	1	—	—	0.6 (3)*	1
Single Issue						
N parties		12		14		18

*If the number of parliaments in which the party is represented deviates from the number of parliaments in the time period it is given in brackets. In this case average proportion of seats relates to that number.

TABLE 2.A.4. *Proportion of parliamentary seats of party families in the Netherlands by time period*

Party family	1946–72 9 parl. % seats	1946–72 9 parl. N parties	1977–98 7 parl. % seats	1977–98 7 parl. N parties	1946–98 16 parl. % seats	1946–98 16 parl. N parties
Communists	5.0	1	1.8 (3)*	1	4.2 (12)*	1
Left Socialists	3.1 (5)*	2	4.5	4	3.9 (12)*	4
Socialists	29.9	2	31.2	2	30.5	2
Total 'Left'	36.6	5	36.5	7	36.5	7
Ecologists						
Liberals	12.0	2	28.4	2	19.2	2
Conservatives						
Religious	50.2	7	33.9	5	43.1	10
Discontent	2.7 (4)*	2	1.0 (4)*	3	1.8 (8)*	4
Regional						
Single Issue	—	—	4.7 (1)*	2	4.7 (1)*	2
N parties		16		19		25

*If the number of parliaments in which the party is represented deviates from the number of parliaments in the time period it is given in parentheses. In this case average proportion of seats relates to that number.

TABLE 2.A.5. *Proportion of parliamentary seats of party families in Germany by time period*

Party family	1949–57 3 parl. % seats	1949–57 3 parl. N parties	1961–80 6 parl. % seats	1961–80 6 parl. N parties	1983–98 5 parl. % seats	1983–98 5 parl. N parties	1945–98 14 parl. % seats	1949–98 14 parl. N parties
Communists	3.7 (1)*	1	—	—	—	—	3.7 (1)*	1
Left Socialists	—	—	—	—	4.1 (3)	1	4.1 (3)*	1
Socialists	32.5	1	42.9	1	38.9	1	39.2	1
Total 'Left'	33.8	2	42.9	1	41.3	2	40.4	3
Ecologists	—	—	—	—	5.9	1	5.9 (5)*	1
Liberals	10.3	1	9.4	1	8.3	1	9.2	1
Conservatives	3.6	1	—	—	—	—	3.6 (3)*	1
Religious	47.3	2	47.8	1	44.5	1	46.5	2
Discontent	4.2 (1)*	2	—	—	—	—	4.2 (1)*	2
Regional	4.5 (1)*	2	—	—	—	—	4.5 (1)*	2
Single Issue	5.5 (1)*	1	—	—	—	—	5.5 (1)*	1
N parties	11	11	3	3	5	5	13	13

*If the number of parliaments in which the party is represented deviates from the number of parliaments in the time period it is given in parentheses. In this case average proportion of seats relates to that number.

TABLE 2.A.6. Proportion of parliamentary votes and seats of party families in the United Kingdom by time period

Party family		1945–74 10 parl. % seats	1945–74 10 parl. N parties	1979–92 4 parl. % seats	1979–92 4 parl. N parties	1997–2001 2 parl. % seats	1997–2001 2 parl. N parties	1945–2001 16 parl. % seats	1945–2001 16 parl. N parties
Communists	votes	0.4 (1)*	1	—	—	—	—	0.4 (1)*	1
	seats	0.3 (1)*	1	—	—	—	—	0.3 (1)*	1
Left Socialists	votes								
	seats								
Socialists	votes	44.5	2	37.8	2	42.0	1	42.5	3
	seats	49.6	2	38.3	2	63.1	1	48.4	3
Total 'Left'	votes	44.5	2	37.8	2	42.0	1	42.5	4
	seats	49.6	2	38.3	2	63.1	1	48.4	4
Ecologists	votes								
	seats								
Liberals	votes	9.7	2	14.6	1	17.6	1	11.9	3
	seats	1.6	2	2.5	1	7.4	1	2.6	3
Conservatives	votes	43.3	1	42.6	1	31.2	1	41.6	1
	seats	47.4	1	56.0	1	25.1	1	46.8	1
Religious	votes								
	seats								
Discontent	votes								
	seats								
Regional	votes	1.4 (8)*	5	3.9	6	5.0	7	2.5 (14)	9
	seats	1.2 (8)*	5	3.2	6	4.2	7	2.2 (14)	9
Single Issue	votes								
	seats								
Others	votes	1.1 (5)*				4.3		1.5 (7)*	
	seats	0.8 (5)*				0.2		0.6 (7)*	
N parties			9		10		10		17

*If the number of parliaments in which the party is represented deviates from the number of parliaments in the time period it is given in parentheses. In this case average proportion of seats relates to that number.

TABLE 2.A.7. *Determining the relevant parties. Involvement in government, Sweden 1944–98*

Parties	% of time in government	Number of Prime Ministers	Single party majority governments	Minimal winning coalition governments	Surplus coalition	Single party minority governments	Minority coalition governments	Caretaker governments	Total number of governments
LS Vänsterpartiet									
SO Sveriges Socialdemokratistiska Arbetareparti	83.1	21	3	3	1	14			21
EC Miljöpartiet de Gröna									
LI Centerpartiet	26.4	3		5			2		7
LI Folkpartiet Liberalerna	16.9	1		2		1	2		5
CO Moderate Samlingspartiet	12.4	1		2			1		3
RE Kristdemokraterna	5.6						1		1
DI Ny Demokrati									
R Mittenpartierna									
R Medborgelig Samling									
Total	19487*	26	3	5	1	15	2		26

*Total number of days September 1944–September 1998 equal 100%
LS Left Socialist, SO Socialist, EC Ecology, LI Liberal, CO Conservative, RE Religious, DI Discontent, R Regional
Bold face: Relevant parties

TABLE 2.A.8. *Determining the relevant parties. Involvement in government, Norway 1945–97*

Parties	% of time in govt	Number of Prime Ministers	Single party majority govt	Minimal winning coalition govt	Surplus coalition	Single party minority govt	Minority coalition govt	Caretaker govt	Total number of govts
COM Norges Kommunistiske Parti									
LS Rød Valgallianse									
LS Sosialistisk Venstreparti									
SO Det Norske Arbeiderparti	71.2	17	6			11			17
LI Senterparti	25.9	2		3			5		8
LI Venstre	18.8			2			3		5
LI Det Liberale Folkeparti									
CO Høyre	19.9	5		3		1	3		7
RE Kristelig Folkeparti	25.9	2		3			5		8
DI Fremskrittsparti									
R Folkeaksjonen Framtid for Finmark									
R Kystpartiet									
Total	20441*	26	6	3		12	5		26

*Total number of days October 1945–September 1997 equal 100%

COM Communist, LS Left Socialist, SO Socialist, LI Liberal, CO Conservative, RE Religious, DI Discontent, R Regional

Bold face: Relevant parties

TABLE 2.A.9. *Determining the relevant parties. Involvement in government, Denmark 1945–2001*

Parties	% of time in govt	Number of Prime Ministers	Single party majority govt	Minimal winning coalition govt	Surplus coalition	Single party minority govt	Minority coalition govt	Caretaker govt	Total number of govts
COM Danmarks Kommunistiske Parti									
LS Socialistisk Folkeparti									
LS Venstresocialisterne									
LS Faelles Kurs									
LS Enheedslisten – De Roed Groenne									
SO Socialdemokratiet	64.0	20		3		12	5		20
LI Venstre	38.0	4		1		2	8		11
LI Det Radikale Venstre	40.0	1		4			5		9
LI Retsforbundet	6.2			2					2
LI Dansk Samling									
LI De Uafhaengige									
LI Liberalt Centrum									
LI Centrum Demokraterne	19.4			1			4		5
CO Konservative Folkeparti	30.3	5		1			7		8
RE Kristeligt Folkeparti	13.2			1			3		4
DI Fremskridtspartiet									
DI Danske Folkeparti									
R Det Sleswigske Parti									
Total	20473*	30		4		14	12		30

*Total number of days October 1945 to November 2001 equal 100%
COM Communist, LS Left Socialist, SO Socialist, LI Liberal, CO Conservative, RE Religious, DI Discontent, R Regional
Bold face: Relevant parties

TABLE 2.A.10. *Determining the relevant parties. Involvement in government, Netherlands 1946–98*

Parties	% of time in govt	Number of Prime Ministers	Single party majority govt	Minimal winning coalition govt	Surplus coalition	Single party minority govt	Minority coalition govt	Caretaker govt	Total number of govts
COM Communistische Partij van Nederland									
LS Pacifistisch-Socialistische Partij									
LS Politieke Partij Radikalen	8.2				1				1
LS Socialistische Partij									
LS Groen Links									
SO Partij van der Arbeid	57.2	7		3	8				11
SO Democraten 66	24.4			1	3			1	5
SO Democratische Socialisten 70	2.0			1					1
LI Volkspartij voor Vrijheid en Democratie	62.0			6	5			1	12
RE Katholieke Volkspartij	56.1	6		3	8			3	14
RE Katholieke Nationale Partij									
RE Nieuwe Roomse Partij									
RE Anti-Revolutionaire Partij	45.1	3		2	6			3	11
RE Christelijk-Historieke Unie	40.7			2	6			2	10

Party						
RE Staatkundig Gereformeerde Partij						
RE Gereformeerd Politiek Verbond						
RE Reformatorische Politieke Federatie						
RE Evangelissche Volkspartij						
RE Christen Democratisch Appel	**29.7**	**6**	**4**	**1**		**1**
DI Rechtse-Volkspartij						
DI Middenstands Partij						
DI Centrumpartij						
DI Centrumdemocraten						
SI Allgemeen Ouderen Verbond						
SI Unie+						
Total	20478*	22	8	10	4	22

*Total number of days May 1946 – May 1998 equal 100%
COM Communist, LS Left Socialist, SO Socialist, RE Religious, DI Discontent, SI Single Issue
Bold face: Relevant parties

TABLE 2.A.11. *Determining the relevant parties. Involvement in government, Germany 1949–98*

Parties	% of time in govt	Number of Prime Ministers	Single party majority govt	Minimal winning coalition govt	Surplus coalition	Single party minority govt	Minority coalition govt	Caretaker govt	Total number of govts
COM Kommunistische Partei Deutschlands									
LS Partei des Demokratischen Sozialismus									
SO Sozialdemokratische Partei Deutschlands	32.3	7		7				1	8
EC Buendnis 90 / Die Gruenen									
LI Freie Demokratische Partei	85.4			16	3			1	20
CO Deutsche Partei	22.0			1	4				5
RE Deutsche Zentrumspartei									
RE Christlich Demokratische Union/ Christlich Soziale Union	73.6	19	1	11	4			3	19
DI Wirtschaftliche Aufbauvereinigung									
DI Deutsche Reichspartei									
R Bayernpartei									
R Suedschleswigscher Waehlerverband									
SI Gesamtdeutscher Block/Bund der Heimatvertriebenen und Entrechteten	3.6				1				1
Total	17909*	26	1	17	4			4	26

*Total number of days August 1949–September 1998 equal 100%

Buendnis 90/Die Gruenen cover all three 'Green' party formations; The Christlich Demokratische Union and the Christlich Soziale Union form a single party (Fraktion) in the parliament.

COM Communist, LS Left Socialist, SO Socialist, EC Ecologist, LI Liberal, CO Conservative, RE Religious, DI Discontent, R Regional, SI Single Issue

Bold face: Relevant party

TABLE 2.A.12. *Determining the relevant parties. Involvement in government, United Kingdom 1945–2001*

Parties	% of time in govt	Number of Prime Ministers	Single party majority govt	Minimal winning coalition govt	Surplus coalition	Single party minority govt	Minority coalition govt	Caretaker govt	Total number of govts
COM Communist Party									
SO Independent Labour Party									
SO Labour Party	37.9	8	7			1			8
SO Social Democratic Party									
LI National Liberal Party									
LI Liberal Party									
LI Liberal Democrats									
CO Conservative Party	62.1	12	12						12
R Scottish National Party									
R Party of Wales									
R Ulster Unionists									
R Ulster Popular Unionist Party									
R UK Unionist Party									
R Democratic Unionist Party									
R United Ireland									
R Social Democratic and Labour Party									
R Sinn Fein									
Others									
Total	20406*	20	19			1			20

*Total number of days July 1945–June 2001 equal 100%

COM Communist, SO Socialist, LI Liberal, CO Conservative, **R** (National) Regional

Bold face: Relevant parties

Electoral Turnout[1]

Kees Aarts and Bernhard Wessels

General elections have become less important for the citizens of modern Western democracies, and therefore the turnout figures have fallen over the past decades. This is at least what many theorists want us to believe, and what has also been suggested in many empirical studies (e.g. Idea 2002: 76–7; Teixeira 1987, 1992; Wattenberg 2000). It is one of the core ideas of the modernization theory introduced in Chapter 1 of this book. But is it also supported by the empirical evidence in Northwestern Europe? This is the question we address in the present chapter.

According to the prevalent view, 'modern' citizens feel more capable of handling their own political affairs, will therefore decide for themselves when and how to get involved in political action, and consequentially will not machine-mindedly go out to vote. This view has in recent years often been rephrased into the expectation that electoral turnout in Western societies will decrease. But it is not shared by everyone. At least two other perspectives on the global development of turnout in elections are encountered.

First, processes of individual modernization include not just the growth of personal autonomy just denoted, but also a rise in the level of formal education. Education is usually seen as a stable co-variate of turnout (Wolfinger and Rosenstone 1980; Blais 2000: 52). With the help of some strong assumptions about the causal mechanism at work, it might be deduced that a rise in the level of education would *ceteris paribus* be associated with a rise in turnout.

Second, whereas modernization suggests a monotone development, another perspective emphasizes the contextual nature of electoral turnout. In the latter perspective, whether citizens vote depends at least to some extent on the alternatives offered to them by the political parties. This perspective thus highlights the supply side of the electoral process.

In the literature on electoral turnout, the combination of the first two—contradictory—views on developments in turnout (increase in personal autonomy and in level of education) is known as the 'puzzle of electoral participation' (Rosenstone and Hansen 1993). Evaluating this puzzle will be our main preoccupation in the first part of the present chapter. In the second part, we investigate how the supply side of elections affects the decision to vote or not.

We investigate the trends in turnout in parliamentary elections in Britain, Germany, the Netherlands, Denmark, Norway, and Sweden over a period of more than 30 years, using macro-level and individual data. Macro-level data on turnout is our point of departure, survey data are introduced where we expect these to add to the macro-overview. We address three questions: Has turnout declined? What are the effects of age, level of education, political interest, and political efficacy on turnout? What are the effects of contextual and election-specific circumstances on turnout?

3.1 HAS TURNOUT DECLINED?

3.1.1 A Matter of Definition?

The notion that electoral turnout has declined over the past decades is widespread, but not as substantiated as one might wish. Perhaps surprisingly, a major problem for the assertion of turnout decline stems from the definition of turnout.

The prime evidence for the presumed decline in electoral turnout comes from the United States. Analysing US data, Teixeira (1987, 1992) pointed to 'the disappearing American voter'. Rosenstone and Hansen (1993), Miller and Shanks (1996), and Wattenberg (2000) also present evidence for a decline, and it has recently been the topic of a major research project (Patterson 2002).

The official turnout figures in the US presidential and congressional elections do show a steady decrease from 1960 to 2000. However, there are good reasons why in this case it might be misleading to trust common knowledge and official figures. These figures define turnout as the percentage of voters in the 'voting age population'. McDonald and Popkin (2001) have shown that the apparent decline in official statistics can almost completely be accounted for by changes in the composition of the 'voting age population'. The denominator in the turnout ratio usually includes aliens without voting rights, a group that has steadily increased over the past decades. When the denominator is redefined as the 'voting-eligible population', the turnout rates show a progressively upward correction over the years, up to almost 6 per cent in 2000. As a result, the 'downward trend' in turnout rates largely disappears (McDonald and Popkin 2001: 969).

This may seem an American peculiarity, but it is more than that. The 'voting age' definition of turnout has become something of a worldwide standard recently. As a result, many authoritive statements on developments in turnout are based on inclusion in the electorate of persons who are not full citizens by legal requirements—a group that, as a result of immigration, has grown in most Western democracies.

The 'voting age' definition of turnout makes some sense in the United States because of the decentralized, voluntary registration procedures there, which result in a comparatively very low registration rate. Hence, defining turnout as a percentage of the registered voters only is not completely satisfying. But for almost all other democracies, it is turnout defined in relation to the number of persons on the electoral list that captures best the power of an electoral system to mobilize its voters (Blais and Dobrzynska 1998: 241). In this chapter we define turnout as the percentage of the registered voters who cast a vote. The exclusion of certain social categories from the computation of turnout levels may of course cover up lamentable situations (Norris 2002: ch. 3), but should in our view not affect the measurement of turnout.

3.1.2   Trends in Turnout, 1945–2002

Whether a decline in turnout is observed, also depends to some extent on the selected *time frame*. The time frame that is selected varies from the past decade to the past two centuries, and it is obvious that the particular selection affects any conclusions on trends. In the latest decade or two, there are signs of a global decrease in turnout (Idea 2002). But looking at the trends in Western Europe since 1945, Topf (1995) emphatically rejects his research hypothesis that electoral participation has declined. The time frame in this chapter is 1945–2002 for the aggregate analyses. For the analyses of survey data, the time frame is (approximately) 1970–2000—the period for which comparable national election study data are available.

The two panels of Fig. 3.1 show the development of turnout, defined as the number of valid votes cast as a percentage of the number of registered voters, for all parliamentary elections since 1945. It should be noted that the Netherlands had compulsory voting until 1970, and turnout figures there show a sharp decline immediately after its abolishment but recover quickly to an internationally average level.

Evidently, turnout in the 1990s tends to be somewhat lower than in the 1970s and 1980s in all six countries, but that is about all that can be said. Recent elections in Germany and in the Netherlands show a slight recovery from the declining trend, but the 2001 British election had an alarmingly low turnout. In Sweden and Norway, the more recent elections also show a decrease compared with the preceding two decades, but in Denmark there is no such development. On the basis of Fig. 3.1 it does not seem warranted to conclude that there is an acute problem with turnout.

3.2   THE PUZZLE OF ELECTORAL PARTICIPATION

3.2.1   The Potential of Individual Level Data

The absence of a secular decrease in voter turnout in the past few decades may be the net result of a number of competing forces on the individual decision to vote or not. That such competing forces are at work, is one of the premises of the literature on modernization processes and voting (Powell 1986; Fuchs and Klingemann 1995; Topf 1995; Wattenberg 2000). Individual level data should therefore show what lies beneath the wavy curves of Fig. 3.1. But what do we expect them to show? Various theoretical arguments have been constructed, which lead to different expectations. We provide a brief overview of these arguments.

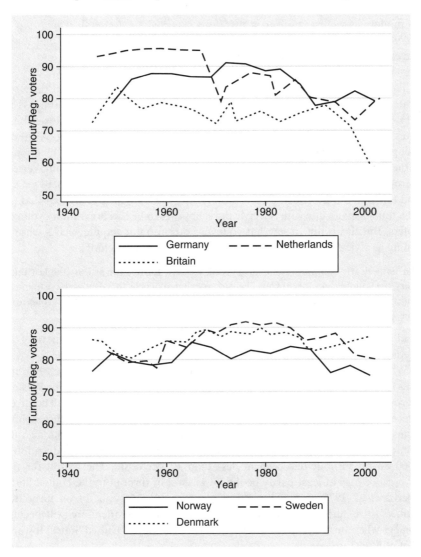

FIG. 3.1. *Turnout in parliamentary elections 1945–2003*
Source: Idea 2002

Fuchs and Klingemann (1995) argue that modernization processes in Western democracies result in 'informed participant citizens', who are characterized by a high sense of personal efficacy and an instrumental orientation towards politics, and who generate new demands on the political system. The political system cannot always respond to all of these demands. A lack of responsiveness of political parties, one major category of actors in the political system, will become evident first in turnout figures, since many other ways for participation are open to modern citizens. Turnout is therefore expected to *decrease, if and only if political responsiveness is low*. It is, however, the general assumption that this is the case, given the successful mobilization of new social movements and—later on—new parties.

Topf (1995) submits that the changing demographic composition of the electorate might account for the apparent lack of evidence of declining turnout (Fig. 3.1). As a result of the changing age composition of the electorate (lower birth rates, more elderly persons) the expectation may be a rise in turnout. Also, the rising level of education—an aspect of individual modernization mentioned earlier—would result in higher turnout. Topf's analyses show that in Western European countries there is indeed a persistent (positive) correlation between age and turnout, but no effect of education. Topf (1995: 46) also points out that the idea that casting your vote is a civic duty, appears to be less firm among younger voters. But this is not to say that younger voters do not acquire such a sense of voting as civic duty later in their lives. Topf (1995: 45) concludes:

Our data clearly confirm...that throughout Western Europe for at least the last thirty years, the youngest electors are less likely to vote than older electors. But we have found no evidence of any general trend towards an increasing difference between these groups over time.

And on the basis of these findings, plus the stable trend lines in turnout, Topf predicts an *increase* in turnout.

While Topf's results do not take into account the developments since 1990, and thus miss the alleged more recent decline, it is notable that his results for Western Europe are not completely in line with those for the United States. The divergence lies in the impact of the level of education on turnout. Rosenstone and Hansen (1993: 135) point to the strong impact of education on turnout in the United States, and Teixeira (1992) estimates that the impact of rising education in 1960–88 on turnout has been no less than 12 per cent.[2] The reason for this divergence may at least partly be the lower level of turnout in the United States (Verba et al. 1978: 6–8). The impact of any explanatory factor on turnout is limited since turnout cannot exceed 100 per cent, and therefore will become smaller when turnout moves from a 40–60 per cent level (United States) towards that ceiling (Europe).

Verba et al., (1995: 48) argue, however, that voting, as an act of political participation, is fundamentally different from other participatory acts in that it requires only a little time, no skills or money. The effect of education on voting is not a direct effect, but runs via what they call 'engagement': political interest, political efficacy, and party identification (1995: 360). They show that once political engagement is taken into account, the independent effect of education on turnout disappears.

3.2.2   The Puzzle

When these various pieces of research are considered together, it appears that education, age, interest, efficacy, and turnout constitute the major parts of a 'puzzle of electoral participation' (Rosenstone and Hansen 1993).[3] This puzzle amounts to the question what the net effect on turnout is of four individual-level characteristics: level of education, age, political interest, and political efficacy. The bivariate relationships between turnout and these four factors display a consistent pattern, which is depicted in Fig. 3.2. Education is negatively correlated with age, and positively with interest, efficacy, and turnout. Age correlates positively with interest and turnout, but negatively with efficacy. Finally, interest and efficacy are positively correlated with each other and with turnout.

We have already seen that the dynamics of turnout in our six countries add up to a basically stable, albeit more recently lower level of electoral participation over the past decades. During the same period, there was a well-documented increase in the level of education in these countries, which would *ceteris paribus* have led to higher turnout, just as the changing age structure would have. But that higher turnout did not happen. Individual modernization theory holds that the sense of personal efficacy has increased (Inkeles, quoted by Fuchs and Klingemann 1995: 12). Finally, political interest is also expected to have increased. This leaves us with the question: How has the net stability of turnout come about?[4]

There are some factors that make a direct assessment of the puzzle of electoral participation awkward, and that leads us towards an indirect test. First, since most of the empirical relationships schematically depicted in Fig. 3.2 are weak, or moderately strong at the best, we cannot take it for granted that the puzzle provides a valid and reliable overview of the factors affecting electoral turnout. There are many other, uncharted forces that change over time and affect electoral

Age	−			
Interest	+	+		
Efficacy	+	−	+	
Turnout	+	+	+	+
	Education	Age	Interest	Efficacy

FIG. 3.2. *Pattern of bivariate relationships*

turnout. Two of these will be dealt with in this chapter, and will be referred to as party alienation and party indifference.

Second, even though national election studies have been run for decades in these six countries, time series of equivalent indicators are surprisingly scarce. In many election surveys, one or more of those indicators are simply absent. The election surveys that are useful from our point of view do not provide comparable time series for indicators of political efficacy or political interest. We therefore assess the empirical status of the puzzle in static rather than dynamic format.

3.3   A FIRST TEST

3.3.1   Indicators and Data

Equivalent measurements of age, education, and turnout are available in all election studies for the six countries in this volume. For interest and efficacy, this is not the case, and the availability of data for these key concepts determines to a large extent the scope of our analyses.

For measuring political interest, we use the direct survey question into subjective political interest (basic format: 'Would you say that you are very, fairly, or not at all interested in politics?', with variations in the root and in the possible answers). This is the indicator that is the most common, and arguably also the most valid single-item measure of political interest. Despite this status, it was excluded from many of the election studies under consideration.

The latter is also true of most indicators of political efficacy. The most frequently found single-item measures of political efficacy read: 'Politics is too complicated for people like me' and 'People like me have absolutely no influence on governmental policies'. These questions highlight what has been termed the internal dimension of efficacy: the feeling that one can personally understand, and take action towards, politics. We have used either of these indicators when they were assessed in the surveys.

Because of missing survey questions[5], we had to exclude many election studies in the individual-level analyses. For each country, each time point for which the appropriate data are available is indicated in Tables 3.1 and 3.2. The variables of interest from these studies have been harmonized, and the studies have subsequently been pooled per country. We have not weighted the various election years, since the numbers of respondents are not very different over the years per country, and since we use the pooled data for testing relationships rather than trends. A final word of caution: Survey data provide information on individual attitudes and behaviour of voters that often cannot be obtained otherwise. However, the survey design has a number of shortcomings, some of which are evidently present in this paper. Reported turnout and political interest are both associated with measurement problems in surveys. Reported turnout suffers especially from overreporting (people say that they voted but in reality they did not vote), but also from stimulus effects due to pre-election interviews (people sometimes vote because a pre-election interview about politics triggers their interest in voting), and from sample selectivity (people who like politics and voting will be more willing to take part in a survey than those who do not). The latter problem, sample selectivity, can also be expected to affect the measurement of political interest: People who are not interested at all in politics, are probably less willing to spend an hour or more talking about politics. These problems are well documented (e.g. Burden 2000). Only in the cases of Norway and Sweden is there an adequate solution for the measurement problem of turnout. Data on reported turnout in the Norwegian and Swedish election studies are validated against the actual turnout data in election records. Therefore, in these two cases we use validated turnout rather than reported turnout.

3.3.2   Logistic Regression Models

Table 3.1 reports six logistic regression analyses, one for each country, of reported turnout on the other elements of the puzzle. The explanatory variables are two socio-demographic characteristics—age in years at the time of the election and highest attained level of education (in three rough categories from low to high); and two attitudinal characteristics—political interest and political efficacy. Finally, the year of the election was included as an 'explanatory' variable, even though the election year in itself does not offer an explanation of turnout. The election year is included in these analyses because it will capture a trend in turnout after political interest and political efficacy have been controlled for.

Table 3.1[6] shows the multivariate effects of a one-unit change in explanatory variables on the odds ratio of voting. For example, the odds of voting to non-voting in Britain increases by a factor 1.025 for each year of age, keeping all other factors constant which means that for each year of age the likelihood of a positive deviation from the average turnout increases by 2.5 per cent.

The impact of age on turnout is positive in all six countries. Education has a positive impact too, but this effect is not statistically significant in Britain and in Denmark. Topf (1995) reports more null findings on the impact of education on turnout. Political interest has a positive impact on turnout in all six countries, and it is strong: By and large, the odds of voting are doubled with every unit increase on the four-point interest scale. In contrast, the indicator of political efficacy shows mixed results. In the Netherlands, Norway, and Sweden, political efficacy has a positive effect on electoral turnout. In Denmark and Germany, however, the impact of efficacy is not statistically significant. In Britain, no suitable survey measure of political efficacy is available. Finally, controlling for interest and efficacy, the year of the election is negatively related with turnout in Britain, Germany, Norway, and Sweden. It should be stressed that this

TABLE 3.1. *Logistic regression models of turnout—I*

	Britain		Denmark		Germany		Netherlands		Norway		Sweden	
	Odds ratio	R.s.e.	Odds ratio	R.s.e.	Odds ratio	R.s.e.	Odds ratio	R.s.e.	Odds ratio	R.s.e.	Odds ratio	R.s.e.
Year	0.974*	0.002	0.992	0.006	0.951*	0.006	1.010†	0.005	0.972*	0.006	0.963*	0.005
Age	1.025*	0.002	1.018*	0.005	1.014*	0.005	1.028*	0.003	1.030*	0.002	1.018*	0.002
Education	1.058	0.037	1.130	0.110	1.579*	0.133	1.494*	0.118	1.310*	0.074	1.306*	0.063
Political Interest	1.903*	0.064	2.850*	0.270	2.744*	0.202	2.222*	0.207	1.927*	0.111	1.832*	0.086
Political Efficacy	n.a.	—	1.114	0.063	1.289	0.167	1.706†	0.182	1.092*	0.031	1.228*	0.054
$N =$	12,974		5,912		6,163		5,685		7,799		16,336	
Pseudo R^2	0.088		0.096		0.141		0.091		0.074		0.056	
Hoshmer-Lemeshow χ^2	83.29, df = 18, p = 0.000		38.67, df = 18, p = 0.003		12.73, df = 18, p = 0.807		24.90, df = 18, p = 0.128		25.99, df = 18, p = 0.100		21.22, df = 18, p = 0.268	
Area under ROC curve	0.703		0.733		0.781		0.728		0.696		0.678	
Elections analysed	1974-F, 1974-O, 1979, 1997, 2001		1971, 1979, 1994, 1998		1972, 1976, 1994, 1998		1971, 1986, 1994, 1998		1981, 1985, 1989, 1993, 1997		1979, 1982, 1985, 1988, 1991, 1994, 1998	

R.s.e.: Robust standard errors; *: p < 0.01; †: p < 0.05; n.a. : not available.

negative relationship does not imply a decrease in turnout in the long run. It is rather to a large extent due to the particular selection of surveys, which in all six countries amounts to a comparison of data from the 1970s or early 1980s with data from the 1990s (and, in the British case, 2001). As we have shown earlier, this particular time frame does show a decrease in turnout in most countries. This is illustrated by the slightly positive impact of the election year on turnout in the Netherlands, which can be explained by the inclusion of the 1971 election when turnout was unusually low (compulsory voting had just been abolished).

At least as important as the individual effects is the fit of the explanatory model as a whole to the survey data. For this purpose, Table 3.1 contains several diagnostics. The first is the pseudo-R^2, a measure indicating the proportion of variance in turnout that can be attributed to the explanatory variables. We note that the proportion of explained variance is rather low, ranging from 0.056 in Sweden to 0.141 in Germany. This model apparently does not explain more than a small fraction of the decision to vote. This is an important finding, since it implies that there are many other factors affecting turnout.

Two other model diagnostics are reported. The χ^2 test evaluates the fit of the actual 'positive' outcomes (voters) to the predicted 'positive' outcomes (voters) in different combinations of values of the explanatory variables.[7] The test shows that the model fits the data in Germany, the Netherlands, Norway, and Sweden, but not in Britain or Denmark. Finally, we conducted Receiver-of-Characteristics (ROC) analyses in order to determine how well the model would predict voting behaviour *and* abstaining behaviour. The 'area under the ROC curve' indicates the likelihood that, for randomly selected respondents, the predicted probability to vote for a voter exceeds that for a non-voter. This likelihood ranges from 0.678 in Sweden to 0.781 in Germany.

Reflecting on the main results of this section, we investigated the effects of level of education, age, political interest, and political efficacy on electoral turnout. There are no data to assess the developments in political interest and political efficacy over the complete time span in which individual modernization would make itself felt. Therefore we provided an approximate first test, pooling the available data per country and including the year of the election into the analyses. The results do not unequivocally support the modernization thesis, but do not bluntly oppose it either. The impact of political interest on turnout is clearly present, but the effect of political efficacy is less pronounced. Age shows the expected relationship with turnout, but in the case of education the findings are not statistically significant in two countries. Finally, we have shown that with these elements of the puzzle of electoral participation, we are able to explain only a very modest part of the individual variation in turnout, and that there are time-related factors which we still have to pinpoint precisely.

3.4 THE CONTEXT OF ELECTORAL PARTICIPATION

In Section 3.3.2 we have considered the impact of two of the three principal kinds of factors emphasized by turnout studies: socio-demographic and socio-psychological factors. Both sets focus on what may be called the 'demand side' of politics; they contrast the voters with the non-voters. Alternatively, we can focus on the supply side of politics, and ask what it is in political life that leads people to vote or not to. In this section we turn to this question.

It is often overlooked that citizens do not make political decisions in a vacuum. Choices take place in a context. Previous studies of the context of political participation have shown that the (institutional) supply side of politics matters for how voters can, and do engage in politics, ranging from the degree of political sophistication of a voting population (Gordon and Segura 1997) to turnout (Powell 1986; Jackman and Miller 1995). It is known that the importance of choice options available to individuals matters, and that turnout decreases by the absence of a realistic candidate or party choice (Campbell et al. 1960).

Converse and Niemi (1971) have pointed to the fact that motivational factors are most important for political participation and have to be differentiated in internalized motivation and external stimulation. Thus, our topic in this section is as to which degree voting participation is influenced by the nature of alternatives presented to citizens in elections. This is a particular and specific aspect of the political context (Plane and Gershtenson 2004: 70). It makes a difference whether political parties offer policy alternatives or not, and whether a race is close or not. Voters compare political offers and make their choice if there is a satisfactory one. This, however, is only a necessary but not sufficient condition to participate in elections.

The policy alternatives that political parties offer can be found in the rhetoric of their leaders and in the election platforms. Because reliable historical data on leaders' rhetoric are not available, we focus on the election platforms. These election programmes are a *nonreactive* source of data on what political parties offer the electorate, in the sense that the programmes do not themselves produce measurement error as survey respondents might do by producing, for example, contrast and assimilation effects (Webb et al. 2000). But supply, in order to meet demand, has to be perceived by the citizens. Thus, in a second stage the individual-level model of turnout introduced earlier in this chapter will be extended by measures of the perceived context.

3.4.1 Election Platforms: The Parties' Offer

Let us start again with the message conveyed by election-level data. The *Comparative Manifestos Project* (CMP) has analysed the contents of all party platforms of the non-negligible parties in parliamentary elections since 1945, for all six countries in our analyses (and for many other countries, too).[8] Sentences in these programmes have been coded into fifty-four thematic topics from seven policy domains. Subsequently, thirteen left-wing topics and thirteen right-wing topics have been identified, and the position of a party platform on the left–right dimension was determined by subtracting the percentage of right-wing topics of the total number of topics mentioned, from the corresponding percentage of left-wing topics (Klingemann et al. 1994). The polarization of an election is then determined by calculating a weighted average distance between the parties on this left–right dimension.

The message that we are after, is contained in Figs. 3.3 and 3.4. Fig. 3.3 shows the development of the left–right polarization of elections over time, for each of the six countries. It is obvious that polarization, thus defined, shows great variation from election to election and between countries. But is it possible to draw additional conclusions? In Germany, the 1960s were a time of very low polarization, but in the 1990s, German party platforms were highly polarized on the left–right dimension. The Netherlands shows little development, but the 1980s and 1990s in this country were clearly less polarized than earlier decades. The Britain shows high polarization in the early Thatcher years, and a quick decline in the 1990s, with the rise of Blair's New Labour. Moving north, Danish elections tend to be more polarized than Norwegian, whereas Sweden shows a depolarization throughout the 1960s and 1970s, and some polarization after-wards.

Figure 3.4 depicts the relationship between the degree of polarization and turnout in elections, by country. The dashed line in each of the panels is the (linear) regression of turnout on polarization; the regression coefficient b and the amount of explained variance by the regression R^2 are also shown in the panels. It shows that the relationship between polarization and turnout is as often positive (Netherlands, Britain, Denmark) as it is negative (Germany, Norway, Sweden). The strength of the relationship varies considerably. The strongest relationships are found in Sweden and the Netherlands. But in Sweden the more polarized elections tend to go together with a clearly *lower* level of turnout, whereas in the Netherlands the relationship is the other way around (for the Dutch case, only elections after the abolishment of compulsory voting have been considered in Fig. 3.4). In the other four countries, the relationship is weak at best.

These findings are probably not surprising for anyone who is a bit familiar with the specifics of elections in each of the six countries. At the same time these findings have neither revealed a trend pointing to depolarization—indicating the 'end of ideology', nor a race to the centre, nor a strong (positive) relationship between polarization and turnout. This means that from this particular perspective there is no reason to assume a trend in turnout development. Rather, situations vary from election to election, and thus election-specific models (Aldrich 1993: 271) or rather models taking into account the particular context

Aarts and Wessels

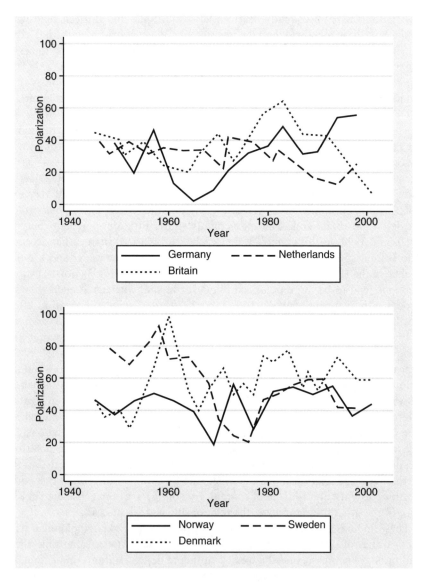

Fig. 3.3. *Polarization in party manifestos 1945–2003*
Source: Idea 2002, Party Manifestos Project

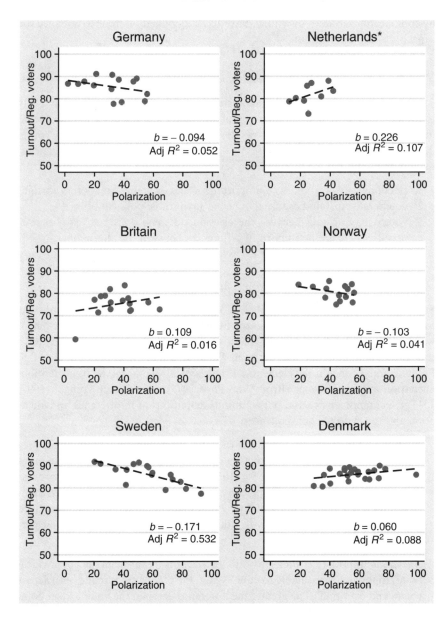

Fig. 3.4. *Turnout and polarization, 1945–2003*
Source: Idea 2002, Party Manifestos Project
*For the Netherlands only elections after abolishment of
compulsory voting (1970) have been considered

by comparable variables over time, have to be identified in order to enhance the capacity to explain turnout.

3.4.2   Individual Level Data

The introduction of election characteristics into the model of turnout obviously follows Downs' insight (1957) that voting decisions are made in terms of expected utility from one's decision. We now take a closer look at the individual voting decision from the Downsian perspective. With regard to abstaining in elections, maximizing expected utility can mean several things:

1. elections may be about so unimportant offices or bodies that voters abstain;
2. voters may abstain because there is no favourable political offer;
3. voters may abstain because the election outcome does not really matter because there are no important differences between the alternatives;
4. voters may abstain because they assume that the result of the race is already fixed; or
5. nothing of this is true, and voters appear at the booth.

Since we are dealing with national elections, which are comparatively important to voters, we do not have to take care of the first point. We also do not deal here with the closeness of an election (point 4). Feld and Kirchgässner (2001) have shown that closeness increases turnout. Thus, we are left with points 2, 3, and 5. Points 2 and 3 concern the elements of the classical spatial model of abstention: alienation and indifference (Brody and Page 1973). Hinich and Munger (1997: 151) give comprehensive and parsimonious definitions of indifference and alienation and the expected consequences:

Indifference: If voters perceive little (no) difference between alternatives, they are less likely to vote. This prediction has both cross-sectional and time series implications: Voters who perceive little distance between alternatives are less likely to vote than voters who perceive large net candidate differentials. Similarly, any given voter is more likely to vote in an election where the perceived difference is large, compared with other elections where the same voter perceives the difference as small.

Alienation: If both (all) alternatives in the election are far from the voter's ideal point, that voter is less likely to vote. Again, the prediction is made both across voters and over time: The greater the difference between the voter's ideal point and the nearest alternative, the less likely is that voter to turn out, compared either with other voters or other elections where perceptions of the difference are smaller.

In formal rational choice terms these definitions and hypotheses imply the following:

TABLE 3.2. *Logistic regression models of turnout—II*

	Britain		Denmark		Germany		Netherlands		Norway		Sweden	
	Odds ratio	R.s.e.	Odds ratio	R.s.e.	Odds ratio	R.s.e.	Odds ratio	R.s.e.	Odds ratio	R.s.e.	Odds ratio	R.s.e.
Year	0.979*	0.002	0.999	0.006	0.962*	0.006	1.014*	0.005	0.976*	0.006	0.965*	0.005
Age	1.024*	0.002	1.018*	0.005	1.014*	0.004	1.026*	0.003	1.031*	0.003	1.016*	0.002
Education	1.110*	0.040	1.147	0.114	1.645*	0.141	1.515*	0.120	1.364*	0.077	1.340*	0.065
Political Interest	1.834*	0.062	2.759*	0.263	2.524*	0.186	2.122*	0.200	1.816*	0.105	1.676*	0.080
Political Efficacy	n.a.	—	1.098	0.062	1.128	0.150	1.638†	0.177	1.087*	0.031	1.180*	0.053
Party Indifference	0.719*	0.041	0.540*	0.062	0.562*	0.063	0.618*	0.064	0.705*	0.057	0.671*	0.047
Party Alienation	0.570*	0.028	0.481*	0.070	0.338*	0.037	0.594*	0.061	0.547*	0.042	0.489*	0.036
$N =$	12,974		5,912		6,163		5,685		7,799		16,336	
Pseudo-R^2	0.102		0.117		0.190		0.109		0.091		0.076	
Hoshmer-Lemeshow χ^2	46.96, $df = 18$, $p = 0.000$		40.93, $df = 18$, $p = 0.002$		14.95, $df = 18$, $p = 0.665$		23.87, $df = 18$, $p = 0.159$		22.77, $df = 18$, $p = 0.200$		24.65, $df = 18$, $p = 0.135$	
Area under ROC curve	0.718		0.753		0.812		0.747		0.717		0.705	
Elections analysed	1974-F, 1974-O, 1979, 1997, 2001		1971, 1979, 1994, 1998		1972, 1976, 1994, 1998		1971, 1986, 1994, 1998		1981, 1985, 1989, 1993, 1997		1979, 1982, 1985, 1988, 1991, 1994, 1998	

R.s.e.: Robust standard errors; *: p < 0.01; †: p < 0.05; n.a.: not available.

Alienation: $|X_A - X_i| > \delta$, where X_A is the position, on some evaluative criterion, of party A, X_i is the voter's ideal point on that criterion, and δ is a region of acceptance (an acceptable difference between X_A and X_i), for all parties A;

Indifference: $|X_A - X_i| \sim |X_B - X_i|$, for all combinations of all parties A and B;

Voting: $|X_A - X_i| < |X_B - X_i|$, for any combination of parties A and B, provided that the voter is not alienated.

We can imagine a number of 'evaluative criteria', referred to in these concepts. The familiar left–right scale is one of them: Both parties and respondents can take positions on this scale, and for the respondent his or her position is then taken to be the ideal point. Other issue and ideology scales can also be selected. However, purely for reasons of data availability (comparable left–right scales or other issue and ideology scales are, with some exceptions, scarce in our country data-sets), we have confined ourselves to another evaluative criterion that is more often available in the data-sets, and this is the *party thermometer question*. Respondents have been asked to indicate how unsympathetic or sympathetic they rate the major parties in an election on a scale usually ranging from 0 to 100 (variants do occur). The respondent's ideal point X_i on this scale obviously is the maximum scale value. Thus, we restrict ourselves to party indifference and party alienation, where conceivably candidates' ratings and policy positions would also provide pertinent criteria.

An *indifferent* respondent can now straightforwardly be made operational as a respondent who assigns his or her highest thermometer rating to more than one political party. An *alienated* respondent is conveniently defined as a respondent whose highest thermometer rating of any party is not in the top quarter of the thermometer scale. Admittedly, the decision to draw the line at the top quarter of the thermometer scale is a bit arbitrary, but it will serve our purposes. It should be noted in passing that someone can be indifferent, but not alienated; alienated but not indifferent; both indifferent and alienated; or none of these.[9]

As with our first test of the puzzle of electoral participation, earlier in this chapter, we refrain from presenting the indifference and alienation variables in a time series format. The number of time points available (i.e. the number of election studies containing the survey questions needed) is too small, and the frequency distributions too dependent on the parties included in the questions. In the following, we evaluate at the individual level the effects of alienation and indifference in combination with the parts of the puzzle introduced in the first sections of this chapter: age, education, political interest, and political efficacy.

Table 3.2 presents the results of a new series of logistic regression runs of turnout, with party indifference and party alienation now included as additional explanatory variables. Both additional variables appear to have a strong negative effect on the decision to vote, as we expected (in logistic regression, odds ratios lower than 1 indicate a negative effect). The effect is particularly strong in Denmark and Germany, but it is highly significant everywhere.

Thus, where polarization measured in party platforms discussed above did not in all six countries point to a positive relationship between supply and 'demand' (the level of turnout), the two survey measures do so. What value should we attach to these partly contradictory findings?

Survey data differ from party platform data because the former are obtained through respondents and the latter not. Whatever the 'objective' situation of party supply may be, the only factor that counts for individual decisions are the *perceptions* of the reality the individuals base their decision on. High polarization of party supply in general does not mean that voters perceive a choice concerning their particular choice set. Respondents who did not vote in an election might be inclined to think that parties are alike, or that no party can be rated highly on a thermometer scale, in order to justify their abstention. Of course, external criteria of party indifference and party alienation being absent, we cannot tell to what extent this is true, but it is intuitively not unlikely.

Returning to Table 3.2, it should be noted that almost all effects of variables that were also included in Table 3.1 remain of the same sign and magnitude after adding party indifference and party alienation. 'Year' still has the same impact in each country as it had in the analyses of Table 3.1, indicating that unmeasured time-related factors are still as important. One exception is the impact of education on turnout in Britain, which is now statistically significant. In all six countries, the amount of explained variance in turnout increases with a few percentage points compared with Table 3.1. Finally, the model fit, as indicated by the Hoshmer-Lemeshow test statistic, is still unsatisfactory in Britain and in Denmark.

3.5 CONCLUSION

Turnout is related to many variables. But even if these relationships are consistent over time and across countries, it is obvious that their explanatory power altogether is rather weak. This probably has to do with the fact that electoral participation has a low-cost, low-benefit nature. Under such circumstances neither an approach concentrating on resources like the SES model, which includes factors such as education and age, nor rational choice considerations, which pertain for example to alienation and indifference, can contribute considerably to the explanation of turnout in terms of R^2. On the other hand, these variables obviously matter considerably for turnout, given the differences between different socioeconomic groups, or between those being alienated, or indifferent, or not. Since the strength of these effects seems to be shaped by the context of an election, it seems to be worthwhile to investigate as to which degree the effects of different variables are shaped by the specific context in a given election, be it the closeness of the race, the campaign strategies, the strategic placement of parties and the like.

Ironically, our results, in a way, underline one of the premises of modernization theory, namely that 'modern' citizens will not machine-mindedly go out to vote. To a large extent, the decision to vote or not depends on uncharted factors. But has there ever been a time, except for compulsory voting periods like in the Netherlands, when citizens did vote more or less automatically?

In all other respects, citizens apparently do not behave according to the patterns suggested by modernization theory. The decision to vote or abstain depends obviously to a larger extent on context factors, that is, the perception of the concrete choice situation, and to an even larger extent on other, unmeasured factors, some of which are time-related, others election-specific or attached to the voter personally.

Notes

1. An earlier version of this chapter was presented at the 2002 Annual Meeting of the American Political Science Association in Boston, MA.
2. That is, turnout in the US presidential elections would have been 12 per cent higher if education would have been the only explanatory factor that changed over time.
3. Adherence to political parties is another piece of the puzzle. We disregard it in this section, but will introduce related concepts—party alienation and party indifference—in one of the following sections.
4. Rosenstone and Hansen (1993) hold that in the United States the sense of political efficacy has gone down in the 1968–88 period; but Listhaug (1995: 267–77) does not find any general trend in Norway, Sweden, Denmark, and the Netherlands, where cross-country variation seems to outweigh longitudinal variation.
5. Another set of questions which were needed in our subsequent analyses are the party thermometer questions (see note 9). Their availability has also determined the inclusion of specific election studies.
6. Results were obtained by using Stata 8 (graphs were also produced by Stata 8).
7. We report the Hosmer-Lemeshow χ^2 rather than the familiar Pearson χ^2, because the former is better suited when there are, as in our analyses, almost as many possible co-variate patterns as observations. In this test, the predicted probabilities of voting have been grouped into twenty quantiles.
8. Our appreciation to Hans-Dieter Klingemann, who made these macro-data available for this volume (see Chapter 2).
9. Parties for which thermometer scores are available in the election studies analysed, are:
   Britain: Conservatives, Labour, Liberals/Liberal-Democrats.
   Denmark 1971: Social-Democrats, Radical Liberal Party, Conservative Party, Liberal Justice Party, Socialist People's Party, Danish Communist Party, Christian People's Party, Liberals, Left Socialists;
   Denmark 1979: as in 1971, and in addition: Centre Democrats, Communist Workers' Party, Party of Schleswig, Progressive Party;
   Denmark 1994: as in 1979, but excluding Liberal Justice Party, Danish Communist Party, Communist Workers' Party, Party of Schleswig, Left Socialists, and including Unity List;

Denmark 1998: as in 1994, and in addition: Danish Peoples Party, Democratic Renewal.

Germany: SPD, CDU/CSU, FDP in 1972 and 1976; in 1994 and 1998 in addition: Greens and PDS.

The Netherlands 1971: small left parties, PvdA, D66, ARP, KVP, CHU, VVD, small right parties.

The Netherlands 1986, 1994, 1998: small left parties, PvdA, D66, CDA, VVD, small right parties.

Norway: Social Left, Labour, Liberal, Christian People's Party, Agrarian Party, Conservative, Progressive party.

Sweden 1979: Left Party, Social Democrats, Centre Party, People's Party Liberals, Moderate Party, Green Party.

Sweden 1982, 1985, 1988: as in 1979, and in addition: Christian Democrats.

Sweden 1991, 1994: as in 1988, and in addition: New Democracy.

Sweden 1998: as in 1988.

4

Social Structure and Party Choice[1]

Maria Oskarson

4.1   THE SOCIAL CLEAVAGE MODEL

That the social position of a voter correlates with his or her party choice is one of the most long lasting and well documented facts in electoral research and political sociology. Ever since the first studies of electoral behaviour it has been known that people occupied in a working class position tend to vote for leftist parties to a higher degree than people in the middle class, and that religiously oriented people tend to vote for Christian Democratic or Conservative parties to a higher degree than people not religiously active (Alford 1963; Rose 1974). This connection between people's social position and party choice is not a coincidence, but tends to be more or less institutionalized in the party systems. The social cleavages of a society are in most cases reflected in the origin of the party systems.

Seymour Martin Lipset and Stein Rokkan (1967) introduced what has become known as 'The Social Cleavage Model' in the book *Party Systems and Voter Alignments*. The introductory chapter presents a theoretical foundation for the process through which groups along a number of social cleavages or division lines, anchored in a society's historical development, were aligned to political parties. Even though the relation between social position and party choice has been studied from many different theoretical perspectives, the social cleavage model remains highly central (see Nieuwbeerta 1995 for an overview; also Franklin et al. 1992: ch. 1). The model states that four social cleavages resulting from historical processes in relation to the national and the industrial revolutions respectively have structured the party systems in the western world. Depending on historical experiences and constitutional decisions at formative moments, combinations of one or more of the cleavages along religious lines (especially the catholic church versus the state), centre/periphery (nation state elites versus geographically peripheral elites), rural/urban (landowners versus industry) or class (employers versus workers) came into shaping the party systems at the time of democratization. Once groups along these social cleavage lines were aligned to the parties, the connection tended to remain through political socialization as well as through party strategies and organization. One of Lipset and Rokkan's main conclusions was that these alignments were extremely stable, and that the party systems therefore were frozen (Lipset and Rokkan 1967: 50; also Rose and Urwin 1970; Maguire 1983). The alignment between social groups and parties has been seen as a main explanation of the stability in European party systems, which is manifested by the fact that the roots of the main parties competing for the votes of the electorate in Europe today are a hundred years old. However, as stated in Chapter 1, it can on good grounds be expected that this traditional relationship between social position and party choice has changed.

A central point in the social cleavage model was that the party systems were not a mere reflection of the cleavage structure. The alignment process could take different routes depending on the institutional context at certain points in the democratization process, and the parties once founded were actors seeking survival and thus had an interest in keeping their alignments to the voters. The parties were seen as actors defining the relevant political cleavages for the voters. This last point was further pronounced by Sartori in his article 'The Sociology of Parties: A Critical Review', where he stated that 'The party is not a "consequence" of the class. Rather, and before, it is the class that receives its identity from the party' (Sartori 1997: 169; also Przeworski and Sprague 1986: 100–1; Bartolini and Mair 1990).

This perspective implies that the importance of social cleavages for party choice does not only depend on the nature or strength of the cleavages, but also on how the parties relate to the cleavages. For example, a radical social democratic party advocating the basic rights and interests of the working class in opposition to the bourgeoisie is more likely to mobilize the working class votes, than a social democratic party located in the ideological centre of the party system addressing the voters as 'ordinary people'. What this implies is quite simple that if there is no party that could be perceived as representing a certain group better than other parties, it is less likely that the group will vote according to a coherent pattern. Cleavage voting refers to the interaction between socio-structural groups and political parties, or in Lipset and Rokkan's terminology 'Social Cleavages and Political Alignments' (Lipset and Rokkan 1967; Sainsbury 1990; also Mair 1997; Curtice 2002).

The social structure of the advanced western democracies is not the same today as it was in the 1950s when the empirical connection between social position and party choice was found for the first time. The industrial societies have evolved into what are sometimes labelled post-industrial societies, where less and less people are engaged in traditional industrial occupations. Trends of secularization have changed the position of religion. The traditional core groups of the social cleavage–based parties have shrunk. The political parties on the other hand have adopted strategies to reach voter groups beyond their traditional 'core groups' as well as to incorporate new political issues. This change of the parties into 'catch all' or 'cartel' parties could be expected to weaken the mobilization of the core groups further. This chapter aims at drawing a picture of this development, as a foundation for the following chapters. Is 'the social cleavage model' still valid?

4.2   WHAT WE KNOW ABOUT THE SOCIAL CLEAVAGE MODEL

Few areas within the field of voting behaviour research have been as contested as social cleavage voting, that is the relationship between social position and party choice. Numerous books and articles have been involved in the debate about whether this relationship persists, has changed or has declined (Dalton et al. 1984; Franklin et al. 1992; Clark and Lipset 1991, 2001; Evans 1999). Most intense has the debate been about the relationship between a voter's class position and party choice, and the general idea of a decline in class voting has been questioned, not the least on methodological grounds (Heath et al. 1985, 1987; Heath et al. 1991; Clark et al. 1993; Manza et al. 1995; Evans 1999). In his comparative study *The Democratic Class Struggle in Twenty Countries* Paul Nieuwbeerta found significant differences in levels of class voting between countries, with the highest levels in Scandinavia and Britain. He also found that 'in many of the countries substantial declines in levels of relative class voting occurred in the post-war period. The declines were largest in the Scandinavian countries, followed by Germany and Britain' (Nieuwbeerta 1995: 195; also Knutsen 2003). Some studies have explicitly taken structural factors such as socio-economic composition, economic development, and organizational structure into consideration in explaining variations in the level of class voting (Franklin et al. 1992; Oskarson 1994; Nieuwbeerta 1995). The general conclusion is that compositional changes are part of the answer to what has changed, but that also the correlation between social position and party choice in many cases has weakened.

Nieuwbeerta's study ended the most intense debates, and the discussion about the importance of social position for party choice has now reached a more nuanced and elaborated state. The development of other cleavages than class is less analysed or contested, but the general conclusion is that social position, all in all, is of decreasing importance for party choice (Franklin et al. 1992; Dogan 2001).

A political perspective on cleavage voting also links the study of cleavage voting to the discussion about how the working conditions of parties and party strategies have changed. The parties are said to be transforming from 'mass parties' mobilizing along cleavage lines, to 'catch all' or 'cartel' parties striving to mobilize all groups in society (Kirchheimer 1966; Katz and Mair 1997: 93–120; Mair 1997; Kitschhelt 1994). Of course these trends are interrelated—if voters are less inclined to vote in accordance with social position, the rationale for the parties is to tone down the group appeal. Even though the argument that cleavage voting can not be understood from 'the voter side' only is not new, it is rarely brought to empirical tests. A main exception is the empirical analysis of Evans et al. (1999: 99) of how polarization along the left–right ideology dimension varies with the level of class voting in Britain. They conclude that '... there is *prima facie* evidence that party positions influence the electorate's perception and, through this, the over-time variation in the voting behaviour of the different social classes'. A similar approach is presented by De Graaf et al. (2001) in an analysis of developments in cleavage voting related to party system change in the Netherlands.

4.3 ANALYSIS OF THE CLEAVAGE MODEL

The social cleavage model includes three central variables or aspects: the strength of the alignments between social groups and the parties organized around the cleavages; the social composition along the central cleavages of a certain society; and also the 'clearness' of the party in representing the social groups. All three aspects of the relation between social groups and parties could on good grounds be expected to change: the relation between an individual's social position and his or her party choice (correlation); the relative sizes of the central social groups (composition); and the strategies and policies presented by the parties (party appeal). This chapter will present the development of the social cleavage model along all three aspects of changes.

The most universal cleavage that could be found in most industrial democracies is the class cleavage, manifested through the Socialist or Social Democratic parties. This cleavage exists in most industrial countries. Also the religious cleavage is important in Europe, especially in countries with both protestant and catholic groups, where large Christian Democratic parties are central in the party systems.[2]

The six countries included in this book are nice examples of countries with party systems well described by the social cleavage model. Two of the countries, Germany and the Netherlands, are clearly two-dimensional with both the class cleavage and the religious cleavage forming the party systems, whilst the four others, Britain, Denmark, Norway, and Sweden are more or less one-dimensional along the class cleavage.

After a general description of the traditional cleavage bases of the party systems the first step explores the voting behaviour of voters belonging to the core groups along the two most central cleavages: class and religion. Are they still loyal to 'their' party? As mentioned earlier we could on good grounds expect this not to be the case. The second step explores the implications of the social structural changes, and the third step takes the polarization in the party systems into consideration, and analyses the relationship between cleavage voting and polarization in the party systems. Does the variation in cleavage voting depend on the degree of polarization in the party systems?

The analysis will concentrate on the relations between voters in the working class and the Social Democratic parties on the one hand, and between religious people and Christian Democratic parties on the other. The limitation of the analysis to the relation between the Social Democratic parties and people in the working class, and between the Christian Democratic parties and the religiously active, does not imply that no other parties or groups matter when it comes to cleavage voting, but that these parties and groups are the most important ones for the social cleavage model.

For most elections analysed here the class variable is based on objective coding. In the Norwegian studies before 1981 only self-placement in occupational groups is available. Therefore, this variable is used for the earlier Norwegian studies. In Sweden a different occupational coding was used before 1976 than in later years. Religious activity is based on church attendance, discriminating between visiting church once a month or more and less frequent visits. Church attendance is measured in all studies except Norway in 1977, Denmark where the question was asked only in 1971 and 1979, and Sweden where the question was introduced in 1988 and asked in every later election study.

4.4   THE CLEAVAGE BASES OF THE PARTY SYSTEMS

The British party system is usually described as basically one-dimensional based on the class cleavage (Butler and Stokes 1974). Before 1918, however, the dominant cleavage was religious, with support for the Conservative Party coming mainly from the established national churches in England and Scotland. When Labour gained support through the introduction of universal franchise in the early 1900s the class cleavage replaced the religious cleavage as the main dividing line in British politics. This does not imply that no other social cleavages are of importance for people's worldviews or party choice, but that no other cleavages traditionally have been aligned to a specific party. Partly this might be seen as a result of the plurality electoral system, which gives very limited chances to minor parties to gain representation. The electoral system strongly supports the development of a one-dimensional party system.

Britain has been the main arena for the debate about whether class voting has declined or not. Due to different operationalizations of class and different measurement techniques the discussion has been centred around the question whether the pattern is best described as 'trendless fluctuation' or 'secular decline'. The former conclusion tends to be the strongest (see Evans et al. 1999 for an overview). Even though religion is not a central cleavage in Britain today, there still remain traces of the traditional pattern that people who adhere to the Church of England and are religiously active tend to vote slightly more for the

Conservative Party than others (Rose and McAllister 1990: 48–9; Kotler-Berkowitz 2001).

That the electoral system is not the only factor deciding the number of cleavages represented in the party system is clear from the Nordic countries. All three Nordic countries included here—Denmark, Norway, and Sweden—have proportional electoral systems and multiparty systems, but still are more or less one-dimensional along the class cleavage. The Nordic countries, especially Norway and Sweden, are often found to have a stronger relationship between class and party choice than most otherwise comparable countries, and also a clear decline of class voting (Franklin et al. 1992; Nieuwbeerta 1995; Knutsen 2001; Andersen 1984). Sweden, as well as Norway, has traditionally also an urban/agrarian cleavage represented in the agrarian parties, but this is of much less importance than the class cleavage. In Denmark the urban/rural cleavage has diminished long ago. In later years occupational sector and gender have gained some importance in all three countries (Knutsen 2001; Berglund 2003a; Oskarson 1992, 1994; Holmberg 2000). In all countries there are also Christian Democratic parties. The Norwegian Christian People's Party was founded in 1933 and is well established in the party system. In Sweden and Denmark the Christian Democratic parties only date back to the 1960s, and in Sweden it was not represented in the Riksdag until 1985. The parties share a traditionalist stand on morality issues, which were important reasons for their origin.

More clearly two-dimensional party systems are found in Germany and in the Netherlands. Both countries have important Christian Democratic parties as well as large Social Democratic parties. In Germany these are the largest parties, with the liberal party FDP, the Green Party and since 1990 the Left-Socialist Party PDS as smaller parties. The social basis of the vote in the western parts of Germany—what used to be the BRD (FRG)—traditionally was defined by class and religion, with signs of weakening ties in later years (Baker et al. 1981; Padgett 1993: 39–41; Nieuwbeerta 1995).

Traditionally, Dutch society has been characterized as a 'three-pillar system' with Catholic and Protestant pillars, in addition to a general or secular one. As part of this pillar system five major political parties dominated Dutch politics in the first half of the twentieth century: two secular parties (a liberal and a socialist party), a Catholic and two Protestant parties. Since the late 1960s the Dutch party system has undergone several changes and splits, and today it is very fragmented. D66 was formed in 1966 and has evolved into a leftist-liberal party with quite clear middle class support (De Graaf et al. 2001: 6). In 1977 the three confessional parties contested the elections with a joint list and formally founded the CDA in 1980. Apart from these changes a number of small parties have evolved, and disappeared again from the party scene. Class voting has never been very strong in the Netherlands, whilst the religious cleavage has been more important for party choice (Nieuwbeerta 1995; De Graaf et al. 2001).

Figure 4.1A–4.1F illustrates the development of the major parties in the six countries since around 1960.[3] Only major parties are included.

As we can see, the parties labelled as the central cleavage parties—the Social Democratic and the Christian Democratic—have remained central actors on the political scene throughout the period. The British Labour Party had a downgoing trend in support between 1964 and 1983, when the third party, the Liberal Democrats, gained support. Since 1983 the Labour Party has increased its vote share, and has come out as the largest party in the elections of 1997 and 2001.

In Germany the Social Democratic Party (SPD) and the Christian Democratic Party (CDU/CSU) have been of approximately the same strength. The Social Democrats enjoyed relatively low support in the 1980s, and have gained since then until they won the chancellorship in 1998. In the Netherlands there have been more fluctuations in the support for the main parties. In the 1960s the support for the religious parties, in particular the catholic KVP, declined very rapidly. Since the merger of the Christian parties ARP, CHU and KVP into CDA in 1977, the CDA has been one of the main parties. However, still in 1963 the KVP alone was as strong as the CDA in 1977. After a strong decrease in the 1990s the CDA managed to reverse this trend and increased its vote share in the two most recent elections. The Social Democrats had a relatively stable and strong period between 1977 and 1989, and more fluctuating support since.

In Norway the Social Democratic Party (DNA) was clearly the dominating party up until the election of 2001, maybe with exception of 1981 when the Conservative Party was a close runner up. In the latest election, 2001, the Social Democrats became insignificantly larger than the Conservative Right Party. The Christian People's Party, KrF, shows a rather stable support at around 10–15 per cent of the votes. In Sweden the Social Democrats have been the largest party at every election, on a fairly stable level. The Danish party system finally, is quite fragmented, as can be seen in Fig. 4.1F. The Social Democratic Party, however, has been the largest party at every election up until 2001, when the very positive trend since the late 1980s for the Liberal Party resulted in a stronger support for the Liberals than for the Social Democrats.

However, that the parties that we here label 'cleavage parties' are still dominant in the national party systems is not the same as saying that the social cleavage model is as applicable as a description of the relation between voters and parties today as it was in the 1960s. The first step in the analysis of the validity of the social cleavage model is the assessment of the relationship between group membership and party choice. Is it still meaningful to talk about class voting and religious voting?

(A)

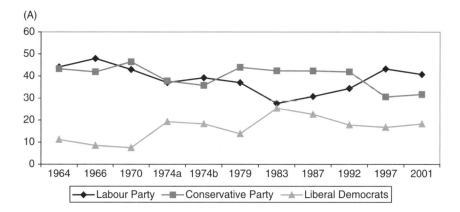

(B)

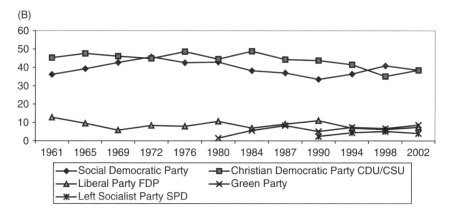

(C)

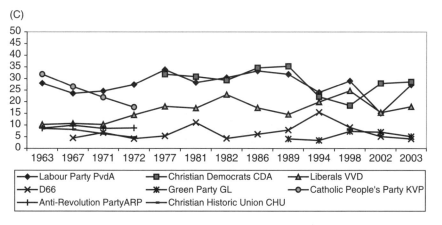

FIG. 4.1. *(A) Party support in Britain, 1964–2001. (B) Party support in Germany, 1961–2002. (C) Party support in the Netherlands, 1963–2003*

(Continued)

(D)

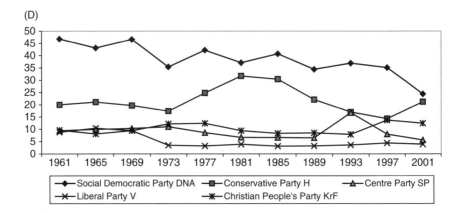

(E)

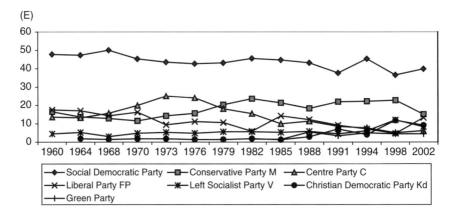

(F)

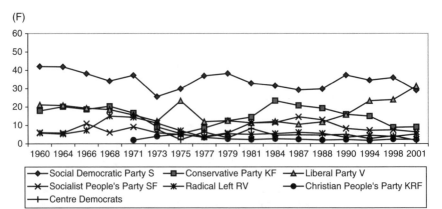

FIG. 4.1. (*Contd.*) (*D*) *Party support in Norway, 1961–2001.* (*E*) *Party support in Sweden, 1960–2002.* (*F*) *Party support in Denmark, 1960–2001*

4.5 TRENDS IN THE RELATION BETWEEN
SOCIAL POSITION AND PARTY CHOICE

The question on how to measure the relation between social position and party choice has been highly debated. For a long time the most widely used measure was the Alford index of class voting, a simple index indicating the proportion of the working class voting for left parties minus the proportion of the middle class voting left (Alford 1963; Nieuwbeerta 1995). For long this index was more or less the definition of class voting. Even if we accept the crudeness in applying dichotomous variables for both class and party vote, one serious drawback remains. The Alford index does not take into account general shifts in party popularity (Nieuwbeerta 1995: 39), and thus risks mixing up changes in the correlation between class and vote with changes in party popularity. An alternative index is therefore the Thomsen index, which is based on the odds for one group, for example manual workers, to vote for left wing rather than right wing parties divided by the odds for non-manual workers to vote left rather than right (Nieuwbeerta 1995: 39–41, 52–5). In this way the general vote share of the parties is controlled for. In order to standardize the odds ratios, the logarithm of the ratios is used, that is, the log odds ratios. This is the measure employed in the following analysis. Figures 4.2A–4.2F present the Thomsen index for class voting, that is, working class voting for Social Democratic parties rather than other parties compared to the non-working class. The same technique is employed for religious voting, that is, religiously active persons voting for Christian Democratic parties rather than other parties compared to non-religious people. The only factor that varies here is the relation between social position and the vote, that is, neither social composition nor party popularity interferes.

In Britain, class voting is on a much higher level than religious voting throughout the period. This is what could be expected, given that there is no purely Christian Democratic Party. Class voting on the other hand is much lower in the year 2001 than in 1964 when the time series begins. The decrease in class voting has, as earlier stated, not been linear. Figure 4.2A shows a quite clear decrease between 1964 and 1970 and, a well known trendless fluctuation during 1972–92, but since 1992 there is a decrease again. This is very much in line with earlier findings (Rose and McAllister 1990; see also Evans 1999 for an overview).

In Germany the index for religious voting in most years is much higher than the index for class voting, indicating that religious voting is much stronger. The Fig. 4.2B does, however, show a slight decrease in religious voting throughout the period. Class voting started on a fairly high level, but decreased steadily during 1961–84. Since then class voting in Germany shows more of a fluctuating pattern.

Also in the Netherlands religious voting is on a higher level than class voting all through the period. The trend for religious voting presented in Fig. 4.2C is clearly

(A)

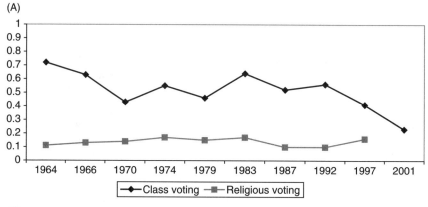

(B)

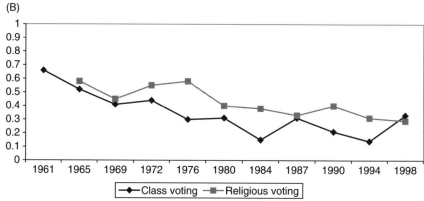

(C)

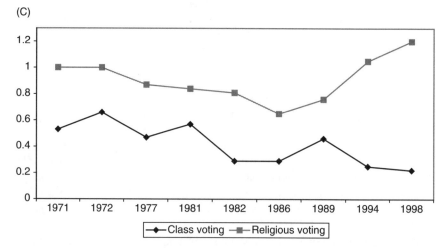

FIG. 4.2. *(A) Class voting and religious voting in Britain. (B) Class voting and religious voting in Germany. (C) Class voting and religious voting in the Netherlands)*

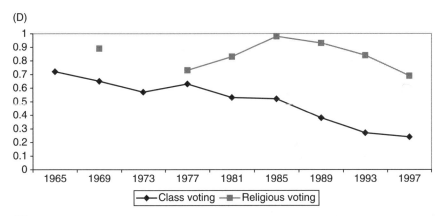

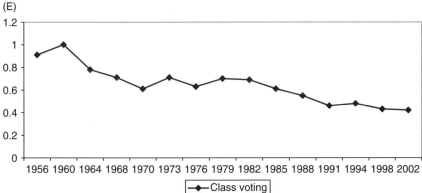

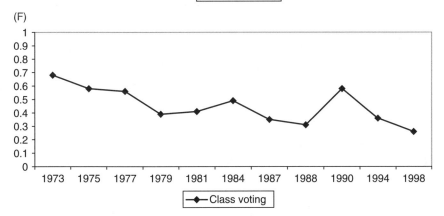

FIG. 4.2. (*Contd.*) (*D*) *Class voting and religious voting in Norway.*
(*E*) *Class voting in Sweden.* (*F*) *Class voting in Denmark*

curvilinear, with a steady decrease between 1971 and 1986 but almost as clear an increase in the period since 1986. Class voting on the other hand is fluctuating on a rather high level in the period 1971–81 and on a lower level since then.

As mentioned earlier, Norway and Sweden are often described as traditionally highly dominated by the class cleavage, but also as the countries where class voting has decreased the most. Figures 4.2D1–2 and 4.2E confirm this. In both countries class voting has decreased steadily. In Sweden the decrease is most pronounced in the 1960s and the 1980s, with more stable patterns in the 1970s and the 1990s. In Norway the decreasing trend is more even. For Norway it is also clear that religious voting is on a higher level than class voting, and shows no monotonous decreasing trend, but rather a curvilinear pattern with a peak in the 1985 election. To label Norway as a clearly unidimensional party system does not seem fully appropriate. Finally, Denmark shows a quite clear decrease in class voting during the 1970s, but more trendless fluctuations ever since (Fig. 4.2F). As mentioned earlier questions about church attendance are only included in two of the Danish studies, and therefore excluded from the analysis here. Table 4.1 summarizes the trends in class voting and religious voting in the six countries. It also presents the β-coefficients and explained variance (R^2) for regression models with the index value for class voting and religious voting respectively as dependent variables and year as independent variable.

For class voting measured with the Thomsen index we have significant and negative β-values for all countries except Britain. The strongest fit is, as expected, found in Sweden and Norway, where we already have observed the most regular decrease in class voting. For Britain the model does not fit very well at all, due to the trendless fluctuation of class voting. According to the figures here, the highest degree of class voting today is found in Sweden and Germany. When it comes to religious voting the linear model does not fit that well. In Britain there is hardly any variation at all, indicated by a β-value hardly discernible from zero. For the Netherlands as well as Norway we already concluded that the trends for religious voting are curvilinear. Only the German case shows a regularly decreasing trend in religious voting indicated here by a significant β-value and a high R^2.

All in all, we can conclude that class voting and religious voting have not vanished totally. Compared to the 1960s, class voting shows a general decrease. During the latest decades the trends are, however, more fluctuating or stable. Religious voting shows less of a linear trend, and is definitely not passé.

4.6 EFFECTS OF CHANGES IN SOCIAL COMPOSITION

Parties closely linked to social groups are quite vulnerable to changes in the social structure. If their core groups decrease in size, this might be directly reflected in the vote share of the parties, unless the party manages to attract new voter

TABLE 4.1. *Trends in class voting and religious voting*

	Britain	Germany	Netherlands	Norway	Sweden	Denmark
Class voting						
Highest value/year	0.72/1964	0.66/1961	0.66/1972	0.72/1965	1.0/1964	0.68/1973
Lowest value/year	0.23/2001	0.14/1994	0.22/1998	0.24/1997	0.42/2002	0.26/1998
Latest value	0.23	0.33	0.22	0.24	0.42	0.26
b	−0.004	−0.010*	−0.014*	−0.015†	−0.011†	−0.012*
R^2	0.246	0.658	0.644	0.918	0.839	0.51
Religious voting						
Highest value/year	0.17/1974	0.58/1965	1.16/1972	0.98/1985		
Lowest value/year	0.10/1987, 1992	0.29/1998	0.29/1982, 1986	0.73/1977		
Latest value	0.16	0.29	1.11	0.69		
b	0	−0.009†	−0.001	−0.002		
R^2	0.001	0.749	0.005	0.048		

Comment: The values in Table 4.1 are taken from Fig. 4.2A–F. The β-values and R^2 are from a regression model with the index value for class voting and religious voting respectively as dependent variables and year as independent variable.
*indicates a 0.05 significance level.
†a 0.01 significance level.

groups. If on the other hand, the party does succeed to attract new groups, the risk is that the 'core voters' no longer recognize the party and thus abandon it. This is what is sometimes labelled 'the Electoral Dilemma'. The Social Democratic parties and the Christian Democratic parties are perfect examples of this. We know that in general the core groups we focus on in this chapter: industrial workers and religiously active people, decreased in size. For example, in many cases the proportion of voters coming from a working class background has decreased from close to 50 per cent of the adult population, to around 30 per cent. The proportion of the electorates who are religiously active has also decreased over the period. For example, in the Netherlands around 60–70 per cent of those interviewed in the elections studies in the 1970s reported that they visited church at least once a month. In the 1990s only around 25 per cent did. Even if the parties receive the same support from these core groups over the years, the societal changes alone would lead to a decrease in support for the parties. On the other hand, this analysis showed that the party loyalty of the social groups also has changed. In order to clarify these developments Figs. 4.3A–F report a contra-factual analysis. We compare the actual vote share of the cleavage parties to the vote share they would have received if the composition of the electorate (that is the proportion of working class and religiously active) had remained the same all through the period studied here, as well as the vote share they would have received if the alignment between the group and the party had remained the same, that is, the same proportion of the group voted for the party today as in the beginning of the time series. The calculation is based on the proportion of those interviewed with known social position and party choice belonging to the group. The actual support for the Social Democratic Party is calculated as:

(% in sample belonging to the working class) × (% of group voting for the party) + (% in sample belonging to the non-working class × % of the non-working class voting for the party).

The same calculation is employed for the Christian Democratic parties, but with religiously active/non-active. The standardization with structural changes held constant means that the groups' proportions are held constant on the value from the first election studied, and with the vote constant the proportion of the groups voting for the party is held constant. The difference between actual support and support when group proportions are held constant are the effects of structural changes, and the difference when voting behaviour is held constant is the effect of changes in the voting tendency of the groups.

For most of the parties, Figs. 4.3A–F show quite mild, but negative, effects of changes in the group proportions, and stronger but also more fluctuating effects of changes in voting behaviour of the groups. The cleavage parties in general would have gained a weaker support than they actually did if class voting or religious voting had not decreased, given the decreasing proportions of the electorates belonging to the core groups of the parties.

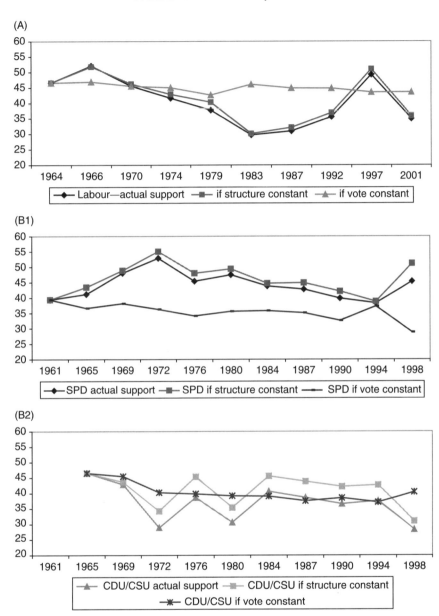

Fig. 4.3. *(A) Effects of changes in social composition in Britain, Labour Party. (B1) Effects of changes in social composition in Germany, Social Democratic Party. (B2) Effects of changes in social composition in Germany, Christian Democratic Party*

(Continued)

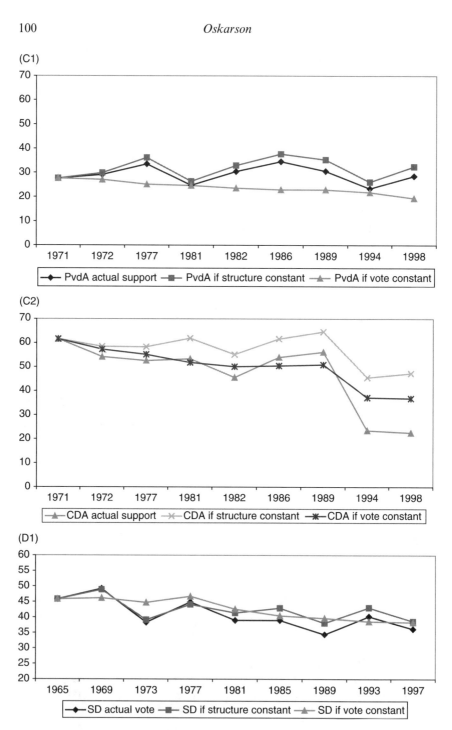

FIG. 4.3. (*Contd.*) (*C1*) *Effects of changes in social composition in the Netherlands, Labour Party.* (*C2*) *Effects of changes in social composition in the Netherlands, Christian Democratic Party.* (*D1*) *Effects of changes in social composition in Norway, Social Democratic Party*

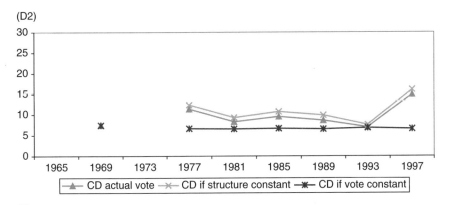

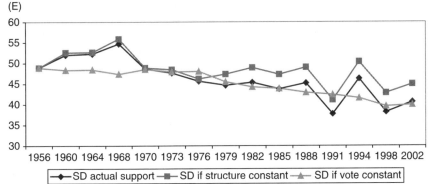

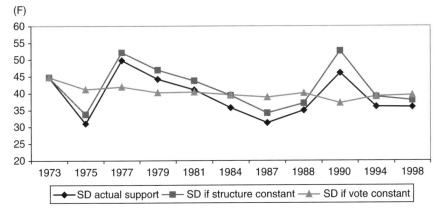

FIG. 4.3. (*Contd.*) (*D2*) *Effects of changes in social composition in Norway, Christian People's Party.* (*E*) *Effects of changes in social composition in Sweden, Social Democratic Party.* (*F*) *Effects of changes in social composition in Denmark, Social Democratic Party*

The varying support for the British Labour Party can not be explained by changes in the proportion of the electorate belonging to the working class. The actual support follows closely the line for the calculated support if the class structure would have remained the same all through the period. Rather, it is variations in the voting behaviour of the classes that show the stronger effect, with negative effects for the Labour Party during the 1980s. The German SPD on the other hand has clearly gained from changes in the voting behaviour of the classes. If class voting had remained the same all through the period the SPD would have been a significantly smaller party today. For the German Christian Democrats on the other hand, the decrease of the proportion of religiously active people is of higher significance than the decrease of the proportion belonging to the working class is for the SPD. The changing voting behaviour among religious and non-religious people has been of smaller importance, except for the elections in 1972, 1980, and 1998. The Dutch Labour Party PvdA would have been slightly larger if the classes would have remained equal in size, but quite significantly smaller if class voting would have remained the same. Only the elections in 1981 and 1994 deviate from this pattern. The Dutch Christian Democrats on the other hand would have been quite a lot larger if the proportion of religiously active people had remained the same as in the early 1970s. But also if the voting behaviour of the religiously active had remained the same, the party would have been larger. Especially in the latest elections it is clear that the CDA has suffered from the secularization process, and has not managed to replace the religiously active voters with secularized voters. The Norwegian Social Democratic Party has suffered only small negative effects of both the structural changes and of changes in voting behaviour of the classes. The party would only have been a couple of percentages larger if group composition or voting behaviour would have remained the same. The small Christian Democratic Party has gained from changes in voting behaviour, that it has managed to attract support from people not religiously active. The Swedish Social Democrats have lost some support due to the changing class composition, and the effect is increasing over the years. The effects of changing class voting on the other hand are both negative and positive over the years. In the 1960s the party gained from increasing support outside the working class, whilst in later years decreasing class voting has a slight negative effect on the strength of the Social Democrats. The Danish Social Democrats also suffer from a small negative effect of changes in class composition. The changing voting behaviour of the classes was compensated for in the late 1970s but not in 1980s. In the latest elections this effect of changing voting behaviour has decreased and is very small.

In Section 4.1 it was stated that the social cleavage model incorporates three central aspects of the relation between society and politics: the social composition along central societal cleavages; the voting behaviour of the central groups along the cleavages; and the degree to which the parties act as representatives for these groups. The analysis so far has shown that the two first aspects of the model—composition and correlation—have changed and have had consequences for the parties. The decreasing sizes of the core groups as well as the decreasing levels of cleavage voting are in most cases compensated by support from outside the core groups, and the parties remain central actors in the party systems. The main exception are the Dutch Christian Democrats, who still are very closely linked to the religiously active group, and thus have decreased in size. From the rather simple analysis here we can conclude that over time the social cleavage model has become less relevant for describing the relationship between voters and parties. That is, however, not the same as stating that it is altogether irrelevant.

4.7 POLARIZATION IN THE PARTY SYSTEM AND THE DECLINE OF THE SOCIAL CLEAVAGE MODEL

As stated earlier, we expect that the impact of social cleavages on party choice will not only depend on how pronounced or widely spread the cleavages are, but also on how the parties relate to the cleavages present in the electorate. If the parties differ in their policy outlook along dimensions strongly related to the cleavages, we would expect the cleavage models to better explain party choice, than would be the case if the parties stand for very much the same policy outlook. Here the analysis will focus on polarization as it can be measured from the party manifestos (see Chapter 2; Budge et al. 2001). In these party manifestos the parties present their analysis of the situation just before an upcoming election, and present their programme for the next mandate period. These manifestos are the actual choices the electorate is facing at the election, and could accordingly be expected to be of importance for their party choice.

The hypothesis stated is that the more polarization there is in the party system, the higher the impact of different cleavages will be. In the following analysis this will be operationalized as the correlations between the index for class voting and religious voting as presented earlier in Figs. 4.3A–F, and polarization indices based on the party manifestos of the parties in every election analysed here.

The indices used are taken from the party manifesto data and represent the range between the parties in the party systems, which is the maximum difference in how a subject area is covered in the manifestos. They are based on general left–right items (PM1), items on planned economy (PM2), items based on market economy (PM3), and items about welfare policy (PM4) respectively. The PM5 index is based on items concerning 'traditional values' in order to catch polarization along the religious cleavage line (Budge et al. 2001).

From the analysis in this chapter it is quite clear that we are dealing with two types of party systems—dual cleavage systems where both the class cleavage and the religious cleavage matter, and single cleavage systems where it is only or mainly class that matters for party choice. As discussed earlier, Germany and the Netherlands are clearly and traditionally considered dual cleavage systems. Here I will also treat Norway as a dual cleavage system since Fig. 4.3D shows a quite high degree of religious voting. Britain, Sweden, and Denmark are more clearly single cleavage systems. When we are analysing the importance of party system polarization along different dimensions, it seems plausible that the relationships between how well the different cleavage models can explain party choice and which dimensions in the party system matter, differ between dual and single cleavage systems. For that reason the correlations in Table 4.2 are presented for all countries taken together, as well as for dual cleavage systems and single cleavage systems separately.

For all countries over half of the correlations (6/10) are significant on at least the 0.05 level. Class voting correlates significantly with 4 of the 5 polarization indices, and only the index measuring polarization regarding traditional values has no significant correlation with class voting. The strongest correlation is found with polarization regarding welfare policies. Religious voting on the other hand correlates only with polarization regarding market economy and traditional values. As expected, all significant correlations are positive, indicating that the higher the polarization is, the higher the level of cleavage voting.

The general result is that the hypothesis that the degree of polarization in the party system at a given election does impact the degree of cleavage voting finds some support. When the differences between the parties are more pronounced, voters tend to be more mobilized along cleavage lines than in less polarized elections.

TABLE 4.2. *Cleavage voting and polarization in the party systems. Pearson's* r

Polarization (party manifesto data)	All countries		Dual-cleavage systems		Single cleavage systems
	Class voting	Religious voting	Class voting	Religious voting	Class voting
PM1 General Left-right	0.280*	0.209	0.081	0.190	0.187
PM2 Planned economy	0.435*	0.249	0.557†	0.496†	0.383*
PM3 Market economy	0.267*	0.461†	0.272	0.334	0.164
PM4 Welfare policy	0.333†	0.278	−0.093	0.109	0.333
PM5 Traditional values	−0.095	0.430†	0.206	0.218	0.427*
N	63	35	26	26	34

*indicates a 0.05 significance level.
†a 0.01 significance level.

4.8 CONCLUSION

The social cleavage model, as formulated by Lipset and Rokkan, implies three relevant aspects in the relationship between social groups and parties—the correlation between group membership and party choice, the social composition of the electorate, and the party appeal of the cleavage based parties. The societal and political developments over the last decades have affected all three aspects. The analysis in this chapter has shown that the correlations between class and party choice in most cases have decreased, at least since the 1960s. Religious voting shows a less general pattern. The weakening support for the cleavage parties from the decreasing core groups of the working class and the religiously active respectively, has in most cases been compensated by support from the growing groups of the middle class and the non-religious. The result is that in general the cleavage parties included here—Social Democratic and Christian Democratic parties—still belong to the largest parties in the party systems. The findings presented in this chapter further support the argument that social cleavage voting must be seen as the result of an interaction between groups in society on the one hand, and the political parties and other significant political actors on the other. They clearly show that we should not overlook changes in party appeals or party strategies when we want to understand the evolution of social cleavage voting. To analyse variations in the relationship between social characteristics of the voter and party choice without considering what happens in the party system is to study cleavage voting without politics.

Notes

1. This chapter was written within the research program 'The Political Sociology of the welfare state—Institutions, Social Cleavages, Preferences' financed by the Swedish Council for Working Life and Social Research and The Bank of Sweden Tercentennary Foundation.
2. The religious cleavage is often described as two-dimensional. There is first the split between religious and secularized, and second between Catholics and Protestants.
3. The election results as well as translations of party names and abbreviations have been accessed from http://www.parties-and-elections.de.

5

Party Identification and Party Choice

Frode Berglund, Sören Holmberg, Hermann Schmitt, and Jacques Thomassen

5.1 INTRODUCTION

In Chapter 4 we found a decline of the impact of traditional cleavage structures on people's party choice, although this decline is less secular than often assumed. As the strong and lasting relationship between social structure on the one hand and people's political loyalties on the other used to be one of the most essential factors of stability in most European democracies, this development might be a threat to political stability.

However, social roots are not the only possible basis for enduring party preferences. An alternative is the direct psychological attachment to a particular party. In the Michigan tradition of electoral research, *party identification* has the function of ensuring people's lasting attachment to a political party. In the original orthodox view party identification is a long-term, affective, psychological identification with one's preferred political party. As such it is even comparable with religious affiliation (Miller and Shanks 1996: 120). Soon after its introduction the analytical usefulness of the concept of party identification in European electoral research became a matter of dispute. In European elections, party identification and party vote tended to coincide and to change in tandem. Thus, one of the most innovative elements of the use of party identification in electoral research, studying the impact of short-term forces on the vote against the baseline of the normal vote, was hardly applicable in the European context (Butler and Stokes 1969; Kaase 1976; Thomassen 1976). However, why this was the case was a matter of dispute. Paradoxically, one interpretation of why at least the directional component of the concept was less useful in the European context compared to the American, was that party identification was much more power-ful in Europe than in the United States. In European parliamentary systems, political parties and not individual politicians are the principal actors in the interaction between voters and governmental institutions, leaving little leeway for individual candidates to run their own campaign for office and offering little incentives for voters to deviate from their party preference in favour of an individual candidate from another party. This is quite different from US politics, in particular in presidential elections, where policy stands and characteristics of the candidates have an important weight in addition to their party background. In a parliamentary democracy with its indirect election of the head of government a split of party identification and the actual vote is less likely. Therefore, it is quite understandable that people in Europe hardly deviate from their party identification. However, this does not prove that party identification is not important. Quite the contrary, it is so important that it dominates all other considerations. Still, if there is hardly a difference between people's party identification and their party choice the analytical usefulness of the directional component of party identification is quite limited (Holmberg 1994), even if party identification is more stable than the vote (Berglund 2000).

According to a different interpretation of the same phenomenon the measurement of party identification in a European context reflects not much more than people's party preference at a particular point in time. According to the *functional model of party identification* (Shively 1979) this is because party identification is less functional to European than US voters. In this view, party identification is a cost saving device providing people with a short cut to all kinds of decisions, including the decision for which party or candidate to vote. However, European voters might not have needed party identification as a cost saving device, because that function was already fulfilled by people's ties to a social class or religion, which in turn were strongly associated with a particular political party. Under these conditions, expressed partisanship will be synonymous with the vote and parties as such will not serve as guides to organize behaviour. Whichever interpretation is correct it is of no consequence for this chapter. In both interpretations the usefulness of the directional component of party identification is rather limited as long as party identification and party choice almost coincide. To what extent this is true is one of the research questions to be answered in this chapter.

The second dimension of the concept of party identification, the strength or intensity component, has never been controversial. There is a general agreement that a variable measuring degree of party attachment is quite useful, no matter how we interpret party identification (Holmberg 1994: 101). As strength of party identification is related to the stability of party choice, both at the individual and the aggregate level, the evolution of the level of party identification is indicative for the stability of the party system.

The logical extension of the argument behind the functional model might be that once the importance of the traditional cleavage structure declines and voters are deprived of their traditional short-cutting device, they will develop an identification with a particular party in the same way as their American counterparts do. In other words, party identification should not necessarily decline in the slipstream of the decline of the relationship between social structure and party system.

However, it is the very same functional theory that contradicts this prediction. The need for an information cost-saving device is supposed to be a function of the political skills of the voters. Modernization and in particular the cognitive mobilization of citizens have increased these skills. The dramatic spread of education in advanced industrial democracies has produced a qualitative change in the political sophistication of citizens. At the same time, these societies have experienced an information explosion through the mass media. Both developments have led to a substantial decrease of information costs. Because of this cognitive mobilization, more voters now are able to deal with the complexities of politics and make their own political decisions. Thus, the functional need for partisan cues to guide voting behaviour is declining for a growing number of citizens (Dalton 1984). As a consequence, we should expect a decline in the level of party identification.

In principle, testing this hypothesis requires not more than an assessment of the development of the level of party identification over time. The hypothesis predicts a secular decline of party identification in advanced industrial democracies. An advantage of the selection of countries in our study is that all six are advanced industrial democracies at about the same level of development. Modernization theory therefore would predict a more or less similar secular decline of party identification in all six countries. This hypothesis will be tested in Section 5.2.

However, even if the development of the level of party identification is consistent with what the theory of modernization predicts, this does not necessarily prove that this development is caused by the mechanisms supposed in functional theory. This theory is based on specific assumptions at the micro-level, which are anything but uncontested (Barton and Döring 1986). In Section 5.3 we will elaborate these assumptions and test to what extent the assumed relations at the micro-level do exist in our data.

The theory of modernization tries to explain changes in politics based on developments in society. As such one might call it a sociological approach, devoid of a political component in the *explanans*. As a reaction to this apolitical approach, an alternative explanation of the development of party identification has been proposed emphasizing developments in the political context, in particular in the *supply side* of politics, rather than social changes. Schmitt and Holmberg (1995) for instance introduce and test the hypothesis that developments and fluctuations in the level of party identification can be explained by simultaneous fluctuations in the level of polarization and the degree of issue conflict between political parties. This approach does not necessarily lead to different predictions than the theory of modernization. In the early 'end of ideology' debate a gradual decline of ideological political differences was predicted as a logical consequence of the decrease of the importance of the cleavage structure. As far as the decline in the level of party identification is a consequence of such a gradual depolarization, it should be a secular decline, just as predicted by the theory of modernization. However, polarization can fluctuate from one election to the other and differ across countries at the same level of modernization. Therefore, in contrast to the theory of modernization, it can explain non-linear fluctuations in the level of party identification. In Section 5.4 we will further discuss this theoretical perspective and test it. Section 5.5 is devoted to party identification as an independent variable: Has modernization and/or a possible decrease in ideological polarization made it less closely tied to the vote?

5.2   THE EVOLUTION OF PARTY IDENTIFICATION

The question whether or not a secular decline in the level of party identification has occurred in advanced industrial democracies and whether modernization is an underlying cause of decline, has been the subject of several previous comparative studies. Schmitt and Holmberg (1995), having studied the developments in fourteen West European countries and the United States until 1992, came to the conclusion: 'If there is an overall tendency, it is of loosening party bonds. But specific developments, by country and party, are so varied that any general "overall" view disguises more than it discloses.' On the basis of a larger number of countries and a longer time span, regressing the year of the survey on trends in partisanship, Dalton (2000*a*) comes to a less ambiguous conclusion. He finds negative trends in seventeen of the nineteen advanced industrial democracies represented in his study.

In this chapter we will see to what extent the trends in partisanship in the six countries included in our study confirm these trends. Limiting ourselves to these six countries might have the disadvantage of a smaller database, but on the other hand it clearly has two major advantages. First, Dalton objects to the study by Schmitt and Holmberg that they include countries which have not yet become advanced industrial societies, and that many time series are too short to reveal effects of cognitive mobilization. An analysis based on national election surveys from Great Britain, Denmark, Germany, the Netherlands, Norway, and Sweden, avoids these problems. All are old democracies, they were traditional industrial societies in the 1960s and have transformed into advanced industrial societies in the 1990s. Second, the limitation to six countries enables us to study the development in these countries in more detail.

The development of the level of party identification for each of the six countries is presented in Fig. 5.1. In two countries the development is pretty much in line with what the modernization thesis would predict. These countries are Britain and Sweden. Although the development in neither country is strictly monotonous, there can hardly be a dispute about the direction of change: 'down we go' (Holmberg 1999). In Britain the decline started in the early 1970s, and continued for more than a decade. The decline came to a halt in the 1980s, that is, in the Thatcher years, but went further in the 1990s. The pattern in Sweden is very similar, although the development over time is a little bit different. After an initial

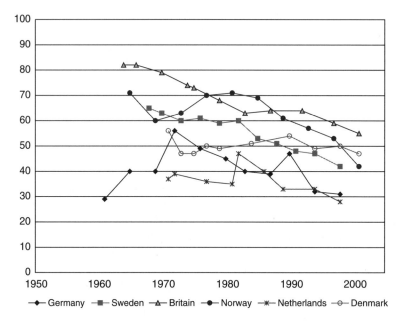

100
90
80
70
60
50
40
30
20
10
0
1950   1960   1970   1980   1990   2000

—◆— Germany —■— Sweden —▲— Britain —●— Norway —✳— Netherlands —○— Denmark

FIG. 5.1. *The evolution of the level of partisanship*

decline in the late 1960s, the trend stabilized in the 1970s, to be followed by a continuous decline ever since.

In the other four countries the development is more complex. In Norway a secular decline can be observed since 1980, but this decline was preceded by an increase in the 1970s after an initial decline in the 1960s. Neither in Denmark nor in the Netherlands can a clear trend be observed. After a sudden decline in the early 1970s, in 1973 to be precise, when all of a sudden the old party system was shaken up, the level of party identification slowly clambered in Denmark, but went down again in the 1990s. In the Netherlands a sudden increase in the 1980s interrupts a trend that otherwise is a negative one. The German trend starts out at about 30 per cent in 1961, reaches its highest level well above 50 per cent in 1972, but then continuously declines, falling back to the 30 per cent mark again—with the major exception of the reunification election in 1990.

So we find compelling evidence that partisanship is declining over time. In all countries partisanship is lower in the late 1990s than in the 1960s and the early 1970s. This is consistent with the theory of modernization. However, it is also clear that partisanship has developed in a more complex way than the modernization thesis would predict. At least part of the development seems to be due to nation-specific characteristics, like Reiter (1989) suggested. It is hard to link the various patterns in the development of partisanship between countries to one general explanation associated with modernization, at least if time is taken as an indicator of the process of modernization. It seems more plausible that the fluctuations and deviations from a linear trend are due to periodical effects and country-specific events.

Given the limited explanatory power of the theory of modernization[1] we will continue our analysis by two consecutive steps. First, in Section 5.3, we will test the micro-theory underlying modernization theory. Second, in Section 5.4, we will—in the spirit of Przeworski and Teune—see to what extent we can replace what seem to be nation-specific causes by more general variables.

5.3 DEALIGNMENT AND COGNITIVE MOBILIZATION

In order to test the validity of the underlying assumptions of modernization theory at the micro-level we first need to specify which aspects of modernization are relevant. These can be derived from functional theory. The functional model argues that partisanship is becoming less relevant for electorates and predicts a lasting loss of loyalties to political parties in general. Current theories of mass politics proposed that party identification had a functional value for citizens in industrial societies, as parties provided political cues that guided them through the complex world of politics, not just regarding the vote, but also in shaping public opinion and in evaluating political events (Campbell et al. 1960). Party identification was of special importance for a certain segment of the electorate, as 'partisanship provides a clear and low-cost voting cue for the unsophisticated voter' (Converse 1975). As political sophistication was not considered to be widespread in industrial society (Converse 1964), the functional value of party identification was considered to be high.

One consequence of the transition to advanced industrial societies is that the functional value of partisanship will decrease. The transition brings about a radical improvement of citizens' political resources. First, because of a sharp rise in the level of education and second, because of the media explosion leads to an increase in the amount of (political) information available. Thus, the media explosion occurs at a moment when citizens are becoming more capable of processing the information they receive. As sophisticated citizens do not need political guidance from parties, this development should lead to a decline of partisanship. This process is usually referred to as the process of *cognitive mobilization*. According to Dalton (1984: 267) this implies that ever more 'citizens possess the skills and resources necessary to become politically engaged with little dependence on external cues. In addition, cognitive mobilization implies a psychological involvement in politics'. However, in our view 'a psychological involvement in politics' should not be included in the definition of cognitive mobilization. Cognitive mobilization literally emphasizes cognitive aspects more than psychological involvement: the second element of Dalton's definition of cognitive mobilization. Also, the main argument of the functionalist model is that modernization leads to a politically more sophisticated electorate that no longer needs the cost-saving device of partisanship to find their way in the world of politics. In this argument political involvement might be considered a possible consequence rather than a factor of cognitive mobilization. Therefore, we will limit the definition of cognitive mobilization to the cognitive element and operationalize it by the level of education. Once we accept this operational definition, cognitive mobilization can only be a cause of a possible decline of party identification when the following conditions are met:

1. The level of education has been increasing over time.
2. There is a stable negative relationship between educational level and the level of party identification; that is, the higher the education, the lower the level of party identification.

When we test these hypotheses, nationally established measures of education are used and recoded into the trichotomy: primary, secondary, and higher education.

In Table 5.1 the development of the level of education is indicated by the percentage of people having received higher education. Obviously, in all countries the level of education has been increasing over time. Therefore, the first condition for cognitive mobilization being a cause of declining partisanship is met. The second condition refers to the relationship between education and party identification.

As can be seen in Table 5.2, education does have a negative effect on the level of party identification. At least all regression coefficients point in the expected direction. However, the effect is not significant in Germany and the Netherlands. In Britain, Norway, and Sweden it has been declining over time. Only Denmark shows a more or less stable and significant effect.

Table 5.3 enables us to look at the relationship between education and partisanship in more detail. This table confirms that at least in Britain, Denmark, Norway, and Sweden the findings are consistent with the cognitive mobilization hypothesis in the sense that there are relatively more independents among people with higher education than among less educated people. However, in the Netherlands and particularly in Germany the pattern contradicts the hypothesis. Also, in Britain, Norway, and Sweden the differences between the different levels of education have become smaller. This is mainly due to a decline of partisanship among people with a low education. This again is the opposite of what the cognitive mobilization hypothesis predicts.

It might be obvious that the level of education is a function of age. The level of education among the population at large has been increasing due to generation replacement. Younger cohorts are much better educated than older cohorts. At the same time age is considered as the most important factor in the development of party identification, not because age in itself is important, but because it is a proxy for the length of time people have had experience with a particular party or the length of time people have been able to confirm their identification with a particular party (Converse 1969, 1976). On the other hand, in the context of the

TABLE 5.1. *The development of education* (Figures are % highly educated)*

	Denmark	Germany	Netherlands	Norway	Sweden	Britain
1960						
1961						
1962						
1963						
1964						2
1965				11		
1966						
1967						
1968					7	
1969				14		
1970					15	3
1971			8			
1972		9	10			
1973				15	10	
1974						5
1975						
1976		14			16	
1977	9		13	14		
1978						
1979	12				20	6
1980		11				
1981			17	16		
1982					23	
1983		12				10
1984	13					
1985				17	25	
1986			19			
1987		12				7
1988					30	
1989			19	19		
1990	20	16				
1991					21	
1992						7
1993				25		
1994	21	20	23		23	
1995						
1996						
1997				24		11
1998		32	23		28	
1999						
2000						
2001						14

*Estimates are based on nation specific indicators of 'higher education'.

Berglund et al.

TABLE 5.2. *Education and strength of party identification* (Figures are regression coefficients, controlled for age and political interest)*

	Denmark	Germany	Netherlands	Norway	Sweden	Britain
1960						
1961						
1962						
1963						
1964						—
1965				−0.13		
1966						
1967						
1968					**−0.21**	
1969				**−0.20**		
1970					**−0.16**	—
1971			−0.04			
1972		−0.01	—			
1973				**−0.16**	**−0.19**	
1974						**−0.21**
1975						
1976		−0.02			**−0.22**	
1977	—		−0.04	**−0.16**		
1978						
1979	**−0.15**				**−0.16**	**−0.15**
1980		—				
1981			−0.05	**−0.12**		
1982					**−0.15**	
1983		−0.01				—
1984	**−0.10**					
1985				**−0.16**	**−0.18**	
1986			−0.06			
1987		−0.03				—
1988					**−0.16**	
1989			—	**−0.15**		
1990	−0.08	−0.07				
1991					**0.07**	
1992						—
1993				−0.03		
1994	**−0.09**	0.00	0.03		**−0.15**	
1995						
1996						
1997				−0.01		−0.06
1998	**−0.16**	0.03	−0.06		**−0.11**	
1999						
2000						
2001				**−0.08**		**−0.09**

*Bold coefficients are significant at the 0.01 level.

Party identification is coded: 1. independent; 2. weak identification; 3. strong identification. Due to a different wording in the Norwegian questionnaire, the coding in 1997 is 1. independent; 2. party identification. Education is coded: 1. primary; 2. high school; 3. higher education.

TABLE 5.3. *Partisanship and education* (Figures are % independents at different educational levels and Pearson's *r*)

	Election year	% primary	% secondary	% higher	Pearson's *r* all	Pearson's *r* under 30
Britain	1964	16	19	32	0.06	0.02
	1970	19	25	31	0.08	0.01
	1974	25	28	39	0.06	−0.01
	1979	29	34	44	0.08	0.04
	1983	37	41	36	0.00	−0.07
	1987	38	40	33	−0.01	−0.06
	1992	37	39	41	0.02	−0.06
	1997	43	40	37	−0.04	−0.04
	2001	34	42	40	0.06	0.07
Denmark	1977	44	49	54	0.07	—
	1979	38	48	48	0.09	−0.09
	1984	70	78	75	0.04	−0.06
	1990	43	53	53	0.08	−0.05
	1994	45	54	60	0.12	−0.05
Germany	1972	39	36	34	−0.04	−0.01
	1976	52	39	34	−0.14	−0.12
	1980	58	45	43	−0.12	−0.17
	1983	60	57	43	−0.09	−0.10
	1987	56	54	52	−0.03	−0.04
	1990	48	42	39	−0.07	−0.02
	1994	69	66	61	−0.06	−0.12
	1998	65	60	46	−0.15	−0.16
Netherlands	1971	67	60	59	−0.06	−0.13
	1977	66	71	57	—	—
	1981	67	66	64	−0.02	−0.05
	1986	58	61	60	0.02	−0.06
	1989	67	74	67	0.02	—
	1994	69	68	61	−0.06	−0.18
	1998	71	75	71	0.01	−0.08
Norway	1965	22	32	33	0.10	0.04
	1969	32	42	53	0.14	0.08
	1973	33	37	49	0.10	0.08
	1977	23	34	36	0.11	0.10
	1981	24	31	34	0.08	−0.01
	1985	24	33	37	0.10	0.01
	1989	29	40	46	0.12	−0.03
	1993	37	46	44	0.04	−0.12
	1997	45	50	42	−0.02	−0.12
Sweden	1968	31	38	53	0.12	0.02
	1970	30	41	49	0.15	0.05
	1973	35	47	55	0.14	0.03
	1976	31	45	48	0.14	0.03

(*Continued*)

Berglund et al.

TABLE 5.3. (*Contd.*)

Election year	% primary	% secondary	% higher	Pearson's r all	Pearson's r under 30
1979	35	48	49	0.12	0.02
1982	35	47	46	0.10	0.01
1985	39	52	57	0.16	0.08
1988	42	50	58	0.14	0.03
1991	48	56	53	0.05	−0.02
1994	44	60	57	0.12	−0.02
1998	47	65	59	0.10	−0.07

party decline thesis, it has been claimed that the life cycle thesis is no longer valid for the post-war generation. Being better educated they are less likely to develop partisanship and something that does not come into being cannot be confirmed either. Regardless which interpretation is correct, it is obvious that in order to assess the net effect of education on partisanship one should control for age. The results of such an analysis are presented in the last column of Table 5.3, where the correlation between education and partisanship for the youngest generation is shown. As far as we are able to discern the predicted relationship in at least some countries, this is no longer the case among the youngest generation. At first, the correlations are lower than among the population at large and then over time turn into the 'wrong' direction. This means that among younger generations people with a lower instead of a higher level of education tend to turn their back to political parties.

Taking all evidence together there is little support for the cognitive mobilization hypothesis and thus for the theory of modernization. Therefore, in Section 5.4 we will turn to the possible alternative explanation of changes in partisanship, focusing on the political context rather than on changes in society.

5.4 PARTY POLARIZATION AND PARTY IDENTIFICATION

Schmitt and Holmberg (1995) tested four political factors as possible causal agents behind decreasing levels of partisanship—the degree of party polarization, the extent of ideological conflicts, the intensity of issue differences, and the evolution of new parties—and found positive, yet weak relationships. The decline in the strength of party identification tended to be related to weakening party polarization, declining ideological conflicts, diminished issue differences, and increases in the number of political parties.

We will not replicate their study in this context. We will, however, test two related hypotheses. Hypothesis number one is tested on the aggregated macro-level using elections as the unit of analysis. It specifies that 'across time and across countries party identification at election time is higher the more polarized political parties are'. This hypothesis implies that if polarization goes up, partisanship will go up as well and go down if polarization decreases.

The hypothesis that the development of party identification is related to the political context is somewhat at odds with the orthodox perspective on party identification as originally developed by the Michigan School of Electoral Research (Campbell et al. 1960) and more recently maintained by Miller and Shanks (1996). In this view party identification is seen as a deep psychological attachment rooted in early-adult socialization and as hardly sensitive to fluctuations in the political context. However, a more revisionist view on party identification sees it as the result of a 'running tally' of retrospective evaluations of party performance (Fiorina 1981). According to this latter view party identification is supposed to vary with the political–institutional context rather than with the social structure of society (Huber et al. 2004).

Our hypothesis states that people's degrees of party attachment will vary between elections depending on the nature of party competition.

The second hypothesis of this section refers to the micro-level and states that people's degree of party identification is related to the extent that they *perceive* ideological differences between relevant political parties. It states that 'people who experience larger differences between parties tend to develop stronger party attachments'.

In order to determine how polarized a party system is at a particular election, we use two data sources. One is the familiar left–right differential derived from the content analyses of party manifestos (see Chapter 2; also Budge et al. 2001). The other one relies on survey evidence and takes the distance between the mean left–right self-placement of party voters as a measure of polarization. Moreover, we consider the left–right distance between the two major parties as well as that of the two polar parties (among those that reached parliamentary representation) as separate and distinct indicators of polarization. With regard to the level of party identification, finally, we look at the proportions of all identifiers and proportions of strong identifiers as two different criteria.

The data in Table 5.4 prove that it is indeed the case that the proportion of party identifiers in national electorates covaries with left–right polarization. Over six countries and about fifty elections, we find that the more polarized a party system is, the more numerous party identifiers are (see first row of Table 5.4). There is clear evidence that party polarization leads to a higher level of party identification no matter what criterion we apply—with one exception: Overall partisanship seems to drop when the ideological distance between the voters of polar parties increases. All other coefficients are positive, two of them statistically significant despite the limited number of cases: Large distances between the two polar parties go along with high proportions of strong party identifiers both according to manifesto data ($r = 0.42$) and survey evidence ($r = 0.32$).

Our first hypothesis implies that variations in polarization within countries across time should lead to variations in the level of party identification. However,

TABLE 5.4. *Left–right polarization and party identification. Pearson's r and n*
(= number of elections) in parentheses

	MRG-based left–right distance two big parties	MRG-based left–right distance two polar parties	Survey-based left–right distance two big parties	Survey-based left–right distance two polar parties
All identifiers	+0.13 (61)	+0.18 (61)	+0.24 (46)	−0.27 (46)
Strong identifiers	+0.21 (59)	+0.42 (59)[†]	+0.29 (44)	−0.32 (44)*
Britain				
all identifiers	−0.45 (10)	−0.59 (10)	+0.38 (7)	+0.38 (7)
strong identifiers	−0.49 (10)	−0.60 (10)	+0.41 (7)	+0.41 (7)
Denmark				
all identifiers	+0.07 (10)	+0.03 (10)	+0.49 (7)	+0.60 (7)
strong identifiers	−0.12 (9)	−0.09 (9)	+0.88 (6)*	+0.67 (6)
Germany				
all identifiers	−0.05 (11)	+0.05 (11)	+0.76 (8)*	−0.04 (8)
strong identifiers	−0.42 (8)	−0.44 (8)	+0.73 (8)*	−0.24 (8)
Netherlands				
all identifiers	−0.18 (9)	+0.30 (9)	+0.53 (7)	+0.74 (7)
strong identifiers	+0.30 (9)	+0.50 (9)	+0.43 (7)	+0.67 (7)
Norway				
all identifiers	−0.51 (10)	−0.07 (10)	−0.44 (7)	−0.20 (7)
strong identifiers	−0.63 (9)	−0.21 (9)	−0.33 (6)	−0.06 (6)
Sweden				
all identifiers	+0.11 (11)	−0.52 (11)	+0.20 (10)	+0.33 (10)
strong identifiers	+0.69 (14)[†]	+0.24 (14)	+0.31 (10)	+0.41 (10)

Source: European Voters Data File; the M(anifesto) R(esearch) G(roup) database (Budge et al. 2001);
and the data collected and reported in the appendix tables of Schmitt 2002.
Note: *$p = 0.05$; [†]$p = 0.01$

the empirical evidence with regard to this specification of the hypothesis is less convincing. The within-country diachronic perspective is conducive to a variety of different patterns. If we start at the bottom of Table 5.5 Sweden is character-ized by a positive co-variation between polarization and partisanship: all but one coefficients seem to indicate that polarization indeed produces partisanship. However, things are exactly the other way round just across the border in Norway: There, rising ideological polarization is accompanied by a decrease of partisanship no matter what criterion we look at. Findings for the Netherlands are similar to the Swedish: the higher the polarization, the more the identification. In the German findings, the particular importance of the two major parties stands out: the farther apart SPD and CDU/CSU voters are ideologically, the more partisanship there is. In Denmark, manifesto-based measures of polarization are hardly correlated with partisanship, while survey-based indicators are: the higher

TABLE 5.5. *Perception of left–right polarization between the two major parties and party identification*

Country	Two major parties	Election	Perceived left–right distance by strength PID (Pearson's r)	Number of cases
Britain	Labour, Conservatives	2001	0.18	2221
Denmark	S, Venstre	1994	0.10	1801
Germany	SPD, CDU/CSU	1980	0.13	1055
		1983	0.15	920
		1987	0.20	1215
		1990	0.06	765
		1998	0.12	1546
Netherlands	PvdA, CDA	1981	0.12	1468
		1982	0.05	674
		1986	0.06	1239
		1989	0.13	1429
		1994	0.06	516
		1998	0.09	1596
Norway	Labour, Conservatives	1973	0.08	892
		1977	0.08	1344
		1981	0.13	1350
		1985	0.06	1923
		1989	0.15	1982
		1993	0.09	1870
Sweden	S, M	1979	0.25	2416
		1982	0.25	2592
		1985	0.18	2535
		1988	0.23	2395
		1991	0.23	2326
		1994	0.19	2154
		1998	0.20	1959

the ideological distance between party electorates, the more partisanship we find. For Britain, finally, the strange finding is that polarization as measured by party manifesto data goes along with declining partisanship, while survey-based polarization coincides with rising partisanship.

It is evident that things are considerably less uniform in individual countries, than one would expect on the basis of the findings of the pooled analysis. Obviously, there are factors intervening in the association between polarization and identification which cannot be controlled for in the bivariate design of the current analysis.[2]

Berglund et al.

TABLE 5.6. *Proportion of loyalists among all identifiers (i.e. including those who did not vote or can not tell which party; figures are %)**

	Denmark	Germany	Netherlands	Norway	Sweden	Britain
1960						
1961						
1962						
1963						
1964						81
1965				84		
1966						77
1967						
1968					87	
1969				85		
1970					86	74
1971			68			
1972		88				
1973	78			85	85	
1974						75
1975						75
1976	78	90			87	
1977	78		72	87		
1978						
1979	81				89	75
1980		88				
1981			?	85		
1982			?		86	
1983		87				74
1984						
1985				86	85	
1986			?			
1987		86				76
1988					82	
1989			72	83		
1990	81	72				
1991					79	
1992						77
1993				76		
1994	82	80	75		82	
1995						
1996						
1997				81		70
1998	81	77	?		77	
1999						
2000						
2001						68

*Empty spaces indicate that the respective information is not available.
A '?' indicates that the recoding of the data does not allow to produce the figure in question.

TABLE 5.7. *Proportion of loyalists among voting identifiers (i.e. excluding those who did not vote or can not tell which party; figures are %)*

	Denmark	Germany	Netherlands	Norway	Sweden	Britain
1960						
1961						
1962						
1963						
1964						91
1965				89		
1966						90
1967						
1968					93	
1969				91		
1970					95	90
1971			91			
1972		92				
1973	81			92	93	
1974						86
1975						87
1976	85	96			91	
1977	87		93	96		
1978						
1979	88				93	88
1980		94				
1981			82	94		
1982			93		92	
1983		93				87
1984						
1985				96	90	
1986			86			
1987		92				86
1988					90	
1989			86	92		
1990	90	86				
1991					86	
1992						87
1993				89		
1994	88	88	82		89	
1995						
1996						
1997				89		87
1998	85	84	83		85	
1999						
2000						
2001						87

In order to test the second hypothesis, in all six countries and across all elections, we created an individual level variable measuring how people perceived the ideological distance on the left–right scale between the Social Democratic Party and the largest of the Conservative parties. This perceived polarization variable turned out to be positively correlated, if only modestly, with people's strength of party attachment in each election studied in each country. Perceptions of large differences go along with stronger degrees of party identification (see Table 5.5).

Of course, correlations do not prove causality. In theory, the relationship could as well have been shaped by self-rationalizations, for example, that people who are strong party identifiers tend to see, and perhaps want to see, large differences between parties. Lacking good panel data we can not disprove this counter-argument, but we have tried to strengthen our test by controlling in multiple regressions for a couple of other variables that we know are, or might be, related to the strength of party identification, for example, people's age, but also level of education. These regression controls did not alter the conclusion. There is a significant relationship between people's perceptions of party conflicts and degrees of partisanship even after relevant controls have been applied. Voters who perceive large party differences tend to have, and maybe also tend to develop, stronger party identifications.

The conclusion of our endeavours in this section is fairly obvious. The pooled analysis clearly indicates that ideological polarization between parties does go along with partisanship, even though this conclusion is not warranted in each country and according to each indicator. What is more: We were able to demonstrate on the level of the individual voter that perceptions of ideological polarization are conducive to partisanship (or caused by it as may well be the case).

5.5 PARTY IDENTIFICATION AND THE VOTE

In this section we change our analytical perspective and look at party identification as an independent rather than as the dependent variable. Is it still the over-deterministic predictor of party choice that it was claimed to be in some of the early publications on European voting behaviour? Or has its impact on the vote been declining over time?

We will determine the proportion of 'loyalists', that is, identifiers who actually vote for their party, for each national election represented in our database. Those who don't are called defectors. Simple as this strategy may sound, it is still a matter of dispute what the appropriate percentage base should be. There are two basic options: all identifiers or only those who actually went to vote. The all-identifiers-option treats non-voting as a 'silent' exit option; in the only-voters-option, these silent defectors are disregarded. We will pursue both paths and start with the former.

In the six countries in this study the proportion of party identifiers who actually support their party in an election varies between 70 and 82 per cent during the 1990s (see Table 5.6). In Germany, Sweden, and Britain the number of loyalists has significantly declined since the 1970s. In Denmark and Norway developments are less spectacular, whereas in the Netherlands, party loyalty has gone up.

In the 1990s, on average three in four West European citizens vote for the party they identify with. However, things look somewhat different if we restrict our analysis to only those identifiers who actually turned out and went to vote. Compared to the 'easy way out' into abstention, voting for another party is clearly a harder criterion for identifying defection rates. And as one would expect, loyalists in this perspective are more numerous, defectors less numerous. But still, in the 1990s, one in seven party identifiers who turn out and vote, do vote for another party than the one they identify with (see Table 5.7). This proportion as well has risen over the past decades in five of the six countries in our study. Denmark is a clear exception. In the 1960s and early 1970s, on average only one in ten identifiers who voted, failed to support their party. So from this perspective as well, party identification and party choice seem to have become more independent than they were a few decades ago.

5.6 CONCLUSION

In this chapter we tested the validity of two alternative theoretical perspectives on the evolution of party identification. According to the first perspective which is based on the theory of modernization, we should expect a secular decline of the level of party identification. The simple reason is that modern citizens—educated and politically skilful as they are—do not need anymore the cue of party identification in order to participate meaningfully in an election.

The second perspective focuses on political rather than social correlates of party identification and predicts less linear developments. Adversary politics, to use Samuel Finer's term, is supposed to be favourable for the development of partisanship while the opposite of it—a broad political consensus across the major parties—is expected to suppress the development of party identification.

Whereas the first perspective predicts a linear decline of partisanship, the second one does not, unless we would expect a linear decline of polarization, which we do not (see Chapter 2). At first sight our findings seem to be consistent with the modernization perspective. Party identifiers have become less numerous over time. However, developments are anything but monotonous in most countries. Also, we found that the micro-theory underlying the theory of modernization is not corroborated. Contrary to what we should expect, cognitive mobilization does not lead to a lower level of party identification.

However, the evidence supporting the second perspective is equally ambiva-
lent. In line with what we expected there is some effect of left–right polarization
on partisanship. Both the analysis of aggregate and individual-level data confirm
that politics matters. The more polarized a party system is, the more partisans we
find. But again, these political correlates of the development of party identification are modest at best, and cannot fully explain what is going on in the six West
European countries under study.

In the final step of our analysis we treated party identification as an independent variable, and tried to assess its predictive power for party choice. On average
three in four partisans actually support the party they identify with, while one in
four abstain from voting or vote for another party. If we restrict this analysis to
voters, the respective proportion rises to six in seven: one in seven voting identifiers vote for another party than the one they identify with. But irrespective of the
way we define the denominator, party identification has lost some of its predictive
power for party choices over the past decades.

Where does all of this lead us to? We believe there are a few insights that we
have added to the body of knowledge in this domain. One is that there is indeed
no monotonous decline in partisanship. Although party identification is on the
way down in all countries investigated, the patterns in this evolution are very
country-specific. Therefore, theoretical perspectives predicting a similar secular
decline of party identification across advanced western democracies, like
the theory of modernization does, can at best explain part of the story. But the
same applies to theoretical perspectives trying to explain fluctuations in the level
of party identification by the political context. Political polarization is one factor
in the evolution of partisanship, but certainly not the only one and perhaps not
even a very powerful one. A final conclusion is that partisanship and the vote
have become more independent over the past decades in Western Europe, which
makes party identification potentially a more powerful analytical instrument
than it was found to be in the early European election studies. How useful it is
as an analytical instrument depends on the extent to which it is possible to explain
deviations from voters' party identification or 'normal vote'. However, that
question is beyond the scope of this chapter.

Notes

1. The results from logistic regressions with partisanship as dependent variable and time as
   explanatory variable (data not shown) prove that not in a single case time explains more
   than 6 per cent of the variance (pseudo-R^2).
2. See Schmitt 2002 for a more complex study design.

6

Value Orientations and Party Choice

Oddbjørn Knutsen and Staffan Kumlin

6.1 VALUE ORIENTATIONS: CONCEPTUAL CONSIDERATIONS

Values are prescriptive beliefs that signify that certain end-states or modes of conduct are personally or socially preferable to other end-states or modes of conduct. Political values are prescriptive beliefs, which individuals would like to see implemented in the political system, and include the forms of political participation by which individuals seek to influence politics.

In European democracies, the most important value conflicts originate in the most crucial socio-political cleavages (see Chapter 4). Of the conflicts fostered by the National Revolution, those related to religious versus more secular values created the most uniform divisions in West European party systems. Christian values focus on the importance of Christian morals and principles in society and politics, and on traditional moral guidelines in school and society in general.

The Industrial Revolution gave rise to economic interest conflicts that were anchored in hierarchical socio-structural variables. The most important political value orientations that emerged from the Industrial Revolution were economic left–right values or left–right materialist values. These value orientations are economic in nature, and they refer in particular to the role of government in creating more economic equality in society versus the need for economic incentives and efficiency. These value orientations incorporate value conflicts related to control, power, and the degree of distribution of resources in the production sphere, and include workers' control and state regulation of the economy versus private enterprise, private property, and the market economy; economic and social equality versus the need for differentiated rewards for stimulating effort (Inglehart 1984: 25; Knutsen 1995a; Lafferty and Knutsen 1984).

The moral value dimension and economic left–right values are often referred to as 'Old Politics' because they capture the essence of the traditional lines of conflict in industrial society. In contrast, 'New Politics' refers to value conflicts emerging from post-industrial society.

There are different ways of conceptualizing the new politics value orientations. According to Inglehart, value conflicts related to *materialist/post-materialist value orientations* reflect the new politics conflict dimension. Inglehart argues that 'new' post-materialist values are deeply rooted and stand in opposition to more trad-itional materialist values. He identifies a 'silent revolution' in which a gradual value change along the materialist/post-materialist dimension takes place. This involves a shift from a preoccupation with physical sustenance and safety values, towards a greater emphasis on belonging, self-expression, and quality-of-life values. The spread of post-materialist values is explained by generational replace-ment, the growth of the new middle class and the spread of higher education (Inglehart 1977, 1990).

Another way of conceptualizing 'New Politics' is represented by *environmental versus economic growth values*. Today this conflict is firmly rooted in the public mind, and in many West European countries conflicts over environmental values seem to be the most manifest expression of the 'New Politics' conflict. A clear manifestation of this is the emergence of green parties that have gained consider-able electoral support in many Western democracies. Furthermore, Flanagan has emphasized in a series of articles that Inglehart's conceptualization of value change combines two dimensions: A *materialist/non-materialist dimension* and *a libertarian/authoritarian* dimension (Flanagan 1987; Flanagan and Lee 1988, 2003). The overarching concept that integrates libertarian values is self-actualization, and the central value orientations within the notion of libertarian values are autonomy, openness, and self-betterment. The authoritarian value orien-tation 'designates a broader cluster of values, which, along with concerns for security and order, includes respect for authority, discipline and dutifulness, patriotism and intolerance for minorities, conformity to customs, and support for traditional reli-gious and moral values' (Flanagan 1987: 1305). The libertarian/authoritarian value orientations are also the central components in Kitschelt's important work (1994, 1995) on changes in the party systems of Western democracies.

Theoretically, it is reasonable to argue that the materialist/post-materialist value orientation incorporates significant aspects of both of the other two post-industrial value dimensions. Therefore it is problematic to use all three in multi-variate analysis since to do so is in a way overcontrolling for some of the same phenomena. As we did not find the most elaborate measure of materialist/post-materialist values, the twelve-item battery, in many election surveys, and the four-item battery was available in only a few surveys, we decided to rely on the other two orientations.

On the basis of the above discussion we have identified the central value dimensions that we will use for analysing the relationship between value orien-tations and party choice:

1. Religious versus secular values or moral values
2. Economic left–right
3. Libertarian/authoritarian
4. Ecology versus growth orientations.

The chapter is organized as follows: Section 6.2 introduces a number of hypotheses about how the impact of various value orientations may have developed over time. Section 6.3 outlines the measurements we have taken in each country to assess the various value orientations. Section 6.4 presents the bivariate correlations between the four sets of value orientations and party choice. In section 6.5 multivariate analyses are carried out to examine and compare the impact of various types of value orientations, and to examine the impact of value orientations while controlling for traditional structural variables. Section 6.6 shifts the theoretical focus from modernization theory to factors related to the political context: Rather than looking for modernization-driven linear shifts in the impact of values over time, we consider the often cyclical changes in perceived party polarization as a factor that may govern the impact of values. Conclusions are drawn in Section 6.7.

6.2 THE IMPACT OF VALUES OVER TIME: WHAT TO EXPECT

The processes of modernization affect the impact of the various value orientations on party choice in at least two ways. The first way is due to a compositional effect. If people's value orientations are changing from, for example, religious to secular values and the correlation with party choice is stable, parties appealing to religious values may decline while secular parties may increase their support. Such compositional effects may be important consequences of value change but they are not results of changes in the *impact* of various value orientations over time. This chapter focuses on the second way value orientations affect party choice, namely, changes in the impact of various value orientations over time. We are testing whether the modernization process implies that voters' value orientations become more or less important for their voting choice over time and that some value orientations become relatively more and others relatively less important over time.[1]

In Chapter 1 two basic hypotheses about the impact of value orientations over time were formulated. These hypotheses are in somewhat more detailed form than the two major hypotheses we are testing in this chapter:

Hypothesis 1. (a) The combined independent impact of value orientations will increase over time, at least initially. This will apply when (b) social background variables are controlled for, and (c) value orientations will increase their combined impact on party choice relatively to the impact of social structure.

Hypothesis 2. (a) The impact of old politics orientations (moral and economic left–right values) will gradually yield to new politics values. This will apply when (b) social background variables are controlled for, and (c) new politics orientations will increase their impact on party choice relatively to the impact of social structure.

Hypothesis 1 is more general than hypothesis 2 and predicts that not only 'new politics' orientations, but political values in general, will become more important over time. Although the major parties founded in religious and class conflicts have lost the commanding position they enjoyed in the 1950s and 1960s, they remain dominant in most party systems. However, with the dissolution of religious networks, and the weakening of class differences, social location is waning as a source of political cues (Dalton and Wattenberg 2000: 277; Franklin et al. 1992; Särlvik and Crewe 1983). We might, however, expect support for the parties that are characterized by the politics of religious and class cleavages to be sustained by values alone. The most plausible argument for this is the notion of 'cognitive mobilization', which refers to the processes by which electors come to 'possess the level of political skills and resources necessary to become self-sufficient in politics' (Dalton 1988: 18). Low levels of education and political information typical of industrial society meant that the average elector relied on social and party cues—'external mobilization'—to manage the complexities of politics. With the expansion of education, especially at the university level, citizens have become politically more sophisticated; with the expansion of political information, particularly the arrival of television, public has come better informed. Thereby, electors have become increasingly independent in political matters; they are seen as being capable of forming their own judgements on political issues, and of making reasonable political decisions, like party choice, rather than following social norms, or relying on the lead given by parties (Dalton et al. 1984: 18–19, 461). This is in accord with evidence of the rise of issue voting (Franklin et al. 1992: 399–403) and the sharp increase in issue diversification (van der Eijk et al. 1992: 413) during the 1970s and the 1980s.

Furthermore, political parties possess considerable ideological and organizational resources, which enable them to change. They are capable of shifting their appeal from focusing on broad social group benefits to more focused political issues and value orientations. At the same time, there is little evidence indicating that parties change their basic ideological positions despite reducing their focus on appealing to social groups (Budge et. al 2001). For example, there are no grounds for presupposing that the values embedded in the politics of class and religious cleavages have faded as class structures have changed and religious affiliations have declined. Unanchored in social divisions, these value orientations may be more fragile but nonetheless, they remain a potent basis for party choice (Knutsen and Scarbrough 1995: 498).

The second hypothesis is derived from the 'new politics' literature, in particular the contribution of Inglehart. According to his *developmental model*, political conflict variables are grouped under the following three headings (Inglehart 1977: 181–2):

1. *Pre-industrial variables* which are more or less ascriptive variables such as religion, language, and ethnicity;

2. *Industrial variables* or achieved variables such as occupation, income, education and membership in trade unions;
3. *Post-industrial variables* which reflect individual-level value orientations, 'particularly those based on post-economic needs', that is, the materialist/post-materialist value orientations.

These three types of variables are related in a developmental sequence because of their origin, and Inglehart tends to see a gradual change from the first two types of variables to the third, and particularly from the second to the third. The process of change in cleavage structure is characterized as a change from a 'class-based to a value-based pattern of political polarisation' (Inglehart 1984: 26–33).

Whereas these two hypotheses lead to the same prediction with regard to new politics orientations, they make different predictions with regard to old politics. Hypothesis 1 predicts a persisting political salience of class and religious orientations but supplemented and pluralized by the advance of new politics orientations. According to this hypothesis both old and new value orientations have become more significant for explaining party choice, in particular when social structure is controlled for. Hypothesis 2 predicts the progressive decline of the salience for party choice of class and religious orientations, to be replaced in due course by new politics conflicts. We interpret Inglehart's thesis of a transformation from old to new politics to include the decline of old politics values in addition to structural dealignment.

We also specify more concrete hypotheses about the impact of each of the two 'old politics orientations' (religious/secular and economic left–right), which in part correspond to the first two hypotheses about the changing impact of the old politics orientations.

The secularization process that has affected all countries in Western Europe is the point of departure for formulating more specific hypotheses about the changing impact of religious involvement and value orientations. There is no doubt that the secularization process has resulted in a smaller religious segment in West European societies (Halman and De Moor 1994; Jagodzinski and Dobbelaere 1995), but the secularization process has less obvious consequences for the impact of religious/secular values than one might expect. One hypothesis predicts that such value orientations have become less important (*the declining correlation hypothesis*), while another predicts a stable impact (*the stable correlation hypothesis*). Both hypotheses take the secularization process for granted. However, according to the *declining correlation hypothesis*, the modernization process and the secularization process in particular may have disrupted religious alignments in the same manner that social class has blurred. Increased social and geographical mobility, and changes in leisure patterns have undermined community integration and social bonds of all sorts, including religious networks. The Catholic Church no longer intervenes in politics and has ceased its active campaigns against parties on the Left, and in the 1970s and 1980s many Catholic clergy and organizations expressed sympathy with leftist policies (Berger 1982). The *stable correlation hypothesis* indicates that religious individuals are still well integrated into a religious network and that, despite comprising a smaller portion of the electorate, they maintain distinct voting patterns. The religious voters have been 'encapsulated' in religious networks and organizations, and still continue to be strong adherents of the religious parties.

A similar argument applies to left–right orientations: As explained above, economic left–right materialist values were central to the emergence of class politics that became predominant in industrial society, and have been very important to the ideological and issue-based political struggle between leftist and rightist political parties. Regarding the development of these values over time, there are two contradicting hypotheses: One implies that left–right materialist value orientations will become less consequential, and the other implies no such decline. According to the first hypothesis (called hypothesis 4 below), economic left–right value orientations will decrease in importance as a consequence of socio-economic and political change. The issues coupled to economic left–right value orientations have become less central to the political agenda, and at the individual level, the experiences that caused these value orientations to become important in explaining party choice, have become less fundamental.

The second hypothesis (called hypothesis 3 below) predicts a transformation of the left–right conflict in which left–right economic value orientations will remain an important predictor of party choice in post-industrial society. The economic left–right cleavage has traditionally been equated with the class cleavage, and economic left–right values have accompanied the class cleavage in the sense that they have been strongly coupled to social class. The transformation of the economic left–right lines of conflict implies that economic left–right values still have a stable and strong impact on party choice despite class and social status realignment. Economic left–right values are increasingly disconnected from social class and other status variables. This creates the potential for the left–right values to have a greater causal effect on party choice when social class is controlled for (Knutsen 1988: 345).

Because of these competing views in the literature we will test which of these alternative hypotheses is corroborated by our data:

Hypothesis 3. The impact of each of the old politics orientations ((a) economic left–right and (b) moral values) on party choice will remain stable or increase over time;

Hypothesis 4. The impact of each of the old politics orientations ((a) economic left–right and (b) moral values) on party choice will decline over time.

The various hypotheses can be summed up as follows:

1. The impact of the total value model, including both old and new politics orientations, will increase over time also when traditional structural

variables are controlled for, and become relatively more important than the traditional structural or social cleavages.

2. New politics value orientations will increase their impact on party choice over time in an absolute sense and relatively, compared with both the traditional structural cleavages (religion and social class) and the old politics orientations. The impact of both the structural variables and the old politics value orientations will decline over time, and new politics orientations will increase their causal impact on party choice, that is, even when traditional structural variables are controlled for.

3. and 4. While all theoretical positions hypothesize that new politics orientations will increase over the long term, there are contrasting hypotheses regarding each of the old politics orientations, they may remain stable and even increase (hypothesis 3), or they may decline (hypothesis 4).

Although these possibilities are included in hypotheses 1 and 2, we discussed the reasons for the various patterns in separate paragraphs since religious/secular and economic left–right values are fairly different conflict lines although they both belong to old politics.

6.3 INDICATORS AND INDEX CONSTRUCTION

The questions in the election surveys often changed from election to election. It is therefore rather complicated to find measurements that can be compared over time. In the face of these difficulties, the following principles have guided our choices: We use political attitudes as indicators of political values because election surveys contain both narrow and more broad-based issue items about voters' policy positions, rather than questions that directly tap a value. Our approach can be justified by the fact that values cannot be observed directly. We consider value orientations to be latent variables that are tapped by constrained (correlated) attitudes. There is a long tradition in political science of analysing attitudinal data to uncover a pattern, or evidence of constraint, among several attitudes. Such evidence is then interpreted as revealing, for example, the influence of ideology and values, or as evidence of a left–right ideology (Campbell et al. 1960: 189–94; Converse 1964; Nie et al. 1976: ch. 8 and 9). This is our approach in this chapter.[2] Evidence of constraint in political attitudes is thought to demonstrate the empirical relevance of the value concept, and the index based on constrained attitudes is thought to tap the value dimension in question. In addition to the empirical constraint criteria it should be possible to interpret an index theoretically in order to represent a value orientation.

The measurements we have developed are thus based on both theoretical criteria and empirical analyses. We have conducted a significant amount of correlation and factor analyses based on surveys from the five countries to examine which indicators should be included in the various measurements. The theoretical criterion is that the factors can be interpreted as tapping the value orientations just discussed.

We relied on indices[3] instead of single indicators. However, sometimes it was impossible to construct indices because only one or two items were available in a time series. At other times several items were available in the surveys, but they were not asked consistently all times. In these instances, we relied on single indicators in order to be able to achieve consistency in measurement over time.[4] In the remainder of this section we explain which items have been included in the various indices and which items have been analysed alone as single indicators.[5]

Factor analyses of the items available in the various surveys in Britain show fairly stable patterns. There are three dimensions: A very pronounced economic left–right dimension; a dimension that contains libertarian/authoritarian items; and a moral dimension.[6] There are few issue or value items in the UK election data before 1974. For the period 1964–70 we rely mainly on single indicators for the various value dimensions. Three such single items are available, two tapping the economic left–right dimension (about nationalization and redistribution), and a third tapping the libertarian/authoritarian dimension (about the death penalty).

For the period from 1974 to 1997 and sometimes to 2001 it is possible to construct more reliable measurements of most of the value orientations, but in some surveys it is not possible to construct the indices because one or more of the items are missing. In the 2001 survey very few items that have been asked in previous surveys are available.

In the Dutch election surveys few issue or value items have been asked repeatedly. Therefore, the best strategy is to rely on single items. No item tapping the libertarian/authoritarian orientations has been asked consistently, although some items have been asked more than once. We therefore picked items having the strongest correlation with party choice from each survey in which more than one item was available, and also picked items that were asked in several subsequent surveys to represent the libertarian/authoritarian dimension. It should be underscored that it is somewhat problematic to compare the strength of the correlation of these orientations over time.

Two sets of items tapping economic left–right orientations are available in the Danish surveys during the period 1971–1998. These were not always asked in the same surveys. One set of items is asked in all surveys from 1971 to 1984, and then again in 1990 and 1998. Another set of items is first asked in 1979 and then again in 1984 and in all subsequent surveys. Two items tapping libertarian/authoritarian values are asked in surveys between 1971 and 1981, and then other items are asked from 1987. One of the items asked in the former surveys is also asked from 1990. A single item tapping ecology/growth values is asked in most surveys since 1981. There is no indicator for religious/secular values in the Danish surveys, so we could not analyse these in Denmark.

Factor analyses show an impressively stable structure, a two-factor pattern comprising an old politics economic left–right dimension and a new politics dimension. Two indices—based on the two batteries of items—have been constructed to tap the economic left–right orientations.[7] The two indices that are constructed for libertarian/authoritarian values are based on different items and cover very different time spans. The correlations based on these different items cannot be directly compared, and we should avoid concluding anything about a rise or fall of libertarian/authoritarian values based only on changes between the periods of 1971–81 and 1987–98. The ecology/growth measurement is based on the mentioned single item.

The economic left–right orientations are covered by several indicators in the Norwegian election surveys and constitute a major dimension according to the factor analyses that we conducted. However, no item is asked consistently from 1969. We have chosen to construct indices based on the items that have been asked in at least three surveys. The index is then constructed on the basis of three to six items.

In most surveys moral/religious value orientations are covered by several items that come out as another major dimension in the factor analyses, but the only question asked in all surveys since 1969 is one about abortion. We have used this to tap the moral/religious dimension.

The ecology/growth dimension is measured by an index comprising three items that are asked in all surveys since 1981. One of these items is also asked in 1977, so it is possible to trace the development for that particular item back to 1977. The factor analyses clearly show that these items constitute a separate dimension.

There are few clear examples of libertarian/authoritarian items in the Norwegian surveys, but the factor analyses reveal a factor comprising several items tapping attitudes towards immigration and foreign aid. It is evident that this factor is a variant of the libertarian/authoritarian dimension. We have constructed two measurements of these orientations, one based on a single item which is available for the whole period 1969–97 about the level of foreign aid, and another which is an index based on two items about immigration policy. We refer to these measurements below as libertarian/authoritarian item and index, respectively.

The items in the Swedish data show a fairly stable factor solution. The economic left–right dimension is revealed as an important and dominant dimension and comprises several items in the data-set. We have constructed one index that is based on two questions that have been included in the Swedish election studies since 1964. We have also constructed a second economic left–right index, which builds on three items that have been included since 1982.

Christian values constitute a separate factor in factor analyses of the various Swedish election surveys. The Christian values index builds on three items. It has a time series that starts in 1982, is interrupted in 1985 and 1988, and then continues throughout the 1990s. Summing up responses to two stimuli, which

are available from 1982 and onwards, was used to create the growth/ecology
scale. Finally, we have constructed an index for libertarian/authoritarian values
based on two items.

6.4 VALUE ORIENTATIONS AND PARTY CHOICE: BIVARIATE CORRELATIONS

In this section we present the strength of the correlations between the various
measurements and party choice over time within each of the countries. We also
test hypotheses 3 and 4 since they involve the impact of the two old politics value
orientations separately.

The dependent variable is 'voting' in the last election. We treat the party choice
variable as a nominal variable, keeping all parties as separate categories. Parties
with only a small percentage of support (and a small N in the various election
surveys) are grouped together under 'other parties'. This category is included in
the calculation of coefficients, but otherwise not reported. The treatment of the
party choice variable is explained below for each country.

The strength of the relationship between party choice and the various value
orientations is measured by the η-coefficient from analysis of variance. This
measure is a standardized measure with values from 0.00 to 1.00. This coefficient
is obtained by reversing the causal order between the variables of party preference and independent value orientations, that is, party preference is treated as the
independent variable.[8]

Britain. In Fig. 6.1A we have shown the strength of the correlations between
two central economic left–right items (nationalization/privatization and redistribution) and one libertarian/authoritarian item (the death penalty for severe
crimes), and party choice[9] for the period 1964–2001. The nationalization item
was not available in 2001, at least not in the previous form, but another item
about privatization was asked in the period 1992–2001 and the correlations for
this item are also included in Fig. 6.1A.[10]

It is evident that the economic left–right issues are totally dominant until the
most recent elections. The correlation between party choice and the nationalization item is 0.48–0.52 for the period 1964–92, and then drops sharply to 0.36 in
1997. As to the redistribution item, the correlation is very strong, but it declines
somewhat in 1997, and then declines dramatically in 2001. The death penalty item
is much more weakly correlated with party choice (0.06–0.15), it increases in
strength from 1992 to 2001, and approaches the redistribution item in 2001.
Regarding the private enterprise item, the strength of the correlation with party
choice is the same as for the nationalization item in 1992, and these two items are
the ones that have the highest correlation with party choice. In 1997 when the
correlation declines significantly for the nationalization item, the decline for the
private enterprise item is considerably smaller, and this item is now the one that is

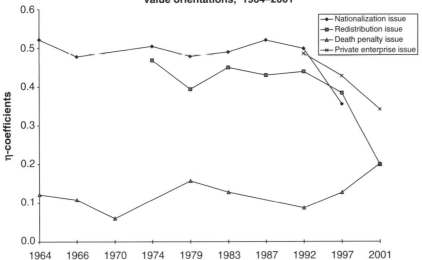

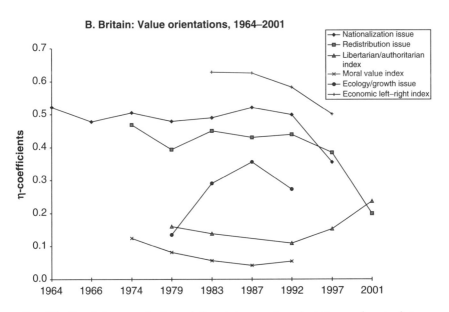

FIG. 6.1. *Trends in strength of correlations between value orientations and party choice*

(*Continued*)

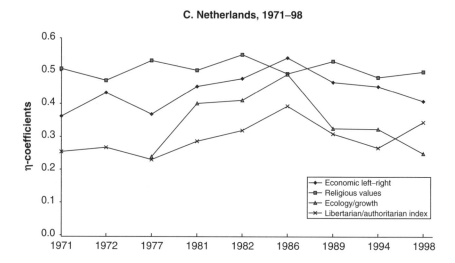

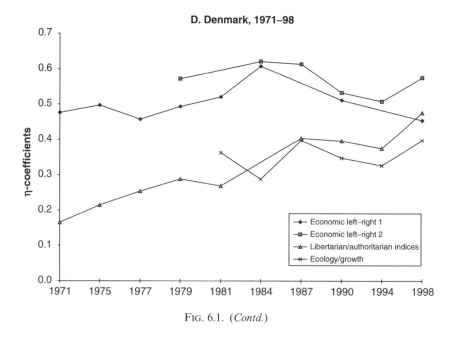

FIG. 6.1. (*Contd.*)

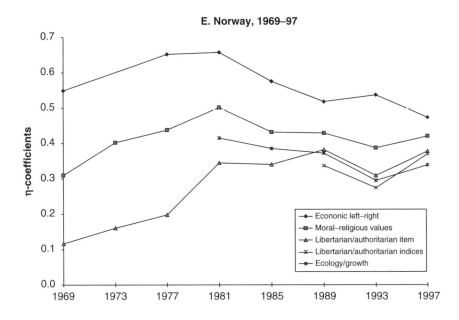

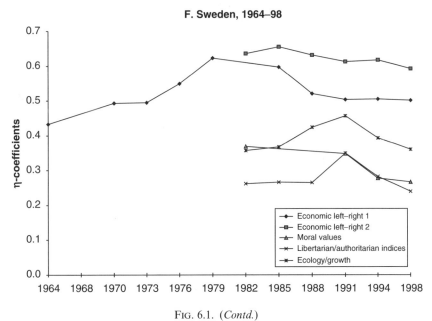

Fig. 6.1. (*Contd.*)

most strongly correlated with party choice of all the items in the survey. However, in 2001 the correlation declines significantly also for this item. This item is nevertheless *the item* that is most strongly correlated with party choice in 2001 compared to all other items examined.

Figure 6.1B shows the correlations between the indices and party choice. The economic left–right index is available for such a short time that we also include the correlations for the nationalization and redistribution item in this figure in order to compare them with the other indices for a longer period of time. The figure shows that the impact of the economic left–right values remains dominant for the period for which we have the possibility to construct the five-item index, but the correlation declines from a very high level (0.63) in the 1980s to 0.50 in 1997.

The impact of the libertarian/authoritarian orientations is fairly low until 1997 when it increases, and this increase continues until 2001. Ecology/growth orientations increase from 1979 to 1987, becoming the second largest after the economic left–right orientations, until they decline somewhat in 1992. The moral values remain weakly correlated with party choice for the period for which we have data.

In summary, the economic left–right orientations have been the dominant political value orientations explaining party choice in Britain. During the 1990s there is a large decline in the impact of these orientations, while the libertarian/authoritarian orientations increase somewhat in importance. The analysis of single items tapping the economic left–right orientations shows nevertheless that some aspects of the left–right views are still most important, while other aspects of the overall economic left–right orientations collapse.

The Netherlands. Figure 6.1C shows the strength of the correlations with party choice[11] for the four value orientations over time. The religious values are strongest correlated with party choice at a fairly high level (0.47–0.53) in all elections except in 1986. The impact of religious values is very stable over time and is not declining.

The impact of the economic left–right orientations is the second largest overall, and the largest in 1986. The correlations increase gradually until 1986 and then decline considerably to the same level as in the 1970s. The two new politics orientations show a lower correlation, but the impact of these orientations also increases until 1986 and then decreases somewhat. However, the correlation of the libertarian/authoritarian dimension increases in 1998 to become relatively more important than the indicator of the ecology/growth dimension.

In summary, the two old politics orientations are dominant in Dutch politics, and they are fairly stable over time, although there is a rise and fall of the economic left–right orientations. The new politics orientations are less important according to the available indicators, but nevertheless of considerable importance in absolute terms, having correlations with party choice of 0.25–0.50.

Denmark. Figure 6.1D shows that the two indices for economic left–right values are dominant in explaining party choice[12] during the 1970s and 1980s. The strength of the correlation increases significantly from the 1970s to the early 1980s, peaks in 1984 (and 1987 for the alternative index), and then declines considerably. The second alternative index is somewhat more strongly correlated with party choice in the surveys in which both sets of items are asked. However, the trends during the 1990s are different for the two indices.

There is a large increase in the impact of libertarian/authoritarian values. A considerable part of the increase takes place from 1981 to 1987, but there is also a considerable increase during the 1970s and in the second half of the 1990s. We note that the libertarian/authoritarian index approaches and even surpasses one of the economic left–right indices in 1998. Regarding the ecology/growth index, there does not appear to be any trend in the fluctuation, but there is a large increase from 1994 to 1998. Given that the measurement is based on only one indicator, the strength of the correlation is remarkably high.

In summary, economic left–right values are dominant in explaining party choice during the 1970s and 1980s in Denmark. The impact of these values declines after the early 1980s but the trend is not constant, given a considerable increase in the correlation for one of the indices from 1994 to 1998. New politics orientations and libertarian/authoritarian values in particular are increasing their impact on party choice remarkably, in particular in the late 1990s, and are approaching the level of impact of the economic left–right orientations.

Norway. It is evident that the economic left–right orientations are fairly dominant in Norway,[13] but that they are declining over time (see Fig. 6.1E). Their impact is largest in 1977 and 1981 (0.65–0.66), and then declines gradually to 0.47 in 1997. A closer examination of the correlation between the various items included in the index and party choice shows that all correlations decline, although the magnitude of the declines varies somewhat. The moral–religious orientations rank second in importance, and increase in importance to 1981 and then decline somewhat.

The correlations between the two new politics orientations and party choice are of fairly similar magnitude. These orientations have a weaker correlation with party choice than the moral dimension. The single indicator of the libertarian/authoritarian values increases gradually in importance until 1981 and then has a fairly stable impact on party choice, apart from 1993 when its impact declines somewhat. We find the same pattern of fairly similar magnitude for the alternative index based on attitudes towards immigrants and immigration policy. The ecology/growth orientations have a fairly large impact on party choice in 1981, but the impact declines gradually until 1993, and then increases somewhat.[14]

In summary, the old politics value orientations are most strongly correlated with party choice among the Norwegian electorate. The impact of economic left–right orientations declines considerably from the early 1980s to the late 1990s, but they remain the value orientations that are most strongly correlated with party choice. The two new politics orientations are also of significant importance, nearly of the same magnitude as the moral orientations. The effects of these orientations are not increasing in importance since the early 1980s in absolute terms, but relatively they have evidently become considerably more important because the impact of the old politics orientations has been declining in recent decades.

Sweden. Looking at the longest available time series, one notices that the impact of economic left–right orientations on party choice[15] rose considerably between 1964 and 1979 (see Fig. 6.1F). However, beginning with the 1982 election, it seems to have receded again: In the 1998 election the correlation between economic left–right and party choice declines to the level of 1970. This latter downward trend is also captured by the 1982–98 index of economic left–right.

In Sweden the index for Christian values consistently has a weaker correlation with party choice than do economic left–right orientations. The impact is fairly stable from the early 1980s to 1991 but declines somewhat thereafter. The impact of growth/ecology orientations also follows a curvilinear pattern over time. But it peaks somewhat later than that of economic left–right (in 1981). The same applies to the libertarian/authoritarian measurement.

The general conclusion is that economic left–right orientations are fairly dominant in explaining party choice in Sweden. The impact of ecology/growth values nearly equals the impact of the economic left–right orientations around 1990, but then declines relative to the economic left–right orientations. The impact of Christian values and of libertarian/authoritarian values also declines somewhat after the 1991 election.

Summarizing the findings for the five countries in our analysis, we find a curvilinear pattern for the economic left–right orientations: The correlations with party choice increase until the 1980s, and then decline during the late 1980s and 1990s. The test of the two competing hypotheses 3a and 4a is therefore somewhat inconclusive. If we compare the strength of the correlations in the 1970s with the late 1990s, the correlations are at the same level or even somewhat higher in the late 1990s in the Netherlands, Denmark, and Sweden, in accordance with hypothesis 3a. In Norway, the correlation in the late 1990s is lower than in the late 1960s and 1970s in accordance with hypothesis 4a. Only in Britain is there a clear long-time trend towards decline, which is found in the elections of 1997 and 2002, in accordance with hypothesis 4a.

It should be underscored that the declining impact of economic left–right orientations from the 1980s to the late 1990s and early 2000s is substantial in all countries. One way of interpreting this decline is to focus on the time lag between the decline of the social class cleavage and the decline of economic left–right orientations, which are associated with that cleavage. While the value conflict remained important and even increased during the 1970s and early 1980s, the class cleavage declined. From the mid-1980s until the 1990s, the economic left–right values tend to follow social class in becoming less important in explaining party choice.

As to the moral orientations there is no consistent trend. There is a decline in Britain and Sweden, a stable correlation with party choice in the Netherlands, and a curvilinear pattern with a peak in the early 1980s in Norway. The test of hypothesis 3b and 4b is therefore also somewhat inconclusive.

6.5 VALUE ORIENTATIONS AND PARTY CHOICE: MULTIVARIATE ANALYSES

In order to test the first two hypotheses, we have to rely on multivariate analyses. Party choice—the dependent variable—is a nominal variable, and therefore conventional multivariate analyses cannot be used. Multinominal logistic regression provides a statistical method for treating dependent nominal variables. This statistical method does not contain any standardized (or unstandardized) coefficients for examining the total impact of the independent variables, neither in the bivariate nor in the multivariate case. However, it contains several measurements aimed at being an equivalent to explained variance or R^2.[16] A frequently used measurement for the explanatory power in multinominal logistic regression is Nagelkerke's R^2 which is the measurement we have used.

6.5.1 *The Impact of Old and New Politics Orientations*

Hypotheses 1 and 2 concern the impact of the whole value model, and the absolute and relative impact of old and new politics orientations. In order to test the relative impact of the old and new politics orientations, we will report the impact of new politics orientations relative to the impact of old politics orientations (as ratios) in both ways that are indicated above:

1. The uncontrolled impact of the new politics orientations compared with the uncontrolled impact of old politics orientations.
2. The impact of new politics in addition to the explanatory power of the old politics orientations when the old politics orientations are entered first into the analysis.

The results are presented in Fig. 6.2.

Since the figure for Britain is somewhat different from those for the other countries, we comment on it after commenting on the figures for the other countries.

In the Dutch data, indicators for both old politics orientations were available for the whole period, and the same applies to some indicators for authoritarian/ libertarian values, while an ecology/growth indicator is available only since 1977. We therefore present the impact of only libertarian/authoritarian orientations

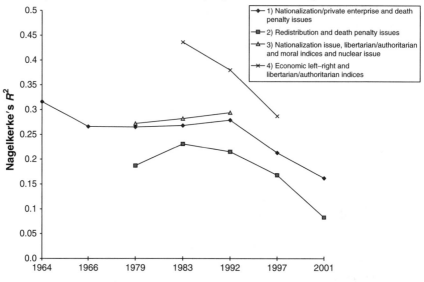

A. Britain:
The impact of the total value model on party choice according to different models

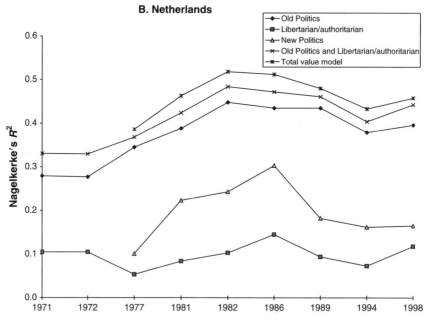

B. Netherlands

FIG. 6.2. *The impact of old politics and new politics value orientations on party choice.*
Results from multinominal logistic regressions

C. Denmark

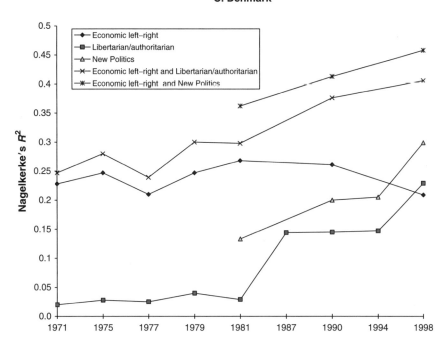

D. Norway

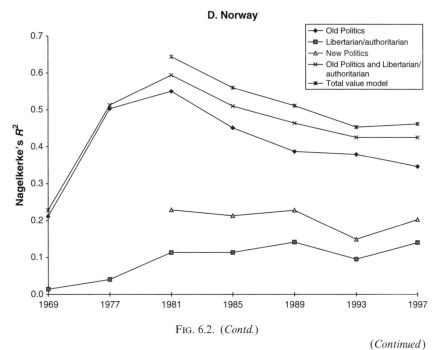

FIG. 6.2. (*Contd.*)

(*Continued*)

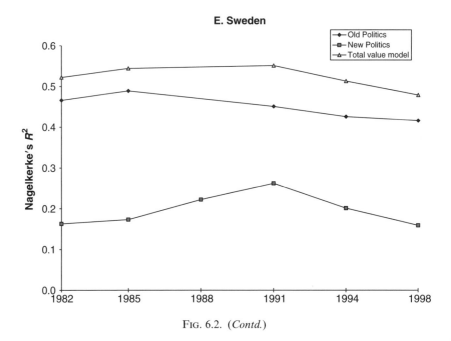

FIG. 6.2. (*Contd.*)

(for the whole period) in addition to the impact of both new politics orientations combined since 1977. As to the impact of the two old politics orientations (see Fig. 6.2B), there is a rapid increase until 1982, then stability until 1989, and then a small decline in the 1990s. The impact of libertarian/authoritarian values fluctuates somewhat, but there is no long-term change, while the total impact of new politics orientations increases substantially until 1986 and then declines considerably due to the decline of the impact of ecology/growth orientations.

The impact of the whole value model increases substantially until 1982, but decreases from 1989, although there is a small increase from 1994 to 1998. In a long-term perspective there is nevertheless a considerable increase. The old politics orientations are fairly dominant for the whole period, but the relative impact of new politics orientations increases greatly from 1977 to 1986, comprising 29 per cent of the impact of old politics orientations in 1977, and 70 per cent in 1986. There is then a decline to 42–43 per cent in 1989–98. The explanatory power of the new orientations in addition to the old is fairly stable: 12 per cent in 1977, 16–19 per cent in the 1980s except for 1989 (10 per cent), and then declining to 14–16 per cent in the 1990s.

In the Danish case, the available measurements of both old and new politics orientations complicate things somewhat. Figure 6.2C shows the impact of the main index for economic left–right orientations, the libertarian/authoritarian orientations, and both of the new politics orientations for the available surveys. Results based on the alternative economic left–right index will be mentioned in the text later.

The main pattern in the Danish case is that the old politics orientations are fairly stable, although peaking in the 1980s[17] and in 1990, and then declining somewhat. The impact of the new politics orientations greatly increases in particular from 1994 to 1998, and is larger than that of old politics orientations in the late 1990s. The dramatic change in the Danish case can be illustrated by comparing the impacts of old politics and libertarian/authoritarian orientations where we have data for a long time span. In 1971 the (uncontrolled) impact of the old libertarian/authoritarian orientations comprises only 9 per cent of the impact of the old politics orientation. In 1990 this has increased to 56 per cent, and in 1998 to 110 per cent. The impact of the two new politics orientations comprises 50 per cent of old politics in 1981, 77 per cent in 1990, and 143 per cent in 1998.

We also find a large increase when we examine how much explanatory power the new orientations contribute in addition to the old: Libertarian/authoritarian orientations add 8 per cent in 1971, 11 per cent in 1981, 44 per cent in 1990, and 94 per cent in 1998. Both new politics orientations add 35 per cent to the explanatory power of old politics in 1981, 58 per cent in 1990, and 119 per cent in 1998. In 1998, new politics orientations have a larger explanatory power than old politics orientations even when the old orientations are entered first into the analysis. This contributes to a pattern whereby the impact of the value model increases substantially over time, and there is no decline from the 1980s or early 1990s as in the other countries.[18]

In summary, the impact of the total value model is increasing over time in the Danish case due to the increasing impact of new politics orientations that approaches the impact of the old politics orientations. The case is partly one of supplementation whereby the new orientations are adding to the explanatory power of the old, and partly one of supplantation (in particular for the main index), whereby the new orientations are replacing the impact of the old. This is exactly what we should expect from Inglehart's theory of a cleavage transformation from old politics to new politics.

In the Norwegian case (Fig. 6.2D), we are able to analyse the impact of the old politics orientations and libertarian/authoritarian values for the whole period 1969–97, and in addition of ecology/growth values from 1981. We see that the impact of old politics orientations increases greatly from 1969 to 1981, and then declines considerably.

The total value model greatly increases its explanatory power from 1969 to 1981, but then its explanatory power declines considerably. When the ecology/growth orientations are included from 1981, they somewhat increase the explanatory power. Nevertheless the pattern is one of decline from 1981 to 1997 for the whole value model.

The impact of libertarian/authoritarian orientations increases over time, but during the period for which we have data for both orientations, the impact of new politics orientations does not increase. The impact of new politics orientations is fairly stable, with a tendency to decrease somewhat in the 1990s. The old politics orientations primarily shape the pattern for the whole value model, showing a sharp increase until 1981, and then a decline. Because of the strong decline of the impact of old politics, the relative impact of new politics increases in the Norwegian case: from 42 per cent in 1981, to 59 per cent in 1989 and 1997. In a longer perspective, we can compare the impact of libertarian/authoritarian values with that of old politics: In 1969, the impact of libertarian/authoritarian values amounts to only 7 per cent of the impact of old politics, increasing to 21 per cent in 1981, and 41 per cent in 1997. When the old politics orientations are entered first into the analyses, new politics orientations increase the explanatory power of the model, from 17 per cent in 1981 to 32 per cent in 1989, and 34 per cent in 1997.

In summary, the impact of the value model can be represented by an inverted 'U' in the Norwegian case, with a sharp increase until 1981, followed by a gradual decline. These changes are reflected in the impact of the whole value model. New politics orientations show a tendency to increase their impact on party choice in a long-term perspective, but they have a fairly stable impact since 1981. Compared to the old politics orientations, the new politics orientations clearly increase their impact relatively over time.

For Sweden we are able to examine the combined impact of the various value orientations for only a brief period because only economic left–right values were available before 1982. We therefore use the alternative (and more comprehensive) index for economic left–right values which does not show as pronounced a decline as the main index which was available for a longer period.[19]

Figure 6.2E shows that the impact of the old politics orientations declines somewhat in recent decades. It should be underscored that in Sweden this decline takes place after a considerable increase in the impact of the dominant old politics orientations, the economic left–right orientations. The new politics orientations increase their impact from 1982 to 1991, and then decline considerably. In 1998 their impact is at the same level as in 1982 and 1985, and at about 60 per cent of the 1991 level. The declines from about 1990 to 1998 are indeed larger for new politics than for old politics orientations, and comprise a significant component of the slight overall decline for the total value model.[20]

The explanatory power of the value model is large in the Swedish case. There is a small increase from 1982 to 1988, followed by a small decline to the late 1990s.[21] The ratio between the old and new politics orientations' explanatory power thus follows an inverted 'U' curve: It increases from 1982 to 1991, and then declines to about the same level as in 1982. The new politics orientations add 11–12 per cent to the explanatory power of the old orientations in 1982 and 1985, and then this increases to 20–22 per cent in 1991 and 1994, but then drops to 15 per cent in 1998.

In the British data it is very difficult to examine all orientations over a longer time period. In Fig. 6.2A we have shown some ways of examining the impact of all value orientations over time based on the same indicators and indices. These measurements are explained in Section 6.3 and are referred to as *models 1–4* in accordance with the numbering in Fig. 6.2A. The two longest time series are based on one economic left–right and one libertarian/authoritarian issue (the death penalty issue). Both models 1 and 2 show a clear decline of the value model. This is caused by the strong decline of the impact of the economic left–right issues as shown in Section 6.4. The third model, which includes indices and indicators for all four value orientations, shows a fairly stable pattern, but these measurements are only available for three elections before 1997. Finally, the fourth model, which includes the comprehensive index for economic left–right orientations and the index for authoritarian values, shows a clear decline. This model generally displays the largest explanatory power, even larger than the four-value orientations model.

The relative strength of old and new politics orientations for explaining party choice can be seen, in the bivariate case, from Fig. 6.1A based on the η-coefficients as to the two first models. For model 1 (regarding the private enterprise item in 1997 and 2001), economic left–right orientations remain dominant, although the death penalty issue approaches the impact of old politics in 2001. According to model 2, it is evident that old politics is dominant until 2001, when the two issues have about the same impact on party choice. According to models 3 and 4 which we are not able to trace after 1992 and 1997, respectively, the old politics orientations are dominant, although new politics orientations are increasing their relative impact. According to model 3, which has the most comprehensive measurement of both old and new politics orientations, the relative impact of new politics increases from 0.19 in 1979 to 0.43 in 1983, and then declines to 0.32 in 1992. According to model 4, the increase is from 0.22 in 1983, to 0.31 in 1997.

In summary, the evidence from the British data is difficult to examine because of the lack of consistent time series. Nevertheless, it indicates that value orientations explain less variance in party choice in the elections of 1997 and 2002. There is also evidence that new politics orientations increase their impact relative to old politics orientations.

6.5.2 The Impact of Value Orientations and Social Cleavages

In this section we will examine the impact of value orientations when traditional old politics social cleavages are controlled for. This analysis examines the causal impact of the value model on party choice because socio-structural variables are prior variables in a causal sense (see Fig. 1.1). The first hypothesis states that value orientations generally (the value model) should increase their causal impact and that the traditional structural cleavages should decline, at least relative to the value model. The second hypothesis implies that new politics orientations should increase their causal impact over time in an absolute sense, and that old politics orientations and the traditional structural variables should decline. We control for religious denomination and social class, and partly for church attendance. These variables are the central old politics structural variables derived from the Lipset–Rokkan model. It should be underscored however, that our conclusions about the relative impact of social structure and value orientations are based solely on these main traditional social cleavages, not on all structural variables.

Church attendance is problematic to use as a control variable because we can expect it to be highly correlated with our measurements of religious values. Research by Jagodzinski and Dobbelaere (1995: 87–96) has shown very strong correlations between church attendance and religiosity or religious/secular values. On the basis of European Values Surveys (I and II) they find that the correlations vary between 0.41 and 0.73 in different countries. Correlations of this magnitude are very rare in survey research. In addition to the strong correlations, there is strong evidence that pronounced changes in religious values are paralleled by similar changes in church attendance. Therefore, these authors assert that church attendance can be used as an indirect measurement of religiosity or religious/secular values. One of the present authors makes the same assertion in several works analysing surveys in which direct measurements of religiosity are not available (see Knutsen 1995a, 1995b, 1997). Due to the strong correlations between church attendance and religious values, one should be careful in controlling for church attendance when examining the impact of religious/secular values which are included in our value model.[22]

Since church attendance is often regarded as a structural variable, we have also done analyses in which it is included, and we report how its inclusion in the structural model influences our findings. However, the results we report in the figures are solely based on social class and religious denomination.

In the Scandinavian election studies, religious denomination is not included. Church attendance is only available in a few of the Danish and Swedish surveys. Therefore, our main social structure model contains social class in these countries.

The results from the main analyses are shown in Fig. 6.3. The lines show:

1. The impact of the structural variables (social class and religious denomination)
2. The controlled impact[23] of old politics values and the total value model[24]
3. The overall impact of both social structure and value orientations (referred to as the whole conflict model in the text)

For Britain we use the first value model (see Fig. 6.2A) in our main analysis since it has the longest time series as well as significant explanatory power. Social

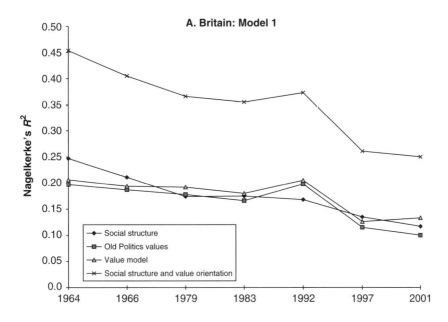

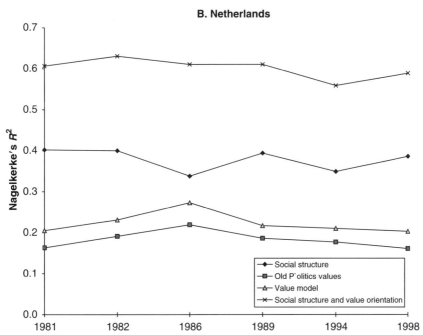

FIG. 6.3. *The impact of social structure and value orientations on party choice*

(*Continued*)

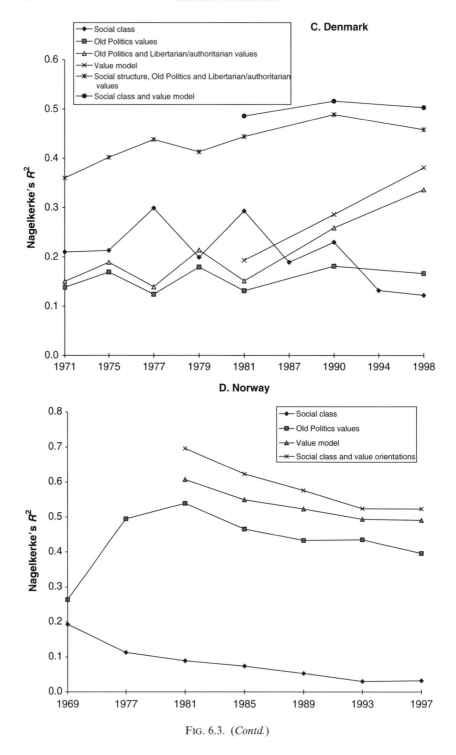

FIG. 6.3. (*Contd.*)

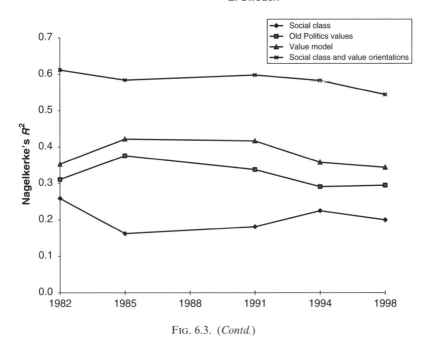

FIG. 6.3. (*Contd.*)

structure and value orientations have fairly equal impact on party choice according to Fig. 6.3A. Both social structure and value orientations have a declining impact over time, and the pattern is one of structural and value dealignment. We note that social structure has a somewhat greater impact than value orientations in the 1960s, and then value orientations have a somewhat greater impact until 1992. Then there is a pronounced decline in the impact of values, so that values and social structure have a fairly equal impact in 1997 and 2001. Social structure contributes to the reduced explanatory power of the whole model from the 1960s until the 1980s, but the large decline from 1992 is mainly explained by the reduced impact of value orientations.

Compared to the explanatory power of the value model when social structure is not controlled for, about 70 per cent remains on average when social structure is entered first into the analyses. This percentage increases gradually from about 65 per cent to 80 per cent.

Church attendance adds less than 0.013 to the explanatory power of the two structural variables in all surveys, and none of the conclusions above is altered in any way if it is included in the structural model.

The analyses of the other models show very similar results. However, for model 4 in which a comprehensive index for economic left–right orientations is used, value orientations have considerably stronger explanatory power than social structure in all three surveys (1983, 1992, and 1997).

In the Dutch data, social class is only available since the 1981 survey, while religious denomination and church attendance are available in all surveys. Figure 6.3B shows the results of the analyses based on religious denomination and social class since 1981, while we refer to the results based on only religious denomination from the 1970s in the text.

Contrary to the British case, social structure is more influential than value orientations for the whole period. The impact of value orientations is on average about 60 per cent of the impact of social structure, and this is fairly stable over time, except in 1986, when the impact of values reaches a peak of 80 per cent. Compared to the explanatory power of value orientations, less than half (44 per cent on average) is left when the structural variables are entered first into the analyses, and this is fairly stable over time, except for a peak in 1986 (53 per cent).

Religious denomination is the more influential of the two structural variables, and is much more influential than (old politics) values in the 1970s. It is in fact more influential than value orientations for the whole period except in 1986, at which time the value model has about the same explanatory power. However, the impact of religious denomination declines considerably during the 1970s, while the impact of value orientations increases. The explanatory power of old politics values increases from 29 per cent to 62 per cent of the impact of religious denomination from 1971 to 1977, and it is probably the case that the relative impact of value orientations would have increased considerably even if social class had been available in the 1970s.

In summary, social structure is considerably more important than value orientations in explaining party choice in the Netherlands. This is a fairly stable pattern over time. However, the analyses of religious denominations and value orientations in the 1970s indicate that there might have been a relative change during the 1970s.

Church attendance adds on average 0.07 to the explanatory power of social structure. The explanatory power of the structural model is even more dominant when church attendance is included, and the conclusions about changes over time would not be changed since the additional explanatory power is fairly constant.

In all the Scandinavian countries the structural model is represented by social class because religious denomination is not available.

The figure for Denmark includes more information than for other countries because we have also included analyses in which the old politics orientations and libertarian/authoritarian values are included, in addition to the three surveys in which the whole value model is available (see Fig. 6.3C). For comparison over a longer time period the analyses based on old politics orientations and libertarian/authoritarian values will be used to represent the whole value model.

The impact of social class fluctuates somewhat but declines after 1990. Value orientations have smaller explanatory power than social class until 1987, except in 1981 when the impact is similar. After 1987, values become more important than social class. Figure 6.3C shows clearly how influential the new politics orientations are in this respect. The large increase in the impact of the value model is exclusively caused by new politics orientations. These changes imply that the relative impact of social class and value orientations changes dramatically over time. In the period 1971–7, the impact of the value model is on average 0.75 of the impact of social class. This ratio increases to 1.13 in 1990, and 2.75 in 1998![25] Value orientations keep on average about 65 per cent of their original strength. This increases gradually from about 60 per cent in the early 1970s, to 80 per cent in 1998.

Church attendance is available in only three Danish surveys, 1971, 1979, and 1987. This variable indeed adds to the explanatory power of social class, in particular in the two surveys in the 1970s. However, the relative impact of value orientations compared to social class and church attendance increases considerably, and surpasses the impact of the former variables in 1987.[26] It is very unlikely that a control for this variable, had one been available, would have changed the dramatic increase in value orientations in the 1990s, and the same applies to the relative impact of social structure (including church attendance) and value orientations.

In Norway, we see from Fig. 6.3D that value orientations are totally dominant when compared to social class for explaining party choice, except in 1969. We note the strong decline of the impact of social class. The impact of old politics values is 1.4 times greater than the impact of social class in 1969. The ratio increases gradually to 14.5 in 1993, and then declines to 12.4 in 1997. The impact of the whole value model is even 15–16 times higher than the impact of social class in 1993 and 1997! Nearly all of the original impact of the value model remains when social class is controlled for, on average 98 per cent. We note, however, a clear tendency towards dealignment in the Norwegian case in the sense that the impact of the whole conflict model declines considerably after 1981, from about 0.70 to 0.52.

Church attendance is available for all surveys. When this variable is included along with social class in the model, it adds from 0.083 to 0.163 to the surveys' explanatory power. Church attendance and social class have an explanatory power of 0.263 in 1969, at which time they approach the explanatory power of value orientations. However, their explanatory power gradually declines to 0.098 in 1997, and the value model adds, gradually over time, 2.5 to 4.5 times as much explanatory power.

In summary, value orientations are very dominant compared to the structural variables included in our structural model in the Norwegian case. Although the impact of value orientations declines from 1981, their relative impact increases because the impact of the structural variables also declines considerably.

The Swedish case is similar to the Norwegian one in the sense that value orientations are dominant (see Fig. 6.3E). The impact of the various components is fairly stable over time, although all components tend to decline in strength. This is reflected in the explanatory power of the whole conflict model, which decreases from 1982 to 1998. Value orientations explain on average 1.9 times as much as social class. This ratio increases from 1.36 in 1982 to 2.30 in 1991, and then declines to 1.72 in 1998. About 70 per cent of the explanatory power of the value model is retained when social class is entered first into the analyses. This ratio is fairly stable over time.

Church attendance is available from 1985 in the Swedish surveys. When it is added to social class, the impact on party choice increases from 0.19 to 0.27, and approaches the impact of value orientations. However, value orientations still have 20 per cent greater explanatory power than social class and church attendance. The relative impact of values peaks in 1991 (40 per cent larger), but is fairly stable for the other surveys (about 20 per cent).

In summary, value orientations are considerably more important than the structural variable(s) in explaining party choice in Sweden, and most of the impact remains when social class (and church attendance) is controlled for.

6.5.3 *Hypotheses 1 and 2 Evaluated against the Findings*

The analyses of hypotheses 1 and 2 formulated in Section 6.2 have shown that value orientations have a large impact on party choice. Based on the averages from the surveys from the period 1980–2001, the Nagelkerke's R^2 are 0.52 in Norway and Sweden, 0.48 in the Netherlands, 0.41 in Denmark, and 0.25 in Britain. However, in Britain, the figure is considerably larger for the model with the largest explanatory power (model 4), 0.37.

In more direct support of hypothesis 1a, the overall impact of value orientations (the total value model) seems to have increased from the 1960s to the 1980s in most countries. Britain, however, appears to be a deviant case, as our analyses based on mostly old politics values have shown. Moreover, only in Denmark do we find a large increase in the overall impact of values. In the Netherlands, there is a small decrease after the peak in 1982, and in Sweden there is a decrease after 1991. The largest decreases are found in Norway (0.18) where there is a gradual decrease from the peak in 1981, and in the United Kingdom (0.12) where nearly all the decrease takes place from 1993 to 2001. This curvilinear pattern is in line with the hypothesis formulated in Chapter 1 that the independent impact of values will initially increase and then decrease.

The inclusion of the traditional socio-structural variables shows that value orientations have a large causal impact compared to the main social cleavages in the Lipset–Rokkan model. Only in the Netherlands does socio-structure have a larger causal impact on party choice than value orientations, while in Britain the impact of the two types of conflict variables are about the same. In both countries the relative impact is fairly stable over time. In the three Scandinavian countries, value orientations have a larger impact than social structure, and the ratio of the explanatory power of the two types of conflict variables increases significantly over time, indicating that value orientations become relatively more important. Hypothesis 1c is then confirmed on the basis of the findings from the Scandinavian countries, but not from Britain and the Netherlands.

Furthermore, most of the impact of value orientations remains, even after structural variables are controlled for. This indicates that most of the bivariate impact of values is not spurious. Only in the Netherlands is the impact of values reduced, on average, to less than half of the original explanatory power (44 per cent), while 60–70 per cent is retained in Britain, Denmark and Sweden, and even 90 per cent in Norway. The reduction caused by the control tends to be smaller over time in all countries except the Netherlands. This is probably associated with the smaller impact of social cleavages on party choice that we find in all countries since the early 1980s, except the Netherlands. All of this means that changes in the relative impact of social cleavages and value orientations are also in accordance with hypothesis 1b.

The combined impact of the old politics value orientations follows a curvilinear pattern in accordance with the pattern for each of the two orientations separately. This is most pronounced in the Netherlands and Norway, but it is also found in Denmark and Sweden. The strongest tendency for old politics orientations to decline from the 1990s is found in Britain, followed by Norway, but it is evident also in the other three countries. This is in accordance with the second hypothesis, which posits a decline in the impact of old politics values.

The new politics orientations have certainly increased their impact on party choice in the long term, in accordance with the second hypothesis. Our analysis shows that their impact has increased from the 1970s to the 1980s. We are not able to trace the development for both sets of new politics orientations from the 1970s for most of the countries, but the evidence we have been able to put forth clearly shows an increase. This applies to the Netherlands, Denmark and Norway, and also to Sweden, although we only have data showing an increased impact from 1982 to 1991 in Sweden. It also applies to the ecology/growth orientations in Britain. However, there is no universal linear trend demonstrating that these orientations increase their impact on party choice from the 1980s. In the Netherlands, the impact peaks in 1986, in Sweden in 1991, and in Norway the impact is largest in the 1980s, and declines in the 1990s. The combined impact of the two new politics orientations peaks in 1983 in Britain as shown in the separate analysis of the new politics orientations in model 3 of Fig. 6.2A, while the impact of libertarian/authoritarian values continues to increase in the 1990s. Only in Denmark is there a clear and almost linear increase of the new politics orientations. Hypothesis 2a is then supported by the data although there is no linear increase in the impact of new politics orientations. The old politics orientations are still more important, but new politics orientations tend to increase their impact relative to the old, as we have seen in the first part of Section 6.4. In a long-term perspective, we find a clear relative increase of the impact of new politics orientations, in accordance with hypothesis 2b, but there is again no linear increase. This is shown in Fig. 6.4, which depicts the ratio of the impact of new politics orientations (uncontrolled) to old politics orientations for the main models we have used in the analyses.

In the Netherlands, Norway, and Sweden, the new politics orientations some-times explain almost half as much as the old politics orientations, but there are again no linear increases. The relative impact of new politics orientations in-creases dramatically in Denmark as the figure shows, placing the relative impact of new politics orientations in Denmark at a much higher level than in the other countries. The relative impact of new politics orientations in Britain is compara-tively lowest, but it increases according to the main measurement.[27]

In order to test hypothesis 2c we have compared the impact of social structure and the impact of new politics orientations. The relative impact of new politics orientations are estimated both from Fig. 6.2 which show the total impact of these values without any controls, and from Fig. 6.4 where we have calculated the impact of new politics orientations as the difference between the impact of the whole value model and the impact of social structure and the old politics orien-tations.

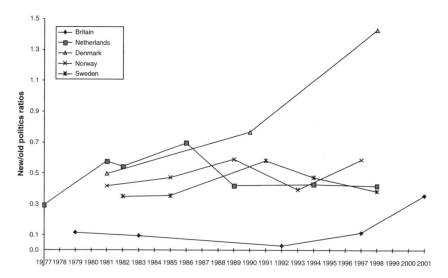

FIG. 6.4. *The ratio of the impact of new politics to old politics value orientations on party, based on the uncontrolled explanatory power*

The results from these calculations are not conclusive. The strongest support for hypothesis 2c is found in Denmark where the impact of new politics orientations increases strongly and that of social class decreases. The ratio increases from 0.21 in 1981 to 1.76 in 1998 even for the controlled model. A similar strong increase takes place in Norway, but in Norway this is first and foremost caused by the strong structural dealignment, and not by an absolute increase in the impact of new politics. In Britain, social structure is more important than new politics orientations even in 2001, but the impact of new politics orientations is increasing relatively to social structure. In the Netherlands and Sweden we do not find a clear increase as in the other three countries. In these countries the relative impact of new politics orientations peaks in 1986 and 1991, respectively, and then declines considerably. In the last elections for which we have data, the relative impact of new politics orientations to social structure is larger than in the first election in Sweden, but on the same level in the Netherlands. In sum, hypothesis 2c is clearly confirmed on the basis of data from three of the five countries.

6.6 POLITICAL VALUES AND POLITICAL CONTEXT

Thus far, we have tested linear developmental hypotheses. While the effects of virtually all value dimensions vary over time, linear predictions derived from variants of modernization theories concerned with topics such as secularization and cognitive mobilization receive modest support. Rather, it is evident that substantial peaks and dips are a common feature of the data. This is especially true for what is still the most important value dimension in West European politics—economic left–right values—in which we have found an inverted U-shaped development over time, with the strongest impact of values in the beginning of the 1980s. In this section we will attempt to account for such non-linear variation in the impact of values by considering a crucial feature of the political context: the extent to which parties manage to communicate large ideological differences to voters.

We expect that the intensity of elite conflict affects the extent to which values matter in political choices among mass publics. This expectation has both empirical and theoretical grounds. Empirically, the initial phases of the US 'belief system debate' (see Converse 1964) led scholars to conclude that US voters were 'innocent of ideology' (Kinder and Sears 1985: 664). That is, whereas US political elites evidently thought about political issues in terms of value-charged ideological labels such as 'conservative', 'liberal', 'left', and 'right', the ordinary American of the late 1950s did not seem to structure his or her political views in a parallel manner. Later studies, however, seemed to show that values and ideology came to play a more important role in the climate of greater disagreement and polarization between parties and candidates that marked the late 1960s and early 1970s (Nie et al. 1976). This period may be contrasted to the first two decades following the Second World War which was a period of relative political calm and economic prosperity. It was a period that lacked significant ideological disagreement between parties and candidates, and during which the US public was less prone to using overarching values as guides to political choices than was later the case.

In related research, comparative inquiries have documented that the European voter is less innocent of ideology than his counterpart across the Atlantic. For instance, based on data from the 1970s and early 1980s, Granberg and Holmberg (1988) reported that ideological constraint, stability, and voting were more widespread in Sweden than in the United States. This difference was attributed not to inherent cultural differences, but to the different nature of political conflict in the two countries. The prediction that emerges from these studies is that the impact of a value orientation on voting will be stronger the more polarized the party system is along that value dimension (for similar discussions, see Niemi and Westholm 1984; Van der Eijk et al. 1996: 357–8; Kumlin 2001; Van Wijnen 2001: ch. 9).

At least three mechanisms may be at play here. First, if party representatives use overarching ideological concepts in a consistent manner, more citizens may be stimulated to do likewise. Expressed differently, if parties present coherent issue packages that are explicitly tied together by labels such as 'left' and 'right', then more voters should learn to use such value-laden concepts themselves.

Second, polarized party conflict may also make it easier for citizens to choose on the basis of values. As Zaller (1992: 44–5) and others have noted, it is easier for people to make value-based political choices if they possess a rich supply of 'cueing information'. This is information about the relationship between their values and the incoming information. People simply cannot use basic values as a reliable guide to choices if they do not have reliable indications as to which party is 'left', 'pro-family', 'pro-market', and so on. On the other hand, when politicians persistently mix ideological cues into their statements, values can begin to function as a perceptual screen with which citizens orient themselves towards the political information flow. They can resist arguments and messages from parties that do not seem to stand for the values they prefer. Conversely, they can accept messages from parties that communicate cues signalling shared values. Another reason why polarized party conflict increases the impact of values is that such conflict generates better and more widely used cueing information.

A third mechanism has to do with affective responses to polarized party conflict. We argued above that if party representatives make frequent use of value-based rhetoric and ideological labels, more citizens will do so too. Moreover, we know that frequently used orientations tend to become more emotionally strong; people feel stronger about opinions and attitudes that they express and use often. In turn, we also know that emotionally strong orientations are typically more accessible in voters' minds, compared to less intense orientations (see Sears 1993: 139; Lavine 2002: 238). More clearly polarized ideological party conflict may thus increase the electoral impact of values by making values more emotionally charged and more accessible in citizens' minds.

Let us now test the hypothesis empirically. In order to measure the extent to which the political context is marked by ideological disagreement and choice, we make use of people's perceptions of party positions along the left–right continuum. That is, for each election we calculated the mean absolute perceived difference between the major left-wing party and the major right-wing party. This variable should be able to tap the extent to which the party system is perceived by voters to offer a wide range of value-related cues and choices, and should therefore have a potential impact on the importance of values in structuring party choice.[28]

Taking an election as the unit of analysis, we regress the explanatory power of the total value model for each election to the mean perceived difference between the major left-wing party and the major right-wing party. The explanatory power of the total value model is measured by the multinomial logistic Nagelkerke's R^2 reported in Fig. 6.2. Our reason for focusing on the total value model, rather than on any of its particular components, is that the left–right semantics have proven to function as encompassing spatial metaphors with a capacity to incorporate aspects of all the value dimensions investigated here (Inglehart and Klingemann 1976: 257–8; Fuchs and Klingemann 1990; Knutsen 1995c; Oscarsson 1998: ch. 8). In other words, previous findings suggest that if a party is perceived to be located to the left, it can mean that it is perceived to be opposed to Christian moral values, that it favours economically leftist policies, that it takes an anti-authoritarian stance, or that it takes some mix of all those positions. In short, a polarized left–right political context provides ideological cues that may make usage of *all* value dimensions easier for voters. Of course, it would have been useful to have access to perceived polarization measurements for all the separate dimensions involved here, but such information has simply not been consistently included in the election studies investigated here.

The results are presented in Fig. 6.5. Since there tend to be quite large differences in the impact of values, especially between Britain and other countries, we find it useful to display a separate regression line for Britain.

The data lend quite some support to the hypothesis. Specifically, the predicted pattern is reflected by both the upper regression line ($r = 0.68$; adjusted $R^2 = 0.43$), as well as by the lower regression line for Britain based on only four cases. In other words, perceived party polarization between major left-side and right-side parties can account for a significant amount of the domestic and transnational variation in the impact of values. For instance, according to the model, it is understandable that the total impact of values in Britain tends to be lower than in other countries, because the perceived ideological distance between major political parties has been smallest there in the elections for which we have valid measurements. Of course, the lower polarization cannot explain all of the difference. By the same token, it follows that the impact of the

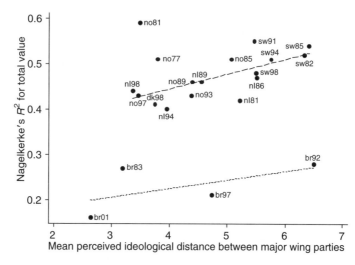

FIG. 6.5. *Party polarization and the impact of values*
Note: The dashed regression line is estimated among all elections except the four
British elections and the outlier Norway 1981 ($r = 0.68$; adjusted $R^2 = 0.43$). If
Norway 1981 is included, the correlation drops significantly ($r = 0.38$; adjusted
$R^2 = 0.09$). The dotted regression line concerns the four British elections.
Abbreviations: br = Britain; nl = The Netherlands; no = Norway;
dk = Denmark; sw = Sweden.

total value model is high in Swedish elections because Swedish voters recognize
larger differences between their two major parties. And it is equally understandable that the impact of values in Dutch and Norwegian elections usually lies
somewhere in the middle.

The models can also be used to understand changes within countries over time.
For example, they help in explaining why the already weak impact of values in
Britain has declined even further in the 1990s. They show us that perceived party
polarization has gradually declined to an all-time low in 2001. Similarly, they
offer an explanation as to why the impact of values in Sweden and the Netherlands has dropped in the 1990s compared to the early 1980s. Again the reason is
that the perceived distance between parties seems to have diminished. Moreover,
in Denmark there is only one election study (1998) for which we have both
perceived polarization data and estimates for the total value model. It is satisfying, however, that this election lies close to the regression line generated
by comparative data. Finally, the Norwegian pattern is the least clear-cut,
particularly the 1981 election, which is an anomaly that breaks the otherwise
relatively consistent pattern. Despite a mere average level of party polarization,
this election produced the strongest effects of value orientations on party choice
that we have been able to record. However, if we leave aside this anomaly (which we

have done in the estimation of the regression line), Norway conforms to the pattern recorded for the other countries in which greater perceived left–right polarization is associated with greater explanatory power of political value orientations.

Finally, it is worthwhile to consider the antecedents of perceived party polarization. If the latter shapes the impact of values, why do people come to form differing perceptions? One troubling possibility is that perceptions are just rationalizations of attitudes and behaviours (Granberg 1993: 70–5; Krosnick 2002: 117–19). More specifically, it is conceivable that voters report larger differences between parties precisely because they are already evaluating politics in terms of overarching value orientations. Of course, this would turn our causal assumption on its head as we have assumed that perceptual variation is at least partly related to differences in the external political–informational context. The contextual factors we have in mind include the messages and cues that parties send to voters through direct campaigning and election manifestos, or indirectly via mass media debates and interviews. In addition, it is likely that media coverage and interpretations offered by journalists have independent effects, in that the media to some extent can choose how to portray differences between parties.

It is in no way the purpose of this chapter to offer a complete test of the proposition that perceived polarization depends on such contextual variables. We have, however, considered empirically one of the potential factors: the extent to which the major parties display ideological differences in election manifestos as measured by data from the MRG. It transpires that there are indeed correlations between the actual party polarization indicated by manifestos and the extent to which voters perceive differences.[29] These observations fit well with those of Oscarsson's study (1998: ch. 9) of party perceptions in Sweden over the last 40 years, which indicated that changes over time in voter perceptions of ideological party positions correspond rather well with actual changes in party ideologies. Findings such as these make it less likely that perceptions are merely products of internal rationalization. Rather, they seem to be related to external contextual conditions that are controlled by parties, the media, and other elite actors. Of course, it is still notable that the correlation coefficients are quite weak, which suggests that election manifestos are but one of the contextual–informational factors at play here.

6.7 CONCLUSIONS

It must be underscored that the linear cognitive mobilization hypothesis (1), predicting a more or less consistent rise in the impact of values over time, only receives support in a long-term perspective. This leads us to an important conclusion: In order to reach a more complete understanding of the variation in value effects, one must also take into account the rather volatile and unpredictable political contexts in which modernization processes take place. In particular, one needs to consider the extent to which the major political actors manage to make voters notice internal ideological differences. This contextual factor appears to regulate the impact of values, whereby the causal mechanisms include the extent to which citizens learn to make use of ideological labels and concepts, the extent to which they receive ideological cues in order to choose on the basis of values, as well as the affective strength with which values are endorsed. In particular, based on our results, we would suggest that the apparent decrease in perceived party polarization in the 1990s has helped reduce the extent to which especially economic left–right values matter for party choice.

While the reasons for such contextual changes in recent years lie beyond the scope of this chapter, a couple of general points can be made. Most importantly, the fall of European communism and the Berlin Wall seem to have had a moderating effect on the leftist sides of West European party systems. Socialist solutions to political problems evidently came to be perceived as less viable throughout the decade. The slogans of 'New Labour', 'die neue Mitte', and the 'third way of Social Democracy' illustrate this trend.[30]

The notion of a deradicalization of the West European left in the last decade is further supported by the party polarization data. Examining ten-year averages for major wing parties, there are clear indications of a decrease in major wing party polarization in most countries examined here. What is more, in the Netherlands and Sweden it is indeed the major Social Democratic parties that have moved towards the centre, although major Conservative parties occasionally contribute to the depolarization of ideological conflict by moving towards the centre from their more radical neo-liberal programmes of the 1980s (particularly in Britain).

All this underscores the major point that the political context created by elite actors in the parties and the media seems to have large short-term and non-linear temporal influences on the salience of political values. Taking the economic left–right in the last decades as an example, it appears as if a long-term trend towards stronger value effects—arguably created by cognitive mobilization—has been strongly offset by recent changes in the electoral context. Of course, an implication here is that the impact of left–right values could very well increase again at short notice if political elites and the media act to widen the perceived ideological gaps between major political alternatives.

In the end, the extent to which political values structure political choices depends on more than linear societal modernization trends. The standpoints and actions of political parties are also influential in this respect.

Notes

1. These changes correspond to ecological and secular realignment, respectively, in the literature on models of electoral change according to the concepts alignment, and realignment (Dalton et al. 1984).

2. van Deth and Scarbrough (1995) use somewhat different arguments to explain why values can be tapped by attitude items. Values are dispositional concepts since they are not directly observable. They are constructs delineating some non-observable processes or phenomena. The concept of value orientations is then used as a heuristic device to facilitate the understanding of attitudes. Attitudes are more concrete beliefs related to a specific situation or object, while values transcend such objects and situations. Values influence attitudes, but the value concept can also be used heuristically, not empirically, in order to capture the value element in attitudes (van Deth and Scarbrough 1995: 38–9).

3. We use unweighted additive indices since we think it is important that the indicators are assigned the same weight in the measurements over time. Otherwise the results might be influenced by the fact that some items are weighted differently in different surveys. The construction of indices is done in the following way with regard to those who answer 'don't know' to a question: They are assigned a neutral middle score on Likert-like items with originally 3–5 categories. On items with more than 5 values, those who answer 'don't know' are assigned the mean score of the variable for the given year.

4. We had to omit Germany from this chapter because issues and value items indicating voters' positions were not available.

5. The detailed question wordings of the various items can be obtained from the authors.

6. Factor analyses comprising a large series of items also showed a separate social equality dimension comprising two items, social equality for women and blacks for the period 1979–97.

7. The index covering the period from 1971 to 1984, and then 1990 and 1998 is called the main or first index, while the other is called the alternative or second index for economic left–right orientations.

8. The η-coefficient between party preference and scales for the sets of value orientations is identical to the Pearson's *r*-coefficient when the different categories of the party preference variable are given their mean scores on these scales, and identical to the canonical correlation coefficient in discriminant analysis with only one discriminating variable (Klecka 1980: 36–7).

9. The party choice variable in the British election surveys comprises Conservative, Labour, and Liberal parties. The Liberal party category also includes the Social Democrats, the Alliance, and the Liberal Democrats.

10. The private enterprise item taps the same aspect of the economic left–right dimension as the nationalization item does, in a new time when privatization, not nationalization, is on the political agenda. It is also formulated more as a principle (political value).

11. The party choice variable comprises 6 categories and one additional category for 'other parties' in the Dutch case. Three of these are the Labour Party (PvdA), the People's Party for Freedom and Democracy (VVD) and D66. The other three categories are based on a collapsing of various parties: The Pacifist Socialist Party, Communist Party, and Radical Party that merged into the Green Left in 1989–90 have been considered as one category for the whole period.

    The predecessors of the Christian Democratic Appeal (CDA) have been collapsed into one category in 1971 and 1972. These parties are the Christian Historical Union

(CHU), the Anti-Revolutionary Party (ARP) and the Catholic People's Party (KVP). These parties merged into CDA in 1977.

Three small Calvinist religious parties have been collapsed into one category. These parties, which often are called Calvinist Fundamentalist parties, are the Reformed Political League (GPV), the Political-Reformed Party (SGP) and the Reformed Political Federation (RPF).

12. The large number of Danish parties has made some collapsing of parties necessary. The analyses are based on the following categories:

    1. Unity List (including its predecessors Left Socialists and Communist Party)
    2. Socialist People's Party
    3. Social Democrats
    4. Radical Liberals
    5. Central Democrats
    6. Christian People's Party
    7. Agrarian Liberals
    8. Conservative People's Party
    9. Progress Party and Danish People's Party (collapsed into one radical rightist category)
    10. Greens, Common Course, and Justice Party are grouped into the 'other party' category

13. The party choice variable comprises the following categories: (1) Communist Party/ Red Alliance, (2) Socialist Left Party and predecessors Socialist People's Party (in 1969) and Socialist Electoral Alliance (1973), (3) Labour Party, (4) Liberal Party, (5) Centre Party (agrarians), (6) Christian People's Party, (7) Conservative Party and (8) Progress Party. The tiny Liberal People's Party (1973–85) is grouped into the 'other party' category.

14. However, according to a single item (included in the index) that has been asked since 1977, the ecology/growth dimension increased considerably in importance from 1977 (0.20) to 1981 (0.30).

15. The party choice variable has the following categories in the Swedish data-set: (1) Left Party (named Left Party Communists 1967–90 and Swedish Communist Party before 1967), (2) Social Democrats, (3) Centre Party (agrarians), (4) People's Party, (5) Conservative Party, (6) Christian Democrats, (7) Green Party (since 1982) and (8) New Democracy (1991–94).

16. Since they do not refer to explained variance, but are only based on some of the same principles, they are called pseudo-R^2.

17. Indeed, we have seen from the bivariate analyses that there was a clear peak in 1984, but because the new politics orientations could not be measured in that survey, 1984 is dropped from the figure.

18. Based on the alternative index for economic left–right values (not shown), we do find the same pattern, i.e. that the impact of new politics orientations approaches the impact of old politics. However, the impact of new politics does not surpass the impact of old politics.

19. For moral values, we have used just one indicator (about Christian values in politics) in the index as our measurement in the multivariate analyses because this indicator was

available also in 1988, while the other two indicators used in the index were not available in either 1985 or in 1988. This indicator is correlated with party choice at about the same level as the index, and the correlation follows the same pattern over time as the index.

20. When we examine the impact of old politics orientations and how much additional variance new politics explains, the impact of old politics declines by 0.035, and new politics by 0.037.

21. The decline is larger when the main index for economic left–right values (index 1) is used, in accordance with the findings from the bivariate analyses (see endnote 17). Using this measurement of economic left–right values, the whole value model reaches 0.50 in 1982 and 1988, and then declines gradually to 0.42 in 1998.

22. We have examined the correlations between church attendance and religious/secular values in the four countries in which both measurements are available. The correlations vary considerably. In the Netherlands and Sweden the correlations are very high, on average 0.487 and 0.472, respectively. They are much lower in Britain and Norway, 0.236 and 0.250, respectively. The high correlations in the former countries make the problem highly relevant. It should be underscored that only when one analyses the impact of value orientations does this problem manifest itself, because the high correlation between church attendance and religious values make it difficult to separate the impact of each of the variables.

23. Except where noted, we refer to the controlled impact of the value orientations below. This also refers to the figures that show only the controlled impact of value orientations, not the uncontrolled impact.

24. This is measured by the change in Nagelkerke's R^2 starting from the analyses in which only social structure is included, and continuing in the analyses in which values are also included.

25. This long-term comparison is based on old politics and libertarian/authoritarian orientations. For the whole value model, the relative impact increases from 0.66 in 1981, to 1.24 in 1990, and 3.12 in 1998.

26. The analysis for 1987 is based on the alternative index for economic left–right values.

27. The more comprehensive model of new politics orientations (model 3) shows, however, a substantially higher ratio for new politics orientations, which is closer to those in the other countries.

28. Consistent with the procedure employed in Chapter 2, the following parties were used: Britain: Labour and the Conservatives; Norway: Labour Party and Conservative Party; The Netherlands: Labour Party (PvdA) and People's Party for Freedom and Democracy (VVD); Sweden: Social Democrats and Conservatives; Denmark: Social Democrats and Liberals (Venstre). The reason for concentrating on major parties is that they often present voters with images of the approximate ideological positions of the two main government alternatives. Moreover, the two major parties generate a large portion of the media coverage and campaign information that reach voters.

29. The correlation between the perceived distance between major parties and the distance between parties according to the manifestos is 0.31 (r); and the correlation between the perceived distance between major parties and the total manifesto ideological range is 0.64.

30. In addition to these short-term observations, scholars have also found theoretical reasons to believe that there has been a long-term decrease in left–right party polarization in Western Democracies. Moreover, utilizing the same comparative manifesto data as this book, Caul and Gray (2000: 211–15) find empirical evidence that this hypothesis stands up well in a comparison of the 1950s and the 1980s.

Left–Right Orientations and Party Choice

Cees van der Eijk, Hermann Schmitt, and Tanja Binder

7.1 INTRODUCTION

The left–right continuum has traditionally been looked upon in electoral research as one of the most important dimensions to describe voters' substantive political orientations. In combination with their perceptions of where the political parties are located on the same dimension, these orientations allow an instrumental mode of electoral choice, much along Downsean lines (Downs 1957). The theoretical status of the left–right concept in electoral studies is therefore inherently different from that of the notion of party identification. The vocabulary of left and right emphasizes, at least implicitly, cognitive-based instrumental modes of electoral behaviour, whereas party identification stresses affect with political parties rather than instrumentality.[1]

Left–right orientations of citizens are customarily found to be one of the most important factors that determine European voters' choices at the ballot box. Their importance for electoral politics and political behaviour is found not to be limited to a direct effect on choice behaviour. Left–right orientations also structure other political orientations with respect to political issues, government performance, and leadership, and they have, via these, also indirect effects on party choice. For this reason, left–right is often referred to as a 'super issue' (the term was probably coined by Inglehart 1984) that encapsulates, impacts upon, and constrains a host of more specific political preferences and orientations. Yet, there is no reason to expect left–right to be always, and everywhere, of equal importance for party choice. Traditionally, the association between left–right and party choice is weaker in some countries—such as Ireland—than in others—such as Denmark.[2] Moreover, there is no reason to expect the electoral importance of left and right to be uniform over time. In Chapter 1 it was suggested that the impact of left–right on electoral choice would initially become stronger in European countries after the 1960s (after controlling relevant other factors), and then decline again in the more recent period. This expectation was based on an analysis of long-term changes in economic, social, and political characteristics of western democracies, some of which were subsumed under the hypothesis of cognitive mobilization. This expectation is in line with the suggestion of political observers who suggested that the electoral importance of left and right declined after the fall of Communism.[3] In view of such previously documented or suggested variations, this book on comparative European voter studies is an excellent venue to investigate cross-national and cross-temporal differences in the importance of voters' left–right orientations for party choice.

When investigating electoral politics, the interpretation of the strength of the association between voters' left–right orientations and their party choice is inextricably linked to the question: What position do these political orientations occupy in a network of (hypothesized) causal relations? To the extent that the left–right position of voters can be regarded as the effect of other variables, its status in a causal network is one of an intervening variable. The most popular of such perspectives in the literature is to regard the left–right position of voters as an expression of their social location. In this reasoning, the social cleavages that contributed to the formation of European party systems still provide meaning to the terms 'left' and 'right' and to voters' individual position on the left–right continuum.[4] This perspective is not uncontested, however, and it is also argued that there is no necessary similarity between erstwhile and current meanings of the terms 'left' and 'right'.[5] In Chapter 1, for example, it was hypothesized that processes of modernization at the social and individual level will gradually reduce the importance of social structure for political orientations, preferences, and behaviour. This hypothesis leads to the expectation that over the course of time, the relation between citizens' left–right placement and their social background becomes increasingly weaker. For obvious reasons, such differences in expectations cannot be settled on the basis of first principles or theoretical arguments only. Which of the different expectations that can be found in the literature is most relevant in which context can only be determined by empirical research. Thus, the relationship between voters' left–right orientations and their place in the structure of society will be investigated in this chapter, in a comparison between countries as well as over time.

Finally, and as already discussed in Chapter 1, we have to take into account that cross-national and cross-temporal variations in the importance of social structure for left–right, and in the importance of left–right for the vote may not only reflect long-term trends and developments, but also differences in the political–institutional context within which voters and parties find themselves. Some conditions may just be more conducive than others for generating associations between left–right orientations and other variables (such as indicators of social location, or electoral behaviour of citizens). As we will see, inter-party relationships and the structure of party competition are particularly important in this respect.

7.2 DATA AND DESIGN OF THE ANALYSES

Our analysis is partially directed to the analysis of developments over time. To obtain a reliable perspective on such developments requires that more than just a few points in time can be compared. We chose to include only those countries in our analyses for which at least five national election studies are available that contain information on voters' left–right positions in addition to information about their party choice and their social structural characteristics. This left us only five countries: Germany, the Netherlands, Denmark, Norway, and Sweden. Even for these countries not all the election studies are useful, as some do not contain the entire information that is necessary for our analyses. Moreover, for some of our analyses there is not sufficient information available for Denmark, so that one section of this chapter is based on no more than four countries. This situation reflects, unfortunately, the often idiosyncratic basis of questionnaire construction, even within a single country over time. Table 7.1 lists for each of the five countries that appear in our analyses the years for which relevant information is available. Because not all of these studies contain the necessary information, some of our analyses will be based on a subset of these studies.

7.3 MEASURING ASSOCIATIONS

The analyses in this chapter focus on the evolution over time of the associations between social structure and left–right orientations of voters on the one hand, and between these left–right orientations and party choice on the other. These associations involve variables at different levels of measurement. Left–right is measured in all studies in a semi-interval manner by self-placement scales containing seven, ten, or eleven categories. Social structure involves a number of

TABLE 7.1. *Election studies included in the analyses of this chapter*

Denmark	Germany	Netherlands	Norway	Sweden
1979	1976	1977	1973	1968
1981	1983	1981	1977	1972
1984	1987	1982	1981	1975
1990	1990	1986	1985	1978
1994	1998	1989	1989	1982
1998		1994	1993	1985
		1998	1997	1987
				1991
				1994
				1998

variables some of which are dichotomous, some nominal, and some ordinal in character (see next section). Party choice is always a nominal level variable.[6] We chose to express the relationship between social structure and left–right in terms of the η^2, that is, in terms of the capacity of the set of variables measuring aspects of social structural background of voters to predict their left–right positions. η^2 can be interpreted as a measure of explained variance, and is identical to the ordinary R^2 one would obtain when the categories of the independent variables (i.e. social structure) are represented by separate dummies. A similar logic for the other association—the one between left–right and vote— would require a quite different method. The predictive power of left–right for party choice cannot be expressed as an η^2, owing to the fact that the dependent variable (party choice) is not measured at interval level but at nominal level. As an alternative one could use a pseudo-R^2 derived from a multinomial or conditional logit analysis, or a measure of predictive power derived from a discriminant analysis. The major drawback of such alternatives is that the two associations that we want to trace over time (and compare between systems) would be assessed in such different ways that they cannot be compared to one another while, as we will see in the next sections, such a comparison is in some instances quite useful.[7] Therefore, we chose to express this second association also in terms of η^2, with left–right as dependent and party choice as independent variable.[8]

7.4   IS OUR WINDOW OF OBSERVATIONS APPROPRIATE?

Some of the expectations about the evolution of the two associations that are at the core of our analyses are derived from a time perspective that is much wider than that covered by our observations. The expectations formulated in Chapter 1 are based on long-term changes in economic, social, and political characteristics of western democracies. It must be kept in mind, however, that the historical 'window' offered to us by our data, is considerably shorter than the duration of this postulated long-term process, and skewed towards the current situation. Even in the five countries that offer the longest period of overtime comparisons for the variables of interest to us, our first observations are for the mid-1970s, or even later, with the exception of Sweden where the first study we can use dates from 1968. The late 1960s and early 1970s are often regarded as a turning point of electoral politics in European countries. During earlier times, cleavage politics allegedly was dominant, while at later times the importance of cleavages for electoral behaviour has greatly diminished.[9] It is thus perfectly possible that the expectations developed in Chapter 1 are entirely correct for a time frame that is not adequately covered by our data. This makes our analyses only partially capable of substantiating, or conversely repudiating, these expectations. We can mitigate this problem, however, by assuming that the character of earlier periods 'lives on' to some extent in the orientations and behaviours of those who were psychologically and politically 'formed' in earlier periods. This reasoning leads us to distinguish in our data between cohorts: groups born and socialized in different historical periods.

Distinguishing between cohorts is also necessary on other grounds. When analysing changes over time, we must acknowledge that a country's population changes in terms of the individuals comprised in it. New voters enter the electorate, old ones die off. The effects of this 'demographic metabolism' are usually relatively limited for a single pair of consecutive elections, but they cumulate with the passage of time. When comparing an electorate in the mid-1970s with that at the end of the 1990s, we usually find that the surviving members of the former comprise no more than 50 per cent of the latter. To the extent that the voters who enter the electorate differ systematically from those who fall away, we obfuscate our view of developments by only analysing entire electorates. We 'control' the changes in the composition of the electorates by performing our analyses for separate cohorts. In the analyses in this chapter we limit ourselves to a fourfold cohort categorization in order to prevent too much clutter, and to avoid severe loss of statistical power owing to small group sizes. We distinguish the following cohorts: born in 1924 or earlier, born in the period 1925–44 (inclusive), born in the period 1945–60 (inclusive), and born in 1961 or later. It is obvious that control of this categorization cannot ensure total comparability between our samples. The continuous process of generational throughput causes the composition of these broad cohorts themselves also to change over the course of time. The post-1960 cohort changes every year by the continuous influx of voters coming of age, while the composition of particularly the pre-1925 cohort changes because of attrition, which will be higher in the older segments of this cohort than in the younger ones. Thus, our cohorts are over time not fully comparable qua composition. In spite of these problems, this differentiation according to cohorts ameliorates considerably the problem of incomparabilities that would exist otherwise.

7.5 SOCIAL STRUCTURE AND LEFT–RIGHT

When assessing changes in the relationship between voters' location in the social structure, and their left–right self-placement, our data pose considerable limitations.

First, our data do not allow us to measure social background in the same manner (let alone in the same detail) as is customary in many sociological theories of societal changes that are cast in terms of class, religion, occupation, region, language, and ethnicity. Therefore, we use background variables that can reasonably be regarded as proxies for the two most potent social cleavages discussed by these theories: class and religion. For this purpose we use as many as possible[10] of the following variables:[11]

- Income of household
- Socio-economic status (sometimes also referred to as subjective social class)
- Presence of one or more union members in the household
- Frequency of church attendance

A second problem we encounter is that the social structural characteristics that are available in our data have been measured differently between countries. This prevents us from pooling our data, and thus forces us to conduct our analyses for each of the countries separately. Even within a single country the set of social structural characteristics that have been measured, and the manner in which this is done is not identical over time, necessitating a kind of 'lowest common denominator' approach in which we focus on those characteristics that have been observed in more or less the same form over time.

As indicated earlier, we not only look at the relationship between social structural characteristics and left–right for the entire electorate at any given moment in time, but we distinguish between cohorts. This yields various statistics for each of the countries in our analyses (e.g. Table 7.2).

Table 7.2 shows (in its last column) that the association between social structure and left–right is at all times very weak. Clearly, there is some variation in the strength of this association, but the changes do not fit a monotonic pattern, as hypothesized by the modernization thesis advanced in Chapter 1.[12] As our series of German data starts only in 1976, it is entirely possible that this association was stronger at earlier times and that it has declined to the levels displayed here before our data started tracking it. But if that were the case, we would expect to find cohort differences, with older cohorts consistently displaying stronger associations between left–right and social structure than younger ones. A comparison of the cohort columns in Table 7.2 reveals the absence of any distinct cohort effects in Germany.[13] If anything, the differences in associations reported in Table 7.2 appear to be of a non-patterned kind, a kind of trendless fluctuation.[14]

Tables similar to Table 7.2 can also be made for the other countries that we analyse: Denmark, Norway, Sweden, and the Netherlands. We report them in an

TABLE 7.2. *Explained variation (η^2) in L/R self-placement with social structure (union membership and church attendance) by cohort—Germany*

Election study	Born before 1925	Born 1925–44	Born 1945–60	Born 1961 and later	Entire electorate
1976	0.10	0.12	0.10	—	0.09
1983	0.03	0.05	0.08	0.10	0.05
1987	0.02	0.07	0.05	0.03	0.05
1990	0.10	0.02	0.03	0.07	0.01
1994	0.13	0.06	0.03	0.04	0.06
1998	0.05	0.06	0.03	0.02	0.02

appendix with this chapter and confine ourselves here to summarizing the main findings:

- The overall level of association between social structure and left–right varies between countries, but to a considerable extent these differences seem to be related to differences in the amount of available indicators for social structural characteristics. Nowhere, however, is this association consistently high. All in all, we find that this association exceeds 0.2 in only 3 (scattered) cases out of a total of 30.
- Which of the social structural variables effectuates most of the overall association differs between countries. In the Netherlands church attendance is comparatively important, in the Scandinavian countries subjective class is of greater importance.
- Over time changes in the overall level of association between social structure and left–right hardly fit any pattern of more or less monotonic decline.[15]
- In none of the countries we find any convincing evidence of systematic cohort effects. The strength of the association we investigate varies between cohorts and years, sometimes even considerably. Yet nowhere do we find that a pattern of intercohort differences repeats itself in even half of the years under observation.
- In some of the countries we find non-negligible period effects: over time differences in the strength of the association between social structure and left–right that affect all cohorts at the same time in the same direction. Later in this chapter we will analyse these differences in more detail.
- In all countries the association between social structure and left–right not only varies in strength between cohorts (albeit in non-systematic ways), but also the character (or 'direction') of the relationship that underlies the η^2 statistic that we use. Indirect evidence hereof can be gained from the tables, when the association is stronger for each of the cohorts separately than for them pooled (i.e. the entire electorate).

Combining all the evidence presented in our tables (and including some additional analyses not reported here) we find in none of the five countries convincing evidence of the decline in the relationship between social structure and left–right that was hypothesized in Chapter 1 of this book. Obviously, the refutation of this hypothesis is not entirely definitive. Our window of observations is limited, and it is possible that the hypothesized change materialized itself before the first observations at our disposal. That would in all likelihood have left traces in the form of systematic cohort differences, of which we do not find clear evidence. Also, breaking down our samples by cohort diminishes the n's upon which our statistics are based. The consequence is an increase in sampling variance (or, stated differently, of the standard errors of the η^2), which may conceivably overwhelm a pattern of systematic decline in association, or a pattern of systematic cohort differences. But such an argument cannot really save the hypothesis, as it would imply that the hypothesized decline is too small to make much of a real world difference amidst other factors that effectuate change (such as period effects). For all practical purposes, then, we have refuted the hypothesis of a declining relationship between voters' social structural characteristics and their left–right orientations.

One interesting implication of our findings so far, which holds for all five countries analysed, is that voters' left–right orientations cannot sensibly be regarded as a reflection of their social position. Sociological reductionism does not help us in understanding where citizens locate themselves on a left–right dimension. The most obvious alternative interpretation of the meaning of people's left–right positions is an autonomous political one. The meaning of left and right is construed in the political domain, which is obviously quite independent from the social structural domain. To the extent that this is true, we would expect variations in the political context to be related to the way in which left–right orientations are associated with other characteristics, including those investigated above. We will present analyses along these lines later in this chapter. Before doing so, however, we turn to questions concerning the association between left–right and party choice.

7.6 LEFT–RIGHT AND PARTY CHOICE

As discussed earlier, the relationship between voters' left–right orientations and their party choice, and possible changes in this relationship, has been a topic of frequent speculation, political commentary, and occasionally of empirical investigation in European countries. We investigate this relation for Germany, the Netherlands, Denmark, Sweden, and Norway. As we did previously for the relation between social structure and left–right, we distinguish between cohorts, in order to trace effects of a past that is unobserved by the available survey information, but that is likely to have left its imprint in systematic differences between cohorts. As discussed earlier, here too we use as a measure of association η^2 (see also endnote 8). For each country our analysis yields a table such as the one for Germany (see Table 7.3). The comparable tables for the other four countries are presented in the appendix to this chapter.

Inspection of Table 7.3 reveals first of all that the association between left–right and party choice is considerably stronger than the one between left–right and social structure. For the entire electorate, this relationship seems to be weaker in the 1990s than in the 1970s and 1980s, but the decline is not monotonous at all. The irregularity of the ups and downs suggests the existence of period effects, but these are weak at best in view of the fact that the rank ordering of the coefficients in the column for the entire electorate is only weakly traceable in the columns for the separate cohorts. Systematic cohort effects are difficult to find, as the pattern

TABLE 7.3. *Explained variation (η^2) in L/R self-placement with party choice by cohort—Germany*

Election study	Born before 1925	Born 1925–44	Born 1945–60	Born 1961 and later	Entire electorate
1976	0.28	0.37	0.29	—	0.32
1983	0.28	0.26	0.37	0.23	0.30
1987	0.30	0.35	0.39	0.32	0.36
1990	0.21	0.28	0.24	0.22	0.23
1994	0.49	0.28	0.24	0.36	0.29
1998	0.29	0.25	0.22	0.25	0.24

of differences between the coefficients is different in each row. In short, we do observe differences, but most of the variation seems to be unpatterned. When inspecting these tables for all countries (compare Table 7.3 with the tables for the other countries in the appendix) we come to the following observations.

In all countries the association between left–right and party choice for the entire electorate is much stronger than the one between left–right and social structure. This association is weakest in Germany, and strongest in Denmark and Sweden.

In some countries, we find noteworthy over-time changes in this association for the entire electorate. In Norway the coefficients vary between a low of 0.31 and a high of 0.62, and in the Netherlands between 0.37 and 0.57. In the other countries the differences over time are more muted. Nowhere, however, do we see a monotonous increase or decline, but rather curvilinear changes, with the highest values in the 1980s. This is the kind of pattern predicted in Chapter 1. Such a pattern is most distinctively found in Norway and the Netherlands, it is more muted in Denmark and Sweden, whereas it is not clearly discernible in Germany. No strong and systematic cohort effects are found to exist. In Norway and Sweden the association is somewhat stronger for the two youngest cohorts compared to the other ones, but we find no such intercohort differences in Denmark, the Netherlands, or Germany.[16]

We find some indications of period effects. These are clearest in the Netherlands and Norway, weaker in Denmark and Sweden, and not clear at all in Germany.

In conclusion, then, one finding stands out across all countries and cohorts: We find no evidence for monotonic changes over time in the association between left–right and party choice. Much of the theorizing that would lead to the expectation of such monotonic changes is, evidently, mistaken empirically. As we remarked in the previous section of this chapter, such expectations are characteristic for some kind of reductionism, in which the political domain is seen as derivative of something else: social structure, modernization, or other factors. So far, we see no evidence of the veracity of such expectations. Therefore, changes over time in associations of left–right with other variables that we observed, have to be explained on a different basis, that also finds its locus in the political domain.

7.7 INTERMEZZO: WHAT WE HAVE LEARNED SO FAR, AND WHAT NOT YET

Our analyses so far focused on the relationship between left–right self-placements of citizens on the one hand and their location in the social structure (as an antecedent) and vote choice (as a consequence) on the other hand. By and large, the results from these analyses can be summarized and interpreted as follows.

The relationship between social background and left–right self-placements is weak, in some countries so weak that there is no room any more for the expectation to be born out that this relationship will weaken over time. In other countries, where the series starts out with a non-negligible relationship between background and self-placement, we indeed do find indications of such a decline. In view of the general weakness of this relationship it is not surprising to find small cohort differences at best. Substantively, these findings seem to imply that left–right identifications of citizens develop quite autonomously. For all kinds of reasons people may consider themselves as located on the left or on the right, and more or less outspokenly so. But they do not do so predominantly because they have a low income, or because they frequently go to church, or reasons like these. Political sociologists might be tempted to conclude from the absence of such social structural rooting that these self-placements are merely ephemeral and of no real political significance. But that would ignore their strong relation with party choice, or other political orientations in terms of issues and candidate evaluations (cf. Kroh 2003). At least we can conclude that those aspects of social structure that are related to the traditional cleavages do not exert much impact on where people locate themselves ideologically between left and right.[17] The political conflicts that gave rise to these cleavages have been 'solved' or at least accommodated long ago, thereby removing conflict as a reinforcing factor in the development of self-identifications. Under such 'pacified' circumstances, socialization by parents and other authorities cannot but imperfectly transmit identification with cleavage groups, an imperfection that is cumulative across successive generations and that results in these old cleavages virtually having lost their political 'steam' after some four generations,[18] that is, somewhere in the 1970s or 1980s. In some of our countries we can still observe the lingering shadows of these cleavages in the data of the oldest cohorts, in other countries we hardly see such a historical footprint. But where we observe that the importance of cleavage factors declines, we also observe for all cohorts that the strength of the association between left–right self-placement and social structural factors varies. It would thus be a mistake to assume that political factors are only responsible for self-placements of younger generations; they evidently impact those of older cohorts as well.[19]

Obviously, our analyses do not totally rule out that people's left–right positions are anchored in their location in the social structure. But then we should consider other aspects of the social structure than the cleavages that originated more than a century ago. Which aspects should these be is not quite clear. The literature in the field points to many social factors that are somewhat correlated with left–right positions, but none of them very strongly so, and none of them yet having been demonstrated to be of real relevance for either left–right positions or voting itself. Any claim for regarding social background as the origin of ideological self-placements thus either becomes quite tenuous, or it has to yield to the idea that the manner in which one's social position influences self-placement is particularistic in nature (cf. Tuckel and Tejera 1983), which actually is a different way to say that social position has lost its structuring power for political orientations and behaviour.

7.8 THE POLITICAL CONTEXT

One of our findings in the previous sections was quite unambiguous: left–right self-placements of voters are strongly related to the choices they make at elections. The strength of this relationship, however, varies considerably over time. This can be observed from the coefficients in the 'entire electorate' column in Table 7.3 and the comparable tables in the appendix. Figure 7.1 presents the changes in this association graphically for the five countries that we analyse.

Although the more or less curvilinear pattern of these associations is in line with the expectation formulated in Chapter 1, it is questionable whether the argument leading to this expectation is correct. The expectation of an initial increase of the *independent* impact of left–right orientations on party choice was based on the supposition that the relationship between social background and left–right orientations would gradually decline. However, since we found that even in the early years of our time series this relationship was already weak, and hardly declined afterwards, this explanation is not very convincing.

One potential alternative explanation of these variations has been ruled out in the previous section: changes in the generational composition of the electorate. Had the throughput of generations been the culprit, we should have observed clear cohort effects in Table 7.3 (and the comparable tables in the Appendix for the other countries), while in fact we did not.

If societal changes cannot explain the variations in Fig. 7.1, an obvious alternative interpretation can, in one form or another, be phrased as 'it's politics, stupid', as discussed in Chapter 1.

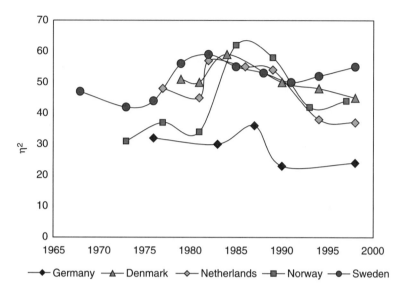

FIG. 7.1. *Association between voters' left–right position and their party choice*

When considering political interpretations, it is tempting to try and interpret the changes in Fig. 7.1 on the basis of whatever specific knowledge one may have about political events and circumstances in each of the countries. Undoubtedly we would then focus on all kinds of country-specific particulars such as changes in the composition of the governing coalition, changes in the 'tone' and content of the public debate on social and political affairs, changes in who contributes to that debate, changes in who occupies top positions in parties and influential interest and pressure groups, and so on. Useful as this may be, it is bound to end up in 'explanations' that are plausible, yet untestable because they are cast in terms of phenomena that are inextricably bound to the same times and places that generated them. Propositions that are testable require, at least in principle, that they be cast in terms that can be applied to characterize a wide variety of contexts. When confronted with variability in the strength of the association between left–right and party choice, we therefore stand to gain from looking at aspects of the political context that relate to left and right. When the terms left and right are powerful heuristics for voters to decide which party to vote for, then the association between their own positions on this continuum and their vote will, *ceteris paribus*, be strong. This will more often be the case when political conflicts are cast in left–right terms, and when the contesting parties in those conflicts are starkly differentiated. In short, we hypothesize that left–right *polarization* is the phenomenon to look at when trying to explain the over-time differences displayed in Fig. 7.1.[20]

Figure 7.2 displays the relationship between left–right polarization on the one hand, and the association between voters' left–right positions and their party choice on the other.[21]

Figure 7.2 supports our expectation to a reasonable extent: for each of the countries we see that the stronger the polarization between the parties in left–right terms, the stronger the effect of left–right voter positions on their choice. The relationships are not perfectly monotonous, but the occasional dips and bumps cannot hide the generally upward sloping character of the graphs.[22] The differences between the lines for the different countries are caused by factors that affect the overall magnitude of the association between voters' left–right positions and their choices, for example the number of parties, their sizes, internal homogeneity, and so on.

This finding nicely complements other findings in the literature. Heath et al. (1991: 220), for example, find that amongst the most important factors effectuating electoral change in Britain in the period 1964–87 are over time variations in perceived distances between parties and variations in ideological polarization. Oppenhuis (1995) and van der Eijk and Franklin (1996) found in a comparative analysis of voting in European countries that the impact of voters' left–right considerations on their vote is stronger when there is more agreement in the electorate as to where the parties are located between left and right.[23] Both

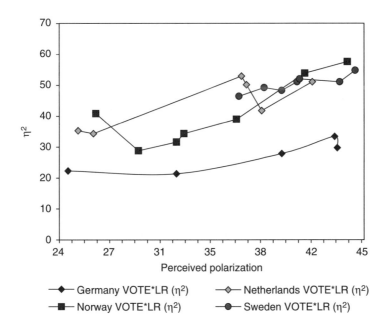

FIG. 7.2. *Left–right polarization and association between left–right voter positions and their party choice*

findings emphasize the instrumental character of party choice. The more parties differentiate themselves in terms of left and right, the more useful the left-right dimension is as a decision-making heuristic. And the more people agree on parties' positions on this dimension, the greater the likelihood that others will correctly interpret the ideological motivation of the vote.

However, ideological voting is not only instrumental. Left–right polarization indicates, over and above the mere ideological spread of electoral choice options, also the intensity of passions involved in party competition, and the heat of the election campaigns. This is why polarization also strengthens party identification (Schmitt and Holmberg 1995) and why it increases the impact of partisanship on the voting decision (Schmitt 2002; Kroh 2003). This is also born out by Chapter 6 on partisanship. Much along those lines, we can conceive polarization as a mechanism that strengthens left–right identifications[24] and thereby increases their impact on the voting decision.

7.9 CONCLUSIONS AND IMPLICATIONS

The main findings from our analyses can be easily summarized in a few points:

1. Voters' left–right position is weakly associated with their location in the social structure.

    (a) The strength of this association varies between countries; it is very weak in Germany, somewhat stronger in Sweden, and of intermediate strength in the Netherlands, Denmark, and Norway. Incomparabilities of available indicators of social structure between the countries undermine substantive interpretations of these inter-country differences.
    (b) The strength of this association varies between cohorts, but not in a systematic fashion that warrants them to be interpreted as 'generational' effects.
    (c) The strength of this association varies over time without a clear trend to be discerned in this variation.

2. Voters' left–right positions are strongly related to party choice.

    (a) The strength of this association varies between countries. Here, too, it is weakest in Germany, but considerably stronger in Sweden, the Netherlands, Denmark, and Norway. These differences reflect differences in party systems (number of parties, size of parties, etc.) which affect the possibilities for left–right orientations to express themselves in party choice.
    (b) The strength of this association varies between cohorts, but not in a systematic fashion that warrants them to be interpreted as 'generational' effects.

(c) The strength of this association varies over time, without any particular kind of trend to be clearly discernible.

(d) In all systems, the over time variation in this association is strongly correlated with the degree of party polarization on the left–right continuum.

The first set of findings, concerning the association between left–right and people's location in the social structure, clearly underline the relative autonomy of the political domain (and most particularly the electoral subdomain) from the social domain of human action and interaction. This means that little mileage can be expected from all kinds of efforts that regard the politics of voters, parties, and elections as reflecting social conditions, social conflicts, and social inequalities. The democratization and electoralization of the pursuit of political power, which is characteristic of western liberal democracies, should indeed imply that the political domain has become quite autonomous from other domains. This should particularly be the case for the processes of electoral politics that are studied in this book. So, whereas the empirical failure of sociological reductionism should not surprise us, the tenacity of the kind of theorizing that leads to it should.

The findings with respect to the association between left–right and party choice are clearly in line with an abundance of results in the literature about the behavioural relevance of these substantive political orientations. The failure of a simple kind of secular change in the strength of this association again points to the autonomous dynamics in the political–electoral domain. This interpretation is forcefully supported by the strong effect of party polarization on this association. Clearly, it is the political context that either promotes or dampens ideological reasoning and thereby affects the possibilities for left–right orientations to express themselves in choice. Some aspects of this context, explaining differences between countries are country-specific, and relate to the long-term traits of the party system and the institutions that define the rules of electoral contests. Over time, differences within countries are, as demonstrated, explicable from variations in the domestic political context.

The findings with respect to the absence of cohort effects are somewhat surprising in view of the fact that various aspects of electoral behaviour are ubiquitously found to be structured by cohort differences. Party choice and electoral participation are frequently found to be systematically different between cohorts (cf. for instance, Schmitt 1987 for the generational basis of electoral support for the Greens in Germany; Franklin 2004 for the generational structure in electoral participation). On the basis of such findings we decided to compare cohorts in the analyses for this chapter. That we did not find any cohort effects may be related to a number of factors. One of the most important is probably that the great majority of our observations are located in a period after the precipitous decline of cleavage politics that was documented for western democracies by Franklin (1992). This decline implied that more room became available for political circumstances to play a role in structuring electoral behaviour, and that the role of social structure declined. The fact that we did not observe much of the latter in our analyses is probably largely due to the differences between Franklin's and our databases. By restricting ourselves to national election studies, our data provide a smaller window of observation for tracing the changes that Franklin found.[25] But what our analyses also point out is that the mere fact that there is more room for political factors to play a role in electoral choice does not imply that this room will be invariably be used to its full extent. It is up to the political parties to make use of it, or not. The differences between parties in terms of ideological polarization are apparently of major importance in this respect. This conclusion leads to other questions: what are the factors that promote polarization or depolarization between parties? This chapter is obviously not the place to address these questions in greater detail.

In view of our emphasis on the relative autonomy of the political realm from other domains of human life it behoves us to dwell a bit upon how we see the nature of the left–right continuum itself. Often the terms left and right are regarded as inextricably linked with specific social and political conflicts (e.g. class conflict), or with specific modes of problem-solving (e.g. state intervention versus markets) or with particular moral values (equality versus freedom). Indeed, at various times and places the left–right dimension has been strongly linked to such conflicts, modes of operation, and values. Yet, there is nothing inextricable about this. Without specification of time and location, the terms left and right have little common meaning, if any at all. The meaning they acquire is the collective outcome of the ways in which numerous individuals interact politically. Most particularly, it is their verbal and symbolic interactions that matter in this context: the way in which people frame conflicts, the way in which they justify their own behaviour, and denounce that of others. Obviously, not everyone counts equally in this respect, as there is no such thing as a power-free dialogue at the level of a society. The collective result of all these framings and interpretations is a set of 'meanings' that is shared to a considerable extent amongst the members of a community, but that is also continuously redefined as a consequence of newly emerging problems, conflicts, and strategies of political actors. So, there is nothing inherently constant about the meaning of left and right.[26] On the short run, and in stable political contexts the question as to which points of view and which preferences go with being left or right seems obvious enough, but in a longer-time perspective these meanings evolve considerably.[27] In short, the 'meaning' of left and right is politically constructed, not by a single individual of group, but through the everyday processes of political cooperation and conflict. Over brief intervals of time, these meanings are usually quite stable, and function as constraints on political thinking and imagination. Yet, over longer periods of time, the ongoing processes of day-to-day politics and, occasionally, the creativity of individuals effectuate changes in these meanings. This process is one of the manifestations of the relative autonomy of the political realm that we emphasized earlier.

Notes

1. This is not to say that no affect is involved in left and right. Left–right self-placements of voters cannot be explicable other than themselves deriving from affect, be it that this does not involve parties but more abstract matters such as ideals, values, and visions of the good society. As a result, it is more than plausible that left–right perceptions are coloured by affect (cf. Inglehart and Klingemann 1976; Granberg and Holmberg 1988).

2. For a comparative analysis of party choice in European countries see van der Eijk and Franklin (1996: 332–65) and van der Eijk et al. (1999: 174–6). The analyses reported there demonstrate that the differences in raw association between left–right and party choice do not only reflect differences in causal effects, but also distributional differences in voters' and parties' positions on the left–right continuum.

3. This is particularly so in the new post-communist democracies (cf. among others Rose and Munro 2003; Tworzecki 2002).

4. Schmitt (1987) for example determines the left–right positioning of the traditional German parties on the basis of their location in the cleavage structure of the German party system.

5. cf. Silverman (1985), Fuchs and Klingemann (1990).

6. Obviously, the nature of our research question does not allow the transformation of party choice to an interval-level variable by extracting only the left–right position of the party voted for. Therefore, it cannot but be represented in our analyses as a nominal level variable. In principle, one can analyse choice by using electoral utilities (adequately measured) for each of the parties on offer as the phenomenon to be analysed (see van der Eijk and Franklin 1996; van der Eijk et al. forthcoming). Such an approach, however, would preclude any comparison across political systems, because such information has—as far as national election studies are concerned— only been collected in the Netherlands. To employ this approach in cross-national comparative analyses is only possible when using the data from the European Elections Studies (1989, 1994, 1999 and 2004). As these studies were conducted at the occasion of the elections to the European Parliament, they do not fit in the design of this volume that focuses on *national* election studies that were conducted at the occasion of elections for *national* parliaments.

7. Moreover, there are other drawbacks associated with those alternatives. Van der Eijk and Kroh (2002) demonstrated that multinomial and conditional logit analyses yield often biased results. The disadvantage of discriminant analysis is that measures of success (i.e. of predictive power) are heavily influenced by the distribution of the dependent variable, rendering their comparison over time problematic.

8. Most of our data derive from post-election surveys. In those instances, endogeneity concerns make it almost impossible to give an unequivocal answer to the question whether party choice or, alternatively, left–right orientation should be considered as the dependent variable (and the other as the independent). This may make our choice for η^2 as the measure of association less problematic than it otherwise would be.

Moreover, we assessed this association also in terms of both Nagelkerke's and Cox and Snell's pseudo-R^2 coefficients derived from a conditional logit analysis. Although the numerical values of these coefficients are obviously different from the η^2 reported in the main text, their patterns of overtime shifts for each of the countries are very similar to those presented in this chapter. Although each of these possibilities has its own drawbacks, they yield substantively similar results.

9. See Chapter 4. Also, cf. Dalton et al. (1984), Crewe and Denver (1985), Franklin et al. (1992).

10. Differences in the content of questionnaires (within countries over time, as well as between countries) necessitate adapting the specification of these analyses to the available data. Wherever possible, we attempted first to maximize comparability over time within each separate country. Where it was impossible to utilize a sufficiently encompassing set of over time comparable background variables within a single country, we ran as many overtime comparisons as possible and report the procedures used and the overall findings in the text.

11. Of these four variables, two derive from questions that were asked for the respondent individually (socio-economic status and church attendance), whereas the other two relate explicitly to the household to which the respondent belongs. The logic of the latter is that social background is believed to be a household characteristic. One could argue, of course, that this makes the strong and not self-evident assumption that households are homogeneous in these respects, and, moreover, that individuals' political orientations and behaviour are strongly determined by this micro-level context. As an alternative, we also investigated the relation between left–right self-placement and background when using for the latter only individual-level data (i.e. individual level income and individual union membership in addition to the two other items that were already individualized). Generally, both approaches yield the same pattern of differences between cohorts and periods. Only when these two approaches result in substantively different findings do we mention and discuss this in the text.

12. One could, of course, be tempted to see a general decline and consider the year 1994 as a single aberrant observation. We feel, however, that the number of time points is too small to warrant such an interpretation. If 1994 is to be considered as an aberrant case, why not consider 1976 so too? Particularly in the case of short time series, one must take care not to fall prey to the so-called 'end-point fallacy' that reifies the beginning and the end of a series of observations, while allowing disturbances from the thus established 'trend' to be explained away on ad hoc grounds.

13. Cohort differences would reveal themselves in a particular pattern of differences between the columns of this table, that is, a particular column (cohort) always exhibiting the strongest (or the weakest) association of all cohorts. Clearly, Table 7.2 does not contain such a pattern. It should be noted in Table 7.2 that the differences in the coefficients between cohorts reveal not only (non-systematic) variations in the strength of the association, but also in the kind ('direction') of relationship. This can be deduced from, for example, the 1990 row of Table 7.2. In this row, each cohort shows an association that is stronger than that for the entire electorate, a result that is caused by the 'direction' of the relationship to be different between the various cohorts, so that combining cohorts necessarily leads to a dampening of the relationship between background and left–right. Because of the weakness of all associations involved it makes no sense to elaborate this in more detail.

14. Obviously, distinguishing between cohorts leads to comparatively small ns upon which the associations in the various cells are based. This leads unavoidably to considerable sampling variation, which by itself would generate the pattern-less

differences between the various cohorts even if the population values of these associations were identical.

15. One might be most tempted to read such a pattern in the table of results for the Netherlands (see Appendix), but even then it hinges particularly on the comparison of the endpoints of our series of election studies. For the risks of such reliance on the end points, see note 12.

16. Again, we want to warn against overinterpretation of the differences between the strengths of these associations between cohorts and over time. Distinguishing between cohorts has its cost in terms of the *n*s, and consequently the standard errors of these coefficients are often non-negligible. Explicit testing for significance would reveal that many pairs of coefficients do not differ significantly. Such binary comparisons are little satisfactory, however, as cohort and period effects would manifest themselves in patterns of differences between columns or rows. Explicit testing for such patterns requires *portmanteau* tests, which are not well developed. We therefore rely in our presentation largely on an informal and *ad oculos* inspection of differences, while keeping in mind the *n*s of the groups involved.

17. One could object to this conclusion on the grounds of our rather 'meagre' possibilities to operationalize these traditional cleavages. These possibilities were indeed poor, as indicated above. But our findings are so strongly in line with those of many other analysts that we feel that our interpretative inference is justified nevertheless.

18. A more extensive argument along these lines can be found in van der Eijk et al. (1992).

19. Moreover, we must be weary of over-stylicization of the past. Certainly, all kinds of information lend plausibility to the notion that cleavages were more important in the past than in recent decades. Yet, historical research in each of these countries tells us also that these cleavages never came close to completely structuring electoral politics, let alone the wider political process.

20. Left–right polarization is a contextual variable that we construct in order to quantify the ideological distance of relevant parties from an ideological centre while taking into account their electoral weight. The measure of polarization that we use is different from the ones used in other chapters of this volume. Our measure is based on voters' perceptions of party locations on the left–right scale. When party positions are defined on the basis of their manifestos, we find no systematic relationship between polarization on the one hand and the association between left–right and the vote on the other hand. This discrepancy in results points to a less-than-perfect linkage between these two operationalizations of polarization. When investigating the association between voters' behaviour and ideological orientations, however, it seems plausible that polarization as perceived by voters is more consequential than polarization as derived from information that is not directly available to most voters.

The actual measure we use is defined by the following formula:

$$IP = \Sigma(|LRm - LRpx| * EPpx / LRm * 100$$

Where:

LRm = the numerical centre of left–right scale;

$LRpx$ = the position of party x on the left–right scale as perceived by the voters; and

$EPpx$ = the proportion of party x of the valid vote in the election under study.

The (spread of the) positions of the various parties on the left–right continuum and their respective sizes determine the value of the polarization coefficient. Parties' sizes are those that result from the election in question. One might object that these sizes are only known *after* the election; we feel that this is not very problematic in the period under observation, when widely available results from opinion polling provide reasonably accurate predictions of parties' performance in the upcoming elections. The positions of parties on the left–right scale that are used in the coefficient of polarization are based on voters' perceptions of where parties stand in this respect; the interpolated median of these perceptions is used here as the position of a party.

21. For the sake of brevity we do not report here the overtime development of our measure of polarization. It is graphically presented in Appendix 2 to this chapter. It is noteworthy that the evolution of this measure for the Netherlands resembles that of a different operationalization of the concept, as was used by Thomassen et al. (2000: 170).

22. These analyses can again only be of an *ad oculos* nature. Ideally, one would run a multivariate analysis with the η^2 as the dependent variable and as independents left–right polarization. In such an analysis each survey would constitute a data point. As the number of usable surveys ranges from five till nine per country, a multivariate analysis would become extremely tenuous. Pooling across countries is not an option as differences in party systems affect the overall magnitude of the η^2. A fixed effects multivariate model cannot solve this, as this would lose the advantage of pooling, namely alleviating low *df*.

    Deviations from a perfectly monotonous relationship are to be expected for a variety of reasons. First, sampling variation will have the effect of disturbing monotonicity; second, variations in the supply-side of electoral politics (which parties are on offer, and what are their characteristics?) will affect the relationship. Finally, other contextual factors may also influence the association between voters' left–right positions and their choice.

23. These findings developed in the context of studies about elections to the European Parliament, and are based on the data of the European Election Studies in 1989, 1994 and 1999, which were conducted in all member states of the EC/EU. See Oppenhuis (1995) and van der Eijk et al. (1996: 355–61) about these effects of perceptual agreement.

24. Knight (1985) discusses these same phenomena and finds it useful to distinguish between 'ideological sophistication' which lends itself to instrumental voting and 'ideological identification' which rather points to the expressive or affective nature of the voting decision. Our data do not enable us to distinguish between these two aspects of ideological voting.

25. Our analyses differ from those by Franklin (1992) not only in terms of which surveys were used, but also the handling of party choice. Franklin dichotomized party choice in left versus right choices. We used the full gamut of choice options in each of the countries, and used therefore also a different measure of association (η^2 versus R^2).

26. See also Silverman (1985).

27. cf. Van der Brug (1996, 1998).

APPENDIX 1

Tables Concerning the Relationship between Social Structure and Left–Right

TABLE 7.A.1.1. *Explained variation (η^2) in L/R self-placement with social structural characteristics (union membership, home ownership, and subjective social class) by cohort—Denmark*

Election study	Born before 1925	Born 1925–44	Born 1945–60	Born 1961 and later	Entire electorate
1979	0.17 [0.09]	0.16 [0.12]	0.16 [0.08]	*	0.13 [0.08]
1981					0.15 [0.08]
1984	0.20 [0.03]	0.13 [0.10]	0.16 [0.13]	0.06 [0.03]	0.13 [0.08]
1990					0.09 [0.07]
1998	*	— [0.04]	— [0.03]	— [0.00]	— [0.02]

*Less than 30 cases. Note that coefficients in parentheses are for the restricted set of predictors union membership and home ownership. For 1981 and 1990, the data file does not contain a suitable age variable to construct cohorts.

TABLE 7.A.1.2. *Explained variation (η^2) in L/R self-placement with social structural characteristics (union membership, church attendance, and subjective social class) by cohort—Netherlands*

Election study	Born before 1925	Born 1925–44	Born 1945–60	Born 1961 and later	Entire electorate
1977	0.25	0.28	0.08	*	0.20 [0.18]
1981	0.19	0.15	0.14	*	0.14 [0.13]
1982	0.22	0.18	0.08	0.13	0.14 [0.13]
1986	0.36	0.08	0.09	0.21	0.13 [0.11]
1989	0.21	0.20	0.13	0.24	0.17 [0.15]
1994	0.09	0.08	0.09	0.06	0.06 [0.05]
1998	0.33	0.10	0.06	0.06	0.07 [0.06]

*Less than 30 cases. Coefficients in parentheses are calculated for a restricted set of predictors including union membership only.

TABLE 7.A.1.3. *Explained variation (η^2) in L/R self-placement with social structural characteristics (union membership, church attendance, and subjective social class) by cohort—Norway*

Election study	Born before 1925	Born 1925–44	Born 1945–60	Born 1961 and later	Entire electorate
1973	0.19	0.20	0.09	0.17	0.16 [0.07]
1977	0.12	0.13	0.13	*	0.11 [0.02]
1981	0.19	0.10	0.14	0.15	0.14 [0.03]
1985	0.28	0.23	0.23	0.13	0.20 [0.03]
1989	0.25	0.17	0.14	0.08	0.14 [0.02]
1993	0.19	0.11	0.07	0.07	0.08 [0.02]
1997	—	—	—	—	— [0.02]

*Less than 30 cases. Coefficients in parentheses are calculated for a restricted set of predictors including union membership only. In 1997, subjective social class was not asked.

TABLE 7.A.1.4. *Explained variation (η^2) in L/R self-placement with social structural characteristics (union membership, church attendance, income, and subjective social class) by cohort—Sweden*

Election study	Born before 1925	Born 1925–44	Born 1945–60	Born 1961 and later	Entire electorate
1968	0.14	0.11	0.12	*	0.11 [0.23]
1988	0.10	0.10	0.15	0.16	0.08 [0.17]
1991	0.08	0.10	0.11	0.11	0.07 [—]
1994	0.23	0.11	0.13	0.06	0.09 [0.18]
1998	0.27	0.09	0.14	0.06	0.08 [—]

*Less than 30 cases. Coefficients in parentheses are calculated for the expanded set of predictors including also subjective social class.

Tables Concerning the Relationship between Left–Right and Party Choice

TABLE 7.A.1.5. *Explained variation (η^2) in L/R self-placement with vote choice by cohort—Denmark*

Election study	Born before 1925	Born 1925–44	Born 1945–60	Born 1961 and later	Entire electorate
1979	0.53	0.41	0.53	*	0.51
1981					0.50
1984	0.51	0.54	0.62	*	0.59
1990					0.55
1994	0.45	0.50	0.52	0.45	0.48
1998	0.47	0.47	0.50	0.39	0.45

*Less than 30 cases. For 1981 and 1990, the data file did not contain a suitable age variable to construct cohorts.

TABLE 7.A.1.6. *Explained variation (η^2) in L/R self-placement with vote choice by cohort—Netherlands*

Election study	Born before 1925	Born 1925–44	Born 1945–60	Born 1961 and later	Entire electorate
1977	0.59	0.46	0.42	*	0.48
1981	0.51	0.43	0.44	0.42	0.45
1982	0.58	0.57	0.56	0.61	0.57
1986	0.58	0.46	0.59	0.64	0.55
1989	0.61	0.55	0.54	0.52	0.54
1994	0.34	0.26	0.43	0.46	0.38
1998	0.36	0.36	0.37	0.38	0.37

*Less than 30 cases.

TABLE 7.A.1.7. *Explained variation (η^2) in L/R self-placement with vote choice by cohort—Norway*

Election study	Born before 1925	Born 1925–44	Born 1945–60	Born 1961 and later	Entire electorate
1973	0.27	0.41	0.44	*	0.31
1977	0.31	0.35	0.52	*	0.37
1981	0.27	0.31	0.46	0.58	0.34
1985	0.60	0.59	0.66	0.64	0.62
1989	0.57	0.52	0.62	0.59	0.58
1993	0.36	0.41	0.44	0.48	0.42
1997	0.36	0.43	0.46	0.48	0.44

*Less than 30 cases.

TABLE 7.A.1.8. *Explained variation (η^2) in L/R self-placement with vote choice by cohort—Sweden*

Election study	Born before 1925	Born 1925–44	Born 1945–60	Born 1961 and later	Entire electorate
1968	0.50	0.46	0.44	*	0.47
1973	0.44	0.40	0.40	*	0.42
1976	0.44	0.39	0.51	*	0.44
1979	0.55	0.54	0.63	*	0.56
1982	0.59	0.60	0.59	0.64	0.59
1985	0.61	0.55	0.54	0.56	0.55
1988	0.53	0.53	0.56	0.56	0.53
1991	0.48	0.48	0.54	0.51	0.50
1994	0.60	0.48	0.54	0.53	0.52
1998	0.52	0.53	0.57	0.57	0.55

*Less than 30 cases.

van der Eijk et al.

APPENDIX 2

The development of Left–Right polarization as perceived by the voters

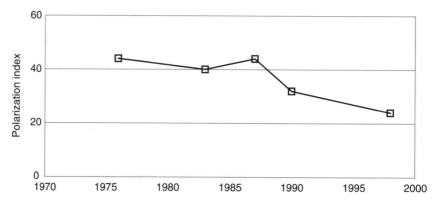

FIG. 7.A.2.1. *Left–right polarization in Germany: 1976–98*

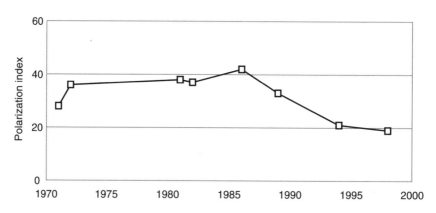

FIG. 7.A.2.2. *Left–right polarization in the Netherlands: 1971–98*

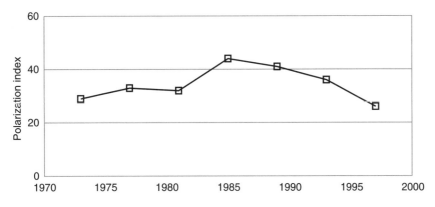

FIG. 7.A.2.3. *Left–right polarization in Norway: 1973–97*

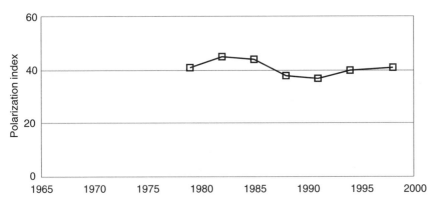

FIG. 7.A.2.4. *Left–right polarization in Sweden: 1968–98*

8

Issue Voting

Bernt Aardal and Pieter van Wijnen

8.1 INTRODUCTION

As noted in Chapter 1, electoral research has been criticized for not taking the political context properly into account when explaining voting behaviour. This critique may be directed towards both the social–psychological approach focusing on long-term party identification (the so-called Michigan school), and the sociological approach focusing on the individual's life-long attachment to particular social groups (the Columbia school). Actually, this critique may also be directed towards theories that focus on the impact of general (end) values or ideological orientations on voting behaviour, without taking notice of the role of specific issues and candidates in the elections.

Although one may argue that the non-contextual criticism does not do justice to all scholars and approaches, it nevertheless illuminates an important challenge for contemporary electoral research. After all, elections are fought over policies and issues that voters, parties, and leaders consider to be important and relevant at the time of the election. If we relegate electoral behaviour to the realm of impersonal social structure and general human values we may indeed risk taking 'politics out of elections.' The aim of this chapter is to address the question: To what extent, and how does 'issue voting' play a role in European electoral behaviour? Is issue voting an important part of individual decision-making in an election campaign? Has issue voting increased over time, and has it now replaced social background as an explanatory variable? In answering these questions, we will focus on the impact of issue priorities on the election outcome.

Before we try to answer the research questions, it may be useful to take a look back at the 'traditional' explanations of vote choice. Are they really devoid of political context? Listhaug (1989) makes a distinction between three different approaches that may serve as a point of departure for this discussion. He distinguishes between: (1) The social–psychological model, (2) The economic (rational) model, and (3) The structural cleavage model. The social–psychological model—with its emphasis on long-term identification with parties—may appear vulnerable vis-à-vis the critique of not being sensitive to the political context of a particular election. However, the model is based upon a causal chain—the so-called funnel of causality—that includes previous political dispositions such as ideology, group adherence, historical experience, and local variations. Thus the original model specification is more dynamic than a rigorous application of 'party identification' alone may suggest (Berglund 2003*b*). Moreover, the model allows temporary deviation from the party line if short-term factors like popular candidates or issues are more important for the voters. Nonetheless, political issues were not a prominent part of US electoral research until the 1970s. In the 1972 presidential election, however, scholars argued that individual attitudes towards the political issues of the day played an important role for the election outcome (Miller et al. 1976; Nie et al. 1976). Since then, research on the importance of issue voting has become standard practise, not only in US election studies (Miller and Shanks 1996), but also in European studies (Borg and Sänkiaho 1995; Borre 2001; Borre and Andersen 1997; Franklin 1985; Heath et al. 2001; Holmberg 2000; Van Wijnen 2001; Aardal et al. 1999).

The second approach, the economic–rational model, is to a large extent directly linked to the political context of an election inasmuch as it presupposes that voters are measuring past performance and future prospects against their self-interests (Downs 1957). A key question in this line of research is: To what extent voters base their vote choice on their personal economic situation (egocentric voting) or on the performance of the national economy (sociotropic voting)? (Kinder and Kiewit 1979, 1981). Although self-interest is not exclusively defined as economic utility, the model tends to pay less attention to non-economic than to economic issues. This is particularly the case for Downs' own contributions. However, scholars who have extended the spatial theories have to a large extent included non-economic issues in their models. This applies both to proximity models (Davis et al. 1970) and directional models (Rabinowitz and Macdonald 1989).

The third approach, the sociological or structural model, appears to be an obvious target for the critique of not being attentive to the political content of elections inasmuch as the social location of voters does not necessarily change much from one election to the other. However, this critique may be more relevant for the Berelson et al.'s approach (1954) than for the Lipset-Rokkan (1967) cleavage model. Sartori (1997) calls the Berelson approach 'sociology of politics' (politics as reflections of social structure), while he labels the Lipset–Rokkan approach 'political sociology' (emphasizing the political *translations* of social structure). One advantage of the Lipset and Rokkan model over the former is that it gives equal attention to any kind of conflict or cleavage: 'Conflicts are not only economic and related to the class structure, but also regional, ethnic, linguistic, religious, and ideological' (Sartori 1997: 173). This means that a variety of political issues may be linked to underlying cleavages. Moreover, the Lipset–Rokkan model focuses on the vital question of how conflicts have been translated or transformed into the political system over time. An important part of the transformation process was the politicization of issues and the creation of collective identities among groups of voters. Contrary to what some scholars seem to believe (e.g. Dalton and Wattenberg 1993: 196–7) the Lipset–Rokkan cleavage model is not deterministic in the sense that political preferences and behaviour can be derived directly from the individual's or the group's location in the social structure of a given society. Moreover, shared political beliefs and values are vital elements both with respect to the emergence and persistence of political cleavages (Bartolini and Mair 1990; Aardal 1994; Knutsen and Scarbrough 1995; Aardal and Waldahl 2004).[1] However, this does not invalidate the argument that values and issues may be more important now than before, relatively speaking. Also, a process of cognitive mobilization has taken place in advanced industrial democracies (Dalton 1984; Dalton and Wattenberg 2000). In these countries, a rise in educational level and in the supply of political information has increased the number of citizens willing, and able, to develop policy preferences. Accordingly, Dalton expects that an increasing number of citizens will vote for parties on the basis of their own policy preferences. As noted in previous chapters, policy preferences increasingly will be less moulded by the citizens' social background—due to individualization and modernization processes. Thus, we can expect that policy preferences in due time will replace social background characteristics as the prime determinants of voting behaviour.

8.2   WHAT IS ISSUE VOTING?

Despite the fact that 'issue voting' has become part of the vernacular of today's electoral researchers, there is a shortage of clear definitions of the concept. In the *International Encyclopedia of Elections*, Dalton (2000*b*: 337) presents 'contemporary electoral choice' in this way:

Today, however, fewer voters approach the election with such sociological or psychological predispositions. Many individuals base their decisions on the issues and candidates of the campaign and the influence of friends, colleagues, and other political cue-givers, which produces an individualization of the voting choice.

He further argues that 'the decline in social group-based voting over time has been matched by an equivalent rise of issue voting' (Dalton 2000*b*: 337). On the surface issue voting seems to be simple and clear-cut; voters are basing their choice on particular issues that are salient at the election in question. But issue voting may mean different things to different scholars. Electoral researchers have used the term issue voting for referring to the electoral impact of either values (ideological orientations), issue positions, issue priorities or performance of political parties (leaders) on issues. As Borre (2001) points out:

Empirical studies of single elections nearly always include one or several chapters on the relationship of issues to party preference. But they go about it in ways that often fit an ad hoc model to the concrete election and which cannot be compared with other survey studies.... It is clear that the assessment of issue voting varies according to the method used.

Borre himself (2001: 13) defines issue voting as comprising the following three elements: (1) Issues about the goals of politics ('values'), (2) Issues as discussions about what should be on top of the agenda (issue salience), and (3) Issue performance in terms of the voters' perceptions of competence and credibility among parties and candidates.

According to Downs (1957) citizens use ideological orientations as yardsticks for developing attitudes on specific issues. The idea that values and ideological orientations are causally preceding attitudes towards issues and issue priorities is widely acknowledged and constitutes the analytical framework of this book (see Fig. 1.1). However, election specific issues may also have an impact in the other direction—by activating latent values or ideological orientations. The latter argument is emphasized by Miller and Shanks (1996; see also Aardal et al. 1999). In the moulding of electoral preferences, there is an interaction effect between ideologies and issues. Whether there is an effect of value orientations on voting behaviour or not, may to a large extent be dependent on election specific issues. The abortion issue may, for example, activate citizens' latent positions on the moral–religious dimension. Without salient issues in elections, there might not be any effect of value orientations on the vote at all.

In theory there is a clear difference between *issues* and *values*. Whereas political values may be defined as 'prescriptive beliefs about which goals (one) would like to see implemented in the political system and about the desired participatory forms to influence politics' (see Chapter 6), political issues are often more narrowly defined—capturing particular policy proposals or political circumstances. In practice, however, it may be difficult to separate sharply between issues and values. In particular, this is the case for structural *position* issues (Lane and Ersson 1987).[2] First, political values may be closely linked to the underlying cleavage structure of a given polity. As argued earlier, this is very much the case for the Lipset–Rokkan cleavage model. Hence, a particular issue may reflect the same latent cleavage as a political value, thus representing deeply embedded predispositions far beyond idiosyncratic, singular phenomena. If this is the case, we would expect to find far more internal consistency among political issues than for instance Converse (1964) did in his classic study. Longitudinal data from Norway, covering the time span between 1977 and 2001, suggests that the internal consistency between attitudes towards political issues actually can be quite high, constituting *issue dimensions* that are stable over time (Aardal 2003). Thus, it may be difficult to separate issues from values. Second, the empirical operationalization of an issue and a value may be so close that it is impossible to maintain the idea of a clear-cut division between 'short-term' and 'long-term' forces. Neither values nor issues can be observed directly, and attitudes towards issues and value orientations are often derived from the same survey questions.

What are the practical implications of this discussion for the present analysis? First of all, part of what may be defined as 'issue voting' has already been taken up in Chapter 6 by Knutsen and Kumlin who analysed the impact of value orientations on the vote. Second, the focus of the present chapter is specifically on issues that were salient at particular elections. Third, the analytical model presented in Chapter 1 (see Fig. 1.1) implicates that we need to control for values and ideological orientations when we analyse the relationship between issues and the vote. But we also have to account for the possibility that the effect of values and ideologies is dependent on salient issues. This implies that alternative analyses have to be conducted, in which the relationship between issues and the vote is not controlled for values and ideologies. Both types of analyses can indicate a range of how important issues are for voting behaviour and the election outcome.

8.3 POSITION AND VALENCE ISSUES

However, all issues are not of the same kind. Stokes (1963) made an important distinction between issues that divide the public into proponents and opponents (position issues), and issues where the public tends to agree on the ends, but not on the means necessary to reach that end (Dalton 2000*b*). Stokes and Dilulio (1993) argue that valence issues systematically have been underestimated as political issues, and that the lack of clear alternatives and issue positions increasingly characterizes modern election campaigns. As a consequence, the salience of a particular issue to some extent has become more important than the issue position of the parties and candidates.[3] The effect of position issues is addressed in proximity theories (Davis et al. 1970; Downs 1957) and in directional theories (Rabinowitz and Macdonald 1989). Valence issues on the other hand are conflicts concerning issue priorities and the competence of political parties and leaders. The effect of valence issues is addressed in theories of retrospective voting (Fiorina 1981; Kinder and Kiewit 1979, 1981) and issue ownership in Section 8.4.

8.4 ISSUE OWNERSHIP

Lately, scholars have been focusing on the fact that political parties tend to acquire a form of 'ownership' of particular issues over time (Ansolabehere and Iyengar 1994; Budge and Farlie 1983; Petrocik 1996). Historically, socialist parties tend to 'own' unemployment in the sense that voters think they are better able to handle this problem than other parties. Conservative parties, on the other hand, tend to 'own' inflation in the sense that voters believe in their ability to do something about it. Issue ownership means that even voters who do not regularly vote for a particular party have a positive evaluation of the party's policy in a particular area. These 'goodwill' measures are usually linked to the party's position in the country's conflict structure (i.e. positions on ideological and value dimensions) or the party's past performance in handling a particular problem while in power. Issue ownership adds a directional element to issue voting inasmuch as it provides a clue with respect to which party will gain or lose voters—given that a particular issue dominates the media agenda. According to the theory of issue ownership, vote preferences are determined by issue priorities and issue competence. Citizens tend to vote for parties that are perceived as competent in the handling of salient issues. Thus, when a particular issue is on top of the agenda in an election campaign, it is not accidental which party benefits most from the issue at the polls.

8.5 EXPECTATIONS

Chapter 6 investigated changes in the electoral impact of value orientations. As mentioned value orientations may be seen as policy preferences that are closely related to position issues. Contrary to Dalton's expectations of an increasing impact of values, however, empirical findings in Chapter 6 indicate that value orientations have not become more important for voting behaviour in West European countries. In this chapter we will investigate to what extent *issue priorities* have become more important for the vote.[4]

The expectation of an increased electoral importance of valence issues can be based on two hypotheses (see Chapter 1). These hypotheses can be regarded as complementary (instead of rival). The first is Dalton's hypothesis that due to cognitive mobilization, citizens are increasingly able to perceive societal problems and to make judgements on the competence of parties in solving these problems.

According to the second hypothesis, there is a negative relationship between party polarization on position issues and the electoral importance of valence issues. When parties take a more polarized stance on position issues, citizens are provided a stronger cue to vote on the basis of these issues instead of valence issues. Based on party manifesto data, Chapter 2 showed that in the last decades, polarization of parties on the left–right dimension has not changed in a uniform and systematic fashion. Using survey data and expert judgements, Knutsen (1999a) documents more uniform trends *within* countries, although the pattern varies *between* countries. In the Netherlands, for example, the decline in left–right polarization is unambiguous, while the polarization has increased in Denmark. Despite the fact that we do not see a unequivocal decline in party polarization in all West European countries, we see downward trends at least in some periods (see also Appendix 2 to Chapter 6).

In sum, we may assume that the degree of polarization in a given polity affects the political 'opportunity structure' and thus the potential for issue voting. In case of a depolarizing party system, one may expect that citizens will resort to other criteria in deciding which party to vote for. One such criterion could be the perceived competence of parties in the handling of valence issues. When voters perceive less substantial differences between party positions on the socio-economic or libertarian–authoritarian value dimension, they might be more tempted to vote on the basis of how competent parties are in, for example, reducing inflation, increasing employment, and reducing environmental pollution.

8.6 ISSUE EFFECTS ON VOTING BEHAVIOUR

The increased focus on issue voting in recent decades must be linked to three important changes in modern societies. First, the weakening bond between social background and party preference. Second, a process of cognitive mobilization in advanced industrial societies. Due to a rise in educational level and political interest, and change in occupation, we can expect that citizens have become more capable to engage in issue voting. Third, the increasing impact of the mass media, and in particular the media's influence on the political agenda during election campaigns. The role of the media is vital in this respect. No matter which definition of 'issue voting' one prefers, an analysis of issue voting must take into account the agenda effect from the mass media. Although one may ask voters about their personal issue preference and correlate that with their vote, 'true' issue voting must be directly linked to the specific issues that dominate the election campaign. More specifically, issue voting to a large extent can be seen as an agenda effect, in particular with regard to the voters' perceptions of which issues are the most salient. Usually the issues that permeate an electoral campaign will also be perceived as important by the voters. However, this is not necessarily so. But, in this chapter we will only look at issues that were perceived as important by the voters themselves.

The research question can be stated as follows: To what extent and how does the voters' perception of important issues during the election campaign affect the voting decision? As mentioned earlier, the idea that issues are important for the voting decision may or may not be related to preconceived notions of issue ownership. If issue ownership is not a part of the equation, one may expect almost random effects of issue salience with respect to which party will stand to gain. However, if issue ownership *does* enter the equation, the expectation will be that the party that owns an issue on top of the agenda will increase its support in the election.

Let us try a simple analysis before we enter the more complex and advanced statistical models. First, we need to identify the most important issues in each election. We restrict ourselves to the most frequently mentioned issues. Although many more issues were mentioned by the voters, we focus on the three issues on top of the voters' own agenda. However, there are some differences in the phrasing of the questions in the original surveys. In four countries (Norway, Sweden, Denmark, and the Netherlands) the question asked was completely open, and the answers were coded by the principal investigators.[5] In two countries (Germany and Britain) the question was closed, presenting pre-selected issues to the voters. Although the question format differs somewhat between the six countries, we believe that these questions at least give an indication of the individual priorities of the voters in each election. The next challenge is to identify the 'issue owner' of each issue—in each election. Ideally we would have preferred to have data based on the voters' own perception of which party they believed had the best policy or policy performance on the specific issues. However, we do not have access to this information for all the countries involved. Because of this lacuna, we have pursued a different strategy. To identify the owners of the various issues, we have relied on judgements by country experts who are all experienced election researchers (see Tables 8.A.1–6 for details).[6]

The first step is to identify the most important issue and the associated issue-owning party (or parties). The most important question, however, is to what extent ownership of one of the top three issues gives the party a boost in the election. Table 8.1 shows the level of support for the issue-owning party among voters who report that the specific issue was important for their vote. Because the parties are very different in size, we present the ratio between support among those who say the issue is important and the overall support of the party at the same election. For party A, this ratio is defined as:

(percentage of voters who think issue X is important, voting for party A) / (percentage of all voters, voting for party A).

This ratio gives an intuitive measure of the extent of 'issue voting'. The following tables will present the results of this initial analysis.

Table 8.1 shows that the issue-owning party (or parties) in average received between 22 and 57 per cent more votes among voters who said that the issue was important, than among voters in general. The average gain across the three most important issues for the issue-owning parties was 26 per cent in the 1970s, 44 per cent in the 1980s, and 31 per cent in the 1990s. According to these measures the issue agenda definitely has an impact on the vote. We do not, however, see a uniform increase in issue voting over time.

If we break down the results by country, we find some interesting differences. Table 8.2 shows the relative strength of the issue-owning party among voters who

TABLE 8.1. *Relative strength of issue-owning party among voters who say that the issue is important*

	1970–9	1980–9	1990+
Issue 1	1.22	1.41	1.23
Issue 2	1.23	1.57	1.29
Issue 3	1.32	1.33	1.40
Average	1.26	1.44	1.31

TABLE 8.2. *Relative strength of issue-owning party among voters who say that the issue is important*

Country	Average
Norway	1.78
Sweden	1.59
Denmark	1.34
Netherlands	1.19
Britain	1.17
Germany	1.07

say that the issue is important in each of the six countries. The three Scandinavian countries—Norway, Sweden, and Denmark are on top of the list, with the Netherlands and Britain in a middle position, and Germany at the bottom.

If we look at the individual elections in each country, we find that Norway is the only country where the issue-owning party has ever received more than twice the percentage of votes among those who say the issue is important than among those who do not say it is important (see Tables 8.A.7–12 for details). However, even in the countries where the 'issue effect' overall is relatively low, we find examples where the issue-owning party has received considerably more votes among the particular issue public. This applies, for example, to the 1977 election in the Netherlands and the 1987 elections in Germany and Britain. Thus, the general conclusion is clear: parties receive considerably more votes among voters who think that the party's own issue is important, than among other voters.

8.7 FROM BIVARIATE TO MULTIVARIATE ANALYSES

In Section 8.6, the bivariate relationship between issues and party choice has been assessed. For a more complete picture of the importance of issues for voting behaviour, it is necessary to control for other variables as well. According to the model presented in Chapter 1, issue opinions and party choice can be influenced both by social background variables and ideological (value) orientations. Thus, the correlation between issue opinions and party choice may be spurious or indirect. In order to assess the 'real' effects of issue opinions on the vote, one has to control for preceding variables in the model.

Multivariate analyses will be performed for measuring the effect of the three most important issues on the vote in elections in the 1970s, 1980s, and 1990s (as described in Tables 8.A.1–6). This effect will be assessed with multinomial logistic regression. The dependent variable is the party voted for.[7] Independent variables are the importance of three issues as perceived by the voters, value orientations, and social background variables. The issue variables are scored 1 if the respondent perceives a certain issue as one of the most important problems of the country (in an open-ended question). Issue variables are scored zero if this is not the case. As mentioned before, issue variables for Britain and Germany are based on closed questions, where respondents can give a rating, indicating the perceived importance of a set of issues. Variables that measure value orientations are the same as used in Chapter 6 on values (socio-economic, libertarian–authoritarian, and ecology–growth values). Social background variables are age, sex, region, church membership, church attendance, social class, working in the private/public sector, level of urbanization, marital status, and union membership.[8]

8.7.1 *The Importance of Issues for the Vote*

In preceding sections the difficulty of measuring the electoral importance of both issues and value orientations has been addressed. One problem concerns the fact that the same survey questions may be used to measure an issue opinion as well as a value orientation. In addition, there is a complex causal relationship between issues and value orientations. Salient issues may activate latent value orientations, which in turn will influence choice of party. And voters may use value orientations as yardsticks to decide which issues are important. In order to establish the explanatory power of issues, the control for preceding variables is vital. If we do control for preceding variables, this may lead to an underestimation of the importance of issue voting. Credit will be given to value orientations which have been activated by salient issues. If we do not control for preceding variables, however, we may overestimate the importance of issue voting. Perceived issue importance may partly be explained by value orientations. In order to account for both mechanisms, we will perform two separate analyses—one controlling for preceding variables and one where we do not control for these variables. Both types of analysis will give an indication of the range of the electoral importance of issues. Explained variance will be measured by McFadden's adjusted ρ^2.

Table 8.3 gives an indication of the explanatory power of the three most important issues in the 1970s, 1980s, and 1990s. For each decade, explained variance is averaged across elections and countries. The table clearly shows that once the vote has been accounted for by social background and value

TABLE 8.3. *Variance explained by issues, across time*

	1970s	1980s	1990s
Controlled for values and social background	0.01	0.02	0.02
Not controlled for values and social background	0.04	0.04	0.03

orientations, the contribution of salient issues to the explained variance is almost negligible. In the 1970s, the three most important issues on average explained 1 per cent of the vote in the six countries. In the 1980s and 1990s, the explained variance was 2 per cent. Controlled for other variables, issues at most explain 4 per cent of the vote (Sweden 1982, Norway 1993). Even when important issues are given more opportunity to explain the vote, issues turn out to be relatively unimportant. When we do not control for preceding variables, the explanatory power on average was 4 per cent in the 1970s and 1980s, and 3 per cent in the 1990s. Issues alone explain at most 9 per cent of the vote (Germany 1987). In the individual countries, no systematic trend can be observed (findings not shown). An exception is Sweden, where the contribution of issues to the explained variance has declined in the past three decades.

Table 8.4 gives an account of differences between countries with respect to how much the three most important issues explain. For each country, the contribution of issues to the explained variance is averaged across election years. When we control for value orientations and social background, there is hardly any difference between countries with respect to the electoral importance of issues. When issues alone are included in the equation, there are substantial differences between countries. In Norway, the three most important issues explain on average 6 per cent of the vote. These issues are slightly less important in Britain, Germany, and Sweden (4–5 per cent). In Denmark and the Netherlands, their importance is almost negligible. Furthermore, our findings indicate a weak relationship between value orientations and perceived issue importance in Denmark and the Netherlands. Although the explained variance is very small, the explanatory power of issues does not change after controlling for value orientations. In the other four countries, there seems to be a stronger relationship. The explanatory power of issues is reduced when value orientations are taken into account.

Our findings demonstrate that the importance of issues in explaining voting behaviour is low in all six countries. This is the case even when only issues explain party choice. Contrary to expectations of modernization theories, salient issues

TABLE 8.4. *Variance explained by issues, by country*

	Controlled for values and social background	Not controlled for values and social background
Norway	0.02	0.06
Britain	0.01	0.05
Germany	0.02	0.04
Sweden	0.02	0.04
Denmark	0.02	0.02
Netherlands	0.01	0.01

have *not* become more important for explaining voting behaviour in the past three decades. Neither can a relationship be observed between party polarization and the electoral importance of issues. There is no relationship between changes in left–right party polarization and trends in the extent to which issues explain the vote, not even in countries where left–right depolarization is unambiguous.

8.7.2 The Effect of Issues on the Election Outcome

The meagre contribution of issues to the explanation of voting behaviour does not preclude a further inquiry into the electoral relevance of issues. Issues can do a poor job in explaining variations in voting patterns, and yet have a substantial potential impact on the election outcome. This has already been shown in bivariate analyses (Tables 8.1 and 8.2). The small contribution of issues to the explained variance can partly be due to the opinion distribution of the electorate. For example, only 10 per cent of the electorate might perceive law and order as an important issue. Accordingly, the distribution of votes over the different parties can to a limited extent be explained by the salience of law and order. This, however, does not preclude that the electoral fate of certain parties is determined by this particular issue. Parties that stress law and order can win a considerable number of votes among people who give priority to this problem. This electoral gain may give them representation in parliament or additional ministerial seats in the new cabinet.

We can estimate the potential electoral impact of issues by calculating vote probabilities for two groups of voters; voters who think that certain issues are important and voters who do not attach importance to these issues. Estimated vote probabilities are derived from multinomial logit models, described in the preceding section. The vote probabilities are estimated for a voter who perceives a certain issue as important and a voter who perceives the issue as not important.[9] For both types of voters, variables for the other two issues and other independent variables are set at the sample mean value.[10] The effect on the vote is defined as the difference between the first and second vote probability.

On the basis of issue ownership theory, we expect that the salience of an issue has the largest positive effect on the probability of voting for the issue-owning party. In other words, when voters attach more importance to a certain issue, it is expected that the party that owns this issue will make the largest electoral gains.

Table 8.5 indicates how often the cases (i.e. specific issues at specific elections) are in accordance with this issue ownership expectation for each country (see Tables 8.A.13–18 for details). In all countries, except the Netherlands, a majority of cases support the expectation that the electoral fortune of the issue-owning party is most dependent on the salience of the issue. In the Scandinavian countries and Germany, a large majority of cases support the expectation. In Britain, 63 per cent of cases show the expected voting pattern. In

TABLE 8.5. *Percentage of cases where issue salience has the largest positive effect on voting for the issue-owning party, by country*

Denmark	0.95
Sweden	0.88
Norway	0.80
Germany	0.75
Britain	0.63
Netherlands	0.43

the Netherlands issue salience has the largest positive effect on voting for the issue-owning party in only 43 per cent of the cases.

The next question is whether issue ownership voting has become more important over time. Table 8.6 gives an indication to what extent voting patterns have been in accordance with the issue ownership theory, in the past three decades. For this purpose, the specific issues in specific election years are aggregated across countries. In the 1970s, 90 per cent of the cases supported issue ownership theory. The proportion was down to 64 per cent in the 1980s and 72 per cent in the 1990s.

Furthermore, Table 8.7 presents the trend in the effect of salient issues on voting for issue-owning parties. For the 1970s, 1980s, and 1990s, we have calculated an average effect on the vote. For each decade, the vote effect is averaged across countries, issues, and election years. In the 1970s, voters who perceived a certain issue as important, on average were 10.5 per cent more likely to vote for the issue-owning party, than voters who did not think the issue was important (controlled for value orientations and social background variables). This effect declined to 8.7 per cent in the 1980s and 8.1 per cent in the 1990s. Looking at the individual countries, we do not find a systematic trend in the issue effect on voting (findings not shown). An exception is the Netherlands, where the electoral position of an issue-owning party has become somewhat more dependent on its own issues in the three preceding decades.

TABLE 8.6. *Percentage of cases where issue salience has the largest positive effect on voting for the issue-owning party, across time*

1970s	1980s	1990s
0.90	0.64	0.72

TABLE 8.7. *Average issue effect on voting for the issue-owning party, across time*

1970s	1980s	1990s
10.5	8.7	8.1

TABLE 8.8. *Average issue effect on voting for the issue-owning party, across countries*

Norway	14.8
Germany	12.1
Sweden	10.2
Denmark	6.7
Britain	6.2
Netherlands	3.9

Table 8.8 shows the difference between the six countries, with respect to the effect of issue salience on voting for issue-owning parties. For each country the table presents effects that are averaged across issues and election years. In Norway, Germany, and Sweden, the vote effect of salient issues is larger than 10 per cent. In these countries, voters who think that a certain issue is important, are on average at least 10 per cent more likely to vote for the issue-owning party (controlled for value orientations and social background variables). This vote effect is moderate in Denmark and Britain (6–7 per cent) and small in the Netherlands (4 per cent).

8.8 CONCLUSION

The main research question in this chapter is to what extent and how the voters' perceptions of important issues affect the outcome of the election and to what extent this affect has changed over time. First of all, it is important to see this chapter and Chapter 6 on value orientations as a whole. 'Issue voting' and 'value voting' are not necessarily very different. Issue positions may be closely linked to underlying value orientations, and perceptions of salient issues may activate latent values. If we, however, focus primarily on issue priorities, we may distinguish issue voting from value voting as being more directly linked to the political context—in terms of salient issues—of a given election.

The initial results of our analyses were quite dismal, showing that issue priorities only to a limited extent were able to explain variations in voting patterns. This holds whether we control for social background and values or not. However, a meagre explanatory power does not necessarily mean that issue voting is non-existent. On the contrary, the above analyses clearly demonstrate that issue voting matters, at least defined as voting for a party that owns an issue that is particularly salient at a given election. In a majority of cases the expectations based on the issue ownership theory were confirmed. If a voter thinks that a certain issue is salient, this has a considerable positive effect on the probability that he or she will vote for the party that is regarded as the owner of the issue.

Although we acknowledge the limitations of our measurements and data, our conclusion nevertheless remains that issues *do* matter in modern elections. However, this does not mean that we subscribe to the popular belief that the vote choice almost entirely is decided by attitudes towards single issues. It is only when we combine the voters' priorities of important issues with their perceptions of which party owns the issue, that we find an effect of some significance.

Moreover, contrary to expectations based on modernization theory, we do not find a secular increase in issue voting over time. Despite a process of individualization, a rise in education and an increase in political information, there has not been an increase in the effect of issue priorities on voting behaviour. Neither has there been a rise in the extent to which issue priorities explain the vote. Also, these findings on voting behaviour do not support the second hypothesis. The decrease in polarization of parties on value dimensions since the 1980s (reported by scholars using expert and survey data) has not been a stimulus for citizens to increasingly base their vote decision on other issue criteria, like issue priorities and issue competence.

To some extent the findings in this chapter may be seen as negative. We do not find the (simple) effects that many commentators and electoral researchers claim are important for the vote choice, and would even increase over time. On the other hand, we do find that issue priorities are linked to perceptions of issue competence, issue ownership, and the vote. The notion that policy preferences— or issues—have 'replaced' social background as prime determinants of voting tends to overlook the fact that even the traditional models of voting behaviour were not devoid of political context. In this perspective, our analysis confirms that election campaigns are still fought over issues that both politicians and voters perceive as important. If a party owns an issue, it stands far better chances in an upcoming election, if only the voters agree with the party that this particular issue deserves particular attention.

Notes

1. Attitudes towards political issues were important even in the early election studies of the 1950s and 1960s (Campbell et al. 1960; McClosky et al. 1960; Valen and Katz 1964).
2. Lane and Ersson (1987) label these kind of issues *structural* issues, referring to the social and structural basis of the cleavage. However, cleavages in the Lipset–Rokkan tradition are not necessarily linked to social groups. Allardt and Pesonen (1967), in their chapter in the Lipset and Rokkan book, show that a cleavage may be non-structural as well, not linked to structurally defined groups (see also Aardal 1994).
3. In practice, it is not always easy to separate ends from means. A certain policy end, for instance, can be seen as a means to achieve a policy end at a higher level of abstraction.
4. Issue priority is particularly important for valence issues. However, issue priority may also be relevant for position issues.
5. This means that we to a large extent are at the mercy of the coding procedures and categories used in each country.

6. Most experts involved are contributors to this book.
7. The following parties have been included in analyses: Denmark: Socialdemokratiet, Venstre, Konservativt Folkeparti, Dansk Folkeparti, Radikale Venstre, Socialistisk Folkeparti, Fremskridtspartiet. Norway: KrF, Høyre, Arbeiderpartiet, Venstre, SV, FrP, Senterpartiet. Sweden: Modernaterna, Socialdemokraterna, Centerpartiet, Folkpartiet, KS, Miljöpartiet De Gröna, Vänsterpartiet. The Netherlands: PvdA, VVD, CDA, D66, Green Left. Britain: Labour, Conservatives, Alliance. Germany: SPD, CDU/CSU, FDP, Greens.
8. The following social background variables have been used for the separate countries. Denmark: region, sex, marital status, level of urbanization, income, working in public sector, union membership. Sweden: marital status, union membership, home ownership, income, church attendance, sex, working in public sector. Norway: age, sex, region, union membership, teetotaller, church attendance, social class. The Netherlands: sex, age, region, union membership, working in public sector, church attendance, social class, level of urbanization. Britain: age, sex, marital status, church attendance, social class, home ownership, union membership. Germany: age, sex, union membership, church attendance, occupation. On request, the authors can provide the data and syntax files with which the logistic regression analyses have been performed.
9. For Britain and Germany, vote probabilities are estimated for voters who give the lowest priority score to an issue, and voters who give the highest priority score to an issue.
10. Vote probabilities are obtained by subsequently substituting the lowest and highest issue salience score in the estimated regression equations. For the other independent variables, the sample mean values are substituted in the equations.

APPENDIX

TABLE 8.A.1. *Great Britain—Three most important issues 1974–92 and issue owner*

Issue	Issue owner	1974	1979	1983	1987	1992
Ricing prices	Conservative..........	1	2			
Problem of strikes	Conservative..........	2	3			
Wage controls	Labour..................	3				
Law and order	Conservative..........		1	2		
Unemployment	Labour..................			1	2	
Social services/health	Labour..................			3	1	
Keep prices down	Conservative..........					1
Up taxes + spend more	Labour..................					2
Equalize income	Labour..................					3
Education	Conservative				3	

TABLE 8.A.2. *Denmark—Three most important issues 1977–98 and issue owner*

Issue	Issue owner	1977	1979	1981	1984	1987	1990	1998
Unemployment	Socialdemokratiet..........................	1	2	1	1	2	1	
Economy	Venstre and Kons. Folkeparti	2	1	2	2	3	3	
Foreign debt	Venstre and Kons. Folkeparti	3	3	3	3			
Environment	SF, VS (and KrF 1987).................					1	2	
Health	Socialdemokratiet..........................							1
Care for the elderly	Socialdemokratiet..........................							2
Immigration	Dansk Folkeparti...........................							3

TABLE 8.A.3. *Germany—Three most important issues 1972–98 and issue owner*

Issue	Issue owner	1972	1976	1983	1987	1990	1994	1998
Stability of prices	CDU/CSU, FDP.................	1	2					
Pension system	SPD......................................	2		2				3
Law and order	CDU/CSU...........................	3	3		3		2	2
(un)Employment	SPD......................................		1	1	1	2	1	1
Decrease public debts	FDP......................................			3				
Environmental protection	Greens................................					2	1	
Better housing	SPD......................................						3	
Economic growth	CDU/CSU, FDP.................						3	

TABLE 8.A.4. *Netherlands—Three most important issues 1977–98 and issue owner*

Issue	Issue owner	1977	1981	1986	1989	1994	1998
Employment	PvdA	1	1	1		2	
Housing	PvdA	2	2				
Subsidies	VVD	3				3	
Economy	VVD		3	3			
Defence	PvdA			2			
Environment	Groen Links				1		
Labour relations	PvdA				2		
Law and order	VVD				3		2
Minority groups	VVD					1	1
Public health	PvdA						3

TABLE 8.A.5. *Norway—Three most important issues 1977–97 and issue owner*

Issue	Issue owner	1977	1981	1985	1989	1993	1997
Moral	Kristelig Folkeparti......................................	1	1				
Tax	Høyre..	2	2				
Employment	Arbeiderpartiet..	3		3	3	2	
Social issues	Arbeiderpartiet..			3	1	1	3	1
Foreign policy	Høyre..			2			
Environment	Sosialistisk Venstreparti/Venstre..................				2		
EU	Senterpartiet..					1	
Family issues	Kristelig Folkeparti......................................						2
Education	Sosialistisk Venstreparti/Høyre....................						3

TABLE 8.A.6. *Sweden—Three most important issues 1982–98 and issue owner*

Issue	Issue Owner	1982	1985	1988	1991	1994	1998
Wage Earners Funds	Moderaterna......................................	1					
Employment	Socialdemokraterna..........................	2	1		2	1	1
Economy	Modernaterna...................................	3				2	
Environment	De Gröna, Centerpartiet.............		2	1	1		
Taxes	Moderaterna......................................		3	2			
Social welfare/health	Socialdemokraterna..........................			3	3	3	2
Education	Folkpartiet..						3

TABLE 8.A.7. *Great Britain—Absolute and relative strength of issue-owning party among voters who say that the issue is important*

	1974		1979		1983		1987		1992	
	Imp	Imp/tot	Imp	Imp/tot	Imp	Imp/tot	Imp	Imp/tot	Imp	Imp/tot
Issue 1	25.0	0.66	54.9	1.17	36.2	1.26	37.0	1.42	33.8	0.74
Issue 2	44.9	1.18	38.7	0.82	49.5	1.10	50.7	1.95	42.5	1.24
Issue 3	42.0	1.03	55.4	1.18	37.3	1.30	40.1	1.09	48.6	1.42
Average		0.96		1.06		1.22		1.49		1.13

TABLE 8.A.8. *Denmark—Absolute and relative strength of issue-owning party among voters who say that the issue is important*

	1977		1979		1981		1984		1987		1990		1998	
	Imp	Imp/tot	Imp	Imp/tot	Imp	Imp/tot	Imp	Imp/tot	Imp	Imp/tot	Imp	Imp/tot	Imp	Imp/tot
Issue 1	46.2	1.04	16.0	1.12	32.5	1.07	33.1	1.04	9.7	1.32	44.0	1.14	33.9	1.08
Issue 2	14.6	1.38	44.3	1.10	21.9	1.57	27.3	1.62	31.7	1.10	20.5	1.38	40.5	1.29
Issue 3	15.9	1.59	15.9	1.12	17.7	1.29	27.6	1.66	24.4	1.51	21.0	1.38	17.1	2.41
Average		1.34		1.11		1.31		1.44		1.31		1.30		1.59

TABLE 8.A.9. *Germany—Absolute and relative strength of issue-owning party among voters who say that the issue is important*

	1972		1976		1983		1987		1990		1994		1998	
	Imp	Imp/tot	Imp	Imp/tot	Imp	Imp/tot	Imp	Imp/tot	Imp	Imp/tot	Imp	Imp/tot	Imp	Imp/tot
Issue 1	23.1	0.97	45.8	1.00	42.1	0.97	43.3	1.06	6.4	1.21	37.3	1.00	43.8	1.02
Issue 2	58.5	1.09	27.2	0.94	43.3	1.00	10.0	1.39	42.8	1.09	40.4	1.07	31.3	1.10
Issue 3	39.1	1.08	50.4	1.11	4.9	0.94	53.2	1.23	43.3	1.11	22.2	1.02	46.8	1.09
Average		1.05		1.02		0.97		1.23		1.14		1.03		1.07

TABLE 8.A.10. *Netherlands—Absolute and relative strength of issue-owning party among voters who say that the issue is important*

	1977		1981		1986		1989		1994		1998	
	Imp	Imp/tot	Imp	Imp/tot	Imp	Imp/tot	Imp	Imp/tot	Imp	Imp/tot	Imp	Imp/tot
Issue 1	36.4	1.02	26.0	1.02	31.9	0.91	7.1	1.34	24.1	1.10	29.1	1.32
Issue 2	49.3	1.38	30.0	1.18	50.8	1.45	36.2	1.12	27.5	1.10	21.9	1.00
Issue 3	25.9	1.76	20.6	1.31	25.0	1.49	13.5	0.97	20.9	0.95	29.6	1.01
Average		1.40		1.17		1.28		1.14		1.05		1.11

TABLE 8.A.11. *Norway—Absolute and relative strength of issue-owning party among voters who say that the issue is important*

	1977		1981		1985		1989		1993		1997	
	Imp	Imp/tot	Imp	Imp/tot	Imp	Imp/tot	Imp	Imp/tot	Imp	Imp/tot	Imp	Imp/tot
Issue 1	31.9	2.77	33.0	3.84	50.5	1.31	40.3	1.20	28.3	1.55	37.1	1.04
Issue 2	46.0	1.97	58.1	1.84	49.4	1.62	19.4	2.51	51.6	1.31	38.4	2.49
Issue 3	75.3	1.71	46.0	1.23	55.1	1.44	38.1	1.14	48.1	1.22	20.2	1.79
Average		2.15		2.30		1.46		1.62		1.36		1.77

TABLE 8.A.12. *Sweden—Absolute and relative strength of issue-owning party among voters who say that the issue is important*

	1982		1985		1988		1991		1994		1998	
	Imp	Imp/tot	Imp	Imp/tot	Imp	Imp/tot	Imp	Imp/tot	Imp	Imp/tot	Imp	Imp/tot
Issue 1	24.4	1.81	58.2	1.33	13.9	1.70	12.8	2.47	56.1	1.22	40.8	1.09
Issue 2	64.9	1.40	11.8	2.58	34.6	2.08	48.7	1.30	28.6	1.40	39.9	1.06
Issue 3	33.7	1.45	38.2	1.93	44.6	0.99	47.3	1.26	54.1	1.18	9.9	2.36
Average		1.55		1.95		1.59		1.68		1.27		1.50

TABLE 8.A.13. *Great Britain—Cases supporting the issue ownership theory in bold. Cases not supporting the theory in parentheses*

	1974	1979	1983	1987	1992
Rising prices	(Labour)	(Labour)			
Strikes	Conserv.	Conserv.			
Wage controls	Labour				
Law and order		Conserv.	Conserv.		
Unemployment			Labour	Labour	
Social services/health			Labour	(Conserv.)	
Prices down					Conserv.
Increased tax/spending					(Alliance)
Equalize income					Labour

TABLE 8.A.14. *Denmark—Cases supporting the issue ownership theory in bold. Cases not supporting the theory in parentheses*

	1977	1979	1981	1984	1990	1998
Unemployment	Soc.dem.	Soc.dem.	(SF)	Soc.dem.	(Soc.dem)	
Economy	Kons./V	Venstre	Venstre	Kons./V	Kons.	
Foreign debt	Kons./V	Venstre	Kons.	Venstre		
Environment					SF	
Health						(Dansk/V)
Care for the elderly						Soc. dem.
Immigration						Dansk F.

TABLE 8.A.15. *Germany—Cases supporting the issue ownership theory in bold. Cases not supporting the theory in parentheses*

	1976	1983	1987	1990	1994	1998
Stable prices	CDU					
Pensions		SPD				SPD
Law and order	CDU		CDU		CDU	CDU
Employment	SPD	(CDU/FDP)	SPD	SPD	(CDU)	(Greens)
Decrease debts		CDU				
Environment			(SPD)	Greens		
Housing				SPD		
Economy growth					CDU	

TABLE 8.A.16. *The Netherlands—Cases supporting the issue ownership theory in bold. Cases not supporting the theory in parentheses*

	1977	1981	1986	1989	1994	1998
Employment	PvdA	(CDA)	(D66)	PvdA	(CDA)	
Housing	PvdA	(CDA/D66)				
Subsidies	VVD				(PvdA)	
Economy		(D66)	(D66)			
Defence			PvdA			
Environment				(D66)		
Job relations						
Law and order				(CDA)		VVD
Minorities					VVD	VVD
Health						(CDA)

TABLE 8.A.17. *Norway—Cases supporting the issue ownership theory in bold.*
Cases not supporting the theory in parentheses

	1977	1981	1985	1989	1993	1997
Moral	KrF	KrF				
Tax	H	H				
Employment	A		A	(H.)	A	
Social issues		A	A	(H.)	A	(KrF)
Foreign policy			(V)			
Environment				(H.)		
EU					Sp	
Family issues						KrF
Education						H

TABLE 8.A.18. *Sweden—Cases supporting the issue ownership theory in bold.*
Cases not supporting the theory in parentheses

	1982	1985	1988	1991	1994	1998
Wage earn	M					
Employment	S	S		S	S	S
Economy	M				(Fp)	
Environment		C	MdG	C		
Taxes		M	M			
Social welfare/health			(C)	S	S	(KS)
Education						Fp

9

Retrospective Voting[1]

Ola Listhaug

9.1 INTRODUCTION

According to modernization theory the modern voters are more likely to be active and independent in making up their mind on election day. The calculus of the new voter may go in different directions, but one likely trend is an increase in the importance of retrospective judgements on the policy record of incumbent parties. Retrospective evaluations can be important along many types of issues where governments have responsibility for policy outcomes. Among issue domains, economics is by far the dominant dimension for the study of retrospective voting. While we would like to cover other aspects of retrospective evaluations, the analytical possibilities of election studies are limited to the economic dimension, at least when one wants to cover most of the countries over time. Although we are primarily interested in retrospective judgements we will also at occasions look into the prospective dimension of economic voting. The relationship between the past and the future is a highly complex and difficult area of research, which the present chapter will only briefly touch upon. Besides assessing the development of economic voting we will attempt to analyse how nation-specific and institutional factors have an impact on the voting model. The general argument of the book leads us to expect a linear trend in the conversion from traditional to modern patterns of voting. But we also expect that this movement is contingent both on national factors like economic cycles and variations in institutional structure.

Economic voting should be assessed within a broader model of voting behaviour. In Europe, Rokkan-type cleavage models have been dominant in explaining voting behaviour. These models have obvious drawbacks. The first and most striking are that cleavages change slowly, and cannot explain political movements in the short run. This is unfortunate especially in times with volatile elections. A second reason is that the cleavages that Rokkan and associates saw as predominant for the formation of political parties and influencing the vote choice of citizens have lost much of their power (Franklin et al. 1992; Chapter 4 of this book). The decline of class voting, the weakening of the power of religion in politics, and the nationalization of electorates in most countries—leaving regional and centre–periphery conflicts behind, have urged students of voting behaviour to look for explanations that go beyond the established cleavage structures: new cleavages, issues, economics, personality, and media, just to mention a few of the most prominent. Lewis-Beck (1988) in particular argued early that economics should have a prominent place together with cleavages and ideology.

Although the observation that the movement of the economy has important political effects is not new, the emergence of the field within empirical science in the 1970s and 1980s is related to the end of a period of strong economic growth after the Second World War, and an increase in inflation and unemployment, and in many countries the three evils in combination. At the same time many governments found that traditional Keynesian policy instruments did not work (Lewis-Beck 1988). The economic problems did not go away with the 1970s and the 1980s. Although inflation rates declined in the advanced economies, unemployment levels in the 1990s remained high by historical standards. To explain the surge in studies of economic voting from what happened in the real world is just one part of the story. Within political science there occurred a marked shift towards models that put stronger emphasis on the individual citizen as actor, often with independence from parties and other collective structures and bonds of loyalty. Many of these models took on a distinctly rational choice character. This shift gave a boost to economic explanations as it became customary to ask about utility of the vote in money terms.

A test of economic voting within a broader set of voting choice models is possible only with survey data. If one wants to do this in a comparative setting, one can either design a new study and collect data for this specific purpose like Lewis-Beck does, or one can rely on available survey data—which is the choice of the European Voter Project. The advantage of this design is that we can monitor aspects of economic voting over an extensive period of time, with interesting variations in economic conditions, political events, and incumbency patterns.

The downside of the approach is, however, considerable. There is weak comparative equivalence in questions across surveys from different countries, and there are also inconsistencies within each national election survey series. This stands in contrast to a well-designed study of the Lewis-Beck type, or to the current designs of the Comparative Study of Electoral Systems, which include an identical module of questions in a large number of national elections studies worldwide. But as of now the latter design does not contain enough data that are useful for the study of economic voting.

With the present data we cannot make strict comparisons across countries, and only limited over time analyses of trends. But we hope to answer some important questions about economic voting. The first question is about the relative importance of economics for vote choice. Is there any support for the hypothesis that economics is replacing cleavages in European elections? To answer this question one should not look at only two time points as one may expect that the impact of economic concerns will vary with the economic conditions at the time of the election, and an investigation over many elections with variations in economic climate would give us a much firmer ground to assess the impact of economic evaluations on the vote.

A second question concerns the internal structure of the economic voting model. In the last twenty years the discussion of the model has been performed along a set of well-defined research questions. The most recent authoritative review of the field sums up the state of the art in nine stylized facts— or empirical generalizations—about voting and popularity functions (Lewis-Beck and Paldam 2000*b*).

There are several points in this review that are relevant for our study. The first is that the economy is important for vote choice, and that the effect of economic changes explains about one-third of changes in the vote. This effect is of course an average, but the size suggests that economic factors are crucial in deciding vote choice and the outcome of elections. The second is that several aspects of economics play a role: growth, unemployment, inflation. The third is that the review states that retrospective evaluations are more important than forward-looking judgements and that concerns for the economic state of the nation beat assessments of personal finances.

Although the review in general is fairly upbeat about what has been achieved, there is still a lot of work to do. A crucial point concerns the stability of economic voting in time and space. It is definitely the stated belief of the reviewers that there is an underlying stability in the pattern, and that the instability is only apparent and not real. If scholars are able to measure coherently and model relevant factors that may intrude on the relationship between the variables of the core model of economic voting, instability will go away, save for 'the routine sources of error which plague any sort of empirical work' (Lewis-Beck and Paldam 2000*b*: 120).

The conclusions of the review by Lewis-Beck and Paldam (2000*b*) do not mean that the controversies are put to rest. It is striking that most of the new findings that are included in the volume by Lewis-Beck and Paldam (2000*a*) come from research on aggregate data, with data from election surveys almost completely lacking. But it is precisely survey data that are needed if we want to study the internal structure of the economic voting model. We hope to cast some further light on questions if voters are retrospective or prospective, and if sociotropic concerns dominate egotropic evaluations. The conclusion that survived from Fiorina (1981: 12–16) is that voters primarily form retrospective evaluations, although Fiorina also makes much effort to align the retrospective model with Downsian theory, which sees the past primarily as a guide to evaluate the future behaviour of governments. More recent research, influenced by the rational expectation revolution in economics, has advocated a stronger version of the forward-looking voter, and shown that there is some empirical merit to support the hypothesis that voters are 'bankers' rather than 'peasants' (MacKuen et al. 1992; Erikson et al. 2000). The 'peasant' model is based solely on assessments of past economic performance or personal experience of the economy. This is a more primitive model (hence the use of 'peasant') than the 'banker' model where the voter incorporates information about the future into personal economic expectations.

Further questions that can be probed with the available data are which parties are rewarded or punished if government is a coalition of two or more parties, and the question of the partisan nature of economic judgements. The first question can be studied by making a distinction between the prime minister's party and the rest of the coalition partners. The idea is that the prime minister is the most important figure in government and support for her or his party will be more strongly affected by the economic evaluations of citizens than support for other parties in the coalition. This hypothesis can be extended and refined in numerous ways by classifying parties according to their share of economic portfolio positions in cabinet (e.g. finance minister, minister for labour and employment). Some parties may have a legacy of economic management, which make them more likely to be judged by economic standards than other parties. More generally, we may replace the simple dichotomy of incumbency and estimate a model where it is possible to compare the economic effects on support for each of the parties and compare the effects within the same model, for example, along the lines of Alvarez and collaborators (2000).

The simple responsibility or reward and punishment model does not take into account that various aspects of the economy will be judged differently by partisan and ideological groups in the electorate. Parties will also have different economic priorities, for example, left parties will put a higher priority on low unemployment while right parties may be more concerned about inflation. The partisan view on economic voting as advocated by Hibbs (1987) and developed in various forms by other scholars (see Carlsen 2000 for a recent overview and test with aggregate data) is of obvious relevance for the countries that we analyse in this chapter.

Some of the optimism that has recently surfaced about the field of economic voting is related to insights from comparative work on the impact of institutional variations across systems. Already Lewis-Beck in his pioneering comparative study of economic voting in the major western democracies suggested that an institutional variable like coalition complexity could reduce the impact of economic evaluations on voting (Lewis-Beck 1988: 110). The argument was more fully developed by Powell and Whitten (1993) as they demonstrated with the help of aggregate data that the clarity of formal electoral arrangements contributes to stronger economic voting. Anderson (2000) extends considerably on the Powell and Whitten analysis as he develops a threefold classification of institutional arrangements that are relevant for economic voting: clarity of responsibility, governing party target size, and the clarity of available alternatives. Clarity of responsibility reproduces the Powell and Whitten index based on one-party rule versus multiparty government, bicameral opposition, decision-making powers for opposition parties, and party cohesion (Anderson 2000: 153–4). The target size argument says that parties that have a greater stake in economic decision-making should be held more responsible for the economy, and that parties that have the most power should be punished more for economic outcomes than less influential parties (Anderson 2000: 154–5). This variable is measured by parliamentary strength and cabinet strength of the prime minister's party (Anderson 2000: 158). Finally, the clarity of available political alternatives must also be taken into account. Anderson hypothesizes that economic voting should be stronger when there are clear alternatives to the current administration, meaning that there are few alternatives, measured by the number of effective parties (Anderson 2000: 155–6). These hypotheses are tested with Eurobarometer data from 1994, and in general receive support.

Lewis-Beck and Nadeau (2000) use the French case to demonstrate that variations in institutional setting within the country affect the relationship between the economy and the vote. They find that the impact is strongest in a presidential election under unified government, and weaker under cohabitation or at European (second order) elections. This finding is also of the clarity variety as cohabitation reduces clarity since both the president and the prime minister are responsible for policy. Similarly, European elections have a focus both on the EU level and the nation, which makes it difficult for voters to assign responsibility for outcomes of policy and promises for the future. The recent enthusiasm for institutional models is not shared by all scholars. In an analysis of Britain, the United States, Germany, Australia, and Spain, Sanders and Carey (2002: 229) find that there are huge variations in economic voting within high clarity countries, and that they have problems in accounting for the results without resorting to vague concepts and ad hoc arguments, or in their terms:

... we recognize that we may be searching for a Holy Grail of economic voting that does not exist. There may in fact be no underlying model that will explain all of the complex features of economic voting that have variously been observed. Rather, there may be, in the final analysis, merely a multiplicity of cultural differences and historical contingencies.

The observation of Sanders and Carey is probably correct. The institutional argument can easily be made very complex if we try to match all the existing configurations that may be important for assessing blame or credit for economic conditions and outcomes. But this is an argument that can be made for most of the mechanisms and variables that affect mass political behaviour. There is always an abundance of detail and context variation that can influence how voters behave at the polls (Dorussen 2002). The goal is always to sort out the most potent factors and to order context accounts and specific events into variables. This probably means that one needs to go beyond institutions as conventionally defined, and include more dynamic context variables. This is exactly the step taken by Nadeau et al. (2002) who create a new clarity index that combines the, largely static, institutional components, with medium- and short-term factors. They test the impact of the new index on patterns of economic voting in eight European countries over a period of sixteen years. The results give additional support to the hypothesis that more clarity, defined in a broader and dynamic manner, increases the strength of economic voting.

9.2 EXPLANATORY MODEL

We investigate three research questions that are related to the standard model of economic voting. First, we study the strength of the relationship between evaluations and the support for incumbent parties and how this relationship is dependent on political leadership and historical context. Second, we ask which aspects of the economy are important: Are voters backward looking or do considerations for future also play a role, and, are evaluations of the economic situation of the country more potent than assessments of the pocketbook? Third, we ask if there is a trend towards increase in economic voting as the traditional cleavage structure declines and a more independent European voter emerges.

To answer the research questions we need to develop a model of the vote that includes economic evaluations in addition to the variables specified in Table 9.1. Preferably, the model should have maximum comparability across time and over countries. With the available survey data only a very limited model can be estimated. We have settled on a baseline model that includes core economic items that are available for each country and measures of cleavages and ideology. We use a measure of subjective class, religious activity, and left–right ideology. In addition we include gender and age. Even this minimum model cannot be estimated in full across elections.

Since we analyse only five countries it is not possible to estimate any systematic impact of institutions. But we present the results in an order that is close to an order from high to low clarity cases: Britain, Germany, Sweden, the Netherlands, and Norway. Britain is the prime example of a majority system with one-party majority governments, and one dominant opposition party. Germany has for most election periods a simple stable majority alternative of a big party (SPD or CDU/CSU), and FDP as junior party. Sweden has a relatively clear institutional structure as government alternatives are rather simple—either social democratic one-party governments or a bourgeois coalition. The government alternatives in the Netherlands and Norway are less clear. The Netherlands has mostly majority coalition governments. In the period covered by our data, minority governments have been the rule in Norway, either the single-party governments of Labour or various bourgeois coalition alternatives.

TABLE 9.1. *Economic voting in Britain.*
Vote for incumbent party. OLS regression

	1997		2001	
	B	Beta	B	Beta
Constant	−0.689		0.195	
State of UK's economy next few years	0.137	0.225*	0.175	0.279*
Retrospective evaluation of household's economy	0.030	0.051†	0.103	0.149*
Subjective social class	0.123	0.138*		
Left–right dimension	0.079	0.363*	−0.059	−0.211*
Church attendance	0.005	0.021		
Gender	−0.062	−0.072*	0.069	0.069*
Age	0.033	0.080*	0.023	0.049†
R^2	0.298		0.189	
($N =$)	1505		1501	

*$p < 0.01$; †$p < 0.05$

Vote: Party choice in recent election (1997: 1 = Conservative Party, 0 = other parties; 2001: 1 = Labour, 0 = other parties).

State of UK's economy next few years: (1 = get worse, 2 = stay about the same, 3 = get better).

Retrospective evaluation of household's economy: Household income compared to last year (1 = worse off now, 2 = stayed about the same, 3 = better off now).

Subjective social class: (0 = working class, 1 = middle class).

Left–right dimension: Self-placement on a scale from 1 to 10 (1 = left, 10 = right).

Church attendance: (0 = never, 1 = less than once a year, 2 = once a year, 3 = several times a year, 4 = once a month or more, 5 = once a week or more).

Gender: (0 = female, 1 = male).

Age: (1 = 17–34 years old, 2 = 35–49 years old, 3 = 50–64 years old, 4 = 65 years old or higher).

9.3 EMPIRICAL RESULTS

In this section we report on the empirical results of the baseline model for Britain, Germany, Sweden, the Netherlands, and Norway.[2] We have excluded elections that do not meet minimum requirements for data, or where coding problems have not been solved. All reported estimates are from OLS regressions. Due to the fact that the dependent variable is dichotomous we have rerun all models using logistic regression. The results from these regressions do not significantly deviate from OLS estimates.

9.3.1 Britain

The analysis for Britain is restricted to the two most recent elections. The first, 1997, was a key election in modern UK electoral history. New Labour led by Tony Blair swept the Conservatives out of office after 18 years in power. The election outcome was not a shock; Labour victory had been long in the making, as for example, argued in many of the contributions in Norris and

Gavin (1997). The part that economics played in the Labour victory equation was also associated with factors that had started to work long before election day. In an analysis of the Conservative campaign Whiteley (1997) argues that the immediate economic conditions moved in a favourable direction before the election, but that the Conservative Party was not able to benefit because the party had lost its reputation for good economic management, partly due to various examples of mismanagement and the 'Black Wednesday' of September 1992 when Britain withdrew from the European Exchange Rate Mechanism. Sanders (1999) emphasizes that the Conservative losses would have been even higher if the economy had not improved at the time of the election.

The evaluation data from 1997 show that there is a very weak effect of retrospective evaluation of the economy of the household on voting for the Conservatives. The effects of future evaluations are much stronger. Voters who are optimistic about the economic future of Britain are much more likely to vote for the Conservatives than those who are pessimistic.

The election of 2001 has some parallels to 1997 in that the incumbent party (Labour) could point to an improving economy. The evaluation figures demonstrate that Labour was able to benefit much more than the Tories in 1997. Both the retrospective evaluations of household economy and the expectation of the state of Britain's economy for the next few years are strongly correlated with support for Labour.

The UK case demonstrates nicely that incumbent parties differ in their ability to exploit the potential benefits of an improving economy. Labour in 2001 was much more successful than the Tories in 1997 to link retrospective economic evaluations to the decision of voting, or not voting, for the party at election day. How decisive this was for the outcome of the two elections, and if a particular legacy of management competence or lack of such competence played a role, cannot be read from the data. The UK results also demonstrate that prospective considerations are of sizeable magnitude, also when compared with social and ideological factors in the vote. For the third question about a trend in economic voting the limited time frame of the UK data prevents us from giving a meaningful answer.

9.3.2   Germany

The analysis of Germany covers the elections from 1972 through 1994, with the two most recent elections representing the united Germany. Previous survey research on Germany, and especially the detailed study of Rattinger (1986) has demonstrated that both incumbency and partisan hypotheses are relevant for explaining vote choice in West Germany for the period 1961–84. Rattinger and Faas (2001) extend this analysis, with similar conclusions, for elections from 1977 to 1998. The Rattinger analyses are limited to economic variables and do not attempt to test economic explanations within a broader model of vote choice.

The German case is interesting from a broader historical perspective. The 'Wirtschaftswunder' of the rebuilding of the country after the Second World War gave the linkage between economics and politics a key position in a political development characterized by consensus across the main political divides. As new economic problems emerged in the 1970s, economics had a polarization effect on politics. In the words of Rattinger (1986: 399), from his overview of the period 1961–84:

Over time, the impact of partisan orientations on economic judgements, i.e. the polarization of such judgements along partisan lines, emerges as strongest for the years from 1972 through 1980, with a clearly visible peak between 1972 and 1976 Bundestag elections, a period with inflation running high and unemployment starting to increase in 1974 following the OPEC oil-shock.

Later, the German reunification brought economic issues to the foreground for two main reasons—East Germany was much poorer than the Western part, and the chosen policy process where a stated goal was to make the living conditions equal in the two parts became extremely costly. The end of the Kohl era at the 1998 election is frequently associated with the effects of economic problems on voters. A detailed examination of this hypothesis clearly shows that voters' evaluation of the economy had become more negative, but the impact of evaluations on party choice was not very strong (Maier and Rattinger 1999).

The results for Germany are laid out in Table 9.2. The time frame of the questions uses the present, instead of a comparison with the past and the present, and there is also some variation in how many categories are used for the various evaluation variables. The main findings are easy to sum up. Collective judgements are clearly more important than personal assessments of the economy. Both present and prospective collective judgements are important, but judgements of the present enjoy an edge over the future. Prospective personal judgements and present personal judgements only achieve statistical significance at two elections each: 1972 and 1990 for prospective evaluations, and 1987 and 1994 for present personal judgements. The observed empirical relationships support the incumbency hypothesis.

The effects of ideology and religion are in line with expectations. When SPD and FDP are in power (1972–6) the signs for left–right ideology and religion are negative, when the CDU/CSU and FDP are in government the signs for both variables are positive. In each of these governments FDP is distinctively the junior partner, which means that the reversal of the signs are explained by the differences in ideological and religious outlook of SPD and CDU/CSU voters in the coalition. Finally, there is no clear time trend in the data. Economic voting varies over the period that we have data for, but the effects of economic evaluations are not generally higher in the 1990s than in the 1970s.

TABLE 9.2. *Economic voting in Germany. Vote for incumbent parties. OLS regression*

	1972		1976		1983	
	B	Beta	B	Beta	B	Beta
Constant	−0.330		0.419		−1.023	
Prospective egocentric economic evaluation	0.098	0.138*	0.038	0.044	0.026	0.030
Present egocentric economic evaluation	−0.015	−0.020	0.007	0.009	−0.012	−0.017
Present general economic evaluation	0.150	0.210*	0.168	0.226*	0.040	0.056†
Prospective general economic evaluation	0.145	0.206*	0.080	0.101*	0.199	0.302*
Left–right dimension			−0.107	−0.488*	0.094	0.417*
Church attendance	−0.091	−0.278*	−0.063	−0.178*	0.031	0.082*
Gender	−0.033	−0.035	−0.040	−0.040	0.042	0.042
Age	−0.004	−0.009	0.002	0.004	0.017	0.037
R^2	0.299		0.500		0.404	
($N =$)	1032		1043		932	

	1987		1990		1994	
	B	Beta	B	Beta	B	Beta
Constant	−1.144		−0.649		−0.911	
Prospective egocentric economic evaluation	0.013	0.013	0.036	0.070†	0.019	0.025
Present egocentric economic evaluation	0.058	0.076*	−0.013	−.028	0.031	0.046†
Present general economic evaluation	0.130	0.172*	0.036	0.068†	0.078	0.101*
Prospective general economic evaluation	0.046	0.059†	0.039	0.103*	0.026	0.035
Left–right dimension	0.103	0.491*	0.0097	0.413*	0.125	0.506*
Church attendance	0.055	0.141*	0.070	0.188*	0.044	0.105*
Gender	0.002	0.002	0.023	0.023	0.011	0.011
Age	0.011	0.024	0.070	0.056	0.047	0.100*
R^2	0.444		0.287		0.376	
($N =$)	1190		788		1382	

*$p < 0.01$; † $p < 0.05$

Vote: Party choice in recent elections (1972 and 1976: 1 = SPD and FDP, 0 = other parties; 1983–94: 1 = CDU/CSU and FDP, 0 = other parties).

Prospective egocentric economic evaluation: (1 = worse, 3 = same, 5 = better).

Present egocentric economic evaluation: (1 = bad, 2 = not that fine, 3 = in between, 4 = good, 5 = very good).

Present general economic evaluation: (1 = bad, 2 = not that fine, 3 = in between, 4 = good, 5 = very good).

Prospective general economic evaluation: (1 = worse, 3 = same, 5 = better).

Left–right dimension: (self-placement on a scale from 1 to 11; 1 = left, 11 = right).

Church attendance: (1 = never or less than once a year, 2 = once a year, 3 = several times a year, 4 = once a month or more, 5 = once a week or more).

Gender: (0 = female, 1 = male).

Age: (1 = 18–34 years old, 2 = 35–49 years old, 3 = 50–64 years old, 4 = 65 years old or higher).

9.3.3   Sweden

Sweden is the country of social democratic dominance, strong left–right divides, and class voting. Sweden has had greater political stability than the other Scandinavian countries. In the period that we study the Social Democratic Party was the incumbent party in five of seven elections, continuing the government hegemony that dates back to the 1930s. The left–right divide has traditionally been associated with a strong degree of class voting. As shown in Chapter 4 the level of class voting has declined in recent decades (see also Oskarson 1994), and much the same is true for other social determinants of the vote like region, place of living, and religion (Holmberg 2000: 106). Other sociological factors of the vote have been rather stable (level of urbanization, sector of employment), or have become more important (gender, age) (Holmberg 2000: 106). Left–right questions are still dominant in Swedish politics although they are off their peak of twenty years ago when the questions of wage earners funds and state control of Swedish industry occupied the political agenda (Holmberg 2000: 119–38).

Sweden has been through economic cycles, which can be read from the net balance of economic evaluations. For personal retrospective evaluations, which has the longest time series of measurement, the net balance was negative in 1976, 1982, and 1994, and positive for the remaining elections. The retrospective assessments of the national economy were strongly negative in 1991 and 1994, and positive in 1985, 1988, and 1998. As noted by Holmberg (2000: 141) incumbent parties have lost votes in all elections that he studied. Since the period covers both economic upturns and downturns it is reasonable to conclude that the economy may play only a modest role in explaining the electoral fortune of government parties in Sweden. His conclusion is, despite of this, that modest retrospective effects of sociotropic judgements do exist (Holmberg 2000: 142). This is also the case for the results that we report in Table 9.3. We find significant effects of backward national evaluations for all elections except 1982. This year is a special case as the incumbent parties at that election were the Centre Party and the People's Party. These parties had the support of less than 30 per cent of the electorate (at the election in 1979), which by Swedish standards was an exceptionally weak minority government (although still stronger than the Ullsten (People's Party) government of 1978–9). The effect of personal retrospective evaluations is clearly more mixed, and this effect fails to achieve significance in four of the elections (1985, 1991, 1994, and 1998).

The Swedish case can be used to shed some light on the effect of forward-looking evaluations. In the first major analysis of economic voting in Sweden, Holmberg (1984) made a strong attack on a study by Miller and Listhaug (1984) which emphasized that there was a link between voting behaviour and prospective evaluations of personal finances. The Holmberg argument was that this link could not be demonstrated since the Norwegian data were from a post-election study (all studies in Norway from 1973 onwards have collected interviews only after the election). Expectations measured after the election could easily be seen as a reflection of the outcome and not as a cause of voting choice. This argument becomes especially critical in elections that lead to a change of government. Sweden has consistently collected pre- and post-election data for all years, and it is possible to estimate the model for both waves. The interesting test for differences between pre- and post-election data comes from elections where governments have changed. We have four such cases in the Swedish material— 1976 (socialist to bourgeois), 1982 (bourgeois to socialist), 1991 (socialist to bourgeois), and 1994 (bourgeois to socialist). We report the results of this

TABLE 9.3. *Economic voting in Sweden. Vote for incumbent parties. OLS regression*

	1976		1982		1985	
	B	Beta	B	Beta	B	Beta
Constant	1.034		−0.022		0.871	
National economy, forward	−0.070	−0.118*	−0.028	−0.067*		
National economy, backward			−0.017	−0.029	0.067	0.169*
Own economy, forward	0.019	0.022				
Own economy, backward	0.102	0.137*	0.051	0.051†	0.004	0.004
Subjective social class	−0.203	−0.195*				
Left–right dimension	−0.092	−0.347*	0.036	0.210*	−0.111	−0.521*
Church attendance					−0.019	−0.037†
Gender	−0.018	−0.018	−0.018	−0.021	−0.048	−0.048*
Age	−0.000	−0.001	0.008	0.095*	0.018	0.038†
R^2	0.281		0.073		0.368	
(N =)	1617		2097		2194	

	1988		1991		1994	
	B	Beta	B	Beta	B	Beta
Constant	0.810		0.960		−0.544	
National economy, forward			−0.013	−0.027	−0.002	−0.007
National economy, backward	0.030	0.069*	0.047	0.074*	0.039	0.051*
Own economy, forward					0.009	0.012
Own economy, backward	0.061	0.059*	0.022	0.022	0.027	0.023
Subjective social class	−0.152	−0.152*			0.089	0.091*
Left–right dimension	−0.094	−0.418*	−0.118	−0.540*	0.137	0.616*
Church attendance	−0.044	−0.080*	−0.035	−0.069*	0.053	0.099*
Gender	−0.033	−0.033	0.014	0.015	−0.020	−0.021
Age	0.030	0.064*	0.021	0.046†	0.010	0.021
R^2	0.290		0.333		0.472	
(N =)	1638		1879		1514	

TABLE 9.3. (*Contd.*)

	1998	
	B	Beta
Constant	0.350	
National economy, forward	0.029	0.077[†]
National economy, backward	0.057	0.136*
Own economy, forward		
Own economy, backward	0.023	0.030
Subjective social class		
Left–right dimension	−0.090	−0.418*
Church attendance	−0.003	−0.006
Gender	0.019	0.019
Age	0.068	0.152*
R^2		0.263
($N =$)		632

*$p < 0.01$; [†]$p < 0.05$

Vote: Party choice in recent Riksdag election (1976, 1985, 1988, 1991, 1998: 1 = SAP, 0 = other parties; 1982: 1 = CP, FP, 0 = other parties; 1994: 1 = MOD, FPL, CP, KD, 0 = other parties).

National economy, forward: 'How do you think that the economic conditions in Sweden will develop in the next few (two or three years, 12 months) years?' (1 = much worse, 2 = no change, 3 = much better).

National economy, backward: 'How has, in your opinion, the Swedish economy changed in the last two or three years (12 months, 1998)?' (1= got worse, 3 = remained about the same, 5 = improved).

Own economy, forward: 'Looking forward two or three years (12 months, 1998), do you believe that your personal economic situation will improve, remain about the same or that it will get worse?' (1 = get worse, 3 = remain about the same, 5 = improve).

Own economy, backward: 'Comparing your own current economic situation not to what it was two or three years ago (12 months, 1998), has it improved, remained about the same or has it got worse?' (1 = got worse, 2 = remained about the same, 3 = improved).

Subjective social class: 'As you know, references is sometimes made to the existence of different classes as societal groups. Is there any class or societal group that you usually think you belong to? Which societal class are you thinking of?' (0 = working class, 1 = middle class).

Left–right dimension: Own position on a scale from 0 (far to the left) to 10 (far to the right).

Church attendance: (1 = never, 2 = more seldom, 3 = a few times a year, 4 = at least once a month).

Gender: (0 = female, 1 = male).

Age: (1 = 18–34 years old, 2 = 35–49 years old, 3 = 50–64 years old, 4 = 65 years old or higher).

analysis in the appendix. When we use data from the pre-election survey the hypothesis of a positive relationship between support for the incumbent parties and forward-looking assessments of the national economy receives support in two of the four elections (1976 and 1991), one has the right sign (1994), and one has the wrong sign (1982). For personal judgements we have only data for two elections. In 1976 we observe support for the hypothesis. In 1994 the sign is correct, but the effect is statistically insignificant. Turning to the post-election data it is striking that all six coefficients are negative, although only two of them are negative and significant, national evaluations in 1976 and 1982. In sum, these results are more encouraging for the hypothesis on forward oriented economic voting than the results for the merged pre-and post-election data in Table 9.3. Finally, we have replaced the vote for the two incumbent parties at the time of the 1982 election with the coalition that governed for most of the period. Adding the Conservative Party to the incumbents does not significantly change the impact of the economic variables at this election.

Summing up our findings from the Swedish data, we find that economic voting is persistent and is not dependent on which of the political blocs are in power. The data give support to the hypothesis of backward-looking incumbency oriented voting with reference to evaluations of the national economy. Evaluations of personal economy are not strongly and consistently related to the vote. The Swedish data cover a period of more than twenty years. Within this time frame there is no discernible trend towards an increase in economic voting in the electorate.

9.3.4   The Netherlands

The Dutch election studies contain only mediated economic survey items. The items ask voters to judge if government policy has a positive or negative impact on personal or collective conditions. We know that mediated items, more than simple items, are affected by political rationalization: Voters who support parties in government are likely to credit government for good economic outcomes while supporters of the opposition parties will be inclined to blame the government for economic troubles. We have not made attempts to sort out the causality of such rationalizations, and the estimates should be interpreted with caution. The items are all about retrospective evaluations (see the footnote to Table 9.4).

A further complication of the Dutch case is the often encompassing coalition governments, which include parties of very different political and ideological stripes. This can render the effects of left–right ideology and religiosity on voting choice quite misleading. This is a general problem that occurs where one wants to compare the effects of economics on support for incumbent party or parties with the impact of other variables that affect the vote. It is theoretically meaningful to use the division between in and out parties for the former question, but it is not equally relevant for the second question. This can clearly be seen in Table 9.4. In 1986 and 1989 there is a strong positive impact of ideology on vote choice. At both elections the centre–right was in power with Lubbers of the Christian CDA as prime minister and the liberal VVD in the coalition. In 1994 Lubbers and CDA were still in power, both with the social democratic PvdA as partners in the coalition. This reverses the sign of the coefficient for ideology, and reduces its size. Finally, in 1998 Kok of the PvdA presided over an ideologically heterogeneous coalition that included VVD and D66, a party slightly to the left of centre. This weakens the impact of ideology on the dichotomous vote variable to nearly insignificance. In this election, the impact of religiosity reaches a record strength,

TABLE 9.4. *Economic voting in the Netherlands. Vote for incumbent parties. OLS regression*

	1986		1989	
	B	Beta	B	Beta
Constant	−0.606		−0.631	
Effect of government policy on general economic situation in last four years	0.092	0.132*	0.145	0.181*
Effect of government policy on personal economy in last four years	−0.008	−0.011	0.052	0.077†
Effect of government policy on employment in the Netherlands in last four years	0.147	0.227*	0.042	0.064
Subjective social class	0.112	0.109*	0.139	0.125*
Left–right dimension	0.070	0.327*	0.076	0.357*
Church attendance	0.000	0.002	−0.011	−0.026
Gender	0.011	0.011	−0.075	−0.075†
Age	0.012	0.026		
R^2	0.354		0.286	
($N =$)	592		705	

	1994		1998	
	B	Beta	B	Beta
Constant	0.047		0.484	
Effect of government policy on general economic situation in last four years	0.101	0.138*	0.098	0.122*
Effect of government policy on personal economy in last four years	0.062	0.084*	0.035	0.051†
Effect of government policy on employment in the Netherlands in last four years	0.085	0.113*	0.040	0.055†
Subjective social class	−0.110	−0.097*	0.031	0.026
Left–right dimension	−0.034	−0.143*	0.015	0.061†
Church attendance	0.058	0.126*	−0.186	−0.421*
Gender	0.017	0.017	−0.048	−0.050†
Age	0.099	0.207*	−0.016	−0.035
R^2	0.154		0.218	
($N =$)	1122		1462	

*$p < 0.01$; †$p < 0.05$

Vote: Party voted for in recent elections (1986: 1 = CDA and VVD, 0 = other parties; 1989: 1 = CDA and VVD, 0 = other parties; 1994: 1 = CDA and PvdA, 0 = other parties; 1998: 1 = PvdA, VVD and D66, 0 = other parties).

Effect of government policy on general economic situation: 'I would now like to ask a few questions concerning what you think about the policies that the government has followed during the past four years. First the general economic situation, do you think that governmental policies have a positive, negative or hardly any effect?' (1 = negative effect, 2 = hardly any effect, 3 = positive effect

Effect of government policy on personal economy: 'And your personal financial situation, has this been positively, negatively or hardly effected by governmental policies?' (1 = negative effect, 2 = hardly any effect, 3 = positive effect).

TABLE 9.4. (*Contd.*)

Effect of government policy on employment: 'And employment in the Netherlands, do you think that governmental policies have had a positive, negative, or hardly any effect?' (1 = negative effect, 2 = hardly any effect, 3 = positive effect).

Subjective social class: 'One sometimes speak of the existence of various social classes or groups. If you were to assign yourself to a particular social class, which would that be? (0 = working class, 1 = middle class).

Left–right dimension: 'It is often said of political beliefs that they are leftist or rightist. Here you have a scale that runs from left to right. When you think of your own political beliefs, where would you place a mark' (Scale ranging from 1 (left) to 10 (right)).

Church attendance: 'How often do you attend religious services?' (1 = never, 2 = several times a year, 3 = at least once a month, 4 = (almost) daily).

Gender: (0 = female, 1 = male).

Age: (1 = 17–34 years old, 2 = 35–49 years old, 3 = 50–64 years old, 4 = 65 years old or higher).

which is explained by the fact that CDA is the dominant party in the opposition while the party at previous time points was in a coalition with major non-religious parties.

The effect of evaluations of the government's impact on the general economic situation is strong and in line with the incumbency hypothesis for all years. The effect of assessments of government's policy on national unemployment is somewhat weaker, but is generally in line with the hypothesis. The assessment of the effect of government policy on personal economy is of about the same magnitude as on national unemployment, with the exception of 1986 where the coefficient has the wrong sign (but is not significant). In sum, the findings for the mediated evaluation items for the Netherlands demonstrate that economic evaluations matter, and that especially retrospective judgements of the overall status of the national economy are important for the support of incumbent parties. There is also some effect of evaluations of personal economic judgements on the vote, but these are weaker than the assessments of the national economy. Again, the empirical strength of the relationship does not show an upwards movement over time.

9.3.5 Norway

Norway has a complex multiparty system. Labour has dominated government since the 1930s. In the post-war period Labour has always formed single-party governments; after 1961 these governments have always been of the minority variety. The non-socialist (bourgeois) parties normally form coalition governments. The most recent bourgeois governments have been in minority in the Storting. The data for Norway cover four elections, 1985–97. Following the defeat of Labour in 1981 the Conservative Party formed a minority government which soon was expanded into a majority coalition with the agrarian Centre Party and the Christian People's Party. These parties were able to remain in power after the election of 1985. This was a period of economic boom, partly fuelled by the implementation of market deregulation policies. The economic evaluations all show a positive balance (this is the difference between positive and negative evaluations; the tables are not shown). The balance is especially strong for retrospective evaluations of the national economy where 9 per cent say that the economy has become worse, and 48 per cent say that the economy has improved. Two of the economic items, prospective and retrospective personal concerns, are not related to support for the incumbent parties, while retrospective collective judgements and evaluation of risk of unemployment have positive links to government support (see Table 9.5).

Labour came back in government in 1986 after the coalition government lost a crucial vote in the Storting. In 1989 the bourgeois coalition returned to power, but had to give way to a new Labour government in 1990 partly due to conflicts over Norwegian membership in the EU which was slowly moving up on the national agenda. The Conservative Party was strongly in favour of membership while the Centre Party was vehemently opposed. More significant for our research, in 1989 there were clear signs that the economy was on a downward slope, and in the next four years would lead Norway into the highest unemployment levels that the country had experienced in the post-war period. The economic problems show up in the economic evaluations of voters, which by now mostly have a negative balance, with an exception for future evaluation of personal finances which has a slightly positive balance. In 1989 only the retrospective collective evaluations are strongly related to voting for the incumbent party, while prospective personal assessments reached a significance at the 0.05-level

TABLE 9.5. *Economic voting in Norway. Vote for incumbent parties. OLS regression*

	1985		1989	
	B	Beta	B	Beta
Constant	−0.754		0.386	
Prospects on own economic situation	0.010	0.013	0.030	0.048[†]
Retrospective evaluations on own economic situation	0.012	0.021	0.019	0.039
Retrospective evaluations on economic situation in the country	0.044	0.079*	0.035	0.090*
Fear of becoming unemployed	0.045	0.069*	0.006	0.011
Subjective social class	0.161	0.164*	−0.186	−0.205*
Left–right dimension	0.123	0.491*	−0.058	−0.262*
Church attendance	0.091	0.124*	−0.035	−0.053[†]
Gender	−0.011	−0.011	−0.028	−0.031
Age	0.028	0.054[†]	0.061	0.128*
R^2	0.434		0.193	
($N =$)	1397		1523	

(Continued)

TABLE 9.5. (*Contd.*)

	1993		1997	
	B	Beta	B	Beta
Constant	0.399		0.374	
Prospects on own economic situation	0.012	0.018	0.050	0.075*
Retrospective evaluations on own economic situation	0.010	0.020	0.021	0.038
Retrospective evaluations on economic situation in the country	0.072	0.149*	−0.002	−0.003
Fear of becoming unemployed	−0.010	−0.020	−0.007	−0.012
Subjective social class	−0.127	−0.135*		
Left–right dimension	−0.058	−0.238*	−0.058	−0.273*
Church attendance	−0.051	−0.080*	−0.036	−0.058[†]
Gender	0.002	0.002	0.011	0.012
Age	0.026	0.053[†]	0.038	0.079*
R^2		0.130		0.083
($N =$)		1610		1784

*$p < 0.01$; [†] $p < 0.05$

Vote: 'Which party or list did you vote for?' (1985: 1 = Conservative, Christian People's Party and Agrarian Party, 0 = other parties; 1989, 1993 and 1997: 1 = Labor, 0 = other parties).

Prospects on own economic situation: 'Let's think forward to the immediate future. Do you believe that your personal financial situation will be about the same as it is now, better than now, or do you feel that it will be worse than it is now?' (1 = worse than now, 2 = about the same as now, 3 = better than now).

Retrospective evaluations on own economic situation: 'We are interested in knowing something about people's current financial situation. Would you say that your financial situation and that of your household is better or worse than it was a year ago?' (1 = worse, 2 = same, 3 = better).

Retrospective evaluation on economic situation in the country: 'Would you say that over the past twelve months, the state of the economy in Norway has got better, stayed about the same, or got worse?' (1 = worse, 2 = about the same, 3 = better).

Fear of becoming unemployed: 'Do you or do you not fear that you yourself or a member of your household may experience unemployment within the next few years?' (1 = yes, 2 = maybe, 3 = no).

Subjective social class: (0 = working class, 1 = middle class).

Left–right dimension: In politics people sometimes talk of left and right. Where would you place yourself on a scale from 1 to 10 where 0 means the left and 10 means the right? (In 1997 the scale is 0 to 10).

Church attendance: (0 = never, 1 = 1–2 times a year, 3 = 3–5 times a year, 3 = 6–10 times a year, 4 = 11–15 times a year, 5 = 16–20 times a year, 6 => 20 times a year, 7 = often).

Gender: (0 = female, 1 = male).

Age: (1 = 18–34 years old, 2 = 35–49 years old, 3 = 50–65 years old, 4 = 65 years old or higher).

and retrospective assessments of personal finances and fear of unemployment were not associated with the vote (Table 9.5).

The economy reached bottom sometime in the first half of 1993 and was on the upturn in the months before the election. The economic evaluations achieve a positive balance at the time of the election, but only the retrospective assessment of the national economy are positively related to support for Labour (Table 9.5).

In 1997, the EU issue had receded, which allowed three of the non-socialist parties to present a competitive government alternative to Labour, and they had some success. The new Labour leader, Torbjørn Jagland, who replaced Gro Harlem Brundtland, decided to step down as a consequence of an election outcome that was slightly below the level of 1993, and would have placed the party in a difficult minority position in parliament. The outcome was a disappointment for the incumbent Labour Party especially when one takes the rapidly improving economy into account. Norway was moving fast into a new economic boom with unemployment falling rapidly. All economic evaluations are strongly positive. The positive balance of retrospective evaluations of the national economy is even stronger than in 1985, with only 2 per cent holding negative assessments and 47 per cent saying that the economy has improved. However, Labour did not benefit from the positive retrospective evaluations as Table 9.5 shows that the impact of egotropic and sociotropic retrospective evaluations is insignificant. In contrast to some of the previous findings, 1997 constitutes an example that prospective evaluations play a role. At the same time this is the only economic item that influences support for the incumbent party.

The findings for Norway show that economic evaluations influence the vote, but the impact is clearly erratic. The retrospective evaluation of the national economy is the most consistent dimension of economic voting, but even this dimension is without impact in the most recent election. With four elections covered by reasonably comparable indicators it is difficult to conclude for the time trend hypothesis, but there is nothing in the data that supports the conclusion that economic evaluations are becoming more important for the vote choice in Norway.

9.4 CONCLUSION

We have demonstrated that the European voter is also an economic voter in the sense that negative evaluations of the economy hurt the electoral fortunes of incumbent parties. Although the effects are quite consistent over time, we also find that political events and institutional factors account for some of the variations that we observe. The weak and irregular effects in Norway can be explained by the dominance of minority governments, a weak opposition, and, at least partly, the EU issue which dominated over economic concerns and probably reduced Labour's ability to benefit from the first stage of the economic recovery in the 1993 election. Similarly, under a different institutional context, the UK Conservative Party in 1997 had less success than Labour four years later to take advantage of an improving economy. These examples may suggest that institutions as well as embedded effects of political events influence the impact of economic evaluations on the vote. The most recent attempt at modelling institutional effects with relevant short-term political factors may then be a step in the right direction, although it makes the economic voting model more complex (Nadeau et al. 2002).

The verdict on the dimensional structure gives credits to most of the candidates: past and present, collectivist and egocentric concerns, unemployment, and economic growth, all play a role at some elections in some of the countries. Overall, judgements of the economy of the country seem to be more important than personal concerns, and the present and the past beat the future.

For those who expected that economic voting would be on the rise, the empirical results are disappointing. For the countries that we have access to time series data for, we find no trends towards an increase in economic voting. The reason for this may be methodological; it is very difficult to establish empirical equivalence of model across time, but also substantial factors may be at work. The economy moves in cycles. The 1970s, which is the starting point for many time series of economic evaluations, was the period of stagflation, putting economic issues to the top of the political agenda while the recent decade has seen a decline in inflation, although unemployment levels have remained high in many countries. The cyclical nature of the economy could render hypotheses derived from modernization theory difficult to validate in the timespan covered by the current investigation.

Finally, we observe that economic effects are of a considerable magnitude in a significant share of the elections, also when compared with the influences of cleavages and ideology. But we note that such comparisons are not always easy to make as coalition governments in some countries are very heterogeneous across social and ideological divides, which makes it difficult to compare hypotheses about incumbency support and general vote choice in the same model.

Notes

1. I thank Lars Grønflaten and Robert Ekle for research assistance
2. Denmark is not included in the present analysis due to lack of variables that are comparable across time.

APPENDIX

TABLE 9.A.1. *Economic voting in Sweden 1976*

	Pre-election study		Post-election study	
	B	Beta	B	Beta
Constant	0.739		1.275	
National economy, forward	0.036	0.058	−0.183	−314*
National economy, backward				
Own economy, forward	0.072	0.083[†]	−0.018	−0.019
Own economy, backward	0.057	0.079[†]	0.102	0.132*
Subjective social class	−0.211	−0.203*	−0.148	−0.143*
Left–right dimension	−0.094	−0.359*	−0.071	−0.264*
Church attendance				
Gender	−0.066	−0.065[†]	0.011	0.011
Age	0.006	0.013	−0.004	−0.008
R^2		0.271		0.362
($N =$)		774		843

$*p < 0.01$; $^†p < 0.05$

TABLE 9.A.2. *Economic voting in Sweden 1982*

	Pre-election study		Post-election study	
	B	Beta	B	Beta
Constant	−0.077		0.072	
National economy, forward	−0.004	−0.008	−0.058	−0.139*
National economy, backward	−0.031	−0.053	−0.007	−0.011
Own economy, forward				
Own economy, backward	0.044	0.044	0.059	0.059[†]
Subjective social class				
Left–right dimension	0.043	0.248*	0.026	0.152*
Church attendance				
Gender	−0.023	−0.028	−0.017	−0.021
Age	0.041	0.103*	0.032	0.084*
R^2		0.082		0.075
($N =$)		976		1121

$^†p < 0.05$; $*p < 0.01$

TABLE 9.A.3. *Economic voting in Sweden 1991*

	Pre-election study		Post-election study	
	B	Beta	B	Beta
Constant	0.800		1.050	
National economy, forward	0.028	0.057[†]	−0.043	−0.094*
National economy, backward	0.032	0.051	0.057	0.088*
Own economy, forward				
Own economy, backward	0.043	0.044	0.006	0.006
Subjective social class				
Left–right dimension	−0.120	−0.527*	−0.113	−0.534*
Church attendance	−0.044	−0.089*	−0.030	−0.058[†]
Gender	−0.004	−0.005	0.031	0.032
Age	0.030	0.067[†]	0.020	0.044
R^2		0.320		0.358
($N =$)		873		1006

*$p < 0.01$; [†]$p < 0.05$

TABLE 9.A.4. *Economic voting in Sweden 1994*

	Pre-election study		Post-election study	
	B	Beta	B	Beta
Constant	−0.626		−0.472	
National economy, forward	0.008	0.024	−0.011	−0.031
National economy, backward	0.056	0.063[†]	0.033	0.048
Own economy, forward	0.019	0.029	−0.007	−0.010
Own economy, backward	0.031	0.026	0.021	0.019
Subjective social class	0.093	0.094*	0.084	0.085*
Left–right dimension	0.135	0.599*	0.139	0.635*
Church attendance	0.051	0.096*	0.054	0.103*
Gender	−0.042	−0.043	−0.000	−0.001
Age	0.027	0.058[†]	−0.008	−0.018
R^2		0.451		0.506
($N =$)		781		733

*$p < 0.01$; [†]$p < 0.05$

10

Party Leaders and Party Choice

John Curtice and Sören Holmberg

10.1 INTRODUCTION

The character and outcome of elections depends on two things—how elections are fought by politicians and what motivations are brought to the voting decision by voters. Both are widely thought to have changed over recent decades. And one of the supposed consequences is that elections have become beauty contests in which voters decide who to vote for on the basis of which party leader they like most rather than which party they think has the best policies or will best represent their interests.

The changes in the motivations of voters that are supposed to have helped change elections into beauty contests have already been elaborated, systematically examined, and analysed in previous chapters. No longer, it is argued, are voters' hopes and aspirations determined by their place in the social structure of society and thus no longer do voters look to political parties to represent the social group to which they belong. Nor do voters have strong emotional attachments to political parties that motivate them to remain faithful to the same party over a lifetime any longer. Lacking such anchors and given the complexities of modern policy-making, voters may even find it difficult to sort out whether the government is to blame for the state of the economy or which party has the best policy. But what they can do is to decide which of the party leaders they like best, in much the same way as they make judgements every day about who they feel they can trust and of whom they need to be wary. Indeed in a complex world where politicians often have to deal with the unexpected, it would seem quite rational to decide how to vote on an assessment of the overall trustworthiness and competence of a party leader rather than the detailed promises made by a party at election time (Page 1978; Kinder 1986).

Meanwhile, if voters are in need of cues about how to vote, then the way that elections are fought certainly appears to have changed in such a way as to encourage voters to focus their attention on leaders (Butler and Ranney 1992; Swanson and Mancini 1996). Television has become the principal medium in which election campaigns are fought and the principal source of information that voters have about an election. Successful television requires two things—pictures and personality. So providing and projecting positive televisual images of their leaders has become more and more important to the way that parties fight their campaigns (Mughan 2000). At the same time, televised debates between party leaders have also become the centrepiece of many a country's election (Smith 1981; LeDuc et al. 1996: 45–8, Esaiasson and Håkansson 2002). Meanwhile party leaders have acquired greater control over the message that their party attempts to sell (Scarrow et al. 2000). In short party leaders have become the most accessible and prominent feature of election campaigns.

There seems every good reason to believe that what voters think of the party leaders should have become a more important influence on how they decide to vote. Television has brought the personalities of party leaders into voters' living rooms at a time when other possible considerations that voters might bring to bear appear either complex or irrelevant. We should then expect to find that party choice has become more closely aligned with leader preference—and that this remains the case even after taking into account the continued residual impact of such influences as social background, party identification, and party issue positions.

Yet, a little thought suggests the need for some circumspection. After all, voters are highly and increasingly cynical about politicians (Norris 1999; Pharr and Putnam 2000), and this alone might lead one to doubt whether voters have come to regard the personality of the party leaders as an important reason to vote one way rather than another. Moreover, there is an important paradox in much of the argument we have put forward so far (King 2002: 4–6). If leaders have indeed become both the most prominent feature of election campaigns and, as Scarrow et al. (2000) have argued, increasingly powerful within their own parties, then perhaps leaders have come increasingly to fashion their parties in their own image. The leader's policy becomes the party's policy. A competent leader creates the impression of a competent party. If that is the case then while we might find that vote choice and leader preference have become increasingly aligned, we will also discover that once we take into account other possible influences, and in particular evaluations of the parties' competence and issue positions, leader preference has no more influence on vote choice now than it did four or five decades ago. The power of the leader lies in their ability to lead and mould their party rather than their ability to appeal to the voters independently of their party.

Meanwhile we also need to bear another important consideration in mind. Throughout this book we have asked whether changes in the way that people vote might be better accounted for by variations in political structure and circumstance rather than trends in social structure. Certainly, how far voters are likely to regard their evaluations of the party leaders as a cue as to how to vote could well be expected to depend on the political structure in which an election is fought. Presidential elections clearly encourage voters to focus on personalities to a far greater degree than do parliamentary ones (McAllister 1996). Yet all of the countries that we are studying in this volume are parliamentary democracies. Moreover in some of our countries, who becomes prime minister depends on a process of post-election coalition formation. As a result voters cannot be sure that even if the party of the most popular leader does secure the most votes that person will necessarily become prime minister. So in these instances at least there is an even weaker incentive to vote on the basis of what voters think of the party leaders.

The political structure may matter in another way too. In particular, there would seem to be little reason to take into account the personality of the leaders of smaller parties in deciding how to vote, as they will have little or no chance of ever achieving the highest office in the land. Meanwhile, the importance of party leaders in how people decide to vote could also depend on the particular circumstances in which an election is fought (King 2002). If there are large differences between the parties in the ideological positions that they put forward, then this might be thought to give voters a stronger incentive to vote on the basis of issues rather than personalities. And perhaps voters will only take the personality of a leader into account when he or she is either particularly liked or especially disliked, and thus evokes a particularly strong reaction from the electorate. In any event if the influence of leaders depends on these kinds of political circumstance, then we might anticipate finding patterns other than a simple secular increase in the importance of leader evaluations.

Certainly there is no consensus in the existing literature that leaders have become an increasingly important influence on voters' choices. In Great Britain, for example, while a number of analysts have argued that evaluations of leaders matter (Butler and Stokes 1974; Graetz and McAllister 1987; Bean and Mughan 1989; Stewart and Clarke 1992; Clarke et al. 2000, 2004), relatively few have attempted to marshal systematically evidence that supports the claim that leader evaluations have become more important. One clear exception is Mughan (2000) who goes so far to argue that one consequence of the growing impact of leader evaluations was that they were decisive in winning the 1992 election for the Conservatives (see also Foley 2000). However, Bartle et al. dispute Mughan's claim (Crewe and King 1994) and argue that evaluations of the leaders have had little net impact on voters' choices at recent elections (Bartle et al. 1998; Bartle 2001; Bartle and Crewe 2002). In Germany, the defeat of the Christian Democrats in 1998 was widely attributed to voters' dislike of Helmut Kohl yet many an academic analysis has failed to demonstrate that evaluations of leaders have become more important (Kaase 1994; Klingemann and Wattenberg 1992; Brettschneider and Gabriel 2002). In Sweden, the independent effect of leader popularity on vote has consistently been found to be very small (Holmberg 1981; Holmberg and Oscarsson 2004). Indeed, even in the United States, there is considerable dispute about the importance of candidate evaluations in presidential elections with those who attest to their importance (Stokes 1966; Kelley and Mirer 1974; Rosenborg et al. 1986) balanced by those who either doubt that they are important or argue that they have at least not become any more important (Miller and Shanks 1982; Shanks and Miller 1990; Wattenberg 1991; Bartels 2002).

Meanwhile, there has as yet been little attempt to examine the proposition that leaders have to come to matter more by testing it in a consistent fashion across a number of countries at once. Filling that gap is the principal aim of this chapter. Equally there has not been much attempt to ascertain the circumstances under which leadership does matter and when not (but see King 2002; Aarts et al. forthcoming), such as whether it matters more for larger parties than for smaller ones. Undertaking such an analysis is our second key task. First, we test a relatively simple proposition: Are voters more likely to vote nowadays for the party of the leader they like best? If they do not, it seems unlikely that leadership evaluations have come to have a greater influence on vote. We then subject the proposition to a stricter test, that is whether leadership evaluations have come to matter more, after we have controlled for some of the other influences on voting behaviour outlined in the earlier chapters. In so doing, we also look at whether the impact of leadership evaluations varies systematically with political structure or circumstance.

10.2   DATA AND METHODOLOGY

Most of the surveys we are analysing in this book asked their respondents to rate each of the main party leaders, most often on an eleven-point scale. The wording of the questions used to administer the scales varied somewhat from country to country; some, for example, asked respondents how good a party leader was, others how much they liked or disliked each leader, but in each case the question elicited an overall summary judgement about each leader. Moreover, in most countries, exactly the same question was asked after each election, easing quite considerably our task of looking at trends over time within each country in the importance of leader evaluations. The biggest exception to these generalizations is Great Britain whose surveys have at different times asked different questions and used different length scales (if indeed a scale was administered at all). We thus need to be aware that some of the differences we find between elections in that country could be an artefact of differences in the way leadership evaluations were acquired, though we aim to minimize that problem by looking only at standardized scores for that country. Meanwhile we should note too that leadership evaluations were not collected in Sweden or Norway until the late 1970s or early 1980s or indeed in the Netherlands until the mid-1980s, thereby reducing the length of the time series that is available to us to analyse for those countries.

But even if we have comparable data about leader evaluations over time, this does not mean that it is easy to examine how the impact of leadership evaluations has changed from election to election. If leadership evaluations influence the way that people vote then we would certainly expect voters to be more likely to support a party if they have a high regard for its leader. Moreover, other things being equal we would expect this likelihood to increase if voters are taking greater cognisance of leaders in deciding how to vote. But such evidence is far from being sufficient to prove that leadership evaluations influence voting behaviour. People may after all decide they like a party leader because they like and perhaps even identify with the party of which a particular leader is the head. Far from being an independent influence on voting behaviour, leadership evaluations may be a consequence of a voting decision that has been made for other reasons. We thus need to be able to demonstrate that leadership evaluations have an influence on voting behaviour independently of whatever people think about a party. Fortunately most of our surveys included questions that acquired evaluations of what people think about the various parties in similar fashion to the questions that were asked about party leaders, and we can thus include these in models of voting behaviour alongside our leader evaluations. But in so doing we need to be aware that this could potentially be too strict a test of the impact of leadership evaluations on voting behaviour. For just as people's views of a leader may be coloured by their view of a party, so they may come to have a favourable view of a party because they like its current leader. However, the risks of this approach are clearly less than not taking into account at all the possibility that leader evaluations are simply the product of party evaluations.

In any event, including party evaluations in our models also serves a further purpose. Leadership evaluations come at the end of the chain of causality being analysed in this book, and so ideally we wish to ascertain how much impact they have independently of the various other influences we have been analysing. We can anticipate that, *inter alia*, party evaluations will reflect some of the other more short-term influences on people's views about the parties, such as retrospective evaluations and issue positions. Even so, we are also able to include in our models direct indicators of three other influences considered in earlier chapters: social structure (measured as social class, religious affiliation, and church attendance), party identification, and value position (usually measured by left–right self-placement). However, as we have no immediate interest here in the relationship between these measures and vote choice, the results for those variables are not reported.

Our analyses typically take the form of a regression model of vote choice for each party at each election, including all those parties that typically won at least 5 per cent of the vote at elections during the period we are analysing. Our dependent variable in each case is thus a dichotomous dependent variable that has the value 1 where the respondent voted for the party in question, and 0 if the respondent voted for a different party, and thus we opt to use logistic regression. Those who said they did not vote are excluded from the analyses.

10.3   A SIMPLE ANALYSIS

We begin, however, by undertaking a simple analysis. To what degree are people more likely to vote for a party if they like its leader? And is there any evidence that this likelihood has strengthened over time? To answer these questions we show in Table 10.1, the results of simple logistic regressions of vote choice against leader evaluations. Note that, for each country, the results for the larger parties appear on the left-hand side of the relevant table, with the smaller parties appearing further to the right.

As we anticipated, it is indeed usually the case that the more someone favourably rates a party leader, the more likely they are to vote for that leader's party. Indeed, every single one of the entries in Table 10.1 is statistically significant. But beyond this two important patterns emerge. The first, and more important, is that there is little or no evidence of a secular increase in the strength of the relationship. In Germany, for example, the coefficients for all three parties were much the same in 1965 as they were in 1998. In Denmark, the coefficients for all of the parties were not that dissimilar in 1998 to what they were in 1971. And in Sweden, the coefficients were much the same in 1982 as they were in 1998. Nowhere is there evidence of a clear and consistent increase in the strength of the relationship. While on its own this does not dispose of the possibility that leadership evaluations have come to have an increasing influence on voting behaviour, it certainly casts some considerable doubt that this indeed is what has happened.

The second pattern to note is that it appears as though leader evaluations are relatively more important for the two largest parties in those countries that are closest to having systems of alternating majority government, Great Britain and Germany. Between 1964 and 2001 power alternated in Great Britain between single-party governments formed by the Conservatives or Labour. And at each of the six elections for which we have data for all three parties in Great Britain, the logistic coefficients for the Conservative and Labour parties are higher than those for the Liberals/Liberal Democrats. Meanwhile, in Germany the SPD and CDU/CSU have usually been the dominant parties in majority coalitions whose chancellor candidates and component parties have been declared in advance of election day. In seven out of nine West German elections, evaluations of FDP leaders are less strongly correlated with vote than are either CDU/CSU or SPD leader evaluations. In contrast, in our remaining four countries there is no systematic evidence that evaluations of the leaders of smaller parties matter less than those of larger party leaders (or equally any evidence that they matter more). It appears that where an election more closely approximates a choice between two alternative heads of government voters may be a little more inclined to take note of the characteristics of the principal protagonists.

So, voters tend to vote for the party of leaders they like. And this seems to be particularly true if a leader is clearly a prospective head of government. But there

TABLE 10.1. *Simple logistic regressions of leader evaluations and vote*

Cell entries are logistic parameter coefficients
Great Britain

	Conservatives	Labour	Liberal/Alliance/ Liberal Democrats
1964	1.06	1.23	na
1966	1.07	1.63	na
1970	1.15	1.51	na
1974 (F)	1.98	1.92	1.27
1974 (O)	1.68	2.24	1.18
1979	1.80	1.54	1.47
1983	1.08	1.06	na
1987	1.62	1.46	na
1992	2.10	1.17	0.84
1997	1.76	1.29	0.87
2001	1.57	2.08	1.01

In 1964–70, leadership evaluations are measured by an eleven-point scale constructed from open-ended like/dislike data. In 1974–9 and 1997–2001, figures are based on eleven-point rating scales, in 1983 a four-point scale, and in 1987 and 1992, five-point scales. Because of these differences all of the scales have been standardized.

Germany

	SPD	CDU/CSU	FDP
1961	0.31	0.51	0.15
1965	0.53	0.55	0.48
1969	na	na	na
1973	1.08	0.54	na
1976	1.03	0.99	0.65
1980	0.85	0.83	0.86
1983	0.76	0.84	0.39
1987	0.62	0.65	0.34
1990	0.50	0.91	0.25
1994	0.57	0.65	0.33
1998	0.48	0.43	0.50

Netherlands

	Labour	Christian Democrats	Liberals	D66
1986	0.59	0.51	0.52	0.75
1989	0.89	0.75	0.55	0.70
1994	0.44	0.46	0.57	0.46
1998	0.44	0.74	0.61	0.39

(*Continued*)

TABLE 10.1. (*Contd.*)

Denmark

	Social Democrats	Liberals	Conservatives	Socialist People's
1971	0.61	0.81	0.46	0.56
1973	0.72	0.95	0.56	na
1994	0.54	0.67	0.72	0.62
1998	0.60	0.67	0.37	0.67

Data on leader evaluations are unavailable for elections between 1973 and 1994.
na = not available

Norway

	Labour	Conservative	Christian	Agrarian	Progress
1981	0.81	0.88	1.10	0.84	0.72
1985	0.79	0.69	0.98	0.95	0.78
1989	0.77	0.58	0.88	0.96	0.73
1993	0.58	0.67	0.78	0.70	0.93
1997	0.58	0.69	0.73	0.74	0.74

Coefficients have been multiplied by 10.

Sweden

	Social Democrats	Moderate	Centre	Liberals	Left
1982	0.67	0.75	0.71	0.60	0.62
1985	0.67	0.79	0.70	0.57	0.87
1988	0.75	0.76	0.81	0.80	0.79
1991	0.71	0.77	0.46	0.78	0.61
1994	0.76	0.74	0.69	0.83	0.58
1998	0.60	0.80	0.85	0.65	0.63

is no sign, so far, that this is any more true now than it was two or three decades ago. Still, perhaps leader evaluations will be found to have become relatively more important once we have taken other possible influences into account. It is to that possibility that we now turn.

10.4   A MORE COMPLEX ANALYSIS

The results of our more complex analysis of the impact of leader evaluations on vote choice are presented in Table 10.2. It shows the regression coefficients and the associated standard errors for leadership evaluations after including the full range of control variables that, we indicated earlier, are intended to capture other possible influences on the vote. Those coefficients that are not significant at

TABLE 10.2. *The Partial impact of leader evaluations on vote choice*

Cell entries are logistic parameter coefficients. Entries in italics are not significant at the 5% level.

Great Britain

	Conservatives		Labour		Liberal/Alliance/ Liberal Democrats	
	Coefficient	Standard Error	Coefficient	Standard Error	Coefficient	Standard Error
1964	0.42	0.13	0.66	0.16	na	na
1966	0.58	0.14	0.72	0.15	na	na
1970	0.40	0.16	0.65	0.18	na	na
1974(F)	0.77	0.17	0.37	0.19	0.46	0.15
1974(O)	0.53	0.15	*0.39*	*0.20*	*0.17*	*0.14*
1979	0.35	0.17	*0.10*	*0.18*	0.32	0.08
1983	0.47	0.13	0.54	0.08	na	na
1987	0.49	0.08	0.29	0.08	na	na
1992	0.66	0.19	*0.13*	*0.15*	0.37	0.17
1997	0.48	0.15	0.33	0.12	*−0.04*	*0.12*
2001	*0.32*	*0.17*	0.75	0.18	*0.20*	*0.14*

Controls: Social class, religion, church attendance (except 2001), left–right position (except 1964–70), party ID, party evaluation.

Germany

	SPD		CDU/CSU		FDP	
	Coefficient	Standard Error	Coefficient	Standard Error	Coefficient	Standard Error
1961	0.15	0.06	0.33	0.05	*−0.04*	*0.06*
1965	0.30	0.05	0.17	0.06	*−0.04*	*0.09*
1969	na	na	na	na	na	na
1972	0.43	0.14	0.24	0.07	na	na
1976	0.28	0.14	0.26	0.11	*0.22*	*0.15*
1980	*0.14*	*0.11*	*0.09*	*0.08*	0.58	0.17
1983	*0.19*	*0.10*	0.25	0.09	*−0.14*	*0.10*
1987	*0.12*	*0.07*	*0.03*	*0.07*	*0.08*	*0.09*
1990	*0.05*	*0.09*	0.38	0.14	*−0.01*	*0.10*
1994	0.29	0.08	*0.01*	*0.08*	*−0.15*	*0.10*
1998	0.23	0.06	0.21	0.06	0.30	0.12

Controls: Social class, religion, church attendance (except 1961), left–right position (except 1961–72 and 1980), party ID (except 1961, 1965), party evaluation.

(*Continued*)

TABLE 10.2. (*Contd.*)

Netherlands

	Labour		Christian Democrats		Liberals		D66	
	Coefficient	Standard Error	Coeffi-cient	Standard Error	Coeffi-cient	Standard Error	Coeffi-cient	Standard Error
1986	*0.07*	*0.20*	0.28	0.13	*0.12*	*0.18*	*0.19*	*0.30*
1989	No party evaluation scores available							
1994	*0.17*	*0.11*	−0.11	0.09	0.15	0.09	*0.00*	*0.09*
1998	*0.12*	*0.09*	0.08	0.12	0.22	0.09	*0.02*	*0.08*

Controls: Social class, religion, church attendance, left–right position, party ID, party evaluation.

Denmark

	Social Democrats		Liberals		Conservatives		Socialist People's	
	Coeffi-cient	Standard Error	Coeffi-cient	Standard Error	Coeffi-cient	Standard Error	Coeffi-cient	Standard Error
1971	0.22	0.04	*0.14*	*0.08*	−0.05	0.07	−0.10	*0.11*
1973	*0.08*	*0.09*	*0.14*	*0.21*	0.05	0.14	na	na
1994	*0.08*	*0.06*	0.34	0.10	0.48	0.12	*0.19*	*0.10*
1998	0.16	0.04	0.13	0.06	−0.08	0.05	0.07	0.07

Controls: Social class (except 1973), church attendance (1971 only), left–right position (except 1971, 1973), party ID (except 1971), party evaluation.
na = not available

Norway

	Labour		Conservative	
	Coefficient	Standard Error	Coefficient	Standard Error
1981	*0.12*	*0.08*	*0.11*	*0.11*
1985	*0.05*	*0.07*	*−0.07*	*0.07*
1989	0.22	0.06	*0.00*	*0.06*
1993	0.14	0.06	0.18	0.07
1997	*0.05*	*0.01*	*0.13*	*0.07*

	Christian		Agrarian		Progress	
	Coefficient	Standard Error	Coefficient	Standard Error	Coefficient	Standard Error
1981	0.41	0.17	*0.03*	*0.17*	*0.11*	*0.15*
1985	*0.03*	*0.11*	*0.23*	*0.13*	*0.02*	*0.12*
1989	0.20	0.11	*0.14*	*0.12*	0.18	0.08
1993	*0.02*	*0.11*	0.18	0.07	0.30	0.12
1997	*0.10*	*0.08*	*0.15*	*0.09*	*0.14*	*0.08*

Controls: Social class, church attendance, left–right position, party ID, party evaluation.
All entries are multiplied by 10.

TABLE 10.2. (*Contd.*)

Sweden

	Social Democrats		Moderate	
	Coefficient	Standard Error	Coefficient	Standard Error
1982	*0.06*	*0.05*	*−0.07*	*0.07*
1985	*0.07*	*0.06*	*0.07*	*0.08*
1988	*0.09*	*0.06*	*−0.02*	*0.08*
1991	*0.01*	*0.06*	0.17	0.07
1994	*0.12*	*0.06*	*−0.05*	*0.07*
1998	0.11	0.05	*0.01*	*0.08*

	Centre		Liberals		Left	
	Coefficient	Standard Error	Coefficient	Standard Error	Coefficient	Standard Error
1982	0.14	0.07	0.37	0.09	*0.03*	*0.09*
1985	*0.11*	*0.09*	−0.15	0.07	*0.13*	*0.12*
1988	*−0.09*	*0.09*	*0.13*	*0.09*	*0.02*	*0.12*
1991	−0.19	0.08	*−0.03*	*0.10*	*0.03*	*0.14*
1994	*0.12*	*0.11*	0.27	0.11	*−0.13*	*0.08*
1998	*0.11*	*0.14*	*0.07*	*0.12*	*0.11*	*0.08*

Controls: Social class, church attendance (except 1982), left–right position, party ID, party evaluation.

the 5 per cent level of probability are shown in italics. Occasionally, one or more of the additional control variables were not available, and details of which ones were included for each election for each country are given at the bottom of each section of the table. However, as discussed earlier, given our particular reliance on party evaluation scores as a mechanism for controlling for the impact of other short-term influences on voting behaviour, we did not undertake an analysis at all if an equivalent party evaluation score was not available.

Unsurprisingly, the introduction of our additional controls reduces the size of our coefficients considerably. For example, whereas the average coefficient for the British Conservative leaders in Table 10.1 was 1.53, here it is only 0.5. Apparently much of the simple bivariate relationship between leader evaluations and vote choice is the product of the tendency of other factors, both to influence how people vote and what they think of the leaders. We might perhaps however still be surprised at how small this analysis suggests the impact of leader evaluations actually is. Well, under half of the over 130 estimates of the impact of leader evaluations in Table 10.2 are statistically significant at the 5 per cent level, while only around a quarter are significant at the 1 per cent level. It seems that while evaluations of party leaders may matter a little to a party's electoral success, it cannot be said that they matter much.[1]

Meanwhile, there is no clearer evidence here that leadership evaluations have come to matter more than was evident from our earlier simpler analysis. For example, in Germany, two of the highest coefficients for the SPD and the CDU/CSU are found in the first two elections in our series, 1961 and 1965. In Denmark, the largest coefficient was recorded (for the Social Democrats) in our first election (1971), while the same is also true in Sweden (for the Liberals). Not that these instances are any evidence of a decline in the impact of leadership evaluations. Rather, there is simply no consistent evidence, or indeed much evidence at all of any kind of secular change in the importance of leadership evaluations.

One other important pattern that we discerned earlier is, however, confirmed: leadership evaluations matter more where something approaching a majoritarian system of alternating government is in place. The only parties for whom most of our estimates of the impact of leadership evaluations are significantly different from zero are the British Conservative and Labour parties together with the German SPD and the CDU/CSU. In our remaining four countries, in contrast, only in Denmark are the coefficients for the two largest parties statistically significant as much as half of the time. Indeed, with just two instances between them of a relationship that is significant at the 1 per cent level, it appears that it has been rare, indeed, for party leaders to matter much at all in the Netherlands, Norway, or Sweden (see also Holmberg and Oscarsson, forthcoming).

But what about the other possible ways in which we have suggested the political circumstances of an election might affect how important leader evaluations are in people's voting decisions? If there is little sign of a secular increase in the importance of leadership evaluations as a result of changes in voters' motivations, is there any evidence that their importance varies within a country according to how far apart the parties are ideologically, or to how popular or unpopular a party leader is? Do leaders only matter when the parties are close to each other ideologically or when a leader is particularly popular or unpopular? In addressing these questions we will focus on the two instances where we have found some consistent and substantial evidence that leadership evaluations do make some difference, that is, for the two largest parties in Britain and Germany.

In Fig. 10.1 overleaf we show how the size of our logistic coefficients for these parties has varied according to the degree of ideological polarization between them. Our measures of ideological polarization are derived from the same source as those in Chapter 2, but note that here our measure is simply the difference between the left–right position of the two major parties and does not take into account the position of the Liberals or the FDP. As we move from left to right along each graph, the scale of the ideological difference between the two main parties becomes greater, and it can be noted that the extent of that difference has varied considerably from one election to another in both countries, though especially so in Great Britain. The coefficients for the Conservatives/CDU are denoted with a diamond, while those for Labour/SPD are displayed with a square.

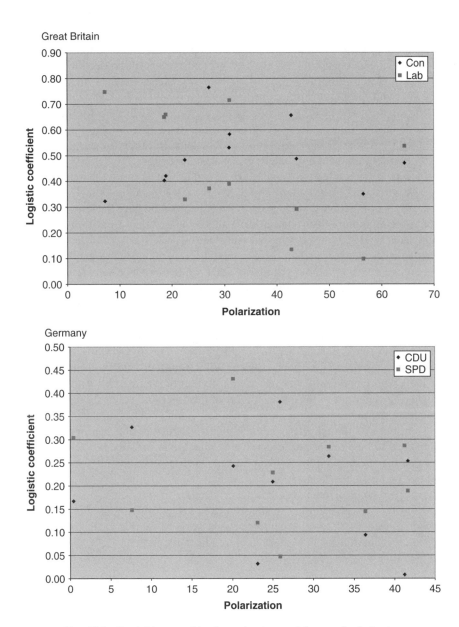

FIG. 10.1. *Partial impact of leader evaluations and degree of polarization*

Neither half of the figure gives any consistent support to the hypothesis. While the coefficient for Labour is highest of all at the British election with the lowest degree of polarization, in 2001, the coefficient for the Conservatives is lowest of all at the very same election. Meanwhile the impact of both the Conservative and the Labour leaders appears to have been around average at the election at which the ideological distance between the parties was greatest—in 1983. In Germany, the SPD and the CDU/CSU were closer to each other ideologically in 1961 and 1965 than they were at any subsequent election, yet the coefficients for the impact of leader evaluations at those elections do not particularly stand out. Meanwhile, we might note that similar inspection of the equivalent data for our four other countries does not lend any weight to the argument either.

In Fig. 10.2 overleaf, we undertake a similar analysis of the relationship between our coefficients and the popularity of the leader in question. To measure the latter we have looked at the proportion of people who gave the leader a rating above the midpoint of the relevant scale and compared that proportion with the equivalent figure for the relevant party evaluation scale. Thus, those leaders who were more likely to secure a positive evaluation from voters than were their party have a positive score on our popularity scale, while those who were less likely to secure a positive rating than their party have a negative rating.

Here too our analysis fails to uncover any apparent relationship. Even though British leaders have on occasion been either a lot more, or a lot less, popular than their party, neither circumstance appears to induce voters to take more notice of what they think of the leaders in deciding how to vote. In Germany, the largest coefficients are found for leaders, such as Willy Brandt in 1972 and Helmut Kohl in 1990, whose popularity was very similar to that of their parties. And again we might note that none of the results for any of the other four countries suggest that leaders matter more when they are particularly popular or unpopular.

So it looks as though that while the political structure of a country makes a difference to how important leader evaluations are in the way people decide to vote, with voters being more likely to take such evaluations into account for parties competing in a majoritarian system, there is rather less evidence that changes in political circumstances from election to election can consistently account for the variation in the importance of leader evaluations. For the most part it appears that the variation from one election to another in the importance of leader evaluations is little more than trendless fluctuation.

10.5 ARE LEADERS SHAPING THEIR PARTIES?

We noted earlier in this chapter, however, one potential problem with the way that we have set about our analysis. If leaders become the prism through which the message of their party is communicated, and if they also tend to become more powerful within their parties, then we might fail to ascertain whether leader

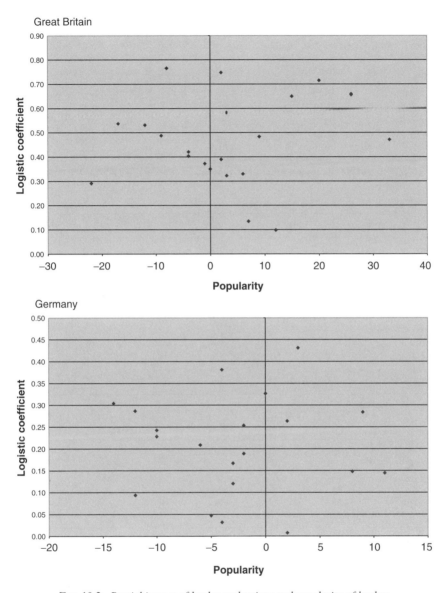

FIG. 10.2. *Partial impact of leader evaluations and popularity of leaders*

evaluations have had greater influence simply because people's evaluations of the parties have become increasingly influenced by their evaluation of the leaders. Such a trend would mean there is increasingly little left for leader evaluations to explain in the statistical analysis that we have undertaken.

TABLE 10.3. *Leader and party evaluation correlations*

Great Britain

	Conservatives	Labour	Liberals/Alliance/Liberal Democrats
1974(F)	0.77	0.77	0.72
1974(O)	0.71	0.80	0.72
1979	0.73	0.69	0.65
1997	0.71	0.75	0.70
2001	0.66	0.80	0.62

Figures calculated only for those years in which eleven-point scales were administered to respondents.

Germany

	SPD	CDU/CSU	FDP
1961	0.45	0.67	0.19
1965	0.61	0.63	0.62
1969	na	na	na
1972	0.87	0.79	na
1976	0.81	0.82	0.65
1980	0.77	0.83	0.68
1983	0.73	0.82	0.68
1987	0.76	0.86	0.59
1990	0.71	0.80	0.46
1994	0.68	0.82	0.61
1998	0.67	0.70	0.56

na = not available

Netherlands

	Labour	Christian Democrats	Liberals	D66
1986	0.81	0.72	0.72	0.64
1989	na	na	na	na
1994	0.68	0.63	0.69	0.70
1998	0.62	0.65	0.72	0.52

na = not available

Denmark

	Social democrats	Liberals	Conservatives	Socialist People's
1971	0.69	0.73	0.61	0.46
1973	0.69	0.79	0.67	na
1994	0.69	0.82	0.69	0.70
1998	0.78	0.82	0.57	0.72

na = not available

TABLE 10.3. (*Contd.*)

Norway

	Labour	Conservative	Christian	Agrarian	Progress
1981	0.77	0.84	0.77	0.74	0.82
1985	0.77	0.77	0.72	0.64	0.76
1989	0.70	0.63	0.71	0.63	0.77
1993	0.69	0.66	0.70	0.77	0.76
1997	0.72	0.69	0.75	0.80	0.83

Sweden

	Social Democrats	Moderate	Centre	Liberals	Left
1982	0.82	0.79	0.77	0.70	0.68
1985	0.83	0.83	0.71	0.76	0.67
1988	0.80	0.81	0.71	0.76	0.66
1991	0.77	0.81	0.67	0.77	0.58
1994	0.80	0.80	0.67	0.75	0.64
1998	0.75	0.75	0.62	0.68	0.66

But if parties have come to be fashioned in the image of their leaders then we would expect voters' ratings of leaders and parties to have become more similar to each other. Table 10.3 examines this possibility by showing the correlation coefficient between party and leader rating for each party and each election. Nowhere is there any consistent evidence of an increase in the strength of the correlation. Denmark perhaps comes closest—three of the four parties show a (mostly small) secular increase in the size of the correlation, though even here the pattern is upset by the Conservatives. Everywhere else what is primarily notable is the consistency of the relationship between party and leader evaluations which rarely falls much below 0.6 or rises much above 0.8. There seems little reason after all to be concerned that we might have missed the growing importance of leadership evaluations simply because our analysis failed to take account of a growing impact of leader evaluations on party evaluations.

10.6 CONCLUSION

In this chapter we have looked at the last link in the chain of influences on voting behaviour that we have been examining in this book. If modernization theory is correct, then leader evaluations are just the kind of short-term influence that should have become more important over the last two or three decades. Yet, however, we have examined the proposition and found scant evidence in support of it. Voters' evaluations of party leaders appear to be as important or unimportant now as they were when they were first measured by the series of surveys we have been analysing. Nothing much seems to have changed.

Part of the reason for this appears to be that the importance of leaders is constrained by the political structure in which elections take place. We uncovered the strongest evidence that leaders matter where a parliamentary election comes closest to mimicking a presidential contest, that is when the next head of government is likely to be the leader of whichever of two large parties can win the most votes without the need to engage in significant post-election coalition bargaining. Of course there are too few countries included in our analysis here to demonstrate that this is indeed systematically the case, though it is in tune with the findings of other research (Curtice, forthcoming; Holmberg and Oscarsson, forthcoming). If the structure of the choice that is offered to voters is one that encourages them to think about the personalities of leaders then it appears they are more likely to do so. Nevertheless, even where that incentive does exist there is no reason to believe that it is any more powerful now than it was two or three decades ago.

On the other hand, we have found little evidence to support the argument that the political circumstances in which an election is fought have a systematic impact on the importance of leader evaluations in influencing the way voters vote. We cannot claim that leader evaluations consistently matter more when ideological differences are less apparent, or when leaders are particularly popular or unpopular. To that degree our principal alternative explanation of why the importance of leader evaluations might fluctuate from election to election has cast little light on our subject. The impact of leaders is, it seems, as variable and unpredictable as are human personalities themselves.

Acknowledgement

The authors are deeply indebted to Sarinder Hunjan of the Social Statistics Laboratory, University of Strathclyde, for running the hundreds of models that underpin this chapter.

Notes

1. Of course the validity of this statement depends on the merits of the controls that are used in the analysis. In particular, some readers may question the inclusion of party identification as a control variable on the grounds that it is, and always has been, too close to vote in most European countries (Thomassen 1976) and that this could be even more true now if party identification has declined as an influence. The coefficients in Table 10.2 are indeed, in general, somewhat larger if party identification is omitted as a control. However, it remains the case that there is no evidence of a secular increase in the impact of leader evaluations. It also remains the case that leadership evaluations appear to matter more in Britain and Germany than they do elsewhere.

Readers may also wish to note that we have further attempted to corroborate the results reported in Table 10.2 by entering into our regression models the difference between a respondent's party evaluation and their leader evaluation instead of the absolute level of their leader and party evaluation. For the most part these models indicated that where Table 10.2 suggests leader evaluations were unimportant, having a higher leader evaluation than a party evaluation was often associated with a lower propensity to vote for a party. Indeed these models identified only three cases when those with a higher leader evaluation than party evaluation were more likely to vote for a party than were those who had a higher party evaluation than leader evaluation.

11

Modernization or Politics?

Jacques Thomassen

11.1 INTRODUCTION

The purpose of this book was to describe and explain the changes in electoral behaviour that occurred in six West European countries in the second half of the twentieth century. In our attempt to explain these changes we systematically tested two alternative theoretical approaches. The first approach is deduced from modernization theory. Modernization theory implies that over time the explanatory power for electoral behaviour of more or less stable structural variables as social class and religion will yield to more short-term factors. Modernization theory also predicts that the decision to vote or not to vote will become more dependent on instrumental orientations, which, other things being equal, will lead to a decline of turnout. The second, and alternative, theoretical approach predicts that changes and variations in patterns of voting behaviour are not due to secular processes in voting behaviour but to variations in the political–institutional context, both between countries and within countries between different elections.

In this final chapter we will summarize what we have learned with regard to the development of patterns of voting behaviour in these European countries and the validity of the two alternative theories. We will do this separately for the two successive decisions people have to make at election time and which at least analytically can be distinguished. First, the decision whether they will vote at all, and second, once they have decided to vote for which party or candidate they will vote.

11.2 TURNOUT

The essence of modernization theory as far as it is relevant for this book is that economic development, the growing size and diversity of the mass media, and the rise of the average level of education gave birth to a new citizen who is politically knowledgeable, self-confident, autonomous in his relations to traditional sources of influence, and politically active.

For two reasons this development is expected to have a negative effect on turnout. First, the increase of political skills will lead to a decreasing relevance of *electoral democracy*. Elections as an institutionalized way for citizens to exert political influence will become less important. Highly competent 'new citizens' are more and more inclined to manage their own affairs and to get themselves directly involved in the process of political decision-making. They will replace conventional forms of political participation by less conventional ones. Political activities directly or indirectly related to elections will become less important within the repertory of political actions. This development will lead to a secular decrease in turnout. Second, modernization will lead to an increasingly *instrumental* orientation towards politics. Voting is something citizens will only do when they have a real choice, that is when it makes a difference to them which party or parties come to power, or when it is clear to them that elections matter for the allocation of power. This instrumental orientation implies that voters will decide from election to election whether they will vote or not. A more instrumental orientation of citizens will make people's decision to vote more dependent on their assessment of the importance of the outcome of a specific election. It does not necessarily mean that turnout will decline. However, if voters' decision to vote or not to vote purely depends on instrumental orientations, the costs of voting will often be perceived to be higher than the possible benefits, making the act of voting an irrational political activity.

The first, and most basic test of modernization theory is whether a decline of turnout has occurred at all. We found that it has, but only in the sense that turnout in the 1990s has tended to be somewhat lower than in the 1970s and 1980s. We did not find a monotonous gradual secular decline of turnout over the past decades. Recent elections in Germany and the Netherlands even show a slight recovery from the declining trend. The trends in turnout, or rather the lack of clear trends, clearly suggest that there is more going on than any theory predicting a secular downward trend can explain. If the empirical facts contradict at least partly our hypothesis, it is time to have another look at the underlying theory. We found that the micro-theory underlying the hypothesis deduced from modernization theory is not corroborated by the correlations found in our data. The expectation deduced from modernization theory that turnout is negatively correlated with education and political efficacy is obviously at odds with the traditional findings in electoral research, thereby creating the 'puzzle of electoral participation'. Our data clearly prove that education is still positively related to turnout. In the case of political efficacy our findings are less unequivocally contradicting modernization theory, but neither do they support it. Therefore, both the lack of a secular decline of turnout and the failure of the micro-theory behind it, ask for an alternative explanation.

Such an alternative explanation is possibly provided by the political–institutional context. In line with rational choice theory the impact of the policy differences (polarization) between political parties as indicated by the content of their party manifestos was assessed. The relationship between polarization and turnout is as often positive as it is negative. Therefore, polarization as indicated by these objective measures cannot possibly explain differences in turnout between elections. However, one might argue that it is not the objective differences between parties that count for voters' decisions, but the differences as they themselves perceive them. Whatever the objective differences, only perceived differences will make a difference. From this perspective an analysis at the individual level was done and turned out to be far more successful. Both indifference (the perception that there is hardly a difference between parties) and alienation (the perception that all parties are far away from the voter's policy positions) do have a negative impact on the decision to vote. However, a possible objection against the (exclusive) use of individual perceptions is that they might be a rationalization of the decision to vote rather than the other way around.

Therefore, neither modernization theory nor the political–institutional approach offer a completely satisfactory explanation for fluctuations in turnout. Modernization theory fails because the decline in turnout does not show the secular pattern it predicts and because the underlying theory at the micro-level had to be rejected. In the case of the political–institutional approach the expected correlations at the micro-level do occur, but because they are not substantiated at the macro-level, some suspicion of the causal direction of these correlations is justified.

11.3 PARTY CHOICE

In Chapter 1 we argued that the same aspects of the process of modernization that might lead to a change in the political involvement of citizens and a decline of turnout can be expected to cause a change in the factors determining voters' party choice. The rise of well-educated and politically skilful citizens undermines the once strong relationship between social structure and politics, between social position and party choice. For the same reason it is becoming more unlikely that people for their lifetime will be loyal to a particular party. Ideologies reflecting traditional cleavages will become less important as a factor determining people's political attitudes and party choice. More and more voters will decide from election to election what party they will vote for, taking into account the issues of the day, the performance of the incumbent government, and their confidence in individual political leaders. Such a development could easily lead to a fragmentation of the party system and to large fluctuations in election outcomes. This is indeed what we found in Chapter 2. Although we did not find a monotonous trend in any of the countries concerned, it is obvious that there is a trend towards higher degrees of fragmentation and volatility. Therefore, at the aggregate level, the developments are as we should expect them to be from the perspective of the theory of modernization. But at the same time our findings offer a clear warning against interpreting these developments as the result of autonomous societal processes only. Electoral laws seem to be at least as important. A minor change of the electoral law in Germany in 1949 and again in 1990 had an immediate effect on the number of parties represented in parliament, whereas in Britain the plurality system prevents a proportional translation of vote shares into seat shares. This is a first indication of the relevance of our alternative explanation that variations in patterns of party choice are not due to a secular process of societal change but to non-secular variations in the political–institutional context.

In the next subsections we will turn to the micro-level. First, we will summarize the expectations and findings for each of the factors we have distinguished in our dynamic model (see Fig. 1.1), and then do the same with regard to the alternative explanation.

11.3.1 The Explanation of Party Choice: Does the Impact of Long-term Factors Decline?

In short, the prediction with regard to the dynamics of the factors of importance for party choice that can be deduced from modernization theory is that over time long-term factors like social background, party identification, and ideological or value orientations will yield to short-term factors like issue and candidate orientations.

The two main factors determining the social cleavage structure in the countries represented in this study were religion and social class, although the weight of these two factors differs from country to country. We expected that over time the impact of voters' class or religious affiliation would decline due to two developments. First, because of a decline of the number of people considering themselves belonging to a particular social class or religion. Second, because over time people of a particular social class or religion would be less inclined to automatically support the political party traditionally related to that particular social class or religion. We clearly found both developments in our analyses.

In this volume we have not specifically focused on the composition effect, that is the decline of the importance of religion and social class because ever more people have disengaged themselves from their social class and/or religious background. This development is well documented elsewhere (Jagodzinski and Dobbelaere 1995; Franklin et al. 1992). Instead we concentrated on the relationship between social background and party choice, that is on the extent to which the social position of those remaining in the social cleavage still is a determining factor of their party choice. On this second aspect the evidence is less unequivocal. The impact of social class shows a clear decline in all six countries if one compares the end points of the trends available to us. However, the course of the trend is different from country to country, suggesting that there is more to it than a simple uniform development in society as the theory of modernization seems to suggest. With regard to religion there is even less of a general trend with the exception of Germany. In the Netherlands, in particular, there is a clear curvilinear pattern, indicating that after a period of decline religion as a basis for party choice is regaining its strength. This development might suggest that parties based on religion are recovering. However, that conclusion would be wrong. What the recovery of the effect of religion on party choice indicates is that the major Christian Democratic Party is still doing well among the shrinking part of the population who still belong to a particular religion but less so among the secularized part of the population. In the previous period the party had been increasing its appeal among non-religious people, thereby weakening the correlation between religion and party choice. Therefore, in order to understand to what extent political parties based on the traditional social cleavages have been able to cope with the changes in society, in particular the changing composition of the population, it is not sufficient to take into account to what extent they are able to mobilize their traditional rank and file. It is at least as important to know to what extent they have been able to compensate their losses due to the secularization process by attracting voters who do not belong to the social groups from which they traditionally attracted their voters. Our analyses clearly indicate that most of the traditional cleavage parties have been able to survive by widening their appeal to a larger part of the electorate than their traditional rank and file. In this respect cleavage voting in most countries has indeed clearly diminished.

The second long-term factor we analysed is party identification. Like in the case of social background the impact of party identification on party choice is expected to decline because of two developments. First, by a decline of the number of people who identify with a political party, and second because of a decline of the extent to which party identification determines party choice. Both effects seem to occur. First, although once more there is not a clear-cut monotonous decline in party identification in all countries, there can be no mistake about the general trend. In the long run the level of party identification has been going down. Second, the extent to which party choice used to be determined by party identification, even to the extent that the one could hardly be distinguished from the other, has declined as well in most of the countries under consideration. This is a second mechanism possibly causing, or perhaps reflecting, a lower predictability of party choice.

As we argued in more detail in Chapter 1, party identification is not the only alternative to social cleavages as a base for more or less stable relations between political parties and voters. In particular, in the European context it has often been argued that ideological or value orientations have the same function. In this book we included two alternative interpretations of the same basic idea. In Chapter 6, value orientations were introduced as the main source of stability in people's party preferences. Value orientations, in the tradition of Lipset and Rokkan, are conceptualized as being part of the cleavage structure. They refer to the *Weltanschauungen* reflecting the different interests on which the traditional cleavage structure is based.

Our expectation was that these orientations would not lose their political significance simultaneously with the social cleavages behind them. People's value orientations are formed during their adolescence and are quite persistent during the rest of their lifetime. As a consequence changes in value orientations among the population at large will only gradually change and will continue to be of importance for people's party choice even when these value orientations are no longer anchored in the social structure. Therefore, we expected that initially the impact of traditional value orientations—controlled for social background variables—would increase rather than decrease. However, as far as these value orientations are the product of the socialization process during people's adolescence when the cleavage structure was still strong, we expected the influence of these orientations to gradually decrease because of generation replacement. As a logical consequence of this argument we expected a curvilinear pattern of the (controlled) impact of traditional value orientations. This expectation was nicely borne out by our data. The predicted pattern was found in all countries with regard to economic left–right values, although both the strength of this pattern and the turning point of the curve differ from country to country. Religious/moral value orientations are less well represented in our data, but as far as they are, they show the same pattern. This implies that at the end of the time period under consideration the impact of traditional value orientations has been declining just like we expected.

But then the question is what will replace them. We introduced two alternative hypotheses which do not necessarily exclude each other but might be valid at successive points in time. The first prediction is that the old value orientations will gradually yield to new politics value orientations, whereas the alternative hypothesis which is more in line with the modernization thesis predicts that because of the process of individualization the explanatory power of all value orientations will gradually decrease. The first hypothesis finds little support. Only in Denmark did we find the expected pattern of a linear increase of the impact of new politics. Everywhere else the impact of new politics orientations followed the same pattern as the traditional value orientations. It increased until the second half of the 1980s and then decreased again. Instead of the new politics value orientation the libertarian–authoritarian dimension has become increasingly important. But its rising strength could not compensate for the declining strength of all other value orientations. As a consequence, with the exception of Denmark, the total impact of value orientations follows the same pattern as traditional value orientations, that is rising until somewhere in the 1980s and declining in the period afterwards, which is consistent with the alternative hypothesis. Therefore, the development of the impact of value orientations seems to be pretty much in line with the expectations formulated in Chapter 1. However, it would be premature to claim that we found conclusive evidence for a gradual decline of the impact of value orientations on party choice. The number of countries in which we found the predicted pattern is very small. In Germany the data we needed were not ascertained whereas Denmark showed a deviant pattern. Also, although we did predict a curvilinear pattern we did not specify when exactly the turning point should be reached. As far as there is a clear turning point it is reached at different times in different countries. Moreover, although the decline of the impact of value orientations in the most recent period is exactly what we should expect according to our interpretation of the theory of modernization, the period to which it applies is still too short to speak of a secular decline. The decline might just as well be due to a period effect caused by a temporal depoliticization. We will come back to this alternative interpretation. Also, the rising impact of the libertarian–authoritarian value dimension indicates that it is anything but impossible that in the longer run new value orientations will replace traditional value orientations.

In our conceptual framework Chapter 7 is functionally equivalent to Chapter 6. But in contrast to Chapter 6 the assumption here is that in the European countries represented in this volume the political cleavage structure can be represented by a single dimension, the left–right dimension. This implies that political parties compete with each other by taking different positions on this dimension whereas voters will vote for the party closest to their own position on the continuum. The expectation with regard to the development of the relationship between left–right and party choice includes several elements. First, we expected that traditionally people's positions on the left–right continuum were to some extent a reflection of their social position, but that this relationship has been declining. Second, we expected that the decline of the impact of the social cleavage structure on people's ideological orientations and their vote would not lead to a simultaneous decline of the impact of left–right orientations on party choice. Quite the contrary, we expected that the independent impact of these orientations would increase, at least initially. Only initially, because as we explained in the context of value orientations we also expected that the process of *individualization* would gradually undermine the impact of any ideological or value orientation. These successive expectations lead to the specific hypothesis that the impact of left–right on party choice, controlling for social background, will show a curvilinear pattern: at first it will increase and then decrease again.

Once again the real world of politics, as revealed by survey research, is more complex than any of these well-defined patterns of change predict. First, we did not find a secular decline of the relationship between people's social background and their left–right orientation, not because it remained high, but because it never was high to begin with, at least not in the period for which we have survey data available. Therefore, there simply was not much room for a decline. Second, we did not find a uniform pattern of change in the relationship between left–right orientations and party choice. Like in the case of value orientations there is some support though for the hypothesis that the development in this relationship follows a curvilinear pattern. In two of the five countries for which this analysis could be done, it was clearly borne out, whereas at least the pattern could be observed in two more countries. This hypothesis was based on the assumption that the relationship between people's social position and their left–right position would gradually decline. However, since this relationship turned out to be quite low from the very beginning of our time series, the explanation for this curvilinear pattern is not very convincing. It would be too simple to claim it as evidence for the validity of the modernization thesis.

11.3.2 The Explanation of Party Choice: Does the Impact of Short-term Factors Increase?

The hypotheses with regard to the three short-term forces—issues, retrospective judgements, and politicians—were formulated as the logical complement to the hypotheses regarding long-term forces. Due to the same developments in society that were expected to lead to a decline of the explanatory power of long-term forces the impact of short-term factors was expected to increase. We can summarize our findings in a single sentence: We found no support whatsoever for a secular rise of the impact of short-term factors. The argument implied by the theory of modernization is that because of the process of cognitive mobilization voters are more and more inclined to base their voting decisions on clearly political grounds, on their assessments and evaluations of the policy views of political parties, and the policy performances and competences of politicians and political parties.

In Chapter 8 the impact of policy issues was assessed. Issue voting implies an evaluation of political parties, an evaluation of which party represents the voter's issue preferences best or which party is best capable of solving the major problems in society. As it is difficult to clearly distinguish the first kind of issues from value orientations (the subject of Chapter 6) Chapter 8 concentrated on the second kind of issues, that is on the impact of voters' assessment of which party is best capable to deal with the major problems in society. We could not find a trace of an increase of issue voting over the period of time our data cover. Moreover, the impact of valence issues on party choice was surprisingly low in all countries at each and every point in time. The contribution of salient issues to the explained variance in party choice is almost negligible.

The analysis of the development over time of impact of retrospective judgements in Chapter 9 leads to a similar conclusion. Retrospective evaluations of the economy are clearly important but there is not a trace of a secular change of the impact of these factors.

Perhaps the most widely believed change in electoral behaviour is the impact of people's judgement of political leaders. The literal visibility of political leaders to the electorate, even on a daily basis in their own living room, has dramatically increased since television has become a major source of information. However, once more this hypothesis does not survive empirical scrutiny. In Chapter 10 we found clear evidence that the more voters favour a party leader, the more likely they are to vote for that leader's party. But once more we found little or no evidence of a secular increase in the strength of this relationship.

Our findings with regard to the hypotheses deduced from the theory of modernization are summarized in the second column of Table 11.1. We formulated similar hypotheses with regard to the impact of each of the long-term forces, social background (social class and religion), party identification, and ideological or value orientations. We predicted a gradual decline of the impact of each of these variables, although we also predicted an initial increase of the impact of ideological and value orientations. All hypotheses predict (at least eventually) a similar monotonous development in each and every country represented in our study. In this strict sense not a single hypothesis survived empirical testing, either because the pattern is not strictly monotonous or/and because one or more countries deviate from the general pattern. However, if we accept deviations from the requirement that developments should be monotonous and exactly similar in each country, we can arrive at the general conclusions as summarized in Table 11.1, in which the variables are grouped as in Fig. 1.1. But because of the deviations from any general pattern we predicted, it should be obvious that all these conclusions can be no more than preliminary, waiting for a replication of our study on a larger number of countries and a longer time period.

The strongest evidence in support of the general hypothesis of a decline of the importance of long-term forces refers to social background. Both social class and religion have lost part of their importance for politics because of a composition

TABLE 11.1. *Summary of empirical findings*

Independent variable	Hypothesis Modernization theory corroborated?	Hypothesis political–institutional context corroborated?
Social background		
(a) Social class		Yes
• Composition effect	Yes	
• Correlation effect	Yes	
(b) Religion		Yes
• Composition effect	Yes	
• Correlation effect	No	
Party identification		Yes
• Composition effect	Yes	
• Correlation effect	Yes	
Value orientations	Yes	Yes
Left–right orientations	No	Yes
Issues	No	No
Retrospective evaluations	No	Casual evidence
Political leaders	No	Polarization: No 'Presidential' contest: Yes

effect. Because both the traditional blue-collar working class and the religiously active part of the population have been shrinking, the natural homeland of labour and confessional parties has become smaller and smaller. In addition to this composition effect the 'correlation effect' has declined as well, at least in the case of social class. Over time it has become less self-evident for members of the working class to vote for a socialist party. In the case of religion we did not find such an evident trend. The general picture of the development of party identification is in line with our expectations. Both the level of party identification and the correlation between party identification and party choice have been declining over time. The case of ideological and value orientations is more complicated. We did find the predicted curvilinear pattern in the relationship between these orientations and party choice, but in particular in the case of left–right orientations the pattern is too weak and the explanation too disputable to claim that the hypothesis based on modernization theory has been corroborated.

The conclusion with regard to all short-term factors, issues, retrospective judgements, and leaders is simple and straightforward: We did not find the slightest evidence in support of the hypothesis that the effect of these factors on party choice would increase over time.

Therefore, instead of finding a gradual shift from left to right in the explanatory power of the factors in Fig. 1.1, as we predicted on the basis of modernization theory, we found that the support for our hypothesis is decreasing the more we move from left to right in Fig. 1.1.

It is also clear that the more we move from left to right, the more we move into the world of real politics. Therefore, it is plausible to think that, in particular, in the case of short-term factors an explanation taking into account the political context of a specific election stands a better chance of surviving empirical scrutiny. Taking into account the political context is exactly what our alternative theoretical approach does.

11.3.3   The Explanation of Party Choice:
The Political–institutional Context

According to this alternative approach, the political–institutional context rather than any development in society is responsible for variations in the explanatory power of particular variables. In this volume we have focused mainly on the polarization between the main political parties as an explanatory variable. Occasionally we could not resist the temptation to take into account more institutional variables like the electoral system or single-party versus multiparty governments. From a theoretical point of view the relevance of these institutional characteristics is indisputable, but because they are rather stable within countries, their only variance is between countries which leaves us with too few cases. Therefore, we were very restrictive in taking such institutional characteristics into account. The advantage of polarization as our main contextual variable is that it can vary not only between countries but within countries between elections as well. There-fore, single elections rather than countries can be taken as the unit of analysis at the aggregate level. Also, the polarization between parties is an excellent measure for the degree to which conflict dimensions are politicized. It is this degree of politicization which is expected to influence to what extent particular variables will be able to influence people's party choice. By politicizing a particular conflict dimension, political parties are able to mobilize the electorate along that con-flict dimension.

The explanatory power of which variables do we expect to vary with the political context? A summary of the hypotheses and our empirical findings is presented in the third column of Table 11.1. The case for two of the three short-term factors is obvious enough. If we expect that voters make up their mind from election to election, and decide which party to vote for on the basis of the issues at stake and their trust in political leaders, it is almost self-evident that the impact of these variables will be related to the extent to which political parties emphasize the differences between them.

In the case of issues our expectations differ though depending on how we define issues. So-called *structural position issues* are neither conceptually nor in oper-ational terms clearly distinguishable from ideological or value orientations. As they are directly related to the main policy dimensions of conflicts, we expect that their impact will increase the more polarized political parties are. And this indeed is what we clearly found in Chapters 6 and 7. There is a clear correlation between polarization and the impact of left–right and value orientations. This finding also sheds another light on the decline of the impact of values on party choice in the second half of the 1980s and the 1990s in most countries. During this same period the polarization between parties, as perceived by the people, decreased in most of these countries, as was shown in Chapter 7. This is one more reason to be sceptical about any attempt to see the decline of the impact of value orientations as evidence for the modernization thesis.

If we define issues as *valence issues*, the important question at election time is in which party voters have the most confidence when it comes to dealing with these issues or problems. We expected that *higher* the impact of such issues, or of issue competence, *less* the polarization between parties. When there is little polariza-tion voters will hardly be able to see the differences in the policy positions of the parties and be more inclined to vote according to their confidence in the issue competence of the parties. This expectation was not borne out. The correlation between valence issues and party choice was so low, to begin with, that it hardly made sense to assess to what extent it was related to polarization.

In the case of retrospective voting it is less clear why it should be related to polarization. Voters can only credit or blame parties in government when it is clear to them which parties are responsible for government policies. It will be more clear in the case of one-party majority governments than in the case of coalition governments or minority governments. However, as argued above, we do not have sufficient cases for a valid test of this kind of hypotheses. Still, in Chapter 9 sufficient casual evidence was presented to sustain the importance of the political and institutional context for the strength of retrospective voting.

In Chapter 10 we found no evidence in support of the hypothesis that polarization increases the extent to which voters take leadership characteristics into account in their decision how to vote. What does seem to matter though is the extent to which a parliamentary election comes close to mimicking a presidential contest, that is when the next head of government is likely to be the leader of whichever of two large parties can win the most votes without the need to engage in post-election coalition negotiations. But once more, this is one of the characteristics that are rather persistent in a particular country and therefore there are simply not enough cases in our analysis to establish this effect in a reliable way. But because it is substantiated by other research we will maintain it as one of the findings of our study.

Whereas it can easily be argued why we should expect a relationship between the political–institutional context and the effect of value orientations, issues and political leaders, it is less clear why we should expect a relationship between polarization and the two remaining long-term factors, social cleavages and party identification. And yet we do find such a relationship in both cases. In line with a more recent insight in the scholarly literature we find that the effect of social class and religion co-varies with the degree of polarization. This means that even class or religious voting does not only depend on the autonomous development of the strength of social class and religion, but also on the extent to which these traditional cleavages are politicized. Basically this observation is anything but new. Following the insights of political sociology rather than the sociology of politics, to paraphrase Sartori, it is obvious that social cleavages are irrelevant for politics as long as they are not politicized. This implies that the political relevance of a particular social cleavage can decline or slumber for a while and then can come back to life. This is then reflected in an erratic rather than a linear pattern over time. A similar argument applies to party identification. The strength of party identification cannot exclusively be explained as the result of an apolitical socialization process but is also related to the difference it makes to identify with one party rather than the other.

11.4 MODERNIZATION AND POLITICS

This, finally, is the strong message of this book. As self-evident as it sounds, but in contrast to some interpretations of the theory of modernization, chapter after chapter we found that electoral behaviour is primarily *political* behaviour that is shaped by the supply side of politics at least as much as by autonomous processes in society. In this respect not much has changed during the period we were able to cover. If this comes as a surprise it is because in parts of the literature the differences between traditional models of voting behaviour and models taking the political context into account are made bigger than they really are. The political context was never irrelevant for voting behaviour. No matter how divided a society is in terms of religion and/or social class, as long as these differences are not politicized, voters cannot be mobilized on this basis. The same argument applies to the political consequences of the process of modernization. No matter how autonomous and competent modern voters are, it depends on political institutions and the behaviour of political parties and political leaders how valuable this competence is. If voters do not see the policy differences between the political parties competing for their votes—as was increasingly the case in the second half of the 1980s and the 1990s in some of the countries in our study—one should not be surprised to find low correlations between voters' policy preferences and their party choice. Key's (1966: 2–3) famous observation that 'Even the most discriminating popular judgement can reflect only ambiguity, uncertainty, or even foolishness if those are the qualities of the input into the echo chamber' is as valid as ever. A similar argument can be made with regard to electoral accountability. As we observed in Chapter 1, the days that mass parties made their political platforms one of the main instruments of electoral competition, and election platforms enabled voters to choose the direction of government are said to be probably over, whereas 'the age of voting on the incumbents' record may be beginning' (Manin 1997: 221). Although we did not find any evidence of such a development, we did present casual evidence suggesting that most of the countries represented in our study are not well prepared for such a development. With the exception of the United Kingdom all of them are consensus democracies according to Lijphart's (1999) typology, at least on the relevant executive-parties dimension. Despite all the superior qualities that are attributed to consensus democracies as compared to majoritarian democracies (Lijphart 1999), a clear weakness is the blurred political accountability caused by the coalition governments that are characteristic for this type of government. And once again we should not be surprised to find that voters do not use a political instrument that is not offered to them. If modernization of society incites voters to a different kind of electoral behaviour, such behaviour is hardly possible without a simultaneous modernization of the political–institutional context.

Appendix 1

Parties, Elections and Parliaments

Hans-Dieter Klingemann

This appendix compiles basic facts and figures of parties, elections, and parliaments of the six countries under study. It is written as a correlate to Chapter 2 and meant to provide detailed information for the interested reader.

A.1.1 SWEDEN

The Swedish party system reflects the class cleavage to a large extent. However, beginning with the 1988 election new parties entered parliament representing environmental interests and Christian values in spite of the 4 per cent threshold of the electoral law. Seats are distributed by proportional representation (modified Sainte-Lague) in two tiers. While the original Swedish five-party system was quite stable until the mid-1980s it changed at the end of the decade to a seven-party system, which from then on also incorporates a religious and an ecology party.

The *Social Democratic Labour Party* (Sveriges Socialdemokratistiska Arbetareparti, SdaP; Socialist) dominates the party system since the beginning of the 1930s. It has strong links with the trade union movement and mainly promotes welfare interests of workers and of the lower middle-class. The *Left Party* (Vänsterpartiet, Vp; Left Socialist) is a second but much smaller party on the left. Founded in 1917 as the Left Social Democratic Party, renamed the Communist Party in 1921, the Left Party—Communists in 1967, and the Left Party in 1990 (which is its present name) it has been represented in each parliament in the time period under study. Although more radical than the Social Democratic Labour Party, the Left Party has never been an obedient follower of Moscow. Rather, it has pursued its own 'Swedish' revisionist programme. For this reason it is classified as belonging to the 'left-socialist' and not the 'communist' party family. For long periods of time minority governments of the Social Democratic Labour Party have relied on the Left Party's support.

There are two liberal parties, the *Centre Party* (Centerpartiet, CP; Liberal) and the *Liberal People's Party* (Folkpartiet Liberalerna, FP; Liberal). Established as the Agrarian Party in 1910 for promoting rural interests, the Centre Party must be regarded a member of the liberal party family today. In the post-Second World War period it has developed a typical liberal profile campaigning for decentralization and for a reduced impact of government on the lives of individuals. The Liberal People's Party (originally formed as a parliamentary group in 1895) draws support from rural free-church movements as well as from professionals and intellectuals. It favours socially progressive policies based on individual responsibility.

The *Moderate Coalition Party* (Moderate Samlingspartet, MSP; Conservative) is the strongest party on the right. Founded in 1904 it was set up to defend the interests of the more privileged. Known as the Conservative Party it adopted its current name only after the 1968 election. The party advocates tax cuts and reduced government interference in the economy. It has long favoured a strong defence policy and Sweden's accession to the EU.

All parties mentioned previously are 'old', founded well before the Second World War. Three new parties have entered Swedish parliament beginning with the 1988 election. The first one was the *Green Ecology Party* (Miljöpartiet de Gröna, Greens; Ecologist). The party called for greater penalties for pollution, the phasing out of nuclear energy, reduced highway construction, and fought the Öresund bridge and tunnel project. It also became a prominent supporter of the 'No' side of the November 1994 referendum on EU membership. The 1994 Social Democratic Labour Party minority government counted on the support of the Green Ecology Party. The same was true in 1998 when Labour had to rely on Green Ecology (and on the Left Party) to avoid a legislative vote of no-confidence. In 1991 two more parties gained representation in parliament: the *Christian Democratic Party* (Kristdemokraterne, Kd; Religious) and *New Democracy* (Ny Demokrati, NyD; Discontent). Formed in 1964 as the Christian Democratic Coalition, the party adopted the name Christian Democratic Community Party in 1987 and its current title in 1996. The party's programme rests on religious principles and wants to promote ethical norms and moral laws protecting a Christian society. It also campaigned for 'cleaner' politics and opposed the introduction of the euro. The Christian Democratic Party can count on the support of the more orthodox part of Swedish protestants. The party entered a minority coalition with the Moderate Coalition Party, the Liberal People's Party, and the Centre Party in October 1994.

New Democracy, which was represented in the 1991 parliament only, campaigned on a populist platform advocating tax cuts, abandonment of the welfare system, and anti-immigration laws—very much in tune with the Progress parties of Norway and Denmark. In 1991 it could send twenty-four deputies to the parliament and subsequently gave crucial support to the centre–right minority government in 1993 and early 1994. After the resignation of its charismatic leader (Count Ian Wachmeister, 'the crazy count') the party failed to achieve the 4 per cent threshold for representation in the following elections. Thus, the parliamentary life of this party was short, indeed. However, the phenomenon demonstrates that flash parties, channelling discontent, can also suddenly hit a party system which demonstrably is one of the most stable in Europe.

Representatives of two small regional electoral alliances gained access to the 1964 and 1968 parliaments. The *Middle Parties* (Mittenpatierna; Regional) were formed in the Gotland constituency, the *Citizens' Coalition* (Medborgelig Saml-ing; Regional) in the Malmö-Helsinborg-Lund-Landskrona constituency. Its deputies joined the factions of other parties and in parliament their organizations did not play a role.

A.1.2 NORWAY

As in Sweden the class conflict has left its imprint on the Norwegian party system. However, the religious dimension has also been politicized. A religious party has been represented in all parliaments of the time period under consideration. Translation of votes into seats is governed by proportional representation (Sainte-Lague). Since 1988 eight of a total of 165 seats are distributed in a second tier. Parties which overcome a 4 per cent hurdle participate in their distribution. The relatively calm period of Norwegian politics, based on its classic five-party constellation came to an end in the early 1970s. Polarization between parties grew in the heated debate about the issue of membership in the EC. When membership was rejected in a national referendum in September 1992 the party system was in disarray. The liberals suffered a split and a populist protest party entered parlia-ment in the 1973 election. This election is considered an 'earthquake' election in Norway by most observers.

The *Norwegian Labour Party* (Det Norske Arbeiderparti, DNA; Socialist) is by far the strongest party both in terms of electoral strength and in terms of governing potential. On average it has held 46 per cent of the seats in parliament and governed 71 per cent of the time period under consideration. Its welfare state programme resembles those of the other Scandinavian socialist parties. The Labour-controlled government supported entrance in the EC in 1972 but was obliged to resign when the proposal was rejected by the Norwegian populace. Three smaller parties to the left of the Labour Party entered parliament, two of which—the *Norwegian Communist Party* (Norges Kommunistiske Parti, NKP; Communist) and the *Red Electoral Alliance* (Rod Valgallianse; Left Socialist)— are no longer represented. The Communist Party had gained seats in the 1945, 1953, and 1957 parliaments. The Red Electoral Alliance won a seat in 1993. It is interesting to note that the Red Electoral Alliance had already tried to form a 'Local List for the Environment and Solidarity' prior to the 1989 election. However, unlike in other countries, their attempt to campaign on an integrated left-socialist and environmental programme has failed mainly because ecological issues had already been taken up by the Liberal Party and the Socialist Left Party early on. Both the Communist Party and the Red Electoral Alliance have lacked of any coalition potential and never participated in government.

The *Socialist Left Party* (Sosialistisk Venstreparti, SV; Left Socialist) was organized as a coalition of the Norwegian Communist Party, the Socialist People's Party, and the Democratic Socialists/Labour Movement Information Committee against Norwegian Membership in the Common Market. This formation participated in the 1973 election and won 10.3 per cent of the seats. In 1975 the members of this alliance committed themselves to the formation of a unified party pursuing a radical left programme and opposing Norwegian entry into the European Community (EC). The Communists finally decided not to dissolve and join the new Socialist Left Party. Subsequently the Socialist Left Party has become a relevant party in the Norwegian party system. Prior to the 1981 balloting, the Socialist Left Party provided the Nordli Labour government with crucial support needed to maintain a slim parliamentary majority. Since 1973 the party is continuously represented in the Norwegian parliament.

Two major parties, the *Centre Party* (Senterpartiet, SP; Liberal) and the *Liberal Party* (Venstre, V; Liberal), and the short-lived *Liberal People's Party* (Det Liberale Folkeparti; Liberal) form the liberal party family in Norway. As in Sweden the Centre Party was originally founded as the Agrarian Party. However, it changed from a party catering to the narrow interests of agriculture to a party which appeals to individualism, market economy, and the middle classes. Trying to assume a position between the left and the right, it consequently changed its name to Centre Party in 1959. The Liberal Party follows a radical liberal programme which more recently is also much concerned with ecological and environmental policies as mentioned earlier. Founded in 1884, it is one of the oldest parties in the Norwegian party system and has been well represented in all parliaments up to 1973. At that time, however, its deputies were split on the projected entry of Norway into the EC. A majority supported membership in the EC while its anti-EC minority decided to participate in a coalition government with the Christian People's Party and the Centre Party—campaigning against membership and for Norwegian national identity. As a consequence the pro-EC faction of the Liberal Party formed the Liberal People's Party. Their new party gained one seat in 1973 and has not held a seat in the parliament since then. By these events the once successful Liberal Party was reduced to two seats in 1973 which it retained in 1977 and 1981. It failed to secure representation in 1985 and 1989 but regained access in the following elections.

The *Conservative Party* (Høyre, H; Conservative), even older than the Liberal Party (founded in 1884), has developed into the strongest party on the right. It advocates support of private investment, elimination of government control in industry, lower taxes, and a strong defence policy. The party participated in seven out of the twenty-six governments of the time period under study.

The *Christian People's Party* (Kristelig Folkeparti, KrF; Religious) has been established at the national level in 1945. Its primary object is maintaining the principles of Christianity in public life. As mentioned previously the Christian People's Party also campaigned against Norwegian entry into the EC to preserve national identity. The party can rely on support of the Lutheran state church and of the protestant free-churches and their various organizations. The Christian People's Party steadily increased its parliamentary representation, held 9.7 per cent of seats in parliament on average and participated in eight of the twenty-six governments.

A populist discontent party, the *Progress Party* (Fremskrittsparti, FrP; Discontent) entered parliament in 1973. Until 1977 it was known as 'Anders Lange's Party for Strong Reduction in Taxes, Rates, and Public Intervention'. The party favours dismantling of the welfare state, stricter immigrations laws, tough anti-crime measures, and opposes membership in the EU. It was invited to join the ruling coalition in 1985 to offset losses of the Conservative Party. Declining the offer the party subsequently held a balance of power in parliament and provided the votes needed to defeat the Willoch government in April 1986. After the 1997 elections the Progress Party emerged as the second largest party in parliament.

Two small regional parties gained access to parliament in 1989 and 1997. In 1989 the *People's Action for the Future of Finmark* (Folkeaksjonen Framtid for Finmark; Regional) sent one representative to parliament. The same was true for the *Coastal Party* (Kystpartiet; Regional) in 1997. They represented interests in the fishing towns of the North. None of these two parties played an important role in the parliaments of 1989 and 1997.

A.1.3 DENMARK

The class cleavage has dominated the formation of the party system in Denmark more than in Sweden or Norway. There was no representation of religious interests in parliament by a religious party until the early 1970s. In addition, the faction of this protestant party is much smaller than the ones of the religious parties in the two other Scandinavian countries. In Denmark the class cleavage has also found a more differentiated expression. Eased by proportional representation (Sainte-Lague) and the very low threshold set by the electoral law for distribution of seats in the second tier (2 per cent) a rather high number of small parties have gained access to the Folketing. This is particularly true of small left and centre parties. However, they enter and leave parliament quite often causing a high degree of change. In the time period under study only four of a total of eighteen political parties were represented in all twenty-three parliaments, six parties entered the Folketing some time after 1945 and are still represented today, while eight parties, which once had sent deputies, are no longer part of the more recent parliaments. Many observers regard the 1973 election as the turning point of the structure of the Danish party system which added three new parties to the four old ones. The core of the party system is formed by the four parties which are characteristic of the party system and have sent deputies to all twenty-three parliaments. This core bears much similarity with the ones of the other two Scandinavian countries. The strongest party on the left is, again, the *Social Democrats* (Socialdemokratiet, SD; Socialist). Its most important centre–right competitors are the *Liberals* (Venstre, V; Liberal), the *Radical Liberal Party* (Det Radikale Venstre, RV; Liberal), and the *Conservative People's Party* (Konservative Folkeparti, KF; Conservative).

Founded in 1871 the dominant Social Democrats mainly represent the interests of industrial labour, advocate a typical welfare state programme trying to achieve full employment, and to guarantee extensive social security benefits. In the course of time the party has been confronted with five smaller parties in parliament which also tried to mobilize the left vote: the *Danish Communist Party* (Danmarks Kommunistiske Parti, DKP; Communist), the *Socialist People's Party* (Socialistisk Folkeparti, SF; Left Socialist), the *Left Socialist Party* (Venstresocialisterne, VS; Left Socialist), *Common Course* (Faelles Kurs, FK; Left Socialist), and the *Red–Green Unity List* (Enhedslisten—De Roed Groenne, EL; Left Socialist).

In the 1940s and 1950s the Danish Communist Party closely followed Soviet policies. It came to a split when Aksel Larsen—at that time still chair of the Communist Party—asked his party to condemn military suppression by Soviet troops of the 1956 Hungarian uprising. When this was denied he and his followers formed the Socialist People's Party. Based on a radical left-socialist (but not on an anti-system programme) the new party outclassed the Communist Party successfully in the following years. The Socialist People's Party has been continuously represented in the Danish parliament since 1960. Despite its more radical orientation it has often acted as an unofficial wing of the Social Democrats, trying to influence platform and voting patterns of the larger party. In this spirit it has pledged conditional support to three minority governments led by Social Democrats. The Danish Communist Party, on the other hand, never recovered from the split in the 1950s and was unable to enter parliaments from 1960 to 1971. In 1973, 1975, and 1977 it came back to parliament on the wings of an anti-EC sentiment in Danish public opinion but did not win any seats since then. In 1975 the party lent support to the left-wing Jorgensen Social Democratic minority government even if it did not enter a formal coalition agreement. The Left Socialist Party was founded by dissidents of the Socialist People's Party who accused their party of origin to have forgotten its Marxist roots. The party was represented in the 1968 and in the 1975 to 1984 parliaments by a small number of deputies. After that time it has lost representation and tries to maintain an identity within the Red–Green Unity List. Three more left-socialist parties need to be mentioned shortly, all of which have gained seats in parliament after 1973. Common Course, a far left pro-trade union, anti-immigration, and anti-EU party, was represented in 1989 but never since. It had little impact on Danish politics. The Red–Green Unity List was launched in 1989 as a coalition of three radical left groupings: the Danish Communist Party, the Left Socialist Party, and the Trotskyist Socialist Workers' Party. In 1991 it was also joined by the Maoist Danish Communist Workers' Party. Strongly opposed to the EU, the Unity List achieved a breakthrough in the 1994 election and was re-elected both in 1998 and 2001. Because of its backing by the far left parties mentioned, it is classified 'left-socialist' and not 'ecologist'. The party seems to have become a more permanent member of the Danish parliament.

The Liberals and the Radical Liberal Party are at the core of the liberal party family in Denmark. As the centre parties of Sweden and Norway, the Danish Liberal Party was also founded in 1870 as an agrarian party to represent the interests of farmers and the rural areas. Today the Liberals stand for individualism in industry and business as opposed to socialism, for reduction of taxation, and adequate defence. Thus, the party has become a member of the liberal party family. The Radical Liberal Party is a social–liberal grouping and it mainly represents small landowners as well as urban intellectuals and professionals. The party advocates strengthening of private enterprise in a social–liberal context. In foreign affairs it is pacifist in outlook and only a lukewarm supporter of European integration. The *Centre Democrats* (Centrum Demokraterne, CD; Liberal) have been formed in 1973 by dissident Social Democrats to protest leftist tendencies in government and its plans for increased taxation. Their programmatic orientation justifies a classification as 'liberal'. The party participated in three Conservative and two Social Democratic led governments and was represented in all parliaments since 1973. However, the Centre Democrats failed to enter the 2001 parliament. All other liberal parties are of minor importance to today's politics. Founded in 1919 the *Justice Party* (Retsforbundet, RF; Liberal) had based its programme on a rather particular economic theory (the so-called 'Grundrententheorie'). It was represented in the six parliaments of the 1945 to 1957 period. The party returned to parliament in 1973 as the only non-socialist party campaigning against Denmark's joining the EU. Not represented in 1975 it sent five deputies to the 1977 and six to the 1979 assemblies. In 1957 and 1960 the Justice Party participated in two minority coalition governments led by the Social Democrats. Three more liberal parties withered away until the mid-1960s. The first one was the *Danish Union* (Dansk Samling, DS; Liberal), followed by the *Independents' Party* (De Uafhaengige, DU; Liberal), and the *Liberal Centre* (Liberalt Centrum, LC; Liberal). The Danish Union, represented in the 1945 parliament, stood for a 'third way' beyond socialism and capitalism. It ceased to exist after 1947. The Independents' Party was founded in 1953 by K. Kristensen, a politician of the Liberals, in protest to the status accorded to Schleswig in the new Danish constitution. The Liberal Centre, formed in 1965 by some members of the Liberal Party who wanted to continue the fiscal policies of T. Kristensen, minister of finance of the K. Kristensen and E. Eriksen governments. The party was dissolved shortly after the 1968 election.

The Conservative Party supports protection of private property, lower taxation, a restrictive fiscal policy, and adequate defence. Founded in 1916 it mainly represents industry and business as well as parts of the Danish middle-class. It has found continuous support to be represented in all parliaments in the time period under study. The Conservatives participated in eight out of thirty Danish governments during that time.

The *Christian People's Party* (Kristeligt Folkeparti, KrP; Religious) gained seats in parliament in 1973. It was formed in 1970 to represent Christian values in politics and in particular to oppose abortion and the liberalization of pornography regulations. The party quickly demonstrated coalition potential and participated in four governments.

The *Progress Party* (Fremskridtspartiet, FP; Discontent), founded in 1972 by Mogens Glistrup, can be described as populist, mobilizing on discontent with the establishment. It campaigned—among other things—for a gradual dissolution of the income tax, against the 'expensive' Danish welfare state, as well as for the abolition of the military and the diplomatic service. While starting as an overly populist party it adopted more moderate political positions in later years. A month prior to the 1990 elections, the party's founder, Mogens Glistrup, was expelled from the parliamentary group for refusing to submit to voting discipline. He came back later as the Progress Party's campaign leader in the 2001 election demanding to expel all Muslims from the country (Andersen 2003: 189). In October 1995 the Progress Party split and the dissident deputies formed the *Danish People's Party* (Danske Folkeparti, DF; Discontent). Entering parliament in 1998 and subsequently supporting the liberal–conservative coalition led by Anders Fogh Rasmussen, its vote share rose to 12 per cent in the 2001 election. It seems likely that the Danish People's Party will consolidate as a more moderate heir of the old populist protest party.

Finally, there is the *Schleswig Party* (Det Slesvigske Parti; Regional) which had been set up to represent the interests of the German minority after parts of Schleswig were unified with Denmark. In the initial years after the Second World War the party did not field own candidates. It won a small number of seats in 1953, 1957, and 1960. In the elections of 1973, 1975, and 1977 the party presented candidates jointly with the Centre Democrats but did not come back on its own.

A.1.4 THE NETHERLANDS

The Dutch party system is formed by both a class cleavage and a religious cleavage which have given rise to liberal, socialist, and religious parties. These parties were the pillars of the 'verzuiling'. The Dutch politics of accommodation and consensus based on this structure of the party system has been aptly described by such authors as Lijphart (1968) or Andeweg and Irwin (2002). This system can also be described as an ideological triangle formed by the liberal, the socialist, and the Christian parties and their three-way relationships (De Beus et al. 1989). Pellikaan et al. (2004: 7–8) aptly describe the major political divisions resulting from the ideological triangle.

The class cleavage ... divides the political universe in two parts: the parties that favor state intervention in the economy in order to guarantee some form of welfare arrangement and the parties that think that government is the problem and not the solution and thus support free *markets*. . . . The second cleavage is the ethic line that separates the political domain in the segment where the parties are supporting the idea that the state should install *moral laws* forbidding abortion, euthanasia and same sex marriage, and the other segment where parties are in favor of a neutral state that leaves these moral decisions in the hands of the citizens itself. . . . The third cleavage is the communitarian line. This line splits ... (the political universe, HDK) into one part where parties acknowledge the need to protect the family as the heart of the society and some aspects of corporatism such as the labour unions that have ties with the Socialist parties as well as with the Christian parties. On the other side of the communitarian–corporatist line we can find the Liberals who are in favor of individual freedom and reject collective notions of communitarianism or corporatism.

While the relative emphasis on these principles decides the pattern of interactions in general, the Dutch 'triangle' was simplified in terms of number of parties involved when the three big confessional parties united to form one interconfessional Christian party which started to contest elections in 1977. This election is described by many observers as a 'critical' election very much so as the 'earthquake' or 'watershed' elections cited for the Scandinavian countries. As known by now, this long-term pattern of a politics of accommodation exploded in the 2002 election. In a penetrating analysis Pellikaan et al. (2004) offer a model which proposes a convincing explanation of this breakdown of the old Dutch party system. The events of 2002, however, are outside the boundaries of the time period under consideration for this chapter.

In the period under study twenty-five parties gained representation in the Dutch parliament. This is the highest number of parties compared to all other countries dealt with in this book. The classification of parties by party family shows one communist, four left-socialist, two socialist, two liberal, ten religious, four discontent, and two single-issue parties. This highlights the overriding importance of the religious parties for Dutch politics. The high number of parties can also be related to the Dutch election law. It rules that the parliament is elected by proportional representation (d'Hondt) in one constituency—an institutional arrangement which greatly facilitates the representation of small parties.

Netherland's Communist Party (Communistische Partij van Nederland; Communist) stood for abolition of capitalism and the monarchy. In later years the party campaigned on an Euro–Communist programme. It was continuously represented in the Dutch parliament up to 1982. In 1946 the Communists were offered to participate in the first post-war government because of its role in the resistance to Nazi Germany's occupation. The party, however, declined the offer and has not shown signs of coalition potential in the following years.

Of the four left-socialist parties only two can be considered important. The small *Pacifist-Socialist Party* (Pacifistisch-Socialistische Partij; Left Socialist) has not shown any coalition potential during the time when it was in parliament while further development of the *Socialist Party* (Socialistische Partij; Left Socialist) is yet unclear. Founded in 1957 by leftist members of the Labour Party and the Communist Party as well as pacifist citizens, the Pacifist-Socialist Party was represented in the nine parliaments starting from 1959 to 1986. The Socialist Party supports a classic left-socialist view with a corporatist link to the labour unions. It entered parliament in 1994 and returned five members in 1998. The *Radical Political Party* (Politieke Partij Radikalen, PPR; Left Socialist), however, a left-socialist party with some Catholic background, was soon included in the 1973–7 Den Uyl government. Founded in 1968 by four deputies of the Catholic People's Party it propagated a more equitable distribution of wealth. The small party (2.2 per cent votes on average) stayed in parliament from 1971 to 1986 and is no longer represented since. The *Green-Left* (Groen Links, GL; Left Socialist) is considered a left-socialist instead of an ecology party. Initially it was organized as an electoral alliance by the Evangelical People's Party, the Radical Political Party, the Pacifist-Socialist Party, and the Communist Party. Like in Norway and Denmark, the Dutch left socialist parties tried to capture a green party's position to regain entry in parliament. Green-Left became a permanent party in 1991 when each of the former constituent alliance parties voted to disband. Their programmatic strategy proved successful. The Green-Left alliance entered parliament in 1989. It also did quite well in the subsequent elections (5 per cent of votes on average) and became the fifth largest party in the 1989 Dutch parliament. The party is on the rise and is about to establish itself in the Dutch parliament.

Of the two socialist parties the largest and most important is the *Labour Party* (Partij van de Arbeid, PvdA; Socialist). Campaigning on a social-democratic programme it contested all sixteen elections of the time period under consideration, governed more than half of this time period (57.2 per cent) and participated in eleven out of twenty-two governments. *The Democratic Socialists '70* (Democratische Socialisten '70, DS '70; Socialist)—founded in 1970 as implied by the name—was a small moderate breakaway from the Labour Party. It stayed in parliament from 1971 to 1977 and participated in the first Biesheuvel (1971–2) government.

As a successor to the Liberal State Party, the *People's Party for Freedom and Democracy* (Volkspartij voor Vrijheid en Democratie, VVD; Liberal) has a long tradition in the Dutch party system. Like the Labour Party it contested all sixteen elections and gained 14.4 per cent of parliamentary seats on average. Although there never was a prime minister coming from their ranks the People's Party for Freedom and Democracy has the longest record as a government party compared to any other party in the Netherlands. It participated in twelve out of a total of twenty-two governments which covered 62 per cent of the total time period under consideration. The second liberal party in the Dutch system are the *Democrats 66* (Democraten 66, D66; Liberal). The party was formed in 1966 as a left-liberal party. In addition to promoting individualism and the market, it advocated to improve accountability of party politics by dropping proportional representation and the direct election of the prime minister. The Democrats 66 established themselves as a successful Dutch party (7.5 per cent of votes on average) and participated as a coalition partner in five governments.

The religious parties constitute the largest group of parties in the Netherlands underlining the historical importance of the religious cleavage in Dutch society. Up to the formation of the *Christian Democratic Appeal* (Christen Democratisch Appel, CDA; Religious) in 1975, which assembled the religious vote into a unified party, religious interests were mainly represented by three larger religious parties. The *Catholic People's Party* (Katholieke Volkspartij, KVP; Religious), successor to the Catholic Electoral League founded in 1897, articulated the interests of the Catholics. The *Anti-Revolutionary Party* (Anti-Revolutionaire Partij, ARP; Religious), founded in 1879, and the *Christian Historical Union* (Christelijk-Historische Unie, CHU; Religious)—a more centrist breakaway from the Anti-Revolutionary Party—organized most of the Calvinist citizens politically. They were not only the strongest religious parties (Catholic People's Party: 28 per cent; Anti-Revolutionary Party: 10.3 per cent; Christian Historical Union: 7 per cent on average in the nine elections they contested) but they were also used to govern the Netherlands. In the time period from 1946 to 1977 the Catholic People's Party participated in all governments, the Anti-Revolutionary Party in eleven and the Christian Historical Union in ten out of a total of fourteen governments. As mentioned earlier these three parties formed the Christian Democratic Appeal in the mid-1970s in an effort to stop the dwindling religious vote. The new inter-confessional party, uniting Catholics and Calvinists in the Netherlands for the first time, proved to be quite successful. It could stop the decline and subsequently stabilize the religious representation in parliament gaining on average 29.9 per cent of the seats in parliament in the seven elections from 1977 to 1998. The party participated in six coalition governments each of which was led by a prime minister of their own party.

The *Political Reformed Party* (Staatkundig Gereformeerde Partij; Religious), founded in 1918 as a breakaway from the Anti-Revolutionary Party, also belongs to the group of the old Dutch parties. It can rely persistently on a small conservative, law and order oriented group of Calvinists which represent about 2 per cent of the vote—enough to return between two or three of the party's candidates to each and every parliament. However, at no time was this party needed to make or break governments. The same is true for the *Reformed Political Union* (Gereformeerd Politiek Verbond; Religious), also Calvinist, and mostly campaigning against permissiveness in social behaviour. Even smaller than the Political

Reformed Party, the Reformed Political Union (on average 1.1 per cent of the vote) can also consistently count to return one or two members to parliament since 1963. Last in the Protestant camp is the *Evangelical People's Party* (Evangelische Volkspartij; Religious), a left-wing breakaway from the Anti-Revolutionary Party. This party promotes a consciously 'progressive policy' and is strongly opposed to the Christian Democratic Appeal. It sent one deputy to the 1982 parliament. As mentioned earlier the party became a constituent member of Groen Links in later years. On the Catholic side, two small and insignificant parties entered parliament and disappeared soon thereafter: the *Catholic National Party* (Katholieke Nationale Partij; Religious) and the *New Rome Party* (Nieuwe Roomse Partij; Religious). Both parties were breakaways from the Catholic People's Party which considered their parent party too liberal on moral issues. The New Rome Party made its appearance in the Dutch parliament only once (1972); the Catholic National Party, present in the 1948 and 1952 parliaments, reunited with the Catholic People's Party in 1955.

None of the agrarian or right-wing discontent parties have shown any coalition potential. The same is true for the two single-issue parties both campaigning as parties for pensioners. The *People's Party of the Right* (Rechtse-Volkspartij; Discontent), founded as the Boerenpartij and renamed in 1977, was set up to protest against the Industrial and Commodity Boards from the mid-1960s to the mid-1970s. The small party (2 per cent seats on average) was represented in five parliaments and disappeared from parliament after 1977. The *Middle Class Party* (Middenstands Partij; Discontent), which protested the influence of big industry and big labour unions, sent two deputies to the 1971 parliament. The *Centre Party* (Centrumpartij; Discontent) and the *Centre Democrats* (Centrumdemocraten; Discontent) were established as extreme right-wing, anti-immigration parties and had ties to the ultra-nationalist Dutch People's Union. The Centre Party sent one (1989) and three (1994), the Centre Democrats six (1994) members to parliament. The *General Association of Elderly People* (Algemeen Ouderen Verbond; Single Issue) and *Union 55+* (Unie+; Single Issue) represent efforts to establish parties for the elderly. They campaigned against a reduction of state pensions and other benefits for senior citizens. In the 1994 parliament the General Association of Elderly People occupied six, the Union 55+ one of the seats.

A.1.5 GERMANY

As in the Netherlands, the German party system reflects the class and the religious (state–church) cleavages. Pappi (1984) also introduced the idea of a (isosceles) triangle to describe the basic conflict structure of the 'old' German party system—much in line with the conceptualization of the Dutch colleagues. As in the Netherlands the major actors in this triangular structure are the Social Democrats, the Liberals, and the Christian Democrats. Their modal policy positions are largely similar to those cited for the Dutch case from the contribution by Pellikaan and colleagues (2004). However, in contrast to the Netherlands, the German post-re-unification party system is also characterized by an important centre–periphery cleavage. This cleavage, which is re-enforced by the federal structure of the German state, has been present before reunification (Roberts 1990) but was of lesser importance for the party system on the federal level. However, its relevance has drastically changed since German reunification. Analysing 'German Unification and Party System Change', Niedermayer (1998: 149–50) states that the dividing line between the western and the eastern part of the German party system is marked by electoral strength and coalition potential of the Party of Democratic Socialism.

The successor of the former GDR's leading party remains marginal in the West, but—by expressing the emerging intra-German center–periphery cleavage—it has established itself as one of the three big parties in the East with considerable relevance for the present structure and future development of the East German party system.

Because the Liberals and the Greens remain marginal in the 'new' Laender, party competition is mainly between the Christian Democrats, the (relatively weak) Social Democrats, and the Party of Democratic Socialism while in the 'old' Laender the competition involves the Christian Democrats, the Social Democrats, the Liberals, and the Greens with the Party of Democratic Socialism being marginal or non-existent. The emergence of the Greens and the growing importance of the centre–periphery dimension has greatly diminished the explanatory power of the triangular model.

The 5 per cent hurdle of the election law has prevented easy access to the German parliament. Translation of votes into seats is governed by proportional representation (Hare-Niemeyer). Half of the seats are allocated by relative majority at the constituency level; the other half is determined by fixed party lists at the state level. In this context it is important to know that parties which fail the 5 per cent criterion can participate in the distribution of votes if they win three seats in a constituency. This rule has helped the German Party to survive in the past as well as the Party of Democratic Socialism. Two special regulations need to be mentioned. The first one applies to the 1949 election; the second to the 1990 election. Both regulations had important consequences for the parties to achieve representation in parliament. In 1949 the 5 per cent hurdle was applied at the Laender level. As a consequence this allowed many regionally based parties entry to the 1949 parliament. In 1990 the Party of Democratic Socialism and the East German Alliance 90/Green Citizens' Movement profited from the ruling of the Constitutional Court to split the territory into a western and an eastern electoral region in which the 5 per cent hurdle was separately applied. While this rule enabled the Party of Democratic Socialism to enter the first all-German parliament, the direct mandate rule was instrumental for the party to be represented in the 1994 parliament.

On the left side of the German party system a communist, a left-socialist, and a socialist party have entered parliaments in the time period under study. Founded in 1863, the *Social Democratic Party of Germany* (Sozialdemokratische Partei Deutschlands, SPD; Socialist) established itself as the most successful party on the left. It became the main competitor to the Christian Democratic/Christian Union parties which governed until 1969. Lacking a response in the electorate the Social Democrats abandoned its original Marxist programme in 1959 and adjusted to the concept of a 'social market economy' in their Bad Godesberg programme. With a powerful base in the larger cities and the more industrialized states, the Social Democrats propagated strong central government, social welfare programmes and a 'normalization' of relations with Eastern Europe. Originally bitterly opposed to German re-armament and integration in the EC, the party changed its political positions before participating in a grand coalition with the Christian Democrats in 1966. West Germany's *Communist Party* (Kommunistische Partei Deutschlands, KPD; Communist) propagated a programme dictated by the Soviet communists. The party was represented in the first German Bundestag, did not win re-election in 1953, and was finally banned by the Constitutional Court in 1956. The *Party of Democratic Socialism* (Partei des Demokratischen Sozialismus, PDS; Left Socialist) entered the German party system in the process of German reunification. Formerly known as the Socialist Unity Party it renamed itself twice. In December 1989 it was called Socialist Unity Party—Party of Democratic Socialism, and shortly thereafter Party of Democratic Socialism the label it still carries today. Dedicated to a state socialist programme the party is almost exclusively represented in the 'new' Laender. Although insignificant in the 'old' Laender it proves to be a significant political player in the 'new' Laender both in terms of electoral strength and, increasingly, also in terms of coalition potential. The party is the main expression of the centre–periphery cleavage and has been classified as a regional party by many observers.

Germany is home to a strong Green party. Founded in 1979, its 1980 programme called for a worldwide ban on nuclear energy, prohibition of the use of chemical and biological weapons, and of the deployment of nuclear missiles in Europe, unilateral disarmament, the creation of a demilitarized zone in Europe, as well as the dismantling of NATO and the Warsaw Pact. Internally divided, their 'realistic' wing, favouring cooperation with the Social Democratic Party finally got the upper hand. In the 1983 election the Greens entered the national parliament and challenged the position of the Free Democrats as the only party able to make and break governments. In the 1990 election the West German Greens unexpectedly failed to pass the 5 per cent hurdle. Hesitant on the issue of German reunification the West German Greens stood for election separately from the common list formed in the new Laender (Alliance 90/Green Citizens' Movement) which gained representation instead. After that interlude the now united party named *Alliance 90/The Greens* (Buendnis 90/Die Gruenen; Ecologist) changed pattern of coalition formation and entered the 1994 and 1998 coalition governments led by Social Democrats.

The liberals are represented by the *Free Democratic Party* (Freie Demokratische Partei, FDP; Liberal). The party stands for free enterprise without state interference but it also advocates a programme of social reforms and has promoted conciliation with Central and Eastern Europe. Profiting from its pivotal position it was included in most coalition governments formed by both the Christian Democrats and the Social Democrats. Until the arrival of the Greens it was the pivotal party in the parliament who could make and break German governments. It stayed in government 85.4 per cent of the time in the period under study.

The *German Party* (Deutsche Partei, DP; Conservative) is the only German party which allows a classification as conservative. Founded as the Lower Saxony State Party in 1945 it advocated federalism, Christian values, protection of private property, reunification of Germany, and promoted interests of German refugees. Their historical ties to the House of Hannover and the 'Welfen' Party explain their preference for constitutional monarchy. The party was represented in the parliaments of 1949, 1953, and 1957. In 1953 and 1957 it profited from the regulation of the electoral law by which parties winning three constituencies participate in the proportional distribution of seats at the national level. As a coalition partner of the Adenauer governments the Christian Democrats made sure that the German Party could win the constituencies necessary by not fielding their own candidates. In 1960 the party split and most of its prominent members joined the Christian Democrats.

Founded in 1945 as an inter-confessional religious party the *Christian Democratic Union* (Christlich Demokratische Union, CDU; Religious) and its Bavarian affiliate, the *Christian Social Union* (Christlich Soziale Union, CSU; Religious) united Catholics and Protestants to sustain German life on the basis of Christian values and principles, and advocating the guarantee of private property as well as freedom of the individual. The two parties agreed that the Christian Democrats would not oppose the Christian Socials in Bavaria while the Christian Socials will not present candidates elsewhere. Since 1949 they have formed a single faction in parliament. The Christian parties formed nineteen out of a total of twenty-six governments and were in power 73.6 per cent of the time period under consideration. Although formally two independent parties the Christian Democratic Union and Christian Social Union are treated as one single party in this analysis. A third religious party, the *German Centre Party* (Deutsche Zentrumspartei, DZ; Religious) was represented in the 1949 and 1953 parliaments. The party wanted to re-establish the tradition of the once important Catholic Centre Party which was founded in 1870 but had to give way to the more successful inter-confessional Christian Democrats.

The *Economic Reconstruction League* (Wirtschaftliche Aufbauvereinigung, WAV; Discontent) and the *German Reich Party* (Deutsche Reichspartei, DRP;

Discontent) are both classified as discontent parties. The nationalistic and anti-parliamentary Economic Reconstruction League tried to mobilize dissatisfied lower middle-class groups in Bavaria and initially cooperated with refugee organizations. The *German Reich Party*, a right-wing extremist party, mostly attracted discontented former Nazi supporters. It sent five deputies to the 1949 parliament. In 1964 the party merged with parts of the former Socialist Reich Party (which had been banned by the Constitutional Court in 1952) to form the National Democratic Party of Germany.

Eased by the particular election law for the first national parliamentary election two regional parties could enter the 1949 Bundestag: the *Bavarian Party* (Bayernpartei, BP; Regional) and the *South Schleswig Voter's League* (Sued-schleswigscher Waehlerverband, SSW; Regional). The Bavarian Party campaigned for an independent Bavaria; the South Schleswig Voter's League represented the interests of the Danish and Friesian minorities and promoted a democratic society on the Scandinavian model. The Bavarian Party has become insignificant. As a minority party the South Schleswig Voter's League is exempted from the 5 per cent threshold rule and consistently obtains representation in the Schleswig-Holstein state legislature.

Finally, the *Refugee Party* (Gesamtdeutscher Block/Bund der Heimatvertrie-benen und Entrechteten, GB/BHE; Single Issue) was set up in 1950 to represent the social interests of the refugees. It mobilized the refugee vote successfully in 1953 and won twenty-seven seats. In 1957 it did not pass the 5 per cent hurdle and was no longer represented in parliament. The Refugee Party participated in the second Adenauer government and held the ministry for refugee affairs. It merged with the German Party in 1961 to form the All-German Party.

A.1.6 THE UNITED KINGDOM

Social class is often cited as the major British cleavage. However, territorial and regional conflicts are also of high importance. They often overlap with and strengthen the class cleavage (Miller 1981). Budge (1998: 130) states:

This sharp territorial contrast underlines the essential political conflict in the United Kingdom, between a coalition of dispersed, peripheral groups (both social and territorial) and a cohesive, centrally located and privileged group supporting the Conservatives—who can thus enhance their electoral appeal as defenders of the 'British' national interest. The restored Liberals, who might have bridged the gap between Labour and Conservatives, have been penalized by the electoral system, which privileges regionally concentrated parties.

Thus, Conservatives have pluralities in the south-east and Labour in the west and north, including Scotland and Wales. The importance of the regions is also reflected by the number of parties in the United Kingdom's parliament. In the period from 1945 to 2001, seventeen political parties were elected to the House of

Commons. This does not seem to square well with the preconceived notion of the United Kingdom as the prototypical two-party system.

For two reasons this high number of parties in parliament can be easily explained. First, there are three parties which were represented in the first post-war parliament only and never thereafter. This relates to the *Communist Party of Great Britain* (Communist), the *Independent Labour Party* (Socialist)—once a founding member of Labour in 1900—and the *National Liberal Party* (Liberal) formed as a consequence of coalition politics during the First World War. Second, but more important are the large number of national–regional parties of Scotland, Wales, and Northern Ireland. In Scotland, the *Scottish National Party* (Regional) was founded in 1934 at the merger of the National Party of Scotland and the Scottish Party. The *Party of Wales*, Plaid Cymru (Regional) emerged in 1925. Both parties sought constitutional, cultural, economic, and social reforms in their regions. Since 1970 and 1974 these parties are continuously represented in the House of Commons although with a small number of members of parliament only. The Scottish National Party and the Party of Wales allied with the Labour Party and the Liberal Democratic Party urging passage of the September 1997 referendum regarding a Scottish Parliament and a Welsh National Assembly. The Northern Irish parties which made it to parliament in the time period under consideration can easily be classified more finely by the degree to which they reject or support reunification of Northern Ireland with the Irish Republic. There have been frequent changes of party labels in both camps. This documentation follows Mackie and Rose (1991: 440) and Rose and McAllister (1982). In that tradition it includes votes for Ulster Unionist candidates with the British Conservative Party and votes for the Northern Ireland Labour Party with the British Labour Party until the 1974 election. The majority of the Northern Ireland delegates to parliament are 'Unionists' who are committed to the maintenance of Ulster's tie with the United Kingdom and to a continued separation from the Irish Republic. The *Ulster Unionists and Loyalists* (Regional)—which cooperate with the Conservative Party at the level of the United Kingdom—is the more moderate party compared to the *Democratic Unionist Party* (Regional). The latter party split from the Unionists in 1971 following a much more radical pro-Union and anti-Catholic programme. The *Ulster Popular Unionist Party* (Regional) and the *Britain Unionist Party* (Regional) which contested the 1992 and 1997 elections also belong to the Unionist's camp. Both parties have gained one seat respectively. Mackie and Rose (1991: 440) have classified individuals, standing under a variety of labels, but having a common allegiance to a united Ireland as *'United Ireland'* (Regional). This classification is followed here, too. United Ireland, the *Social Democratic and Labour Party* (Regional) as well as *Sinn Fein* (Regional) advocate reunification of Northern Ireland with the Irish Republic. The Social Democratic and Labour Party is the more moderate unification party. It proposes the eventual reunification of Ireland by popular consent. A much more radical, pro-unification position on the issue is propagated by Sinn Fein, a party founded in 1905. Sinn Fein has won seats in the House of Commons in 1997 and 2001 but it has never taken them up as a sign of their fundamental opposition to Westminster's policy on the Irish issue.

The five Scottish, Welsh, and Irish national–regional parties (plus 'United Ireland') which advocate devolution or separation, as well as the two Irish parties which campaign in favour of the United Kingdom send only a small number of deputies to Westminster. However, they are by no means unimportant to British politics. In fact they do, indeed, indicate the regional issue and they clearly play an important role in Scotland, Wales, and Northern Ireland.

Three parties formed a new one with the former *Liberal Party* (Liberal) as its core. In 1981 a group of liberal Labour dissidents formed the *Social Democratic Party* (Socialist) which campaigned for European integration, devolution, the introduction of a system of proportional representation, and welfare state policies. The Social Democratic Party concluded an agreement with the Liberal Party in 1982 and the two parties jointly contested the elections of 1983 and 1987 as an 'Alliance'. After the 1987 election a merger was proposed and formally approved leading in 1988 to the creation of the *Social and Liberal Democrats* (Liberal). Its shorter name was adopted in 1989. In 1977–8 the Liberals entered into a parliamentary accord with the Labour Party. Thus, after a long time out of power the Liberal Party permitted one of the two major parties to continue in office as a minority government. After the 1997 election the Liberal Democrats announced cooperation with the new Labour government and a special cabinet committee was established for regular consultation in areas of common interest. It must also be noted that on the regional level the Liberal Democrats entered coalition governments with the Labour Party both in Scotland (1999) and Wales (2000).

The British first-past-the-post-election law, however, greatly discriminates against the liberal parties. From 1945 to 1987 the Liberal Party had won an average of 10.3 per cent of the vote which translated into 1.7 per cent of the total number of seats in the House of Commons. For the period between 1992 and 2001 these figures were 17.7 per cent and 6 per cent for the Liberal Democrats respectively. Thus much of the stability of the acclaimed simple and clear-cut system of two-party competition between Labour and Conservatives is engineered by the electoral system. Budge (1998: 126) states this succinctly. 'Yet this impressive continuity and stability rests on one very narrow base—the electoral system.... It protects the two largest parties up to a point where a competitor gets less than 30 percent of the vote.'

The Labour Party and the Conservative Party have dominated parliament for decades. The *Labour Party* (Socialist) mainly represents the interests of the working class although under Tony Blair it has recently broadened its programmatic appeal. The *Conservative Party* (Conservative) advocates the rights of private property, a traditional moral order, and encourages market forces. The twelve Conservative governments covered 68 per cent of the time period under consideration and the eight Labour governments covered the rest of it. All British governments have been majority governments with the exception of the first Wilson cabinet which was a minority government supported by the Liberals as mentioned earlier.

TABLE A.1.1. *Key characteristics of political parties. Age, presence in parliament, average proportion of seats and votes, Sweden 1944–98*[1]

Parties	Foundation	Seats first	Seats last	Continuous	Seats			Votes		
					Mean	SD	N	Mean	SD	N
LS Vänsterpartiet	**1917**	**1944**	**1998**	**Yes**	**4.7**	**2.5**	**18**	**5.7**	**2.2**	**18**
SO Sveriges Socialdemokratistiska Arbetareparti	**1889**	**1944**	**1998**	**Yes**	**46.2**	**3.7**	**18**	**44.6**	**3.3**	**18**
EC Miljöpartiet de Gröna	**1981**	**1988**	**1998**	**No**	**5.2**	**0.6**	**3**	**4.8**	**0.8**	**3**
LI Centerpartiet	**1910**	**1944**	**1998**	**Yes**	**14.4**	**5.5**	**18**	**13.8**	**5.3**	**18**
LI Folkpartiet Liberalerna	**1934**	**1944**	**1998**	**Yes**	**14.3**	**6.2**	**18**	**14.0**	**5.9**	**18**
CO Moderate Samlingspartiet	**1904**	**1944**	**1998**	**Yes**	**17.8**	**4.4**	**18**	**17.5**	**3.9**	**18**
RE Kristdemokraterna	**1964**	**1991**	**1998**	**Yes**	**7.9**	**3.9**	**3**	**5.8**	**4.9**	**3**
DI Ny Demokrati	1991	1991	1991	Yes	7.2	*	1	6.7	*	1
R Mittenpartierna	1964	1964	1968	Yes	*	*	*	0.6	0.4	2
R Medborgelig Samling	1964	1964	1968	Yes	†	†	†	1.6	0.1	2
Others	1944	1944	1998	Yes	1.8	1.4	18	1.8	1.4	18

*1964: 2 deputies joined the Folkpartiet Liberalerna; 1968: 2 deputies joined the Centerpartiet, 1 deputy joined the Folkpartiet Liberalerna

†1964: 1 deputy joined the Folkpartiet Liberalerna and 1 deputy joined the Moderate Samlingspartiet; 1968: 3 deputies joined the Centerpartiet, 1 joined the Folkpartiet Liberalerna

[1]In Tables A.1.1 to A.1.6 data in bold typeface refer to relevant parties. The following abbreviations are used: COM = Communist, LS = Left-Socialist, SO = Socialist, EC = Ecologist, LI = Liberal, CO = Conservation, RE = Religious, DI = Discontent, R = National Regional, SI = Single Issue.

TABLE A.1.2. *Key characteristics of political parties. Age, presence in parliament, average proportion of seats and votes, Norway 1945–97*

Parties	Foundation	Seats first	Seats last	Continuous	Seats			Votes		
					Mean	SD	N	Mean	SD	N
COM Norges Kommunistiske Parti	1923	1945	1957	No	3.3	3.5	3	6.8	4.5	3
LS Rød Valgallianse	1993	1993	1993		0.6		1	1.1		1
LS Sosialistisk Venstreparti	1961	1961	1997	No	4.9	3.8	9	6.5	2.8	9
SO Det Norske Arbeiderpartiet	1887	1945	1997	Yes	46.4	5.6	14	41.4	5.0	14
LI Senterparti	1920	1945	1997	Yes	9.9	3.6	14	9.1	2.6	14
LI Venstre	1884	1945	1997	No	7.1	5.1	12	7.8	3.9	12
LI Det Liberale Folkeparti	1972	1973	1973		0.6		1	3.4		1
CO Høyre	1884	1945	1997	Yes	20.9	6.0	14	20.8	5.0	14
RE Kristelig Folkeparti	1933	1945	1997	Yes	9.7	2.8	14	9.8	1.8	14
DI Fremskrittsparti	1973	1973	1997	No	6.8	6.0	6	8.0	4.9	6
R Folkeaksjonen Framtid for Finmark	1989	1989	1989		0.6		1	0.3		1
R Kystpartiet	1997	1997	1997		0.6		1	0.4		1
Others		1945	1997	Yes				2.8	2.1	14

TABLE A.1.3. *Key characteristics of political parties. Age, presence in parliament, average proportion of seats and votes, Denmark 1945–2001*

Parties	Foundation	Seats first	Seats last	Continuous	Seats Mean	SD	N	Votes Mean	SD	N
COM Danmarks Kommunistiske Parti	**1919**	**1945**	**1977**	**No**	**5.2**	**2.7**	**9**	**5.3**	**2.9**	**9**
LS Socialistisk Folkeparti	**1959**	**1960**	**2001**	**Yes**	**8.5**	**3.3**	**17**	**8.2**	**3.1**	**17**
LS Venstresocialisterne	1967	1968	1984	No	2.8	0.4	6	2.7	0.6	6
LS Faelles Kurs	1987	1987	1987		2.3		1	2.2		1
LS Enheedslisten—De Roed Groenne	**1989**	**1994**	**2001**	**Yes**	**2.9**	**0.6**	**3**	**2.8**	**0.4**	**3**
SO Socialdemokratiet	**1871**	**1945**	**2001**	**Yes**	**36.4**	**4.8**	**23**	**35.6**	**4.7**	**23**
LI Venstre	**1870**	**1945**	**2001**	**Yes**	**19.9**	**6.5**	**23**	**19.0**	**5.9**	**23**
LI Det Radikale Venstre	**1903**	**1945**	**2001**	**Yes**	**7.2**	**3.2**	**23**	**7.1**	**3.0**	**23**
LI Retsforbundet	**1919**	**1945**	**1979**	**No**	**4.2**	**1.9**	**9**	**4.2**	**1.9**	**9**
LI Dansk Samling	1937	1945	1945		2.7		1	3.1		1
LI De Uafhaengige	1953	1960	1964	Yes	3.1	0.4	2	2.9	0.6	2
LI Liberalt Centrum	1965	1966	1966		2.3		1	2.5		1
LI Centrum Demokraterne	**1973**	**1973**	**1998**	**Yes**	**5.1**	**2.0**	**11**	**4.8**	**1.9**	**11**
CO Konservative Folkeparti	**1893**	**1945**	**2001**	**Yes**	**15.8**	**4.9**	**23**	**15.5**	**4.7**	**23**
RE Kristeligt Folkeparti	**1970**	**1973**	**2001**	**No**	**2.9**	**0.9**	**11**	**2.9**	**1.0**	**11**
DI Fremskridtspartiet	**1973**	**1973**	**1998**	**Yes**	**8.9**	**4.6**	**11**	**8.8**	**4.6**	**11**
DI Danske Folkeparti	**1995**	**1998**	**2001**	**Yes**	**10.0**	**3.6**	**2**	**9.7**	**3.3**	**2**
R Det Slesvigske Parti	1919	1953	1960	Yes	0.6	0.0	3	0.4	0.1	3
Others	1919	1945	2001	Yes				2.6	1.8	23

TABLE A.1.4. *Key characteristics of political parties. Age, presence in parliament, average proportion of seats and votes, the Netherlands 1946–98*

Parties	Foundation	Seats first	Seats last	Continuous	Seats			Votes		
					Mean	SD	N	Mean	SD	N
COM Communistische Partij van Nederland	1909	1946	1982	Yes	4.2	2.7	12	4.3	2.7	12
LS Pacifistisch-Socialistische Partij	1957	1959	1986	Yes	1.6	0.8	9	1.9	0.7	9
LS Politieke Partij Radikalen	1968	1971	1986	Yes	2.1	1.3	6	2.2	1.3	6
LS Socialistische Partij	1994	1994	1998	Yes	2.3	1.4	2	2.4	1.6	2
LS Groen Links	1991	1989	1998	Yes	4.9	2.1	3	5.0	2.0	3
SO Partij van der Arbeid	1946	1946	1998	Yes	29.9	3.3	16	28.8	3.2	16
SO Democraten 66	1966	1967	1998	Yes	7.6	3.8	10	7.5	3.6	10
SO Democratische Socialisten 70	1970	1971	1977	Yes	3.3	2.4	3	3.4	2.4	3
LI Volkspartij voor Vrijheid en Democratie	1948	1946	1998	Yes	14.4	5.8	16	14.1	5.6	16
RE Katholieke Volkspartij	1945	1946	1972	Yes	29.1	5.3	9	28.0	5.1	9
RE Katholieke Nationale Partij	1948	1948	1952	Yes	1.5	0.7	2	2.0	1.0	2
RE Nieuwe Roomse Partij	1971	1972	1972		0.7		1	0.9		1
RE Anti-Revolutionaire Partij	1879	1946	1972	Yes	10.4	1.8	9	10.3	1.8	9
RE Christelijk-Historieke Unie	1908	1946	1972	Yes	7.8	1.4	9	7.8	1.4	9

(*Continued*)

TABLE A.1.4. *Key characteristics of political parties. Age, presence in parliament, average proportion of seats and votes, the Netherlands 1946–98 (Contd.)*

Parties	Foundation	Seats first	Seats last	Continuous	Seats			Votes		
					Mean	SD	N	Mean	SD	N
RE Staatkundig Gereformeerde Partij	1918	1946	1998	yes	2.0	0.2	16	2.1	0.2	16
RE Gereformeerd Politiek Verbond	1952	1963	1998	yes	1.0	0.3	11	1.1	0.4	11
RE Reformatorische Politieke Federatie	1977	1981	1998	yes	1.3	0.6	6	1.4	0.4	6
RE Evangelische Volkspartij	1981	1982	1982		0.7		1	0.7		1
RE Christen Democratisch Appel	**1975**	**1977**	**1998**	**yes**	**29.9**	**6.5**	**7**	**29.0**	**6.4**	**7**
DI Rechtse- Volkspartij	1958	1963	1977	yes	2.0	1.6	5	2.1	1.6	5
DI Middenstands Partij	1971	1971	1971		1.3		1	1.4		1
DI Centrumpartij	1982	1982	1982		0.7		1	0.8		1
DI Centrumdemocraten	1989	1989	1994	yes	1.3	0.9	2	1.7	1.1	2
SI Allgemeen Ouderen Verbond	1994	1994	1994		4.0		1	3.6		1
SI Unie+	1994	1994	1994		0.7		1	0.9		1
Others	1946	1946	1998	yes	0.7			1.9	0.5	16

COM Communist, LS Left Socialist, RE Religious, DI Discontent, SI Single Issue
Bold face: Relevant parties.

TABLE A.1.5. *Key characteristics of political parties. Age, presence in parliament, average proportion of seats and votes, Germany 1949–98*

Parties	Foundation	Seats first	Seats last	Continuous	Seats Mean	Seats SD	Seats N	Votes Mean	Votes SD	Votes N
COM Kommunistische Partei Deutschlands	1918	1949	1949		3.7		1	5.7		1
LS Partei des Demokratischen Sozialismus	1946	1990	1998	Yes	4.1	1.4	3	4.0	1.4	3
SO Sozialdemokratische Partei Deutschlands	1863	1949	1998	Yes	39.2	4.9	14	37.5	5.3	14
EC Buendnis 90 / Die Gruenen*	1980	1983	1998	Yes	5.9	2.8	5	6.6	1.3	5
LI Freie Demokratische Partei	1948	1949	1998	Yes	9.2	2.4	14	8.9	2.1	14
CO Deutsche Partei	1945	1949	1957	Yes	3.6	0.6	3	3.6	0.4	3
RE Deutsche Zentrumspartei	1870	1949	1953	Yes	1.6	1.3	2	2.0	1.6	2
RE Christlich Demokratische Union/Christlich Soziale Union†	1945	1949	1998	Yes	46.3	5.2	14	44.1	5.3	14
DI Wirtschaftliche Aufbauvereinigung	1945	1949	1949		3.0		1	2.9		1
DI Deutsche Reichspartei	1949	1949	1949		1.2		1	1.8		1
R Bayernpartei	1946	1949	1949		4.2		1	4.2		1
R Suedschleswigscher Waehlerverband	1948	1949	1949		0.3		1	0.3		1
SI Gesamtdeutscher Block/Bund der Heimatvertriebenen und Entrechteten	1950	1953	1953		5.5		1	5.9		1
Others		1949	1998	Yes				3.8	2.3	14

*Buendnis 90/Die Gruenen cover all three 'Green' party formations
†The Christlich Demokratische Union and the Christlich Soziale Union form a single party (Fraktion) in the parliament

TABLE A.1.6. *Key characteristics of political parties. Age, presence in parliament, proportion of seats and votes, the United Kingdom 1945–2001*

Parties	Foundation	Seats first	Seats last	Continuous	Seats			Votes		
					Mean	SD	N	Mean	SD	N
COM Communist Party	1920	1945	1945		0.3		1	0.4		1
SO Independent Labour Party	1932	1945	1945		0.5		1	0.2		1
SO Labour Party	**1900**	**1945**	**2001**	**Yes**	**48.3**	**9.3**	**16**	**41.2**	**6.3**	**16**
SO Social Democratic Party	1981	1983	1987	Yes	0.8	0.1	2	10.7	1.3	2
LI National Liberal Party	1918	1945	1945		1.7		1	2.9		1
LI Liberal Party	**1852**	**1945**	**1987**	**Yes**	**1.7**	**0.6**	**13**	**10.3**	**5.2**	**13**
LI Liberal Democrats	**1988**	**1992**	**2001**	**Yes**	**6.0**	**2.6**	**3**	**17.7**	**0.8**	**3**
CO Conservative Party	**1834**	**1945**	**2001**	**Yes**	**46.8**	**11.2**	**16**	**41.6**	**5.7**	**16**
R Scottish National Party	1934	1970	2001	Yes	0.7	0.5	9	1.7	0.6	9
R Party of Wales	1925	1974	2001	Yes	0.5	0.1	8	0.5	0.1	8
R Ulster Unionists	1892	1974	2001	Yes	1.6	0.4	8	1.0	0.4	8
R Ulster Popular Unionist Party		1992	1992		0.2		1	0.1		1
R UK Unionist Party		1994	1994		0.2		1	0.1		1
R Democratic Unionist Party	1971	1992	2001	Yes	0.5	0.2	3	0.4	0.2	3
R United Ireland	1945	1945	1987	No	0.3	0.1	10	0.4	0.1	10
R Social Democratic and Labour Party	1970	1974	2001	Yes	0.3	0.2	8	0.5	0.1	8
R Sinn Fein	1905	1997	2001	Yes	0.5	0.2	2	0.6	0.2	2
Others		1945	2001	Yes				1.5	1.2	16

TABLE A.2.1. *Election results: Proportion of valid votes, degree of fragmentation and volatility, Sweden 1944–98*

Party	Sept. 1944	Sept. 1948	Sept. 1952	Sept. 1956	June 1958	Sept. 1960	Sept. 1964	Sept. 1968	Sept. 1970	Sept. 1973	Sept. 1976	Sept. 1979	Sept. 1982	Sept. 1985	Sept. 1988	Sept. 1991	Sept. 1994	Sept. 1998
Vänsterpartiet	10.3	6.3	4.3	5.0	3.4	4.5	5.2	3.0	4.8	5.3	4.8	5.6	5.6	5.4	5.8	4.5	6.2	12.0
Sveriges Socialdemokratistiska Arbetareparti	46.6	46.1	46.1	44.6	46.2	47.8	47.3	50.1	45.3	43.6	42.8	43.2	45.6	44.7	43.2	37.7	45.3	36.4
Miljöpartiet de Gröna															5.5		5.0	4.0
Centerpartiet	13.6	12.4	10.7	9.5	12.7	13.6	13.2	15.7	19.9	25.1	24.1	18.1	15.5	12.4	11.3	8.5	7.7	5.1
Folkpartiet Liberalerna	12.9	22.8	24.4	23.8	18.2	17.5	17.0	14.3	16.2	9.4	11.1	10.6	5.9	14.2	12.2	9.1	7.2	4.7
Moderate Samlingspartiet	15.8	12.3	14.4	17.1	19.5	16.6	13.7	12.9	11.5	14.3	15.6	20.3	23.6	21.3	18.3	21.9	22.4	22.9
Kristdemokraterna														0.3		7.1	4.1	11.8
Ny Demokrati																6.7		
Mittenpartierna							0.3	0.9										
Medborgelig Samling							1.5	1.7										
Others	0.7	0.1	0.1	0.1	0.0	0.1	1.8	1.5	2.3	2.4	1.8	2.2	3.9	2.0	3.6	4.4	2.2	2.6
Fragmentation*	0.71	0.70	0.69	0.70	0.70	0.69	0.71	0.69	0.71	0.71	0.72	0.72	0.70	0.72	0.74	0.78	0.72	0.78
Volatility†		11.3	3.1	3.4	7.3	3.7	4.3	6.1	8.8	8.6	3.0	6.4	7.4	8.4	7.4	18.2	14.7	14.7

*Rae's F

†Pedersen's V

Table A.2.2. *Election results: Proportion of valid votes, degree of fragmentation and volatility, Norway 1945–97*

Party	Oct. 1945	Oct. 1949	Oct. 1953	Oct. 1957	Sept. 1961	Sept. 1965	Sept. 1969	Sept. 1973	Sept. 1977	Sept. 1981	Sept. 1985	Sept. 1989	Sept. 1993	Sept. 1997
Norges Kommunistiske Parti	11.9		5.1	3.4										
Rod Valgallianse													1.1	
Sosialistisk Venstreparti					2.4	6.0		11.2	4.2	4.9	5.5	10.0	7.9	6.0
Det Norske Arbeiderparti	41.0	45.7	46.7	48.3	46.8	43.1	46.5	35.3	42.3	37.2	40.8	34.3	36.9	35.0
Senterpartiet	8.0	7.9	9.4	9.3	9.4	9.9	10.5	11.0	8.6	6.7	6.6	6.5	16.7	7.9
Venstre	13.8	13.1	10.0	9.6	8.8	10.4	9.4	3.5	3.2	3.9			3.6	4.5
Det Liberale Folkeparti								3.4						
Høyre	17.0	18.3	18.4	18.9	20.0	21.1	19.5	17.4	24.8	31.7	30.4	22.2	17.0	14.3
Kristelig Folkeparti	7.9	8.4	10.5	10.2	9.6	8.1	9.4	12.3	12.4	8.9	8.3	8.5	7.9	13.7
Fremskrittsparti								5.0		4.5	3.7	13.0	6.3	15.3
Folkeaksjonen Framtid for Finnmark												0.3		
Kystpartiet														0.4
Others	0.4	6.6	0.0	0.3	3.0	1.4	4.7	0.9	4.5	2.2	4.7	5.2	2.6	2.9
Fragmentation*	0.76	0.72	0.72	0.70	0.71	0.74	0.71	0.80	0.73	0.74	0.72	0.79	0.79	0.80
Volatility†		12.7	9.8	2.5	6.3	6.8	8.6	23.0	18.1	12.8	6.7	14.8	17.5	16.4

*Rae's F

†Pedersen's V

TABLE A.2.3. Election results: Proportion of valid votes, degree of fragmentation and volatility, Denmark 1945–2001

Party	Oct. 1945	Oct. 1947	Sept. 1950	Apr. 1953	Sept. 1953	May 1957	Nov. 1960	Sept. 1964	Nov. 1966	Jan. 1968	Sept. 1971	Dec. 1973	Jan. 1975	Fe. 1977	Oct. 1979	Dec. 1981	Jan. 1984	Sept. 1987	May 1988	Dec. 1990	Sept. 1994	Mar. 1998	Nov. 2001
Danmarks Kommunistiske Parti	12.5	6.8	4.6	4.8	4.3	3.1						3.6	4.2	3.7									
Socialistisk Folkeparti							6.1	5.8	10.9	6.1	9.1	6.0	5.0	3.9	5.9	11.3	11.5	14.6	13.0	8.3	7.3	7.6	6.4
Venstresocialisterne										2.0			2.1	2.7	3.7	2.7	2.7						
Fælles Kurs																		2.2					
Enheedslisten—De Roed Groenne																					3.2	2.7	2.4
Socialdemokratiet	32.8	40.0	39.6	40.4	41.3	39.4	42.1	41.9	38.3	34.2	37.3	25.7	29.9	37.0	38.3	32.9	31.6	29.3	29.8	37.4	34.6	35.9	29.1
Venstre	23.4	27.6	21.3	22.1	23.1	25.1	21.1	20.8	19.3	18.6	15.6	12.3	23.3	12.0	12.5	11.3	12.1	10.5	11.8	15.8	23.3	24.0	31.2
Det Radikale Venstre	8.2	6.9	8.2	8.6	7.8	7.8	5.8	5.3	7.3	15.0	14.3	11.2	7.1	3.7	5.4	5.1	5.5	6.2	5.6	3.6	4.6	3.9	5.2
Retsforbundet	1.9	4.5	8.2	5.6	3.5	5.3						2.9		3.3	2.6								
Dank Samling	3.1																						
De Uafhaengige							3.3	2.5															
Liberalt Centrum									2.5														
Centrum-Demokraterne												7.8	2.2	6.4	3.2	8.3	4.6	4.8	4.7	5.1	2.8	4.3	2.3
Konservative Folkeparti	18.2	12.4	17.8	17.3	16.9	16.6	17.9	20.1	18.7	20.4	16.7	9.2	5.5	8.5	12.5	14.5	23.5	20.8	19.3	16.0	15.0	8.9	9.1
Kristeligt Folkeparti												4.1	5.3	3.4	2.6	2.3	2.7	2.4	2.0	2.3		2.5	2.3
Fremkridtspartiet												15.9	13.6	14.6	11.0	8.9	3.6	4.8	9.0	6.4	6.4	2.4	
Danske Folkeparti																						7.4	12.0
Det Slesvigske Parti					0.5	0.4	0.4																
Others	0.0	1.8	0.3	1.2	2.6	2.3	3.3	3.6	3.0	3.7	7.0	1.3	1.8	0.8	2.3	2.7	2.2	4.4	4.8	5.1	2.8	0.4	2.3
Fragmentation*	0.78	0.74	0.75	0.75	0.74	0.74	0.74	0.73	0.76	0.78	0.78	0.86	0.82	0.81	0.80	0.83	0.81	0.83	0.83	0.79	0.79	0.79	0.79
Volatility†	15.9	15.9	10.4	3.1	3.8	3.8	14.4	2.5	9.6	12.1	9.4	34.6	19.6	19.2	12.0	12.9	10.8	9.6	6.4	12.6	11.7	13.7	15.2

*Rae's F
†Pedersen's V

TABLE A.2.4. *Election results: Proportion of valid votes, degree of fragmentation and volatility, the Netherlands 1946–98*

Party	May 1946	July 1948	June 1952	June 1956	Mar. 1959	May 1963	Feb. 1967	Mar. 1971	Nov. 1972	May 1977	May 1981	Sept. 1982	May 1986	Sept. 1989	May 1994	May 1998
Communistische Partij van Nederland	10.6	7.7	6.2	4.8	2.4	2.8	3.6	3.9	4.5	1.7	2.1	1.8				
Pacifistisch-Socialistische Partij					1.8	3.0	2.9	1.4	1.5	0.9	2.1	2.3	1.2			
Politieke Partij Radicalen								1.8	4.8	1.7	2.0	1.7	1.3			
Socialistische Partij															1.3	3.5
Groen Links														4.1	3.5	7.3
Partij van de Arbeid	28.3	25.6	29.0	32.7	30.4	28.0	23.6	24.6	27.3	33.8	28.3	30.4	33.3	32.0	24.0	29.0
Democraten 66							4.5	6.8	4.2	5.4	11.1	4.3	6.1	7.9	15.5	9.0
Democratische Socialisten 70								5.3	4.1	0.7						
Volkspartij voor Vrijheid en Democratie	6.4	7.9	8.8	8.8	12.2	10.3	10.7	10.3	14.5	18.0	17.3	23.1	17.4	14.6	20.0	24.7
Katholieke Volkspartij	30.8	31.0	28.7	31.7	31.6	31.9	26.5	21.8	17.7							
Katholieke Nationale Partij		1.3	2.7													
Nieuwe Roomse Partij									0.9							
Anti-Revolutionaire Partij	12.9	13.2	11.3	9.9	9.4	8.7	9.9	8.6	8.8							
Christelijk-Historische Unie	7.8	9.2	8.9	8.4	8.1	8.6	8.1	6.3	4.8							
Staatkundig Gereformeerde Partij	2.1	2.4	2.4	2.3	2.2	2.3	2.0	2.4	2.2	2.1	2.0	1.9	1.7	1.9	1.7	1.8
Gereformeerd Politiek Verbond						0.7	0.9	1.6	1.8	1.0	0.8	0.8	1.0	1.2	1.3	1.3
Reformatorische Politieke Federatie											1.3	1.5	0.9	1.0	1.8	2.0
Evangelische Volkspartij												0.7				
Christen-Democratisch Appel										31.9	30.8	29.4	34.6	35.4	22.2	18.4
Rechtse Volkspartij						2.1	4.8	1.1	1.9	0.8						
Middenstands Partij								1.4								
Centrumpartij												0.8				
Centrumdemocraten														0.9	2.5	
Algemeen Ouderen Verbond															3.6	
Unie 55+															0.9	
Others	1.0	1.6	2.1	1.6	2.0	1.6	2.6	2.5	1.1	1.9	2.3	1.4	2.5	1.4	1.8	2.7
Fragmentation*	0.79	0.80	0.80	0.76	0.78	0.79	0.84	0.86	0.85	0.75	0.78	0.76	0.73	0.74	0.82	0.80
Volatility†		5.6	6.1	6.7	5.7	5.4	10.8	13.4	12.6	44.0	9.2	9.8	11.3	7.9	21.9	17.1

*Rae's F

†Pedersen's V

TABLE A.2.5. *Election results: Proportion of valid votes, degree of fragmentation and volatility, Germany 1949–98*

Party	Aug. 1949	Sept. 1953	Sept. 1957	Sept. 1961	Sept. 1965	Sept. 1969	Nov. 1972	Oct. 1976	Oct. 1980	March 1983	Jan. 1987	Dec. 1990	Sept. 1994	Sept. 1998
Kommunistische Partei Deutschlands	5.7													
Partei des Demokratischen Sozialismus												2.4	4.4	5.1
Sozialdemokratische Partei Deutschlands	29.2	28.8	31.8	36.2	39.3	42.7	45.9	42.6	42.9	38.2	37.0	33.5	36.4	40.9
Buendnis 90/Die Gruenen[1]										5.6	8.3	5.1	7.3	6.7
Freie Demokratische Partei	11.9	9.5	7.7	12.8	9.5	5.8	8.4	7.9	10.6	7.0	9.1	11.0	6.9	6.3
Deutsche Partei	4.0	3.3	3.4											
Deutsche Zentrumspartei	3.1	0.8												
Christlichdemokratische Union/ Christlichsozial Union	31.0	45.2	50.2	45.4	47.6	46.1	44.9	48.7	44.5	48.8	44.3	43.8	41.5	35.1
Wirtschaftliche Aufbauvereinigung	2.9													
Deutsche Reichspartei	1.8													
Bayernpartei	4.2													
Suedschleswigscher Waehlerverband	0.3													
Gesamtdeutscher Block/Bund der Heimatvertriebenen und Entrechteten		5.9												
Others	5.9	6.5	6.9	5.6	3.6	5.4	0.8	0.8	2.0	0.4	1.3	4.2	3.5	5.9
Fragmentation*	0.79	0.69	0.64	0.64	0.61	0.60	0.58	0.58	0.61	0.61	0.65	0.68	0.68	0.69
Volatility†		20.7	8.5	9.5	5.3	5.2	5.8	3.8	4.2	9.9	5.7	7.2	7.1	7.6

[1] Die Gruenen and Buendnis 90 ran as independent parties in 1990. Die Gruenen failed to pass the 5% hurdle. Buendnis 90 reached the quorum in East Germany and represented the Greens in parliament. 5.1% is the proportion of votes for Die Gruenen and for Buendnis 90 together; 1.2% is the proportion for Buendnis 90.

*Rae's *F*

†Pedersen's *V*

TABLE A.2.6. *Election results: Proportion of valid votes, degree of fragmentation and volatility, the United Kingdom 1945–2001*

Party	July 1945	Feb. 1950	Oct. 1951	May 1955	Oct. 1959	Oct. 1964	Mar. 1966	June 1970	Feb. 1974	Oct. 1974	May 1979	June 1983	June 1987	Apr. 1992	May 1997	June 2001
Communist Party of Britain	0.4															
Independent Labour Party	0.2															
Labour Party	48.0	46.1	48.8	46.4	43.8	44.1	48.0	43.1	37.2	39.3	36.9	27.6	30.8	34.4	43.2	40.7
Social Democratic Party												11.6	9.7			
National Liberal Party	2.9															
Liberal Party	9.0	9.1	2.6	2.7	5.9	11.2	8.5	7.5	19.3	18.3	13.8	13.7	12.8			
Liberal Democrats														17.9	16.8	18.3
Conservative Party	36.8	43.4	48.0	49.7	49.4	43.4	41.9	46.4	37.9	35.8	43.9	42.4	42.3	41.9	30.7	31.7
Scottish National Party								1.1	2.0	2.9	1.6	1.1	1.3	1.9	2.0	1.8
Party of Wales									0.5	0.6	0.4	0.4	0.4	0.5	0.5	0.7
Ulster Unionists and Loyalists									1.5	1.5	1.3	1.4	1.2	0.8	0.8	0.8
Ulster Popular Unionist Party														0.1		
Britain Unionist Party															0.0	
Democratic Unionist Party										0.2	0.2	0.4	0.3	0.3	0.3	0.7
United Ireland	0.4	0.4	0.4	0.6			0.5	0.6								
Social Democratic and Labour Party									0.5	0.5	0.4	0.4	0.5	0.5	0.6	0.6
Sinn Fein															0.4	0.7
Others	2.3	1.0	0.2	0.6	0.7	0.9	1.1	1.3	0.9	0.9	1.5	1.0	0.7	1.7	4.6	4.0
Fragmentation*	0.62	0.59	0.53	0.54	0.56	0.60	0.59	0.59	0.68	0.68	0.65	0.71	0.70	0.67	0.69	0.70
Volatility†		6.9	7.3	2.4	3.4	5.9	4.4	5.9	15.3	3.2	8.7	11.9	3.1	23.6	12.4	3.4

*Rae's F
†Pedersen's V

TABLE A.3.1. *Election results: Proportion of seats in parliament, degree of fragmentation and volatility, Sweden 1944–98*

Party	Sept. 1944	Sept. 1948	Sept. 1952	Sept. 1956	June 1958	Sept. 1960	Sept. 1964	Sept. 1968	Sept. 1970	Sept. 1973	Sept. 1976	Sept. 1979	Sept. 1982	Sept. 1985	Sept. 1988	Sept. 1991	Sept. 1994	Sept. 1998
Vänsterpartiet	6.53	3.5	2.2	2.6	2.2	2.2	3.4	1.3	4.9	5.4	4.9	5.7	5.7	5.4	6.0	4.9	6.3	12.3
Sveriges Socialdemokratistiska Arbetareparti	50.0	48.7	47.8	45.9	48.1	49.1	48.5	53.7	46.6	44.6	43.6	44.1	47.6	45.6	44.7	39.5	46.1	37.5
Miljöpartiet de Gröna															5.7		5.2	4.6
Centerpartiet	15.2	13.0	11.3	8.2	13.9	14.7	15.5	16.7	20.3	25.7	24.6	18.3	16.1	12.6	12.0	8.9	7.7	5.2
Folkpartiet Liberalerna	11.3	24.8	25.2	25.1	16.5	17.2	18.5	14.6	16.6	9.7	11.2	10.9	6.0	14.6	12.6	9.5	7.5	4.9
Moderate Samlingspartiet	17.0	10.0	13.5	18.2	19.5	16.8	14.2	13.7	11.7	14.6	15.8	20.9	24.6	21.8	18.9	22.9	22.9	23.5
Kristdemokraterna[‡]														0.3		7.5	4.3	12.0
Ny Demokrati																7.2		
Mittenpartierna							0.3	0.9										
Medborgelig Samling[§]							1.5	1.7										
Total number of seats	230	230	230	231	231	232	233	233	350	350	349	349	349	349	349	349	349	349
Fragmentation*	0.68	0.67	0.68	0.69	0.68	0.68	0.69	0.64	0.70	0.70	0.71	0.71	0.68	0.70	0.73	0.76	0.71	0.77
Volatility[†]		13.5	3.9	5.1	9.1	2.6	3.3	6.5	9.2	8.9	2.7	6.5	7.2	8.6	6.4	18.5	13.4	14.3

*Rae's F

[†]Pedersen's V

[‡]There was an electoral alliance of the Centerpartiet and the Kristdemokraterna in 1985. 1 candidate of the Kristdemokraterna entered parliament.

[§]Mittenpartierna. 1964: 2 deputies joined the Folkpartiet Liberalerna; 1968: 2 deputies joined the Centerpartiet, 1 deputy joined the Folkpartiet Liberalerna.
Medborgelig Samling. 1964: 1 deputy joined the Folkpartiet Liberalerna and 1 deputy joined the Moderate Samlingspartiet; 1968: 3 deputies joined the Centerpartiet and 1 deputy joined the Folkpartiet Liberalerna.

TABLE A.3.2. *Election results: Proportion of seats in parliament, degree of fragmentation and volatility, Norway 1945–97*

Party	Oct. 1945	Oct. 1949	Oct. 1953	Oct. 1957	Sept. 1961	Sept. 1965	Sept. 1969	Sept. 1973	Sept. 1977	Sept. 1981	Sept. 1985	Sept. 1989	Sept. 1993	Sept. 1997
Norges Kommunistiske Parti	7.3		2.0	0.7	1.3	1.3								
Rod Valgallianse													0.7	
Sosialistisk Venstreparti								10.3	1.3	2.6	3.8	10.3	7.9	5.5
Det Norske Arbeiderparti	50.7	56.7	51.3	52.0	49.3	45.3	49.3	40.0	49.0	42.6	45.2	38.2	40.6	39.4
Senterpartiet	6.7	8.0	9.3	10.0	10.7	12.0	13.3	13.6	7.7	7.1	7.6	6.7	19.4	6.7
Venstre	13.3	14.0	10.0	10.0	9.3	12.0	8.7	1.3	1.3	1.3			0.6	3.6
Det Liberale Folkeparti								0.7						
Høyre	16.7	15.3	18.0	19.3	19.3	20.7	19.3	18.7	26.5	34.2	31.9	22.4	17.0	13.9
Kristelig Folkeparti	5.3	6.0	9.3	8.0	10.0	8.7	9.3	12.9	14.2	9.7	10.2	8.5	7.9	15.2
Fremskrittsparti								2.6		2.6	1.3	13.0	6.1	15.2
Folkeaksjonen Framtid for Finnmark												0.6		
Kystpartiet														0.6
Total number of seats	150	150	150	150	150	150	150	155	155	155	157	165	165	165
Fragmentation*	0.69	0.63	0.68	0.67	0.69	0.72	0.69	0.76	0.66	0.69	0.68	0.76	0.75	0.77
Volatility†	8.7	8.7	9.4	2.7	4.1	5.4	6.0	17.4	18.2	11.6	4.9	19.0	16.2	20.1

*Rae's F

†Pedersen's V

Table A.3.3. Election results. Proportion of seats in parliament, degree of fragmentation and volatility, Denmark 1945–2001

Party	Oct. 1945	Oct. 1947	Sept. 1950	Apr. 1953	Sept. 1953	May 1957	Nov. 1960	Sept. 1964	Nov. 1966	Jan. 1968	Sept. 1971	Dec. 1973	Jan. 1975	Feb. 1977	Oct. 1979	Dec. 1981	Jan. 1984	Sept. 1987	May 1988	Dec. 1990	Sept. 1994	Mar. 1998	Nov. 2001
Danmarks Kommunistiske Parti	12.2	6.1	4.7	4.7	4.6	3.4						3.4	4.0	4.0									
Socialistisk Folkeparti							6.3	5.7	11.4	6.3	9.7	6.3	5.1	4.0	6.3	12.0	12.0	15.4	13.7	8.6	7.4	7.4	6.9
Venstresocialisterne										2.3			2.3	2.9	3.4	2.9	2.9						
Fælles Kurs																		2.3					
Enhedslisten—De Roed Groenne																					3.4	2.9	2.3
Socialdemokratiet	32.4	38.5	39.6	40.9	42.3	40.0	43.4	43.4	39.4	35.5	40.0	26.3	30.3	37.1	38.9	33.7	32.0	30.5	31.4	39.4	35.4	36.0	29.7
Venstre	25.7	33.1	21.5	22.2	24.0	25.7	21.7	21.7	20.0	19.4	17.1	12.6	24.0	12.0	12.6	11.4	12.6	10.9	12.6	16.6	24.0	24.0	32.0
Det Radikale Venstre	7.4	6.8	8.1	8.7	8.0	8.0	6.3	5.7	7.4	15.4	15.4	11.4	7.4	3.4	5.7	5.1	5.7	6.3	5.7	4.0	4.6	4.0	5.1
Retsforbundet	2.0	4.1	8.1	6.0	3.4	5.1						2.9		3.4	2.9								
Dank Samling	2.7																						
De Uafhaengige							3.4	2.9															
Liberalt Centrum									2.3														
Centrum-Demokraterne												8.0	2.3	6.3	3.4	8.6	4.6	5.1	5.1	5.1	2.9	4.6	
Konservative Folkeparti	17.6	11.5	18.1	17.5	17.1	17.1	18.3	20.6	19.4	21.1	17.7	9.1	5.7	8.6	12.6	14.9	24.0	21.7	20.0	17.1	16.0	9.1	9.1
Kristeligt Folkeparti												4.0	5.1	3.4	2.9	2.3	2.9	2.3	2.3	2.3		2.3	2.3
Fremkridtspartiet												16.0	13.7	14.9	11.4	9.1	3.4	5.1	9.1	6.9	6.3	2.3	
Danske Folkeparti																						7.4	12.6
Det Slesvigske Parti	—				0.6	0.6	0.6																
Total number of seats	148	148	149	149	175	175	175	175	175	175	175	175	175	175	175	175	175	175	175	175	175	175	175
Fragmentation*	0.78	0.72	0.75	0.74	0.72	0.73	0.75	0.71	0.75	0.76	0.75	0.85	0.82	0.81	0.79	0.82	0.80	0.81	0.81	0.77	0.78	0.79	0.78
Volatility†	15.7	15.7	13.0	2.4	3.8	3.5	14.3	2.3	9.8	12.0	8.0	34.3	19.5	18.9	11.5	13.3	11.5	8.6	6.3	12.0	11.4	12.0	14.3

*Rae's F
†Pedersen's V

TABLE A.3.4. *Election results: Proportion of seats in parliament, degree of fragmentation and volatility, the Netherlands 1946–98*

Party	May 1946	July 1948	June 1952	June 1956	Mar. 1959	May 1963	Feb. 1967	Mar. 1971	Nov. 1972	May 1977	May 1981	Sept. 1982	May 1986	Sept. 1989	May 1994	May 1998
Communistische Partij van Nederland	10.0	8.0	6.0	4.0	2.0	2.7	3.3	4.0	4.7	1.3	2.0	2.0				
Pacifistisch-Socialistische Partij					1.3	2.7	2.7	1.3	1.3	0.7	0.7	2.0	0.7			
Politieke Partij Radicalen								1.3	4.7	2.0	2.0	1.3	1.3			
Socialistische Partij															1.3	3.3
Groen Links														4.0	3.3	7.3
Partij van der Arbeid	29.0	27.0	30.0	34.0	32.0	28.7	24.7	26.0	28.7	35.3	29.4	31.3	34.7	32.7	24.7	30.0
Democraten 66							4.7	7.3	4.0	5.3	11.3	4.0	6.0	8.0	16.0	9.3
Democratische Socialisten 70								5.3	4.0	0.7						
Volkspartij voor Vrijheid en Democrazie	6.0	8.0	9.0	9.0	12.7	10.7	11.3	10.7	14.7	18.7	17.3	24.0	18.0	14.7	20.7	25.3
Katholieke Volkspartij	32.0	32.0	30.0	33.0	32.7	33.3	28.0	23.3	18.0							
Katholieke Nationale Partij		1.0	2.0													
Nieuwe Roomse Partij									0.7							
Christen-Democratisch Appel										32.7	32.0	30.0	36.0	36.0	22.7	19.3
Anti-Revolutionaire Partij	13.0	13.0	12.0	10.0	9.3	8.7	10.0	8.7	9.3							
Christelijk-Historische Unie	8.0	9.0	9.0	8.0	8.0	8.7	8.0	6.7	4.7							
Staatkundig Gereformeerde Partij	2.0	2.0	2.0	2.0	2.0	2.0	2.0	2.0	2.0	2.0	2.0	2.0	2.0	2.0	1.3	2.0
Gereformeerd Politiek Verbond						0.7	0.7	1.3	1.3	0.7	0.7	0.7	0.7	1.3	1.3	1.3
Reformatorische Politieke Federatie											1.3	1.3	0.7	0.7	2.0	2.0
Evangelische Volkspartij												0.7				
Rechtse Volkspartij						2.0	4.7	0.7	2.0	0.7						
Middenstands Partij								1.3								
Centrumpartij												0.7				
Centrumdemocraten														0.7	2.0	
Allgemeen Ouderen Verbond															4.0	
Unie 55+															0.7	
Total number of seats	100	100	100	100	150	150	150	150	150	150	150	150	150	150	150	150
Fragmentation*	0.78	0.79	0.79	0.75	0.76	0.78	0.82	0.84	0.84	0.73	0.77	0.75	0.71	0.73	0.82	0.79
Volatility†		4.0	5.0	7.0	5.0	6.0	10.0	13.2	13.3	44.6	9.4	10.0	11.4	7.3	22.7	16.7

*Rae's *F*

†Pedersen's *V*

TABLE A.3.5. Election results: Proportion of seats in parliament, degree of fragmentation and volatility, Germany 1949–98

Party	Aug. 1949	Sept. 1953	Sept. 1957	Sept. 1961	Sept. 1965	Sept. 1969	Nov. 1972	Oct. 1976	Oct. 1980	March 1983	Jan. 1987	Dec. 1990	Sept. 1994	Sept. 1998
Kommunistische Partei Deutschlands	3.7													
Partei des Demokratischen Sozialismus												2.6	4.5	5.4
Sozialdemokratische Partei Deutschlands	32.6	31.0	34.0	38.1	40.7	45.2	46.4	43.2	43.9	38.8	37.4	36.1	37.5	44.5
Bündnis 90/Die Grünen										5.4	8.5	1.2	7.3	7.0
Freie Demokratische Partei	12.9	9.9	8.3	13.4	9.9	6.1	8.3	7.9	10.7	6.8	9.3	11.9	7.0	6.4
Deutsche Partei	4.2	3.1												
Deutsche Zentrumspartei	2.5	0.6												
Christlich-Demokratische Union/ Christlich-Soziale Union	34.6	49.9	54.3	48.5	49.4	48.8	45.4	49.0	45.5	49.0	44.9	48.2	43.8	36.6
Wirtschaftliche Aufbauvereinigung	3.0													
Deutsche Reichspartei	1.2													
Bayernpartei	4.2													
Südschleswigscher Wählerverband	0.3													
Gesamtdeutscher Block/Bund der Heimatvertriebenen und Entrechteten		5.5												
Others	0.8													
Total number of seats	402	487	497	499	496	496	496	496	497	498	497	562	672	669
Fragmentation*	0.75	0.64	0.58	0.60	0.58	0.55	0.57	0.57	0.59	0.60	0.64	0.62	0.66	0.66
Volatility†		20.8	7.7	9.2	3.5	4.5	3.4	3.6	3.5	9.0	5.6	8.6	9.4	8.0

*Rae's F

†Pedersen's V

TABLE A.3.6. *Election results: Proportion of seats in parliament, degree of fragmentation and volatility, the United Kingdom 1945–2001*

Party	July 1945	Feb. 1950	Oct. 1951	May 1955	Oct. 1959	Oct. 1964	Mar. 1966	June 1970	Feb. 1974	Oct. 1974	May 1979	June 1983	June 1987	Apr. 1992	May 1997	June 2001
Communist Party of Britain	0.3															
Independent Labour Party	0.5															
Labour Party	61.4	50.4	47.2	44.0	41.0	50.3	57.8	45.7	47.4	50.2	42.4	32.2	35.2	41.6	63.6	62.5
Social Democratic Party												0.9	0.8			
National Liberal Party	1.7															
Liberal Party	1.9	1.4	1.0	1.0	1.0	1.4	1.9	1.0	2.2	2.1	1.7	2.6	2.6			
Liberal Democrats														3.1	7.0	7.9
Conservative Party	31.1	47.7	51.4	54.8	57.9	48.3	40.2	52.4	46.8	43.6	53.4	61.1	57.9	51.6	25.0	25.2
Scottish National Party								0.2	1.1	1.7	0.3	0.3	0.5	0.5	0.9	0.8
Party of Wales									0.3	0.5	0.3	0.3	0.5	0.6	0.6	0.6
Ulster Unionists and Loyalists									1.7	1.6	1.6	2.3	2.0	1.4	1.5	0.9
Ulster Popular Unionist Party														0.2		
Britain Unionist Party															0.2	
Democratic Unionist Party										0.2	0.2	0.2	0.2	0.5	0.3	0.8
United Ireland	0.3	0.3	0.5	0.3			0.2	0.5								
Social Democratic and Labour Party									0.2	0.2	0.2	0.2	0.5	0.6	0.5	0.5
Sinn Fein															0.3	0.6
Others	2.8	0.2			0.2			0.3	0.3						0.2	0.4
Total number of seats	640	625	625	630	630	630	630	630	635	635	635	650	650	651	659	659
Fragmentation*	0.52	0.52	0.51	0.51	0.50	0.51	0.50	0.52	0.56	0.56	0.53	0.52	0.54	0.56	0.53	0.54
Volatility†	16.6	16.6	3.9	3.4	3.3	9.8	8.2	13.0	6.1	3.8	9.8	10.2	3.7	10.5	27.1	2.0

*Rea's F

†Pedersen's V

TABLE A.4.1. *Left–right positions of relevant Swedish political parties as derived from party election programmes, 1944–98*

Year	Vp	SdaP	Greens	CP	FP	MSP	Kd	NyD	Polarization	Range
1944	7.7	**−39.0**		19.0	9.5	**26.3**			23.65	65.3
1948	**−42.0**	−32.4		−6.3	19.5	**50.0**			39.32	92.0
1952	**−37.4**	−35.8		−9.6	13.2	**40.9**			34.27	78.3
1956	**−52.0**	−39.0		−3.6	−16.5	**53.7**			41.13	105.7
1958	**−54.6**	−27.3		9.5	25.5	**57.6**			46.20	112.2
1960	−26.3	**−57.7**		3.5	6.5	33.7			35.93	91.4
1964	−36.2	**−39.7**		−17.9	−37.2	**60.4**			36.58	100.1
1968	−29.9	−35.8		−12.9	**−48.5**	25.3			28.41	73.8
1970	−32.0	**−39.7**		−8.4	−28.6	**0.1**			17.20	39.8
1973	−23.1	**−23.2**		−17.2	−10.1	6.6			12.10	29.8
1976	**−22.6**	−15.8		−15.6	**0.7**	−1.8			10.10	23.3
1979	**−49.0**	−15.9		−9.1	−22.4	**14.3**			23.32	63.3
1982	**−40.7**	−26.6		−12.5	−3.3	**22.9**			25.08	63.6
1985	**−26.5**	−13.7		−7.1	11.4	**58.9**	−6.8		27.92	85.4
1988	−30.8	**−47.7**	−7.1	−16.8	1.7	**37.3**			29.57	85.0
1991	**−32.6**	−22.3		−8.5	1.4	38.0	−6.8	**42.8**	29.73	75.4
1994	**−29.5**	7.8	−3.8	1.8	−7.8	**41.7**	−4.7		20.94	71.2
1998	**−31.1**	−18.4	−23.6	3.3	9.5	**22.5**	−1.2		20.73	53.6
Mean	**−32.7**	−29.0	−11.5	−6.0	−4.2	32.7	−4.9	**42.8**	27.90	72.7
SD	13.8	15.0	10.6	10.0	19.9	19.7	2.7		9.87	24.8

TABLE A.4.2. *Left–right positions of relevant Norwegian political parties as derived from party election programmes, 1945–97*

Year	SV	DNA	SP	V	H	KrF	FrP	Polarization	Range
1945		**−43.4**	**23.3**	−19.5	4.7	−13.0		26.27	66.7
1949		**−30.4**	3.8	−4.5	12.7	**17.0**		18.67	47.4
1953		**−34.0**	7.4	−28.4	10.7	**17.3**		23.62	51.3
1957		**−33.0**	4.7	−5.8	**11.1**	9.9		17.32	44.1
1961	**−47.1**	−37.7	−8.3	−17.9	3.4	**8.9**		22.94	56.0
1965	**−54.0**	−43.7	−26.3	−34.3	−7.2	**−7.0**		19.58	47.0
1969		**−34.0**	−19.6	−27.3	**−9.9**	−22.0		9.32	24.1
1973	−33.8	−37.2	−19.5	**−38.2**	−17.2	−9.5	**61.8**	31.00	100.0
1977	**−40.8**	−36.5	−19.4	−24.9	−10.6	**−6.6**		14.12	34.2
1981	**−36.8**	−29.1	−21.6	−28.0	6.5	−6.5	**35.7**	25.85	72.5
1985	**−42.4**	−33.8	−24.3		−7.2	−12.9	**37.4**	27.23	79.8
1989	**−44.4**	−34.9	−23.7		−4.8	−21.8	**27.0**	24.96	71.4
1993	**−31.5**	−21.9	−14.0	−14.5	17.3	5.1	**46.1**	27.57	77.6
1997	**−23.4**	−21.7	−10.9	−8.5	7.0	−0.7	**27.3**	18.31	50.7
Mean	**−39.4**	−33.7	−10.6	−21.0	1.2	−3.0	**39.2**	21.91	58.8
SD	9.1	6.5	14.9	11.1	10.5	13.0	13.1	5.95	20.2

TABLE A.4.3. *Left–right positions of relevant Danish political parties as derived from party election programmes, 1945–2001*

Year	DKP	SF	EL	SD	V	RV	RF	CD	KF	KrF	FP	DF	Polarization	Range
1945	**−31.5**			−29.2	**31.1**	−11.0	11.4		−0.2				24.76	62.6
1947	**−19.3**			−18.1	−2.4	−5.2	**29.2**		7.8				17.94	48.5
1950	**−32.3**			−13.9	17.5	0.0	10.2		**19.1**				20.08	51.4
1953	**−21.1**			−17.1	2.9	−12.8	**15.5**		3.6				14.49	36.6
1953	**−18.6**			−13.7	19.1	−2.8	**21.4**		13.6				17.47	40.0
1957	**−38.1**			−27.3	36.6	−11.1	12.7		**39.0**				33.39	77.1
1960		**−69.4**		−42.1	17.6	−12.0			**53.8**				51.02	123.2
1964		**−35.1**		−22.8	4.5	−14.3			**15.9**				21.55	51.0
1966		**−24.2**		−11.8	7.2	−7.7			**35.7**				23.13	59.9
1968		**−29.9**		−6.6	6.4	−14.4			**17.0**				19.10	46.9
1971		−31.9		**−45.1**	4.2	−13.5			**36.2**				33.12	81.3
1973	−23.2	**−29.9**		−15.2	**39.4**	−12.0	3.5	6.8	25.8	24.4	13.4		24.88	69.3
1975	**−38.0**	−28.0		−31.1	8.9	4.6		2.0	**36.2**	25.1	21.8		28.60	74.2
1977	−30.6	**−35.8**		−27.6	16.5	−23.3	9.4	**21.7**	18.7	21.0	5.5		24.67	57.5
1979		**−60.4**		−23.5	4.3	−40.0	1.3	37.4	24.0	22.4	**43.2**		38.14	103.6
1981		**−45.8**		−9.4	17.4	−3.3		36.8	**55.0**	14.1	34.2		32.89	100.8
1984		**−50.8**		−42.0	17.9	−18.1		29.4	34.7	10.5	**44.7**		37.56	95.5
1987		**−43.1**		−30.6	**19.0**	−25.0		2.0	−4.5	5.8	11.5		23.25	62.1
1988		**−45.9**		−29.4	32.5	−14.1		17.3	**36.0**	3.4	28.0		31.97	81.9
1990		−19.0		**−41.9**	10.1	−30.4		0.0	15.6	16.7	**28.2**		26.25	70.1
1994		**−36.6**	−36.0	−22.1	**57.4**	−21.6		−4.1	10.6		43.7		36.63	94.0
1998		−36.2	**−39.8**	−6.6	32.9	−18.4		7.0	21.2	24.7	**36.0**	17.8	29.51	75.8
2001		**−26.2**	−17.0	−20.4	**42.0**	−20.8			39.8	23.4		15.0	29.45	68.2
Mean	−28.1	−38.1	−30.9	−23.8	19.3	−14.2	12.7	14.2	24.1	17.4	28.2	16.4	27.82	70.9
SD	7.7	13.2	12.2	11.6	15.2	10.0	8.6	15.1	16.0	7.9	13.7	2.0	8.41	36.6

TABLE A.4.4. *Left–right positions of relevant Dutch political parties as derived from party election programmes, 1946–98*

Year	PPR	GL	PvdA	D66	DS70	VVD	KVP	CDA	ARP	CHU	Polarization	Range
1946			**-27.3**			5.6	-13.2		12.0	**18.9**	19.60	46.2
1948			**-25.3**			-4.0	4.8		7.5	**16.2**	15.75	41.5
1952			**-36.4**			**19.2**	10.3		11.2	16.2	19.52	55.6
1956			**-24.5**			13.0	-0.2		6.5	**16.1**	15.73	40.6
1959			**-27.0**			**10.9**	-19.5		10.6	6.2	17.65	37.9
1963			**-33.5**			3.7	-25.6		0.5	-13.8	16.75	37.2
1967			**-38.7**	-26.2		1.8	-2.5		-6.0	**4.8**	16.94	43.5
1971	-39.2		**-46.1**	-23.8	-24.5	**-11.7**	-26.2		-17.7	-26.5	11.19	34.4
1972	**-45.8**		**-45.8***	-45.8	-13.0	**16.4**	-21.5		-21.5	-21.5	21.01	61.9
1977	**-37.8**		**-45.4**	-24.0	-15.7	**7.2**		-11.7			19.42	52.6
1981	**-31.2**		-29.5	-27.6		**5.8**		-21.5			13.67	37.0
1982	**-24.5**		-22.2	-18.4		**20.8**		-11.0			16.97	45.3
1986	-18.8		**-22.6**	-10.0		7.4		-5.5			12.22	30.0
1989		**-28.0**	-21.5	-11.7		0.7		-10.8			11.35	28.7
1994		**-23.6**	-8.0	-1.9		**6.4**		4.7			12.12	30.0
1998		**-31.5**	-22.5	-13.7		**8.4**		-5.3			16.17	39.9
Mean	**-32.9**	**-27.7**	**-29.8**	-20.3	-17.7	7.0	-10.4	-8.7	0.3	1.8	16.00	41.4
SD	10.0	4.0	10.6	12.2	6.0	8.3	13.8	8.0	12.7	17.8	3.13	9.4

*PPR, PvdA, D66 coalition; KVP, ARP, CHU coalition

TABLE A.4.5. *Left–right positions of relevant German political parties as derived from party election programmes, 1949–98*

Year	PDS	SPD	GRE	B'90/GRE	GRE/B'90	FDP	DP	CDU/CSU	GB	Polarization	Range
1949		**−30.6**				−1.9	**17.1**	15.0		20.00	47.7
1953		**−18.5**				**−2.2**	−16.7	−4.1	**−26.7**	10.57	24.5
1957		**−33.8**				−7.2	−7.5	**27.8**		23.14	61.6
1961		−7.6				**−13.1**		**0.0**		6.60	13.1
1965		−11.6				**−9.9**		**−12.0**		1.05	2.1
1969		**−15.7**				−10.7		**−6.8**		4.45	8.9
1972		**−17.2**				**3.8**		2.9		10.50	21.0
1976		**−29.7**				−13.2		**2.2**		15.95	31.9
1980		**−27.7**				−6.5		**8.7**		18.20	36.4
1983		−24.1	**−38.4**			2.2		**17.5**		24.25	55.9
1987		−24.2	**−29.3**			4.9		−1.1		15.71	34.1
1990	**−39.8**	−26.2			−16.7	**−2.0**		−3.3		16.42	37.8
1994	**−34.6**	−17.5		−24.4		1.3		**33.7**		27.05	68.3
1998	**−50.0**	−7.8		−29.5		3.3		**17.2**		27.87	67.2
Mean	−41.5	−20.9	−33.8	−27.0	−16.7	−3.7	−2.3	7.0	−26.7	15.84	36.5
SD	7.8	8.4	6.5	3.6		6.4	17.5	13.5		8.36	21.5

TABLE A.4.6. *Left–right positions of relevant British political parties as derived from party election programmes, 1945–2001*

Year	Labour	LibDem	Alliance	Liberal	Conservatives	Polarization	Range
1945	**−32.2**			−18.4	**12.5**	22.35	44.7
1950	**−23.9**			**16.5**	−9.0	20.20	40.4
1951	**−28.3**			**2.2**	−8.6	15.25	30.5
1955	**−33.1**			**6.0**	−19.9	19.55	39.1
1959	**−31.7**			**−7.5**	−16.5	12.10	24.2
1964	−26.0			**−27.1**	−7.1	10.00	20.0
1966	**−21.6**			−12.4	**9.4**	15.50	31.0
1970	**−22.9**			**21.2**	−4.3	22.05	44.1
1974–02	**−35.9**			−30.2	**−8.8**	13.55	27.1
1974–10	**−32.8**			−12.8	**−1.9**	15.45	30.9
1979	**−31.9**			−21.0	**24.6**	28.25	56.5
1983	**−40.7**		−8.8		**23.6**	32.15	64.3
1987	**−13.2**		−9.7		**30.6**	21.90	43.8
1992	**−27.3**	−20.1			**15.5**	21.40	42.8
1997	**−7.6**	−6.2			**14.9**	11.25	22.5
2001	−10.1	**−10.3**			−3.0	3.65	7.3
Mean	**−26.2**	−12.2	−9.2	−7.6	**3.2**	17.79	35.6
SD	9.4	7.1	0.6	17.1	15.5	7.14	14.3

Appendix 2

The European Voter Data Base

Ingvill C. Mochmann and Wolfgang Zenk-Möltgen

A.2.1 INTRODUCTION

The Central Archive for Empirical Social Research at the University of Cologne (http://www.gesis.org/ZA) is the archive for the European Voter dataset. The data used in the chapters of this book are made available to the scientific community on the Internet (http://www.gesis.org/Eurolab/EVoter). The purpose is to give the interested researcher the opportunity to work with the national subsets and integrated subsets of the national election studies at the same level as the principal investigators and authors of the chapters in *The European Voter*. The data and additional information has been made available by the principal investigators and their teams. All data and documentation relevant for *The European Voter* have been integrated and stored in a database under the ZA CodebookExplorer (see Zenk-Möltgen and Mochmann 2000; Mochmann et al. 2000; Luijkx et al. 2003) by the authors of this appendix.

A.2.2 CONTENTS OF THE DATABASE

Countries and Time Period

The database contains a folder for each of the countries analysed in *The European Voter* (i.e. Denmark, Germany, Britain, the Netherlands, Norway, and Sweden). Each country folder consists of subsets for each election study used in the analyses, as well as one integrated country file including all time periods for a country. The time periods covered by the data differ among the countries and range from nine to fourteen elections. Altogether, the database covers the time period from 1956 to 2001.

Study Descriptions

For each integrated country file a study description is included in the database which informs about the overall size of the integrated data file and contains special information regarding the respective subsets, for example weighting, recoding. Furthermore, the English versions of the original study descriptions have been included in the database. The purpose of this is to give the user information concerning the overall size and contents as well as objective of the original dataset from which the subsets have been built. A database description informs about all integrated country files included in the database.

Data Files

Statistical Packages for the Social Sciences (SPSS) files are included for all subsets and all integrated files which can be downloaded to conduct analyses in SPSS. The database also allows the user to carry out simple analyses over the Internet. The subsets include variables from the following areas: general background variables, occupation and class, other variables related to the cleavage model (such as religion, urbanization, region), political interest and involvement, variables regarding parties (such as party members, party identification), party and party leader sympathy, political participation, left–right positions, economy, values, ideology, national issues, and voting. The coding of the value labels has been harmonized across time and nations. Not all variables are available for all countries at all time periods. Details on available variables can be found in the study descriptions and/or in the variable correspondence lists.

Trends

The database includes trends of the variables by thematic categories. Each variable the integrated country files has been assigned to a trend folder. This facilitates immediate comparative analyses of the trend per country.

Additional Information

PDF files containing variable correspondence lists are available as well. These lists refer to the original variable in the original dataset for each of the variable included in the subsets for each period in time. Here you will also find other information if this has been provided by the participating countries.

A.2.3 USAGE OF THE DATABASE

The database can be accessed with the ZA Codebook Explorer Online Version. The database is available at http://www.gesis.org/Eurolab/EVoter/. Further details both on the contents of the database and the technical aspects of the database can be found there.

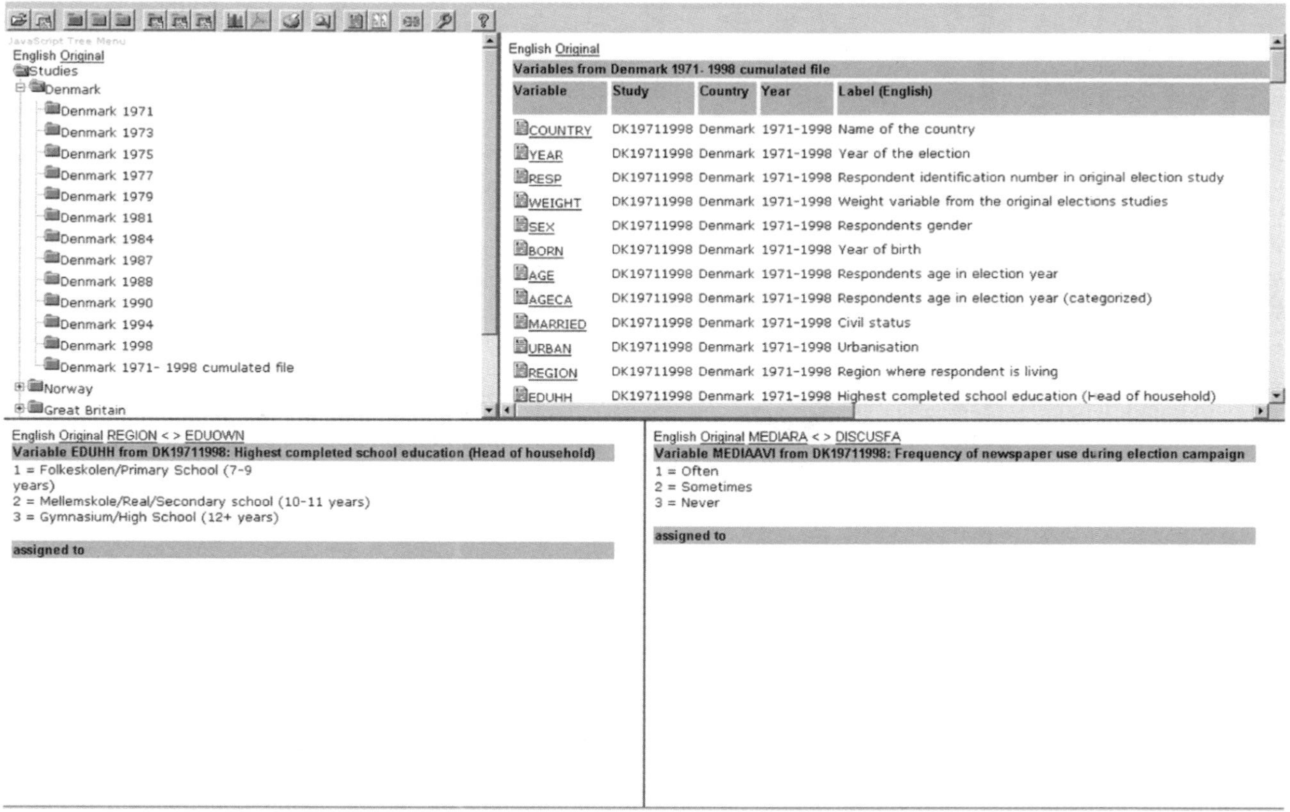

Fig. A.2.1. *The Explorer View 'Studies' of the ZA CodebookExplorer online version*

Analysis:

Study: [NL19711998 ▾]

Variable 1: [POLINTR subjective interest politics   ▾]

Variable 2: [YEAR election year   ▾]

Weighting: ● None
           ○ Variable [▾]

                                            ○ Frequency   Crosstab Options:
                                            ● Crosstab   ○ Counts
                                            ○ Descriptives   ● Column Percent
                                            ○ Comparison   ○ Row Percent
                                                                    ○ Total Percent

                                                    [Run Analysis]

Results:

Crosstab Table

POLINTR by YEAR from NL19711998

Value	Label	Missing	1971	1972	1977	1981	1982	1986	1989	1994	1998	Sum	Valid Sum
		☑											
	SYSMIS	☑	-	-	-	-	-	-	-	-	-		0
1	not interested at all	☐	42,6	48,3	39,4	31,6	25,6	27,2	22,6	21,5	25,9		33,4
2	fairly interested	☐	44,2	35,7	49,6	54,4	58,4	56,4	633	65,6	64,6		53
3	very interested	☐	11	14,7	11	13,5	15,9	16	14,1	12,7	9,5		12,9
998		☐	1,4	0,8	-	0,4	0,1	0,2	-	0,2	-		0,5
999		☐	0,8	0,5	-	0	-	0,1	-	-	-		0,2
Sum													
Valid Sum			100	100	100	100	100	100	100	100	100		100

FIG. A.2.2. *Example analysis of political interest by year for the Netherlands*

After logging in, the Explorer View 'Studies' will be displayed (see Fig. A.2.1). This View contains folders for countries and their election years. By selecting a year (or the integrated file) the respective variables are listed. If available, the question and answer texts can be displayed in either English or the original language.

The menu bar at the top allows opening also the Explorer View 'Trends', the Study Descriptions View, the Analysis Window, or the Additional Information Window. The Explorer View 'Trends' (▣) has the same structure as the Explorer View 'Studies', but it contains a folder for each trend of the integrated country datasets. The Study Descriptions View (▦) can be used to browse through the background information of the surveys. The analysis function (▦) can give an overview on the distribution of frequencies. By selecting the election year of the cumulative datasets as a crosstab variable, a trend analysis can be performed (see Fig. A.2.2). The Additional Information Window (▨) opens a list of PDF files which can be downloaded or viewed directly.

The Extended Search Window (▨) gives the possibility to search keywords in variables, question texts, or descriptions. Detailed information about the ZA CodebookExplorer functionalities can be found in the Help function (▨).

References

Aardal, B. (1994). 'Hva er en Politisk Skillelinje? En Begrepsmessig Grenseoppgang (What is a Political Cleavage? A Conceptual Demarcation)', *Tidsskrift for Samfunnsforskning*, 35: 217–48.

—— (ed.) (2003). *Velgere i Villrede... En Analyse av Stortingsvalget 2001* (Confused Voters... An Analysis of the 2001 Storting Election). Oslo: N W Damm & Søn.

—— and Waldahl, R. (2004). 'Political Cleavages in a Media-Driven Environment', in H. M. Narud and A. Krogstad (eds.), *Elections, Parties and Political Representation*. Oslo: Universitetsforlaget.

—— Valen, H., Narud, H. M., and Berglund, F. (1999). *Velgere i 90-årene* (Voters in the 1990s). Oslo: NKS-Forlaget.

Aarts, K., Blais, A., and Schmitt, H. (eds.) (forthcoming). *Party Leaders and Democratic Elections*. Oxford: Oxford University Press.

Adams, J., Clark, M., Ezrow, L., and Glasgow, G. (2003). *Understanding Change and Stability in Party Ideologies: Do Parties Respond to Public Opinion or to Past Election Results?* Paper presented at the Annual Meeting of the Public Choice Society, Nashville, TN, 21–23 March 2003.

Aldrich, J. H. (1993). 'Rational Choice and Turnout', *American Journal of Political Science*, 37: 246–78.

Alford, R. A. (ed.) (1963). *Party and Society. The Anglo-American Democracies*. Chicago: Rand McNally.

Allardt, E. and Pesonen, P. (1967). 'Cleavages in Finnish Politics', in S. M. Lipset and S. Rokkan (eds.), *Party Systems and Voter Alignments*. New York: Free Press.

Alvarez, R. M., Nagler, J., and Willette, J. R. (2000). 'Measuring the Relative Impact of Issues and the Economy in Democratic Elections', *Electoral Studies*, 19: 237–53.

Andersen, J. G. (1984). 'Decline of Class Voting or Changes of Class Voting? Social Class and Party Choice in Denmark in the 1970s', *European Journal of Political Research*, 12: 243–59.

—— (2003). 'The General Election in Denmark, November 2001', *Electoral Studies*, 22: 186–93.

Anderson, C. J. (2000). 'Economic Voting and the Political Context: A Comparative Perspective', *Electoral Studies*, 19: 151–70.

Andeweg, R. B. (1982). *Dutch Voters Adrift: On Explanations of Electoral Change 1963–1977*. Leiden.

—— and Irwin, G. A. (2002). *Governance and Politics of the Netherlands*. Houndsmill: Palgrave.

Ansolabehere, S. and Iyengar, S. (1994). 'Riding the Wave and Claiming Ownership over Issues: The Joint Effect of Advertising and News Coverage in Campaigns', *Public Opinion Quarterly*, 58: 335–57.

Baker, K. L., Dalton, R. J., and Hildebrandt, K. (1981). *Germany transformed: Political Culture and the New Politics*. Cambridge, MA: Harvard University Press.

Banks, A. S. (ed.). (1976, 1977, 1978, 1979) *Political Handbook of the World: 1976–1979.* New York: McGraw-Hill.

—— (ed.). (1985) *Political Handbook of the World: 1984–1995.* Binghamton, NY: CSA Publications.

—— and Jordan, R. S. (eds.). (1975) *Political Handbook of the World: 1975.* New York: McGraw-Hill.

—— and Muller, T. C. (eds.). (1998 & 1999) *Political Handbook of the World: 1998–1999.* Binghamton, NY: CSA Publications.

—— Muller, T. C., and Overstreet, W. R. (eds.). *Political Handbook of the World: 2000–2002.* Binghamton, NY: CSA Publications.

—— and Overstreet, W. R. (eds.). (1980, 1981, 1982, 1983) *Political Handbook of the World 1980–1983.* New York: McGraw-Hill.

—— Day, A. J., and Muller, T. C. (eds.). (1995, 1996, 1997) *Political Handbook of the World: 1995–1997.* Binghamton, NY: CSA Publications.

Barnes, S. H. and Kaase, M. (eds.) (1979). *Political Action: Mass Participation in Five Western Democracies.* Beverly Hills, CA and London: Sage.

Bartels, L. (2002). 'The Impact of Candidate Traits in American Presidential Elections', in A. King (ed.), *Leaders' Personalities and the Outcomes of Democratic Elections.* Oxford: Oxford University Press.

Bartle, J. (2001). 'Why Labour Won – Again', in A. King (ed.), *Britain at the Polls 2001.* Chatham, NJ: Chatham House.

—— 'The General Election in Britain, June 2001', *Electoral Studies,* 22: 166–73.

—— and Crewe, I. (2002). 'The Impact of Party Leaders in Britain: Strong Assumptions, Weak Evidence', in A. King (ed.), *Leaders' Personalities and the Outcomes of Democratic Elections.* Oxford: Oxford University Press.

—— Crewe, I., and King, A. (1998). *Was it Blair who Won It? Leadership Effects in the 1997 British General Election.* Colchester: University of Essex Papers in Government and Politics, no. 128.

Bartolini, S. and Mair, P. (1990). *Identity, Competition, and Electoral Availability: The Stabilization of European Electorates 1885–1985.* Cambridge: Cambridge University Press.

Barton, T. and Döring, H. (1986). 'Weakening Partisanship and the Higher Educated in Britain', *European Journal of Political Research,* 14: 521–42.

Bauer-Kaase, P. (2001). 'Politische Ideologie im Wandel? – Eine Laengsschnittanalyse der Inhalte der politischen Richtungsbegriffe "links" und "rechts" ', in H. -D. Klingemann and M. Kaase (eds.), *Wahlen und Waehler.* Wiesbaden: Westdeutscher-Verlag, 207–43.

Bean, C. and Mughan, A. (1989). 'Leadership Effects in Parliamentary Elections in Australia and Britain', *American Political Science Review,* 83: 1165–79.

Bell, D. (1988). *The End of Ideology: On the Exhaustion of Political Ideas in the Fifties,* 2nd edn. Cambridge, MA: Harvard University Press.

Berelson, B., Lazarsfeld, P. F., and McPhee, W. (1954). *Voting.* Chicago: University of Chicago Press.

Berger, S. (1982). 'Introduction: Religion in West European Politics', *West European Politics,* 5 (2): 1–7.

Berglund, F. (2000). 'Party Identification – Nothing but the Vote?' *Acta Politica,* 35: 37–63.

—— (2003*a*). 'Valget i 2001 – Skiljelinjemodellens Endelikt?', in B. Aardal (ed.)., *Velgere i Villrede.* Oslo: NKS-Forlaget.

Berglund, F. (2003*b*). *Partiidentifikasjon og Politisk Endring: En Studie av Langsiktige Tilknytninger Blant Norske Velgere 1965–1997* (Party Identification and Political Change: A Study of Longitudinal Attachments among Norwegian Voters). Oslo: Institutt for Statsvitenskap, Universitetet i Oslo.

Bille, L. (1990). 'Denmark: The Oscillating Party System', in P. Mair and G. Smith (eds.), *Understanding Party System Change in Western Europe*. London: Frank Cass.

Blais, A. (2000). *To Vote or not to Vote: The Merits and Limits of Rational Choice Theory*. Pittsburgh: University of Pittsburgh Press.

—— and Dobrzynska, A. (1998). 'Turnout in Electoral Democracies', *European Journal of Political Research*, 33: 239–61.

Borg, S. and Sänkiaho, R. (eds.) (1995). *The Finnish Voter*. Tampere: The Finnish Political Science Association.

Borre, O. (2001). *Issue Voting. An Introduction*. Aarhus: Aarhus University Press.

—— and Andersen, J. G. (1997). *Voting and Political Attitudes in Denmark*. Aarhus: Aarhus University Press.

Brettschneider, F. and Gabriel, O. (2002). 'The Nonpersonilization of Voting Behavior in Germany', in A. King (ed.), *Leaders' Personalities and the Outcomes of Democratic Elections*. Oxford: Oxford University Press.

Brody, R. A. (1978). 'The Puzzle of Political Participation in America', in A. King, *The New American Political System*. Washington, DC: American Enterprise Institute.

—— and Page, B. I. (1973). 'Indifference, Alienation, and Rational Decisions', *Public Choice*, 15: 1–17.

Budge, I. (1994). 'A New Theory of Party Competition: Uncertainty, Ideology, and Policy Equilibria Viewed Comparatively and Temporally', *British Journal of Political Science*, 27: 647–58.

—— (1998) 'Great Britain: A Stable, but Fragile, Party System?' in P. Pennings and J. E. Lane (eds.), *Comparing Party System Change*. London: Routledge, pp. 125–36.

—— and Farlie, D. (1983). *Voting and Party Competition*. London: Wiley.

—— Klingemann, H. -D., Volkens, A., Bara, J., and Tannenbaum, E. (2001). *Mapping Policy Preferences: Estimates for Parties, Electors and Governments 1945–1998*. Oxford: Oxford University Press.

Burden, B. C. (2000). 'Voter Turnout and the National Election Studies', *Political Analysis*, 8: 389–98.

Butler, D. and Ranney, A. (eds.) (1992). *Electioneering: A Comparative Study of Continuity and Change*. Oxford: Clarendon Press.

—— and Stokes, D. E. (1969). *Political Change in Britain*. New York: St Martin's Press.

—— and Stokes, D.E. (1974). *Political Change in Britain*, 2nd edn. London: Macmillan.

Campbell, A., Converse, P.E., Miller, W.E., and Stokes, D.E. (1960). *The American Voter*. New York: Wiley.

Carmines, E. G. and Huckfeldt, R. (1996). 'Political Behavior: An Overview', in R. Goodin and H. -D. Klingemann (eds.), *A New Handbook of Political Science*. Oxford: Oxford University Press.

Carlsen, F. (2000). 'Unemployment, Inflation and Government Popularity – are there Partisan Effects?', *Electoral Studies*, 19: 141–50.

Castles, F. and Mair, P. (1984). 'Left-Right Political Scales: Some "Expert" Judgments', *European Journal of Political Research*, 12: 73–88.

Caul, M. L. and Gray, M. M. (2000). 'From Platform Declarations to Policy Outcomes: Changing Party Profiles and Partisan Influence over Policy', in R. J. Dalton and M. P. Wattenberg (eds.), *Parties without Partisans: Political Change in Advanced Industrial Democracies*. Oxford: Oxford University Press.

Clark, T. N. and Lipset, S. M. (1991). 'Are Social Classes Dying?', *International Sociology*, 6: 397–410.

—— and Lipset, S. M. (eds.) (2001). *The Breakdown of Class Politics: A Debate on Post-Industrial Stratification*. Washington, DC: Woodrow Wilson Center Press.

—— Lipset, S. M., and Rempel, M. (1993). 'The Declining Political Significance of Social Class', *International Sociology*, 8: 293–316.

Clarke, H., Ho, K., and Stewart, M. (2000). 'Major's Lesser (Not Minor) Effects: Prime Ministerial Approval and Governing Party Support in Britain since 1979', *Electoral Studies*, 19: 255–73.

—— Sanders, D., Stewart, M., and Whiteley, P. (2004). *Political Choice in Britain*. Oxford: Oxford University Press.

Converse, P. E. (1964). 'The Nature of Belief Systems in Mass Publics', in D. Apter (ed.), *Ideology and Discontent*. New York: Free Press.

—— (1969). 'Of Time and Partisan Stability', *Comparative Political Studies*, 2: 139–71.

—— (1975). 'Public Opinion and Voting Behavior', in F. Greenstein and N. Polsby (eds.), *Handbook of Political Science*. Reading: Addison-Wesley.

—— (1976). *The Dynamics of Party Support: Cohort-Analyzing Party Identification*. Beverly Hills, CA: Sage.

—— and Niemi, R. G. (1971). 'Non-Voting Among Young Adults in the United States', in W. J. Crotty, D. M. Freeman, and D. S. Gatlin (eds.), *Political Parties and Political Behavior*. Boston, MA: Allyn & Bacon.

—— and Pierce, R. (1986). *Political Representation in France*. Cambridge, MA: Belknap Press.

Crewe, I. and Denver, D. (1985). *Electoral Change in Western Democracies: Patterns and Sources of Electoral Volatility*. London: Croom Helms.

—— and King, A. (1994). 'Are British Elections Becoming More "Presidential"?', in M. K. Jennings and T. Mann (eds.), *Elections at Home and Abroad: Essays in Honor of Warren E. Miller*. Ann Arbor, MI: University of Michigan Press.

Curtice, J. (2002). 'The State of Election Studies: Mid-life Crisis or New Youth?', *Electoral Studies*, 2002: 161–8.

—— (forthcoming). 'Elections as Beauty Contests: Do the Rules Matter?', in K. Aarts, A. Blais, and H. Schmitt (eds.), *Party Leaders and Democratic Elections*. Oxford: Oxford University Press.

Dalton, R. J. (1984). 'Cognitive Mobilization and Partisan Dealignment in Advanced Industrial Democracies', *Journal of Politics*, 46: 264–84.

—— (1988). *Citizen Politics in Western Democracies*. Chatham, NJ: Chatham House.

—— (1996). 'Comparative Politics: Micro-behavioral Perspectives', in R. Goodin and H-D. Klingemann, *A New Handbook of Political Science*. Oxford: Oxford University Press.

—— (2000a). 'The Decline of Party Identification', in R. Dalton and M. P. Wattenberg (eds.), *Parties without Partisans: Political Change in Advanced Industrial Democracies*. Oxford: Oxford University Press.

Dalton, R. J. (2000*b*). 'Influences on Voting Behavior', in R. Rose (ed.), *International Encyclopedia of Elections*. London: Macmillan.

—— (2000*c*). 'Value Change and Democracy', in S. Pharr and R. D. Putnam (eds.), *Disaffected Democracies. What's Troubling the Trilateral Countries?* Princeton, NJ: Princeton University Press.

—— (2002). *Citizen Politics. Public Opinion and Political Parties in Advanced Industrial Democracies*. 3rd edn. New York: Chatham House.

—— and Wattenberg, M. P. (1993). 'The Not So Simple Act of Voting', in A. Finifter (ed.), *Political Science: The State of the Discipline II*. Washington, DC: The American Political Science Association.

—— and Wattenberg, M. P. (eds.) (2000). *Parties without Partisans: Political Change in Advanced Industrial Democracies*. Oxford: Oxford University Press.

—— Flanagan, S. C., and Beck, P. A. (eds.) (1984). *Electoral Change in Advanced Industrial Democracies: Realignment or De-alignment?* Princeton, NJ: Princeton University Press.

Davis, O. A., Hinich, M. J., and Ordeshook, M. P. (1970). 'An Expository Development of a Mathematical Model of the Electoral Process', *American Political Science Review*, 64: 426–48.

Day, A. J. (ed.) (1988). *Political Parties of the World*. 3rd edn. Chicago: St James Press.

De Beus, J. W., Lehning, P. B., and Doorn, J. A. A. van (1989). *De Ideologische Driehoek: Nederlandse Politiek in Historisch Perspectief*. Amsterdam: Boom.

De Graaf, D., Heath, A., and Need, A. (2001). 'Declining Cleavages and Political Choices: The Interplay of Social and Political Factors in the Netherlands', *Electoral Studies*, 20: 1–15.

Dogan, M. (2001). 'Class, Religion, Party: Triple Decline of Electoral Cleavages in Western Europe', in L. Karvonen and S. Kuhnle (eds.), *Party Systems and Voter Alignments Revisited*. London: Routledge.

Dorussen, H. (2002). 'Conclusions', in H. Dorussen and M. Taylor (eds.), *Economic Voting*. London: Routledge.

Downs, A. (1957). *An Economic Theory of Democracy*. New York: Harper & Row.

Dunleavy, P. (1996). 'Political Behavior: Institutional and Experiential Approaches', in R. Goodin and H-D. Klingemann (eds.), *A New Handbook of Political Science*. Oxford: Oxford University Press.

Duverger, M. (1951). *Les Partis Politiques*. Paris: Armand Colin.

Erikson, R. S., MacKuen, M. B., and Stimson, J. A. (2000). 'Bankers or Peasants Revisited: Economic Expectations and Presidential Approval', *Electoral Studies*, 19: 295–312.

Ersson, S. and Lane, J. E. (1998). 'Electoral Instability and Party System Change in Western Europe', in P. Pennings and J. E. Lane (eds.), *Comparing Party System Change*. London: Routledge.

Esaiasson, P. and Håkansson, N. (2002). *Besked Ikväll!*. Värnamo: Etermedier i Sverige.

Evans, G. (ed.) (1999). *The End of Class Politics? Class Voting in Comparative Perspective*. Oxford: Oxford University Press.

—— Heath, A., and Payne, C. (1999). 'Class: Labour as a Catch-All Party?' in G. Evans and P. Norris (eds.), *Critical Elections: British Parties and Voters in Long-Term Perspective*. London: Sage.

Evans, J. A. J. (2002). 'In Defence of Sartori: Party System Change, Voter Preference Distributions and Other Competitive Incentives', *Party Politics*, 8: 155–74.

Feld, L. P. and Kirchgässner, G. (2001). 'Erwartete Knappheit und die Höhe der Wahlbeteiligung: Empirische Ergebnisse für die Neunziger Jahre', in H-D. Klingemann and M. Kaase (eds.), *Wahlen und Wähler – Analysen aus Anlass der Bundestagswahl 1998*. Wiesbaden: Westdeutscher-Verlag.

Fiorina, M. F. (1981). *Retrospective Voting in American National Elections*. New Haven: Yale University Press.

Flanagan, S. C. (1987). 'Value Changes in Industrial Societies', *American Political Science Review*, 81: 1303–19.

—— and Lee, A. -R. (1988). *'Explaining Value Change and its Political Implications in Eleven Advanced Industrial Democracies'*. Paper presented at the 14th World Congress of the International Political Science Association. Washington, 28 August – 1 September.

—— —— (2003). 'The New Politics, Culture Wars, and the Authoritarian-Libertarian Value Change in Advanced Industrial Democracies', *Comparative Political Studies*, 36: 235–70.

Foley, M. (2000). *The British Presidency: Tony Blair and the Politics of Public Leadership*. Manchester, IN: Manchester University Press.

Franklin, M. N. (1985). 'Assessing the Rise of Issue Voting in British Elections Since 1964', *Electoral Studies*, 37–56.

—— (1992). 'The Decline of Cleavage Politics', in M. N. Franklin et al. (eds.), *Electoral Change: Responses to Evolving Social and Attitudinal Structures in Western Countries*. Cambridge: Cambridge University Press.

—— (1996). 'Electoral Participation', in L. LeDuc, R. G. Niemi, and P. Norris (eds.), *Comparing Democracies: Elections and Voting in Global Perspective*. London: Sage.

—— (2004). *Voter Turnout and the Dynamics of Electoral Competition in Established Democracies Since 1945*. Cambridge: Cambridge University Press.

—— Mackie, T. K., and Valen, H. (eds.) (1992). *Electoral Change: Responses to Evolving Social and Attitudinal Structures in Seventeen Democracies*. Cambridge: Cambridge University Press.

—— van der Eijk, C., and Oppenhuis, E. (1996). 'The Institutional Context: Turnout', in C. van der Eijk and M. N. Franklin (eds.), *Choosing Europe? The European Electorate and National Politics in the Face of European Union*. Ann Arbor, MI: University of Michigan Press.

Fuchs, D. and Klingemann, H-D. (1990). 'The Left-Right Schema', in M. K. Jennings and J. W. van Deth (eds.), *Continuities in Political Action: A Longitudinal Study of Political Orientations in Three Western Democracies*. Berlin: Walter de Gruyter.

—— —— (1995). 'Citizens and the State: A Changing Relationship?', in H-D. Klingemann and D. Fuchs (eds.), *Citizens and the State*. Oxford: Oxford University Press.

Gallagher, M., Laver, M., and Mair, P. (2001). *Representative Government in Modern Europe*. 3rd edn. New York: McGraw-Hill.

Gordon, S. B. and Segura, G. M. (1997). 'Cross-National Variations in the Political Sophistication of Individuals: Capability or Choice?', *Journal of Politics*, 59: 126–47.

Graetz, B. and McAllister, I. (1987). 'Popular Evaluations of Party Leaders in the Anglo-American Democracies', in H. Clarke and M. Czudnowski (eds.), *Political Elites in the Anglo-American Democracies*. DeKalb, IL: Northern Illinois University Press.

Granberg, D. (1993). 'Political Perception', in S. Iyengar and W. J. McGuire (eds.), *Explorations in Political Psychology*. London: Duke University Press.

—— and Holmberg, S. (1988). *The Political System Matters: Social Psychology and Voting Behavior in Sweden and the United States*. Cambridge: Cambridge University Press.

Grofman, B. (1996). 'Political Economy: Downsian Perspectives', in R. Goodin and H-D. Klingemann (eds.), *A New Handbook of Political Science*. Oxford: Oxford University Press.

Gross, H. and Rotholz, W. (1999). 'Das politische System Norwegens', in W. Ismayr (ed.), *Die politischen Systeme Westeuropas*. Opladen: Leske + Budrich.

Halman, L. and De Moor, R. (1994). 'Religion, Churches and Moral Values', in P. Ester, L. Halman and R. de Moor (eds.), *The Individualizing Society: Value Change in Europe and North America*. Tilburg: Tilburg University Press.

Hazan, R. Y. (1995). 'Attacking the Centre: "Moderate-Induced Polarization" in Denmark and the Netherlands', *Scandinavian Political Studies*, 18: 73–95.

Heath, A. F., Jowell, R., and Curtice, J. (1985). *How Britain Votes*. Oxford: Pergamon Press.

—— —— —— (1987). 'Trendless Fluctuation: A reply to Crewe', *Political Studies,* 35: 256–77.

—— Jowell, R. M., and Curtice, J. K. (2001). *The Rise of New Labour: Party Policies and Voter Choices*. Oxford: Oxford University Press.

—— Jowell, R., Curtice, J., Evans G., Field, J., and Witherspoon S. (1991). *Understanding Political Change: The British Voter 1964–1987*. Oxford: Pergamon Press.

Heidar, K. (1990). 'Norway: Levels of Party Competition and System Change', in P. Mair and G. Smith (eds.), *Understanding Party System Change in Western Europe*. London: Frank Cass.

Helms, L. (2004). 'The Federal Election in Germany, September 2002', *Electoral Studies*, 23: 143–9.

Hibbs, D. A., Jr. (1987). *The Political Economy of Industrial Democracies*. Cambridge, MA: Harvard University Press.

Hinich, M. J. and Munger, M. C. (1997). *Analytical Politics*. Cambridge: Cambridge University Press.

Holmberg, S. (1981). *Svenska Väljare*. Stockholm: Liber.

—— (1984). *Väljare i Förandring*. Stockholm: Liber.

—— (1994). 'Party Identification Compared across the Atlantic', in M. K. Jennings and T. E. Mann (eds.), *Elections at Home and Abroad: Essays in Honor of Warren E. Miller*. Ann Arbor, MI: University of Michigan Press.

—— (1999). 'Down and Down We Go: Political Trust in Sweden', in P. Norris (ed.), *Critical Citizens: Global Support for Democratic Governance*. Oxford: Oxford University Press.

—— (2000). *Välja Parti* (Choosing Party). Stockholm: Norstedts Juridik AB.

—— and Gilljam, M. (1987). *Väljare och Val i Sverige*. Stockholm: Bonniers.

—— and Oscarsson, H. (2004). *Väljare. Svenskt Väljarbeteende under Femtio år*. Stockholm: Norstedts Juridik AB.

—— —— (forthcoming). 'Party Leader Effects on the Vote', in K. Aarts, A. Blais, and H. Schmitt (eds.), *Political Leaders and Democratic Elections*. Oxford: Oxford University Press.

Huber, J. (1989). 'Values and Partisanship in Left-Right Orientations: Measuring Ideology', *European Journal of Political Research*, 17: 599–621.

—— Kernell, G., and Eduardo L. Leoni. (2004). *The Institutional context and party attachments in establishes democratics*. Unpublished paper.

—— and Inglehart, R. (1995). 'Expert Interpretations of Party Space and Party Locations in 42 Societies', *Party Politics*, 1: 73–111.

Idea. (2002). *Voter Turnout Since 1945: A Global Report*. Stockholm: International IDEA.

Inglehart, R. (1977). *The Silent Revolution – Changing Values and Political Styles among Western Publics*. Princeton, NJ: Princeton University Press.

—— (1984). 'The Changing Structure of Political Cleavages in Western Society', in R. J. Dalton, S. Flanagan, and P. A. Beck (eds.), *Electoral Change in Advanced Industrial Democracies*. Princeton, NJ: Princeton University Press.

—— (1990). *Cultural Shift in Advanced Industrial Society*. Princeton, NJ: Princeton University Press.

—— and Klingemann, H-D. (1976). 'Party Identification, Ideological Preference and the Left-Right Dimension among Western Publics', in I. Budge, I. Crewe, and D. Farlie (eds.), *Party Identification and Beyond: Representations of Voting and Party Competition*. London: Wiley.

Ismayr, W. (1999). 'Das Politische System Deutschlands', in W. Ismayr (ed.), *Die Politischen Systeme Westeuropas*. Opladen: Leske + Budrich.

Jackman, R. W. and Miller, Ross M. A. (1995). 'Voter Turnout in the Industrial Democracies during the 1980s', *Comparative Political Studies,* 27: 467–92.

Jagodzinski, W. and Dobbelaere, K. (1995). 'Secularisation and Church Religiosity', in J. W. van Deth and E. Scarbrough (eds.), *The Impact of Values*. Oxford: Oxford University Press.

Jahn, D. (1999). 'Das Politische System Schwedens', in W. Ismayr (ed.), *Die Politischen Systeme Westeuropas*. Opladen: Leske + Budrich.

Kaase, M. (1976). 'Party Identification and Voting Behaviour in the West German Election of 1969', in I. Budge, I. Crewe, and D. Farlie (eds.), *Party Identification and Beyond: Representations of Voting and Party Competition*. London: Wiley.

—— (1994). 'Is there Personalization in Politics? Candidates and Voting Behaviour in Germany', *International Political Science Review*, 15: 211–30.

—— and Bauer-Kaase, P. (1998). 'Zur Beteiligung an der Bundestagswahl 1994', in M. Kaase and H. -D. Klingemann (eds.), *Wahlen und Wähler: Analysen aus Anlass der Bundestagswahl 1994*. Wiesbaden: Westdeutscher-Verlag.

—— and Klingemann, H. -D. (1994). 'Electoral Research in the Federal Republic of Germany', in J. J. A. Thomassen (ed.), *The Intellectual History of Election Studies. Special Issue of the European Journal for Political Research*. Dordrecht: Kluwer, pp. 343–66.

Katz, R. S. and Mair, P. (1997). 'Party Organization, Party Democracy, and the Emergence of the Cartel Party', in P. Mair (ed.), *Party System Change: Approaches and Interpretations*. Oxford: Clarendon Press.

Kelley, S., Jr. and Mirer, T. (1974). 'The Simple Act of Voting', *American Political Science Review,* 68: 572–91.

Key, V. O. (1966). *The Responsible Electorate*. Cambridge: Harvard University Press.

Kinder, D. R. (1986). 'Presidential Character Revisited', in R. Lau and D. Sears (eds.), *Political Cognition*. Hillsdale, NJ: Lawrence Erlbaum.

Kinder, D. R. and Kiewit, D. R. (1979). 'Economic Discontent and Political Behavior: The Role of Personal Grievances and Collective Economic Judgements in Congressional Voting', *American Journal of Political Science,* 23: 495–527.

—— —— (1981). 'Sociotropic Politics', *British Journal of Political Science,* 11: 129–61.

—— and Sears, D. O. (1985). 'Public Opinion and Political Action', in G. Lindzey and E. Aronson (eds.), *Handbook of Social Psychology.* New York: Random House.

King, A. (2002). 'Do Leaders' Personalities Really Matter?', in A. King (ed.), *Leaders' Personalities and the Outcomes of Democratic Elections.* Oxford: Oxford University Press.

Kirchheimer, O. (1966). 'The Transformation of the Western European Party Systems', in J. LaPalombara and M. Weiner (eds.), *Political Parties and Political Development.* Princeton, NJ: Princeton University Press.

—— (1997). 'The Catch-All party', in P. Mair (ed.), *The West European Party System.* Oxford: Oxford University Press. (Originally published in J. Lapalombara and M. Weiner (1966), *Political Parties and Political Development*).

Kitschelt, H. (1994). *The Transformation of European Social Democracy.* Cambridge: Cambridge University Press.

—— (1995). *The Radical Right in Western Europe – A Comparative Analysis.* Ann Arbor, MI: University of Michigan Press.

Klecka, W. R. (1980). *Discriminant Analysis.* Beverly Hills, CA: Sage.

Klingemann, H-D. (1979). 'Measuring Ideological Conceptualizations', in S. H. Barnes and M. Kaase (eds.), *Political Action: Mass Participation in Five Western Democracies.* Beverly Hills, CA and London: Sage.

—— and Wattenberg, M. (1992). 'Decaying versus Developing Party Systems: A Comparison of Party Images in the United States and West Germany', *British Journal of Political Science,* 22: 131–49.

—— Hofferbert, R. I., and Budge, I. (1994). *Parties, Policies, and Democracy.* Boulder, CO: Westview Press.

Knight, K. (1985). 'Ideological Sophistication Does Matter', *Journal of Politics,* 47: 828–53.

Knutsen, O. (1988). 'The Impact of Structural and Ideological Party Cleavages in West European Democracies: A Comparative Empirical Analysis', *British Journal of Political Science,* 18: 323–52.

—— (1995a). 'Left-Right Materialist Value Orientations', in J. W. van Deth and E. Scarbrough (eds.), *The Impact of Values.* Oxford: Oxford University Press.

—— (1995b). 'Party Choice', in J. W. van Deth and E. Scarbrough (eds.), *The Impact of Values.* Oxford: Oxford University Press.

—— (1995c). 'Value Orientations, Political Conflicts and Left-Right Identification – A Comparative Study', *European Journal of Political Research,* 28: 63–93.

—— (1997). 'The Partisan and the Value-Based Components of Left-Right Self-Placement: A Comparative Study', *International Political Science Review,* 18: 191–225.

—— (1998). 'Expert Judgements of the Left-Right Location of Political Parties: A Comparative Longitudinal Study', *West European Politics,* 21: 63–94.

—— (1999a). 'Left-Right Party Polarization among the Mass Publics: A Comparative Longitudinal Study from Eight West European Countries', in H. M. Narud and T. Aalberg (eds.), *Challenges to Representative Democracy.* Bergen: Fagbokforlaget.

Knutsen, O. (1999b)*Left-Right Polarization in West-European Party Systems: A Compara-tive Longitudinal Study Based on Judgments by Political Experts*. Oslo: Department of Political Science: Working Paper 7/1999.

—— (2001). 'Social Class, Sector Employment, and Gender as Party Cleavages in the Scandinavian Countries: A Comparative Longitudinal Study, 1970–95', *Scandinavian Political Studies*, 24: 311–50.

—— (2003). *Overall and Traditional Left-Right Class Voting in Eight West-European Countries: A Comparative Longitudinal Study 1975–1997*. Paper presented at the Euro-pean Consortium of Political Research's Joint Sessions of Workshops, Edinburgh, 2003.

—— and Scarbrough, E. (1995). 'Cleavage Politics', in J. van Deth and E. Scarbrough (eds.), *The Impact of Values*. Oxford: Oxford University Press.

Kotler-Berkowitz, L. (2001). 'Religion and Voting Behaviour in Great Britain: A Reassess-ment', *British Journal of Political Science*, 31: 523–54.

Kroh, M. (2003). *Parties, Politicians and Policies – Orientations of Vote Choice across Voters and Countries*. Ph.D. dissertation, University of Amsterdam.

Krosnick, J. A. (2002). 'The Challenges of Political Psychology: Lessons to be Learned from Research on Attitude Perception', in J. H. Kuklinski (ed.), *Thinking About Political Psychology*. Cambridge: Cambridge University Press.

Kühnel, S. M. and Fuchs, D. (1998). 'Nicht Wahlen als Rationales Handeln: Anmerkun-gen zum Nutzen des Rational-Choice Ansatzes in der Empirischen Wahlforschung', in M. Kaase and H. -D. Klingemann (eds.), *Wahlen und Wähler: Analysen aus Anlass der Bundestagswahl 1994*. Wiesbaden: Westdeutscher-Verlag.

Kumlin, S. (2001). 'Ideology-Driven Opinion Formation in Europe: The Case of Attitudes towards the Third Sector in Sweden', *European Journal of Political Research*, 39: 487–518.

Lafferty, W. and Knutsen, O. (1984). 'Leftist and Rightist Ideology in a Social Democratic State: An Analysis of Norway in the Midst of the Conservative Resurgence', *British Journal of Political Science*, 14: 345–67.

Lane, J. -E. and Ersson, S. O. (1987). *Politics and Society in Western Europe*. Beverly Hills, CA and London: Sage.

Lane, J. -E. and Ersson, S. O. (1994). *Politics and Society in Western Europe*. London: Sage.

Lane, J. -E. and Ersson, S. O. (1999). *Politics and Society in Western Europe*. London: Sage.

Lavine, H. (2002). 'On-Line versus Memory-Based Process Models of Political Evalu-ation', in K. R. Monroe (ed.), *Political Psychology*. Mahwah, NJ: Lawrence Erlbaum.

Lazarsfeld, P. E., Berelson, B. R., and Gaudet, H. (1948). *The People's Choice. How the Voter Makes Up his Mind in a Presidential Campaign*. 2nd edn. New York: Columbia University Press.

LeDuc, L., Niemi, R., and Norris, P. (1996). 'Introduction: The Present and Future of Democratic Elections', in L. LeDuc, R. Niemi, and P. Norris (eds.), *Comparing Dem-ocracies: Elections and Voting in Global Perspective*. Thousand Oaks, CA: Sage.

Lepszy, N. (1999). 'Das Politische System der Niederlande', in W. Ismayr (ed.), *Die Politischen Systeme Westeuropas*. Opladen: Leske + Budrich.

Lewis-Beck, M. S. (1988). *Economics and Elections: The Major Western Democracies*. Ann Arbor, MI: University of Michigan Press.

—— and Nadeau, R. (2000). 'French Electoral Institutions and the Economic Vote', *Electoral Studies*, 19: 171–82.

Lewis-Beck, M. S. and Paldam, M. (eds.) (2000*a*). 'Special Issue: Economics and Elections', *Electoral Studies*, 19, 113–22.

—— —— (2000*b*). 'Economic Voting: An Introduction', *Electoral Studies*, 19: 113–21.

Lijphart, A. (1968). *The Politics of Accomodation: Pluralism and Democracy in the Netherlands*. Berkeley, CA: University of California Press.

—— (1999). *Patterns of Democracy: Government Forms and Performance in Thirty-Six Countries*. New Haven and London: Yale University Press.

Lipset, S. M. and Rokkan, S. (1967). 'Cleavage Structures, Party Systems and Voter Alignments: An Introduction', in S. M. Lipset and S. Rokkan (eds.), *Party Systems and Voter Alignments: Cross-National Perspectives*. New York: Free Press.

Listhaug, O. (1989). 'Gamle og Nye Modellar i Valforskinga: eit Oversyn (Old and New Models in Electoral Research: An Overview)', *Tidsskrift for Samfunnsforskning*, 30: 339–60.

—— (1995). 'The Dynamics of Trust in Politicians', in H-D. Klingemann and D. Fuchs (eds.), *Citizens and the State*. Oxford: Oxford University Press.

Luhmann, N. (1981). *Politische Theorie im Wohlfahrtsstaat*. Muenchen: Olzog.

—— (1984). *Soziale Systeme*. Frankfurt: Suhrkamp.

Luijkx, R., Brislinger, E., and Zenk-Möltgen, W. (2003). European Values Study 1999/ 2000 – A Third Wave: Data, Documentation and Database on CD-ROM. in ZA-Information, Nr. 52, S. 171–83.

Macdonald, S. E. and Rabinowitz, G. (1998). 'Solving the Paradox of Nonconvergence: Valence, Position, and Direction in Democratic Politics', *Electoral Studies*, 17: 281–300.

Mackie, T. T. and Rose, R. (1991). *The International Almanac of Electoral History*. rev 3rd edn. London: Macmillan.

MacKuen, M. B., Erikson, R. S., and Stimson, J. A. (1992). 'Peasants or Bankers? The American Electorate and the U.S. Economy', *American Political Science Review* 86: 597–611.

Maguire, M. (1983). 'Is There Still Persistence? Electoral Change in Western Europe 1948–1979', in H. Daalder and P. Mair (eds.), *Western European Party Systems: Continuity and Change*. London: Sage.

Maier, J. and Rattinger, H. (1999). 'Economic Conditions and the 1994 and 1998 Federal Elections', *German Politics*, 8 (2): 33–47.

Mair, P. (1990). 'Continuity, Change and the Vulnerability of Party', in P. Mair and G. Smith (eds.), *Understanding Party System Change in Western Europe*. London: Frank Cass, pp. 169–87.

—— (1997). *Party System Change: Approaches and Interpretatations*. Oxford: Clarendon Press.

—— and Mudde, C. (1998). 'The Party Families and Its Study', *Annual Review of Political Science*, 1: 211–29.

—— and Smith, G. (eds.) (1990). *Understanding Party System Change in Western Europe*. London: Frank Cass.

Mallory, W. H. (ed.). (1932–1962) *Political Handbook of the World: 1932–1962*. NewYork: Harper.

—— (ed.). (1963–1967) *Political Handbook of the World: 1963–1967*. New York: Harper & Row.

—— (ed.). (1968) *Political Handbook of the World: 1968*. New York: Simon & Schuster.

Manin, B. (1997). *The Principles of Representative Government*. Cambridge: Cambridge University Press.

Manza, J., Hout, M., and Brooks, J. (1995). 'Class Voting in Capitalist Democracies since World War II: Dealignment, Realignment or Trendless Fluctuation?' , *Annual Review of Sociology*, 21: 137–62.

McAllister, I. (1996). 'Leaders', in L. LeDuc, R. Niemi, and P. Norris (eds.), *Comparing Democracies: Elections and Voting in Global Perspective*. Thousand Oaks, CA: Sage.

McClosky, H., Hoffman, J. P., and O'Hara, R. (1960). 'Issue Conflict and Consensus among Party Leaders and Followers', *American Political Science Review*, 54: 406–27.

McDonald, M. P. and Popkin, S. L. (2001). 'The Myth of the Vanishing Voter', *American Political Science Review*, 95: 963–74.

Miller, A. H., Miller, W. E., Raine, A. S., and Brown, T. A. (1976). 'A Majority Party in Disarray: Policy Polarization in the 1972 Election', *American Political Science Review*, 70: 753–78.

—— and Listhaug, O. (1984). 'Economic Effects on the Vote in Norway', *Political Behavior*, 6: 301–19.

Miller, W. (1981). *The End of British Politics?* Oxford: Clarendon Press.

Miller, W.E. (1994). 'An Organizational History of the Intellectual Origins of the American National Election Studies', in J. J. A. Thomassen, *The Intellectual History of Election Studies. Special Issue of the European Journal for Political Research*. Dordrecht: Kluwer.

—— and Shanks, M. (1982). 'Policy Directions and Presidential Leadership: Alternative Interpretations of the 1980 Presidential Election', *British Journal of Political Science*, 12: 299–356.

—— —— (1996). *The New American Voter*. Cambridge, MA: Harvard University Press.

Mochmann, E., Oedegaard, I.C., and Mauer, R. (1998). *Inventory of National Election Studies in Europe 1945–1995*. Bergisch Gladbach: Edwin Ferger Verlag.

—— —— Mauer, R., and Zenk-Möltgen, W. (2000). BTW-DISC 2000. Continuity Guide der deutschen nationalen Wahlstudien 1949–1998, ZA Codebook Explorer Version 2.1, ZA.

Mughan, A. (2000). *Media and the Presidentialization of Parliamentary Elections*. Basingstoke: Palgrave.

Nadeau, R., Niemi, R. G., and Yoshinaka, A. (2002). 'A Cross-National Analysis of Economic Voting: Taking Account of the Political Context Across Time and Nations', *Electoral Studies*, 21: 403–23.

Nannestad, P. (1999). 'Das Politische System Daenemarks', in W. Ismayr (ed.), *Die Politischen Systeme Westeuropas*. Opladen: Leske + Budrich.

Nie, N., Verba, S., and Petrocik, J. R. (1976). *The Changing American Voter*. Cambridge, MA: Harvard University Press.

Niedermayer, O. (1998). 'German Unification and Party System Change', in P. Pennings and J. E. Lane (eds.), *Comparing Party System Change*. London: Routledge.

Niemi, R. G. and Wesholm, A. (1984). 'Issues, Parties, and Attitudinal Stability: A Comparative Study of Sweden and the United States', *Electoral Studies*, 3: 65–83.

Nieuwbeerta, P. (1995). *The Democratic Class Struggle in Twenty Countries 1945/1990*. Amsterdam: Thesis Publishers.

Norris, P. (1999). 'Introduction: The Growth of Critical Citizens?', in P. Norris (ed.), *Critical Citizens: Global Support for Democratic Governance*. Oxford: Oxford University Press.

Norris, P. (2002). *Democratic Phoenix: Political Activism Worldwide*. New York: Cambridge University Press.

—— and Gavin, N. T. (eds.) (1997). *Britain Votes 1997*. Oxford: Oxford University Press.

Oppenhuis, E. (1995). *Voting Behavior in Europe*. Amsterdam: Het Spinhuis.

Oscarsson, H. (1998). *Den Svenska Partirymden. Väljarnas Uppfattningar av Konfliktstrukturen i Partisystemet 1956–1996*. Göteborg: Department of Political Science, Göteborg University.

Oskarson, M. (1992). 'Sweden', in M. N. Franklin, T. K. Mackie, and H. Valen (eds), *Electoral Change: Responses to Evolving Social and Attitudinal Structures in Seventeen Democracies*. Cambridge: Cambridge University Press.

—— (1994). *Klassröstning i Sverige*. Stockholm: Nerenius & Santérus.

Padgett, S. (ed.) (1993). *Parties and Party Systems in the New Germany*. Aldershot: Dartmouth Publishing.

Page, B. (1978). *Choices and Echoes in Presidential Elections: Rational Man and Electoral Democracy*. Chicago: University of Chicago Press.

Pappi, F. U. (1984). 'The West German Party System', *West European Politics*, 7: 7–26.

Parsons, T. (1969). *Politics and Social Structure*. New York: Free Press.

Patterson, T. (2002). *The Vanishing Voter: Civic Involvement in an Age of Uncertainty*. New York: Knopf.

Pedersen, M. N. (1979). 'The Dynamics of European Party Systems: Changing Patterns of Electoral Volatility', *European Journal of Political Research*, 7: 1–26.

Pellikaan, H., De Lange, S., and van der Meer, T. (2004). *The Dutch Parliamentary Election of 2002: Christian-Judaic-Humanistic Culture versus Islamic Culture as a New Line of Conflict*. Paper presented at the Annual Meeting of the American Political Science Association, Chicago, IL: USA, September 2004.

Pennings, P. (1998). 'The Triad of Party System Change: Votes, Office and Policy', in P. Pennings and J. E. Lane (eds.) (1998). *Comparing Party System Change*. London: Routledge.

—— and Lane, J. E. (eds.) (1998). *Comparing Party System Change*. London: Routledge.

Petrocik, J. R. (1996). 'Issue Ownership in Presidential Elections, with a 1980 Case Study', *American Journal of Political Science*, 40: 825–50.

Pharr, S. J. and Putnam, R. D. (eds.) (2000). *Disaffected Democracies: What's Troubling the Trilateral Countries?* Princeton, NJ: Princeton University Press.

Plane, D. L. and Gershtenson, J. (2004). 'Candidates' Ideological Locations, Abstention, and Turnout in U.S. Midterm Senate Elections', *Political Behavior*, 26: 69–93.

Powell, G. B. (1986). 'American Voter Turnout in Comparative Perspective', *American Political Science Review*, 80: 17–43.

Powell, G. B., Jr. and Whitten, G. D. (1993). 'Cross-National Analysis of Economic Voting: Taking Account of the Political Context', *American Journal of Political Science*, 37: 391–414.

Przeworski, A. and Sprague, J. (1986). *Paper Stones: A History of Electoral Socialism*. Chicago: University of Chicago Press.

—— and Teune, H. (1970). *The Logic of Comparative Social Inquiry*. New York: Wiley-Interscience.

Rabinowitz, G. and Macdonald, S. E. (1989). 'A Directional Theory of Issue Voting', *American Political Science Review*, 83: 93–121.

Rae, D. (1971). *Political Consequences of Electoral Law*. New Haven: Yale University Press.

Rattinger, H. (1986). 'Collective and Individual Economic Judgments and Voting in West Germany, 1961–1984', *European Journal of Political Research*, 14: 393–419.

—— and Faas, T. (2001). 'Wahrnehmungen der Wirtschaftslage und Wahlverhalten 1977 bis 1998', in H-D. Klingemann and M. Kaase (eds.), *Wahlen und Wähler*. Wiesbaden: Westdeutscher-Verlag.

Reif, K. and Schmitt, H. (1980). 'Nine Second-Order National Elections: A Conceptual Framework for the Analysis of European Election Results', *European Journal of Political Research*, 8: 3–44.

Reiter, H. (1989). 'Party Decline in the West: A Skeptic's View', *Journal of Theoretical Politics*, 1: 325–48.

Roberts, G. K. (1990). 'Party System Change in West Germany: Land-Federal Linkages', in P. Mair and G. Smith (eds.), *Understanding Party System Change in Western Europe*. London: Frank Cass, 98–113.

Rose, R. (ed.) (1974). *Electoral behaviour: A Comparative Handbook*. New York: Free Press.

—— and McAllister, I. (1982). *United Kingdom Facts*. London: Macmillan.

—— —— (1986). *Voters Begin to Choose: From Closed-Class to Open Elections in Britain*. London: Sage.

—— —— (1990). *The Loyalties of Voters: A Lifetime Learning Model*. London: Sage.

—— and Munro, N. (eds.) (2003). *Elections and Parties in New European Democracies*. Washington, DC: CQ Press.

—— and Urwin, D. (1970). 'Persistence and Change in Western Party Systems Since 1945', *Political Studies*, 18: 287–319.

Rosenborg, S., Bohan, L., McCafferty, P., and Harris, K. (1986). 'The Image and the Vote: The Effect of Candidate Presentation on Voter Preference', *American Journal of Political Science*, 30: 108–27.

Rosenstone, S. J. and Hansen, J. M. (1993). *Mobilization, Participation, and Democracy in America*. New York: Macmillan.

Sainsbury, D. (1990). 'Party Strategies and the Electoral Trade-off of Class-Based Parties. A Critique and Application of the "Dilemma of Electoral Socialism" ', *European Journal of Political Research*, 18: 29–50.

Sanders, D. (1999). 'Conservative Incompetence, Labour Responsibility and the Feelgood Factor: Why the Economy Failed to Save the Conservatives in 1997', *Electoral Studies*, 18: 251–70.

—— and Carey, S. (2002). 'Temporal Variations in Economic Voting: A Comparative Cross-National Analysis', in H. Dorussen and M. Taylor (eds.), *Economic Voting*. London: Routledge.

Sani, G. and Sartori, G. (1983). 'Polarisation, Fragmentation and Competition in Western Democracies', in H. Daalder and P. Mair (eds.), *Western European Party Systems: Continuity and Change*. London: Sage.

Sartori, G. (1976). *Parties and Party Systems*. Cambridge: Cambridge University Press.

—— (1997). 'The Sociology of Parties: A Critical Review', in P. Mair (ed.), *The West European Party System*. Oxford: Oxford University Press. Originally published in O. Sammer (ed.) (1968), *Party Systems, Party Organizations and the Politics of New Masses*.

Särlvik, B. and Crewe, I. (1983). *Decade of Dealignment: The Conservative Victory of 1979 and Electoral Trends in the 1970s*. Cambridge: Cambridge University Press.

Scarrow, S., Webb, P., and Farrell, D. (2000). 'From Social Integration to Electoral Contestation: The Changing Distribution of Power within Political Parties', in R. Dalton and M. Wattenberg (eds.), *Parties without Partisans: Political Change in Advanced Industrial Democracies*. Oxford: Oxford University Press.

Schmitt, H. (1987). *Das Parteiensystem der Bundesrepublik Deutschland. Eine Einführung aus politik-soziologischer Perspektive*. Hagen: Fern-Universität [Studienbrief in drei Kurseinheiten].

—— (2002). 'Partisanship in Western Europe and the US: Causes and Consequences'. Paper prepared for presentation at the Annual Conference of the American Political Science Association in Boston, MA, 27 August to 1 September.

—— (2004). 'Parteibindungen, Links-Rechts-Orientierungen und die Wahlentscheidung in Deutschland und Frankreich', in J. W. Falter, O. W. Gabriel, and B. Wessels (eds.), *Wahlen und Wähler: Analysen aus Anlass der Bundestagswahl 2002*. Opladen: Westdeutscher-Verlag.

—— and Holmberg, S. (1995). 'Political Parties in Decline?', in H-D. Klingemann and D. Fuchs (eds.), *Citizens and the State*. Oxford: Oxford University Press.

Sears, D. O. (1993). 'Symbolic Politics: A Socio-Psychological Theory', in S. Iyengar and W. J. McGuire (eds.), *Explorations in Political Psychology*. Durham: Duke University Press.

Shanks, M. and Miller, W. (1990). 'Policy Direction and Performance Evaluation: Complementary Explanations of the Reagan Elections', *British Journal of Political Science*, 20: 143–235.

Shively, W. P. (1979). 'The Development of Party Identification among Adults', *American Political Science Review*, 73: 1039–54.

Sigelman, L. and Yough, S. N. (1978). 'Left-right Polarization in National Party Systems – A Cross-National Analysis', *Comparative Political Studies*, 11: 355–79.

Silverman, L. (1985). 'The Ideological Mediation of Party-Political Responses to Social Change', *European Journal of Political Research*, 13: 69–93.

Smith, A. (1981). 'Mass Communications', in D. Butler, H. Penniman, and A. Ranney (eds.), *Democracy at the Polls*. Washington, DC: American Enterprise Institute.

Stebbins, R. P. and Amoia, A. (eds.). (1973). *The World This Year: 1971–1973 (supplement to the Political Handbook and Atlas of the World: 1970)*. New York: Simon & Schuster.

Stewart, M. and Clarke, H. (1992). 'The (Un)importance of Party Leaders, Leader Images and Party Choice in the 1987 British Election', *Journal of Politics*, 54: 447–70.

Stokes, D. (1963). 'Spatial Models of Party Competition', *American Political Science Review*, 57: 368–77.

—— (1966). 'Some Dynamic Elements of Contests for the Presidency', *American Political Science Review*, 60: 19–28.

—— and Dilulio, J. J. (1993). 'The Setting: Valence Politics in Modern Elections', in M. Nelson (ed.), *The Elections of 1992*. Washington, DC: Congressional Quarterly Press.

Sturm, R. (1999). 'Das Politische System Grossbritanniens', in W. Ismayr (ed.), *Die Politischen Systeme Westeuropas*. Opladen: Leske + Budrich.

Swanson, D. and Mancini, P. (1996). *Politics, Media and Modern Democracy*. New York: Praeger.

Taylor, M. and Herman, V. (1971). 'Party Systems and Government Stability', *American Political Science Review* 65: 28–37.

Teixeira, R. A. (1987). *Why Americans Don't Vote: Turnout Decline in the United States 1960–1984*. New York: Greenwood Press.

—— (1992). *The Disappearing American Voter*. Washington, DC: Brookings Institution.

Thomassen, J. J. A. (1976). 'Party Identification as a Cross-National Concept: Its Meaning in the Netherlands', in I. Budge, I. Crewe, and D. Farlie (eds.), *Party Identification and Beyond: Representations of Voting and Party Competition*. London: Wiley.

—— (2000). 'From Comparable to Comparative Electoral Research', in J. van Deth, H. Rattinger, and E. Roller, *Die Republik auf dem Weg zur Normalität? Wahlverhalten und Politische Einstellungen nach Acht Jahren Einheit*. Opladen: Leske + Budrich.

—— Aarts, C. W. A. M., and Van der Kolk, H. (eds.) (2000). *Politieke Veranderingen in Nederland 1971–1998. Kiezers en de Smalle Marges van de Politiek*. Den Haag: SDU.

Topf, R. (1995). 'Electoral Participation', in H-D. Klingemann and D. Fuchs (eds.), *Citizens and the State*. Oxford: Oxford University Press.

Tromp, B. (1990). 'Party Strategies and System Change in the Netherlands', in P. Mair and G. Smith (eds.), *Understanding Party System Change in Western Europe*. London: Frank Cass.

Tuckel, P. and Tejera, F. (1983). 'Changing Patterns in American Voting Behavior, 1914–1980', *Public Opinion Quarterly*, 47: 143–202.

Tworzecki, H. (2002). *Learning to Choose: Electoral Politics in East-Central Europe*. Cambridge: Cambridge University Press.

Valen, H. (2003). 'The Storting Election in Norway, September 2001', *Electoral Studies*, 22: 179–85.

Valen, H. and Katz, D. (1964). *Political Parties in Norway*. Oslo: Universitetsforlaget.

Van Deth, J. W. and Scarbrough, E. (1995). 'The Concept of Values', in J. W. van Deth and E. Scarbrough (eds.), *The Impact of Values*. Oxford: Oxford University Press.

Van der Brug, W. (1996). *Where is the Party? Voters Perceptions of Party Positions*. Amsterdam: University of Amsterdam.

—— (1998). 'The Informed Electorate: Political Perceptions and Party Behaviour', *Acta Politica*, 33: 20–55.

Van der Eijk, C. and Franklin, M. N. (eds.) (1996). *Choosing Europe? The European Electorate and National Politics in the Face of Union*. Ann Arbor, MI: University of Michigan Press.

—— and Kroh, M. (2002). 'Alchemy or Science? Discrete Choice Models for Analysing Voter Choice in Multi-Party Contests'. Paper presented at the Annual Meeting of the American Political Science Association, Boston, August.

—— and Niemöller, K. (1992). 'Netherlands', in M. Franklin, T. Mackie, and H. Valen (eds.). *Electoral Change: Responses to Evolving Social and Attitudinal Structures in Western Countries*. Cambridge: Cambridge University Press.

—— —— (1994). 'Election Studies in the Netherlands', in J. J. A. Thomassen, *The Intellectual History of Election Studies. Special Issue of the European Journal for Political Research*. Dordrecht: Kluwer, pp. 323–42.

—— Franklin, M. N., and Oppenhuis, E. (1996). 'The Strategic Context: Party Choice', in C. van der Eijk and M. N. Franklin (eds.), *Choosing Europe? The European Electorate and National Politics in the Face of Union*. Ann Arbor, MI: University of Michigan Press.

——, —— and Van der Brug, W. (1999). 'Policy Preferences and Party Choice', in H. Schmitt and J. J. A. Thomassen (eds.), *Political Representation and Legitimacy in the European Union*. Oxford: Oxford University Press.

—— Franklin, M., Mackie, T., and Valen, H. (1992). 'Cleavages, Conflict Resolution and Democracy', in M. N. Franklin, T. Mackie and H. Valen (eds.), *Electoral Change: Responses to Evolving Social and Attitudinal Structures in Western Countries*. Cambridge: Cambridge University Press.

—— Van der Brug, W., Kroh, M., and Franklin, M. (forthcoming). 'Rethinking the Dependent Variable in Voting Behavior–on the Measurement and Analysis of Electoral Utilities', *Electoral Studies*, vol. 24.

Van Wijnen, P. (2001). *Policy Voting in Advanced Industrial Democracies. The Case of the Netherlands 1971–1998*. Enschede: University of Twente.

Verba, S., Schlozman, K. L., and Brady, H. E. (1995). *Voice and Equality: Civic Voluntarism in American Politics*. Cambridge, MA: Harvard University Press.

Verba, S., Nie, N. H., and Kim, J. (1978). *Participation and Political Equality: A Seven-Nation Comparison*. Chicago: University of Chicago Press.

Visser, M. (1998). *Five Theories of Voting Action*. Enschede: University of Twente.

Volkens, A. and Klingemann, H-D. (2003). 'Parties, Ideologies and Issues: Stability and Change in Fifteen European Party Systems 1945–1998', in K. R. Luther and F. Mueller-Rommel (eds.), *Political Parties in the New Europe – Political and Analytical Challenges*. Oxford: Oxford University Press.

Wattenberg, M. P. (1991). *The Rise of Candidate-Centred Politics: Presidential Elections of the 1980s*. Cambridge, MA: Harvard University Press.

—— (2000). 'The Decline of Party Mobilization', in R. J. Dalton and M. P. Wattenberg (eds.), *Parties Without Partisans: Political Change in Advanced Industrial Democracies*. Oxford: Oxford University Press.

Webb, E. J., Campbell, D. T., Schwartz, R. D., and Sechrest, L. (2000). *Unobtrusive Measures*. rev edn. Thousand Oaks, CA: Sage.

Wende, F. (ed.) (1981). *Lexikon zur Geschichte der Parteien in Europa*. Stuttgart: Kroener.

Wessels, B. (2004). 'The German Party System: Developments after Unification', in W. Reutter (ed.), *Germany on the Road to Normalcy: Policies and Politics of the Red-Green Federal Government (1998–2002)*. New York: Palgrave Macmillan.

Whiteley, P. (1997). 'The Conservative Campaign', in P. Norris and N. T. Garvin (eds.), *Britain Votes 1997*. Oxford: Oxford University Press.

Widfeldt, A. (2003). 'The Parliamentary Election in Sweden, 2002', *Electoral Studies*, 22: 778–84.

Woldendorp, J., Keman, H., and Budge, I. (2000). *Party Government in 48 Democracies (1945–1998): Composition – Duration – Personnel*. Dordrecht: Kluwer.

Wolfinger, R. E. and Rosenstone, S. J. (1980). *Who Votes?* New Haven: Yale University Press.

Wolinetz, S. (1988). *Parties and Party Systems in Liberal Democracies*. London: Routledge.

Zaller, J. R. (1992). *The Nature and Origins of Mass Opinion*. Cambridge: Cambridge University Press.

Zenk-Möltgen, W. and Mochmann, E. (2000). Der Continuity Guide der deutschen Wahlforschung und der ZA CodebookExplorer. In Klein, M. u.a. (ed.): 50 Jahre Empirische Wahlforschung in Deutschland. Wiesbaden: Westdeutscher Verlag 596–614.

Index